SOE

the scientific secrets

This book is dedicated to Douglas Everett,
a man of stature, modesty,
kindness and tremendous enthusiasm

SOE

the scientific secrets

FREDRIC BOYCE AND DOUGLAS EVERETT

FOREWORD BY M.R.D. FOOT

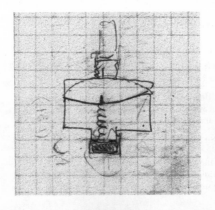

The
History
Press

Title page: The sketch in Everett's notebook showing the
principle of the 'air leak' or 'disc time' delay – Newton's
hoped-for temperature independent time delay.

First published in 2003 by Sutton Publishing

This edition published 2009 by
The History Press
The Mill, Brimscombe Port
Stroud, Gloucestershire, GL5 2QG
www.thehistorypress.co.uk

Reprinted 2010, 2013, 2016

British Library Cataloguing in Publication Data.
A catalogue record for this book is available from the British Library.

ISBN 978 0 7524 5329 3

Typesetting and origination by The History Press
Printed in Great Britain

CONTENTS

FOREWORD

The history of SOE seems to spring a never-ending run of surprises: here are some more. For several years past, the Imperial War Museum's secret war gallery has exhibited a set of SOE's tools – some of them gruesome – for forwarding its tasks of subversion and sabotage. Many of SOE's surviving papers have now gone public, and the Public Record Office has published two of the catalogues in which the tools were listed. This book explains how, why and where they were designed.

It is by two scientists, one of whom has just died – his survivor dedicates the book to him; Everett served in SOE himself, and his co-author Boyce shared in the task of clearing up after it, so they write with inside knowledge, always an advantage when dealing with a secret service. They present a clear scientific account of the ways SOE's inventors worked, and summarise the results; some of them well enough known, others partly or entirely new.

There is a mass of detail, for instance, on Operation Braddock, the proposal to drop small incendiaries into Germany, to be picked up by slave labourers and used to start fires; Mackenzie mentions this in his recently released in-house history of SOE, but here it is handled fully (the results were disappointing). There is also a lot of new detail on Periwig, Templer's attempt to convince the German security authorities that there was an active resistance movement in Germany in the last winter of the war; Leo Marks's dark hints are here spelled out in full. SOE has often, wrongly, been accused of dealing in biological warfare; the authors are able to rebut this charge, but do have a disconcerting passage on research intended to disrupt the digestion of members of the Wehrmacht. This never reached the point of attempted action.

These pages give a vivid picture of how hard SOE's scientists worked, and how informally; they were free of many constraints of service discipline, and encouraged to think laterally. George Taylor and Tommy Davies from SOE's governing Council gave them plenty of starting impetus, and D.M. Newitt, the head of scientific research, kept all of them up to the mark.

SOE: The Scientific Secrets

Needless to say, he recruited on the old boy net – there was no other safe way of doing so; the results justified the method. He and six of his colleagues became Fellows of the Royal Society. Inter-service and inter-secret-service jealousies marred corners of the story, and will probably be blown up by the ignorant into attempts at sensation; they did not much hinder the war effort. With the passage of time it is getting less and less easy to remember that SOE was a fighting service, formed to help win a world war.

A good deal of mud was thrown at SOE by Marxists who maintained that it was a tool of capitalism. Many of its members did come from large firms; but they were there to beat a bad enemy, not to serve any commercial interest. One of the large firms that supplied several senior men was the great textile firm of Courtauld's; and after the war Courtauld's looked after Newitt, funding a chair for him at Imperial College London.

He would have enjoyed this account of his and his colleagues' role in aiding a critical victory.

M.R.D. Foot

ACKNOWLEDGEMENTS

The authors would like to express their gratitude to the many individuals and organisations who have helped in the writing of this book. In particular, they thank Professor D.W.J. Cruickshank, FRS, for his recollections and photographs; John van Riemsdijk for supplying information and material; Elizabeth Howard-Turner for the gift of the late Agnes Kinnersley's Station IX scrap book; and Tony Brooks for his first-hand account of sabotaging railway wagons.

Duncan Stuart, the SOE Adviser to the Foreign and Commonwealth Office, was always helpful with advice and information from files prior to their official release. Christopher J. Tompkins made an excellent sectionalised drawing of the Time Pencil and Lady Cicely Mayhew translated the German on the Pigeon Post form.

Of the organisations contacted during the research for this work, the MoD Pattern Room, then in Nottingham, and the Royal Signals Museum at Blandford Camp were most helpful in permitting photographs to be made of key items of SOE equipment.

The portrait of Professor D.M. Newitt, FRS, was obtained with the assistance of the Royal Society, while the biographical details of some of the engineers were drawn from documents made available by the Institution of Mechanical Engineers.

Other organisations which contributed are the Public Record Office at Kew who never failed to come up with any of the over two hundred files consulted; the Royal Navy Submarine Museum at Gosport; the Airborne Forces Museum at Aldershot; and the Imperial War Museum whose photographic, audio and document archives were used. It is worth noting here that the IWM contains a fascinating exhibition devoted to the SOE.

Finally we would like to thank the following individuals with whom conversations have elicited numerous small but interesting points in this history: George I. Brown, Graden Carter, H. Woodend, Eric Slater, Mrs Mary Fields, Bill Mack, Tom Rae and the late Leo Marks who sadly died during the writing of this book.

FB
DHE

PREFACE

T he history of the Special Operations Executive (SOE) and the exploits of some of its agents in Occupied Europe have been the subject of many books published in the last fifty years. As security has, little by little, been relaxed and the Public Record Office (PRO) has released previously secret material into the public domain, a clearer and more complete picture has emerged. However, despite the publication by the PRO of the *Secret Agent's Handbook of Special Devices* and the release of the official *Secret History of SOE* by W. Mackenzie, there has been so far no detailed account of the development of equipment and techniques upon which the success of subversive activities relied. Though not having the same dramatic impact as stories of the daring deeds of agents, such an account is important in setting their deeds in perspective. As noted by Professor M.R.D. Foot, this aspect of SOE's history 'awaits reliable treatment in print'. This book attempts to fill that gap.

The main objectives of the book are threefold. First, to present a coherent account of the role of technical support in the evolution of overall SOE policies and their relation to the grand strategies of the Allies. Second, to describe in some detail the research leading to the development, production and distribution of a wide range of devices and supplies for the use of agents. Finally, to make an assessment of the importance of the work of the various R&D establishments set up by SOE in the early stages of the war and which provided much of the impetus for the development of new devices.

Relatively few of the personnel brought in to staff the research establishments were professional soldiers, and those that were had been trained in conventional military rather than in guerrilla warfare. Apart from a few seconded from Government departments, the majority of those recruited for research positions were young graduates with only a short period of research experience. Consequently much of the research started virtually from scratch and it was done by what were effectively amateurs who were faced with a steep learning curve to be surmounted on a challenging time scale. Not surprisingly, many of the initial ideas were reached ad hoc and depended on research to establish their technical validity and bring them to fruition. Ingenuity, imagination and enthusiasm were the characteristics most apparent in the staff. Perhaps the most striking feature of their activities was the very wide range of topics with which they became involved. They ran from high explosive technology to chemical and biochemical devices; from the techniques of air supply to incendiarism; from camouflage to underwater warfare; and from radio communications to weaponry.

Much of the work involved collaboration with the Operational Directorates of SOE and with other Government and military research establishments. Despite the political problems which beset SOE from time to time, these close links were effective and mutually beneficial.

One of the authors of this book, the late Douglas Everett, was recruited by SOE in 1942, worked at the research station at The Frythe near Welwyn (Station IX) and was later in charge of the User Trials Section with special responsibility for Air Supply Research. He therefore had first-hand knowledge of many of the topics dealt with. Some of his notebooks have survived, and together with several of his reports released by the PRO have formed the basis for several chapters. Fredric Boyce was an ICI engineer whose contact with and interest in SOE was fired by his involvement in the clearance of dangerous material left by them when The Frythe was acquired by ICI in 1946. He has been responsible for researching over 200 files at the PRO which have filled in many details of the organisation and development of SOE's technical operations.

The outcome is a well-documented account of a major contribution to the effective exploitation of scientific and technical skills in support of the often heroic efforts of the SOE agents worldwide.

ONE

INTRODUCTION

On the night of 14 May 1941, a 29-year-old German spy by the name of Karel Richard Richter descended by parachute into a field near London Colney in Hertfordshire. After burying his parachute and other incriminating items, including by mistake his emergency rations, he went into hiding. If he had set off up the Great North Road and managed to avoid detection he would have reached, after a few miles on the left, the entrance to a fine estate. A notice on the gate revealed that this was War Office property and that entry was forbidden without written permission. An armed guard in a discreetly placed hut kept watch on the gates. The drive beyond the gates wound up through a plantation of mature trees – Cypress, Redwood and Wellingtonia – interspersed with banks of rhododendrons in full bloom. Through the trees he might have caught sight, silhouetted against the sky, of a red-brick Victorian mansion at the top of the rise. There was little to suggest that this was a specially protected property. There were no high fences topped with barbed wire and no guard dogs. Had he hidden in the undergrowth and waited until morning he would have observed the arrival of a few dozen girls – typists or secretaries perhaps – and the departure of a car carrying three or four men, some in uniform, some in civilian clothes. During the day a little traffic would enter or leave and in the evening the girls went and those who had spent the day away elsewhere would return. To the casual observer, even a German spy, there was little to arouse curiosity. Many companies, some of them with Government contracts, had been evacuated from London to avoid the bombing, but maintained daily contacts with their headquarters. Unfortunately for him, Richter, who had spent three days without food or drink, was quickly arrested and convicted as an enemy spy. Prisoner 13961's short stay in the UK ended in a struggle on the gallows in Wandsworth Prison at 9 a.m. on 10 December.[1]

The mansion he would have stumbled upon was The Frythe at Welwyn in Hertfordshire, known then by its cover name as part of the Inter-Services Research Bureau (ISRB). These initials concealed its true identity. It was in fact one of the highly secret establishments set up early in the Second World War by the Special Operations Executive (SOE) to carry out sabotage and subversion against the enemy in occupied Europe using unconventional and often ungentlemanly means. SOE's very existence was a closely guarded secret – denied even by the Government in the Commons. To those working at The Frythe it was simply ISRB Station IX and to many of them the initials SOE meant nothing. Nor would many have known that it had other cover names (of non-existent departments!) such as MO1(SP) in the War Office, NID(Q) at the Admiralty and AI10 at the Air Ministry. Those members of its staff who in the course of their work were required to visit other military establishments were issued with passes identifying them as from MO1(SP). Sentries and security officers rarely recognised these initials but were usually satisfied when told they stood for Military Operations 1 (Special Planning). It was not until some time after the war that the very existence of SOE was allowed to be mentioned in public.

Station IX was the main centre for the Research, Development and Supplies Directorate of SOE and, as will be described later, played a pivotal role in the evolution of new and improved weaponry, equipment and techniques for use by its agents in occupied Europe and worldwide. Over the years glimpses of this work and some of the products which evolved have been given, often incidentally, in accounts of the history of SOE and the exploits of its agents published since the war. However, the authors of many of these books were constrained by security considerations. Those who were not personally involved have had to rely on the limited amount of information available to them at the Public Record Office (PRO), and on the discreet recollections of those who were. The belated release by the PRO of most of the surviving SOE files, supplemented by personal recollections of those who are now free to speak, has made available in the public domain new evidence to fill some of the gaps. Exhibits relating to its work are displayed in a number of museums including the Imperial War Museum in London, the Airborne Forces Museum at Aldershot, the Royal Signals Museum at Blandford Camp and in a small local museum at Arisaig in Western Scotland. But the full stories behind the invention and development of its weapons have until recently remained buried in the archives. A major problem facing historians attempting to compile a definitive account of the organisation arises from the fact that in the rapid and piecemeal development of SOE there was no Central Registry for its documents and no rational filing system. The departmental papers are scattered, incomplete and often confusing. Towards the end of hostilities a Central Registry was set up but only a quarter of the work of reclassifying the papers into a common system had been completed when the organisation was eventually disbanded in 1946. Unfortunately, a large proportion of the records of SOE have been lost, partly by deliberate destruction at the end of the war, some in a serious fire at the Baker Street headquarters, and many by weeding over half a century. One estimate is that over 80 per cent of the archives had been lost and the remainder were classified.

The situation has, however, changed dramatically in the last few years as most of the surviving SOE files have been opened to the public and now provide material for a more extensive study of its activities. It is interesting that some of the files which were said to have been lost have come to light. A number of important books have now collected together information hitherto unavailable. They include *The Secret History of SOE* by William Mackenzie (2000), written between 1945 and 1947 but not allowed to be published for a further 55 years; the *Secret Agent's Handbook of Special Devices* (2000); and even more recently *SOE Syllabus* (2001). But none of these provides an account of the research and development of SOE weaponry and equipment, nor of the distinguished band of scientists and engineers who were recruited to solve the wide range of problems arising from this new form of warfare.

In the following chapters an attempt is made to present as full a picture as possible, based largely on the available documentation together with personal recollections of a few of those who were involved. Sadly, many of those who could have answered some of the outstanding questions have taken their secrets to the grave: Time continues to reap its harvest month by month.

A large number of abbreviations and symbols were used throughout the conflict. An explanation of them is given in Appendix C.

TWO

WHAT WAS THE SPECIAL OPERATIONS EXECUTIVE?

The Special Operations Executive (SOE) was formed in mid-July 1940 at the height of the crisis following Dunkirk and the fall of France. It brought together three existing secret organisations: Section D of the Secret Intelligence Service (SIS) otherwise known as MI6; the Military Intelligence Research unit (MI(R)) of the War Office formerly known as General Staff (Research) or GS(R); and Electra House, attached to the Foreign Office and mainly concerned with propaganda.

As early as March 1939 the existence of three organisations tackling much the same work was seen as an anomaly. Certain duplication of effort was taking place between MI(R) and D Section, something the country could ill afford. It wasted valuable time and there was a tendency for production aspects of the work to take precedence over vital research. The first paper to address this problem was prepared in June 1939. Over the next few months there followed various initiatives attempting to solve the problem of co-ordination.

Reorganisation was discussed in a complex series of meetings held in June and July 1940 involving, in various combinations, the CIGS, Lord Gort; the Foreign Secretary, Lord Halifax; the Chief of GS(R), Col Holland; Mr Hugh Dalton; Mr Clement Attlee; and representatives of SIS. They dealt among other things with the sensitive problem of the military or civilian control of a merged organisation. The solution was to some extent a compromise between political interests, but the details of the discussions, said to have been acrimonious, leading to agreement cannot, according to W. Mackenzie in his *Secret History of SOE*, be traced from the papers available. The final document proposing the setting up of an organisation to be called the Special Operations Executive under the Chairmanship of Dalton was signed on 19 July by Neville Chamberlain (then Lord President of the Council following his resignation as Prime Minister on 10 May 1940). Churchill had already, on 16 July, offered the Headship of SOE to Hugh Dalton, the 53-year-old Minister of Economic Warfare (MEW), with the now much-publicised exhortation to 'set Europe ablaze'. Ironically, it was on this very day that Hitler signed his Führer Directive No. 16 for the planning of Operation Sea Lion, the invasion of Britain. The SOE Charter was finally approved by the War Cabinet on 22 July. In retrospect it seems somewhat anomalous that it was placed, not under any of the parent ministries, but under the Ministry of Economic Warfare. The reasons were a consequence of the complex political negotiations which preceded its formation. Each of the constituent organisations had been set up independently before the war in 1938 with objectives which were loosely defined and overlapping. The new organisation was given a more specific task of promoting sabotage and subversion through its own covert agents and with supplying arms, equipment and agents to resistance movements throughout occupied Europe and beyond. When they were amalgamated to form SOE they each brought with them a good deal of historical baggage which, throughout the war, coloured relations between SOE and its parents. These political problems, though they were of major importance in the general progress of SOE, did not have any significant influence on its scientific and technical work.

Implementation of the Charter took a little time. Control of Section D and Electra House passed from the Foreign Office to MEW on 16 August, while the formal dissolution of MI(R) followed in October. Meanwhile SOE's London Headquarters was moved in October 1940 to 64 Baker Street, where it adopted its public cover name of the Inter-Services Research Bureau. It was quite separate from MEW in Berkeley Square. Dalton remained as head until in 1942 he was replaced by Lord Selborne, also aged 53. To appreciate the development of the scientific and technical aspects of SOE's work it is important to set the scene by outlining the history of those components which came together to form SOE. Electra House, which was set up in 1938 by Lord Hankey and headed by Sir Campbell Stuart, was mainly concerned with propaganda and had little impact on the research and development work of SOE. Attention is, therefore, here restricted to Section D (MI6) and GS(R) (later known as MI(R)). The formal relationship between them is difficult to disentangle, but some of their technical work certainly overlapped.

5

SECTION D

In April 1938 the then head of the SIS, Admiral Sir Hugh Sinclair, arranged for the secondment of Maj Lawrence Grand, RE, from the War Office to SIS to carry out a study and to report on the possibilities of creating a British organisation for covert offensive action. Germany and Italy had already conducted such operations in countries which they later overran, and the possible existence of a Fifth Column in Britain was not entirely ruled out.[1] Grand had no experience of secret service work but he had ideas and enthusiasm and a persona which earned the admiration of all who worked with him. His personal energy was much needed for time was not on his side – by now, Austria had been occupied by Germany. Grand was promoted to Colonel, given the symbol D and set up the Devices Section of MI6, to be called Section D and with the cover name of Statistical Research Department of the War Office. Section D's terms of reference were:

a) To study how sabotage might be carried out
b) to produce special sabotage ammunition
c) to make experiments on carrying out sabotage
d) to train saboteurs
e) to study methods of countering sabotage.

The use of aggressive action was precluded as long as peace held.

At first the Section consisted of only two officers. Among those recruited by Grand in December 1938 was Cdr A.G. Langley RN who set in motion and pursued energetically work on the research and development of ideas and stores needed to meet the above objectives. In particular, his small group was concerned with the design of time fuses and switches of various types and of explosives and incendiary devices. Section D was originally based at SIS's head office at 54 Broadway but soon expanded to the adjacent Caxton House. In the early months of 1939, as the threat of war grew ever closer, Horace Emery of SIS arranged for the manufacture of the first batch of Time Pencil fuses to Langley's design. Articles made in Germany and Italy which might be suitable for concealing or camouflaging weapons were collected and contacts established with organisations which could be of use in war, such as various Service Departments, the Research Department at Woolwich Arsenal, the British Scientific Instrument Research Association, the Royal Society, Imperial Chemical Industries, Shell Oil

Company, the Railway Executive, etc. On the outbreak of war, most of Section D's staff moved with the Government Code and Cipher School (GCCS), the forerunner of GCHQ, to Bletchley Park (Station 'X') although some went to The Frythe.

By the middle of 1939 a small magazine for explosives and incendiaries had been built at Bletchley and work had started on full scale experiments with weapons.[2] This was not universally popular as it was judged that it was incompatible to have explosives and decoding work on the same site. Furthermore, GCCS's work was expanding rapidly and Section D was forced to find accommodation for Langley's work elsewhere. In November 1939 it was moved to Aston House at Stevenage in Hertfordshire which was given the title Signals Development Branch Depot No. 4, War Office. In 1941 it became War Department Experimental Station 6 (ES6 WD), recognising its parent MI6. On the formation of SOE it became known also as Station XII. Langley took with him a small group of about seven officers, two laboratory technicians, five other ranks (O/Rs) and secretarial staff. Among those who moved to Aston House were Dr Drane (in command); Capt L.J.C. Wood (later Colonel and in command of the Station); Capt C.R. Bailey; Mr Colin Meek, a Scientific Civil Servant and explosives expert on secondment from Woolwich Arsenal and another un-named, possibly Douglas Barnsley; and, on a part-time basis, Mr Eric Norman. The laboratory assistants were Mr G. Doe and Mr B.S.M. Stalton. Dr F.A. Freeth was also concerned with this group.

Also recruited by Grand was a group of distinguished amateur sailors from the Royal Cruising Club including Frank Carr, the Assistant Librarian of the House of Lords, Roger Pinckney, the architect of Melbourne Cathedral and Augustine Courtauld, Arctic explorer. They had all been recruited to familiarise themselves with parts of the continental coastline which could be of strategic importance in wartime. Attached to this group was Gerry Holdsworth who was later to set up the Helford Base in Cornwall.[3] Meanwhile, Section D had established agents and offices in Sweden, Norway, Holland, Spain, and France. However, within a few months of the outbreak of war it had lost contact with nearly all of its overseas agents, and it was soon apparent that most had been arrested by the Germans. Its work was, inevitably for such a novel enterprise, largely a process of trial and error which was overtaken by the progress of the war before significant results could be obtained. As a result, after the fall of France neither Section D nor any other

Allied covert organisation had any agents on the Western European mainland, although a number remained in the Balkans and the Middle East.

GS(R)

In 1938 a section was set up in the War Office by the Deputy CIGS, Sir Ronald Adam, known by the innocuous title of General Staff (Research). It was to research into the problems of tactics and organisation under the DCIGS. It produced a number of papers of which two are of interest but have not been found: 'Considerations from the Wars in Spain and China with Respect to Certain Aspects of Army Policy' and 'An Investigation of the Possibilities of Guerrilla Activities'. In December 1938 Lt Col J.F. Holland, RE, was appointed head of the group. His experience of irregular warfare in Ireland and India had influenced the writing of the latter paper. With Col Grand of Section D, Holland produced a joint paper dated 20 March 1939 dealing with the possibility of guerrilla actions against Germany if they overran Eastern Europe and absorbed Rumania. The formal objectives of GS(R) were similar to those of Section D:

a) To study guerrilla methods and to produce a guerrilla Field Service Regulations Handbook incorporating detailed tactical and technical instructions, as they applied to various countries
b) To evolve destructive devices suitable for use by guerrillas and capable of production and distribution on a wide enough scale to be effective
c) To evolve procedures and machinery for operating guerrilla activities if it were decided to do so subsequently.

As the Military Intelligence Directorate expanded in response to the increasing threat of war in the spring of 1939, GS(R) changed its name to Military Intelligence (Research) or MI(R). Holland's section was first housed in Caxton House, adjacent to Grand's Section D, but on the outbreak of war it was moved to the War Office building. In the spring of that year Holland was authorised to appoint two Grade II staff officers to MI(R). The first was another Royal Engineer, Maj M.J.R. Jefferis, later Sir Millis Jefferis, to work on guerrilla devices. His unit was based initially at 36 Portland Place, but when they were bombed out in Autumn 1940 they moved to The Firs, a Tudor mansion at Whitchurch near Aylesbury which became known as MI(R)c. Also known as 'Winston Churchill's Toyshop',[4] it produced a string of inventions, several of which, like those from Section D, became the basis for the development of devices which were later adopted both by SOE and the regular Army Engineers. However, this unit became increasingly concerned with larger-scale military hardware such as anti-tank weapons, the destruction of concrete pillboxes and the clearance of minefields. On the formation of SOE it was specifically excluded from the transfer of MI(R) to SOE and remained independent as MD1 under the patronage of Churchill and his friend and scientific adviser, Prof Lindemann (later Lord Cherwell).

For the second of these posts Holland chose Maj Colin Gubbins, RA. This appointment was to prove crucially important in the later development of SOE. Gubbins's first task was to work on two pamphlets: 'The Partisan Leader's Handbook';[5] and 'The Art of Guerrilla Warfare'. The second of these was written in collaboration with Holland, while a third, 'How to Use High Explosives', was written by Jefferis. They drew heavily on the experiences of Lawrence (of Arabia) and of operations in Palestine, Ireland, the North-West Frontier and Russia. Surprisingly, there was not at this time a single book to be found in any library in any language on these subjects. In fact, none of these pamphlets was published in England although they were distributed widely in Europe and South-east Asia.

With the formation of SOE, MI(R) was combined with Section D.

THE BIRTH OF SOE

SOE had a difficult birth and suffered recurring post-natal pains. The incorporation of Section D with MI(R) to form one body responsible to an Executive Director, to be called CD, required many changes both in structure and personnel. There were hard decisions to be taken and several heads rolled. Both Grand and Holland had made internal enemies and returned to pursue their distinguished military careers: they both ended up as Maj-Gens. Many other staff left or were transferred to other duties.

The first to fill the post of CD in August 1940 was the 58-year-old Sir Frank Nelson who had to build up SOE almost from nothing. Nelson was a businessman, a former Conservative MP and former Vice-Consul at Basle in Switzerland, where he had had some involvement with SIS. He undertook his task with great enthusiasm and dedication, but ruined his health and was obliged to resign in May 1942 after eighteen months.

Initially SOE was divided into three Branches: SO1 (Propaganda), SO2 (Active Operations) and SO3 (Planning). Of these SO1 was the subject of arguments with the Ministry of Information and the Foreign Office and was soon taken over and incorporated in the Political Warfare Executive (PWE) controlled by the Foreign Office. Useful sidelights on the early years before SOE and PWE parted company are contained in *The Secret History of PWE* by David Garnett. SO3, in the words of M.R.D. Foot, 'proceeded to strangle itself in festoons of paperwork'[6] and had disintegrated by the end of September 1940. This left SO2, which now took on the mantle and title of SOE. At this stage, with the exception of a few Regular Army officers, the whole staff was amateur. Mercifully, the organisation was free from the minor bureaucracy of a Government department. This led to a looser and more flexible arrangement, which was not without its disadvantages.

SOE was financed by secret funds from the Ministry of Economic Warfare and for some time (certainly until the end of 1942) its officers were paid monthly in crisp, white £5 notes – until the Inland Revenue became aware that some people were not paying income tax! It is sometimes said that those paid from SOE funds were exempt from tax. This may well have been true of its agents, but not for the rest of its personnel.

Nelson inherited two deputies. Maj, later Col George Taylor from Section 6 was in charge of operations, including the re-establishment of Country Sections, while Col F.T. (Tommy) Davies from MI(R) took control of 'facilities' which included training, supplies and stores. Both were ruthless and efficient and played important roles in SOE throughout the war.

George Taylor was an Australian business tycoon who had joined SIS and Section D before the war. He influenced the organisational structure and later was to play a major role in Balkan and Middle Eastern affairs.

Col Davies, the son of a General and a Director of Courtaulds, had joined MI(R) as a Captain in the Grenadier Guards shortly before the outbreak of war. In 1939 he was a member of the MI(R) mission (No. 4 Military Mission) to Poland which arrived at its destination the day war broke out but returned within a few days since there was little it could do. In May 1940, Davies paid a hasty trip to Amsterdam to destroy or remove certain securities, and a few weeks later led a raiding party to the Courtauld factory in Calais and succeeded in removing large quantities of platinum before the Germans arrived. As well as being deputy for Nelson, he was also his personal assistant and as such was responsible for the setting up of the training sections. By the end of 1941 he had become the Director of Research, Development and Supplies with the code symbol AD/Z, a post he held for the rest of the war.

On Nelson's retiral his post as CD went, early in May 1942, to his then deputy, Sir Charles Hambro, a successful city banker and a Director of the Great Western Railway and of the Bank of England. He had been in charge of the Scandinavian Section for two years. His many other responsibilities meant that he was unable to spend as much time on SOE business as the post demanded. By the spring of 1942 Dalton had been replaced by Lord Selborne. Following personal difficulties with Selborne, Hambro was sacked in September 1943. His replacement was Brig (later Maj Gen) Gubbins who, as recorded above, had joined SOE in November 1940 and been Hambro's deputy.

Colin McVean Gubbins was in many ways the ideal leader of SOE. A professional soldier born in Tokyo, Japan on 2 July 1896, he had seen service in the First World War, and in Northern Russia and gained valuable experience when he fought as a Major against the Irish Republican Army in the Irish Civil War in 1921. He was a small, wiry Scotsman who was described as 'quiet-mannered, quiet-spoken, energetic, efficient and charming', 'a still waters run deep sort of man' and 'a born leader of men'. He was on the staff of MI(R) in the spring of 1939 when, under the shadow of the approaching conflict, he wrote the two pamphlets on clandestine warfare referred to above. Later that year he became the senior staff officer to the British Military Mission in Poland and was in overall charge of the MI(R) group there. As it was, his efforts to set up a Polish resistance force were thwarted by the lightning speed of the German advance and he was fortunate to get out in time to Paris where he was promoted to Lt Col. In April 1940 he was brought back to select and train troops for the assault on Norway at Narvik. He was then engaged in the setting up of the Auxiliary Units in Britain to fight a guerrilla war against German invaders should they land. By November that threat had diminished and he was put in charge of Operations and Training in Dalton's SOE, together with responsibility for the Polish and Czechoslovakian sections. After Hambro's demise he remained as CD for the rest of the war having had to suffer the loss of his elder son in an SOE operation at Anzio,

Italy in February 1944. He was knighted for his work and died in Stornoway, Scotland on 11 February 1976. A full biography, *Gubbins and SOE*, written by Peter Wilkinson and Joan Bright Astley, was published in 1993.

Gubbins's influence on the direction and overall policies of SOE was crucial. Throughout his association with the organisation from 1940, his period as deputy to Hambro, and his own period as CD to the end of the war, his personality and drive played a major role in developing and executing SOE policies. The team which grew up around him realised the vital importance of scientific and technical support in areas which were regarded traditionally as outside the normal military concern. As a result, SOE was able to provide the resistance movements in Europe and the Middle and Far East with substantial specialist support in the way of supplies, equipment and technical innovation. This was made possible through the work of the Directorate of Research, Development and Supplies under Col Tommy Davies and his Director of Scientific Research, Dr Dudley Newitt. The nature and extent of the activities of the DSR Sections form the subject matter of the rest of this book.

THREE

SOE RESEARCH AND DEVELOPMENT ESTABLISHMENTS

From October 1940 the headquarters of SOE were in Baker Street, London. Its true purpose was obscured in the title Inter-Services Research Bureau which was displayed prominently for all to see on the blast wall protecting the main entrance of no. 64. In the course of the war it took over a number of office buildings in the adjacent streets and squares and gave them identities which were even more obscure. Wartime organisations undertaking highly secret work required accommodation and facilities for research and testing under conditions which would not arouse curiosity. To satisfy this demand the Government exercised its wide-reaching powers to requisition public and privately owned properties needed to meet the national emergency. Apart from the administrative offices around Baker Street, SOE acquired several other types of property. Establishments concerned with experimental work, storage and production were mostly in Hertfordshire and were denoted by Roman numerals. Those housing training schools, denoted by Arabic numerals, were mainly in three groups: paramilitary schools were in remoter areas of Western Scotland north of the Caledonian Canal; the so-called 'Finishing Schools' concerned with subversion and propaganda were around Beaulieu in Hampshire; the operational schools were located in Leicestershire, Gloucestershire, Oxfordshire and several counties further south. In addition, the Signals, Polish and Norwegian Sections had a number of schools and there were Parachute Schools in Cheshire, Northamptonshire, Hertfordshire and Surrey. By its very nature it was inevitable that SOE would tend to use large houses on substantial estates, and in some quarters it was supposed frivolously that SOE stood for 'Stately 'Omes of England'. In fact, SOE was in the second league in this respect. For example, SIS was in part housed in Woburn Abbey.

The Directorate of Research, Development and Supply under Tommy Davies (AD/Z) had its main stations in and around Hertfordshire. The more important of this group were Station IX at The Frythe near Welwyn, which had been taken over by Section D in August 1939 and later received the Experimental Section when it was moved from Station XII in 1941; Station XII at Aston House near Stevenage, to which the combined Section D and MI(R) moved from Bletchley Park in November 1940; Station XV, the Thatched Barn road-house at Borehamwood, which housed the Camouflage Section; and Station VI at Bride Hall, Ayot St Lawrence, which housed the Arms Section. Each of these had limited living accommodation for staff, although many of those employed in them lived locally in rented houses or flats. A full list of SOE Stations in this Directorate is given in Appendix A.

THE FRYTHE, STATION IX

It is believed that the name Frythe came from the old English word Ffrid (pronounced Freeth) which referred to an area of wooded country rather than a specific location. There is a 1260 record of land at Welwyn being owned by a John del Frith and the Prioress of Holywell. The Wilshere family took a 60-year lease on the property in 1539 but, at the dissolution of the monasteries, Henry VIII gave The Frythe to Sir John Gostwick, the Wilsheres remaining as tenants. Sir William Gostwick, Sir John's brother, sold the estate to William Wilshere in 1547.

The Wilshere family prospered and their social status rose from 'yeoman' to 'gentleman'. From time to time the house was leased to other families but they retained their ownership. In 1838 William Wilshere, who was then MP for Great Yarmouth, decided to enhance his status by commissioning the Hertford architect Thomas Smith to design the present mansion on the site of the earlier house and this was completed in 1846 in the then fashionable Gothic-revival style. An impressive portico was added in 1870 together with a clock tower without a clock face. The time was announced by chimes and so that hearers knew which quarter of which hour was being chimed, it struck first the hour and then the quarter in question. So at a quarter to midnight it must have kept people awake for a long time![1] There was an air of opulence and history about the grand staircase and the stained glass windows characteristic of the style adopted by the upwardly mobile classes in the nineteenth century. One of the dining rooms housed an organ which was still serviceable in the late 1950s and, indeed, was played on festive occasions. But the gargoyled façade which hid the true antiquity of the estate did not impress everyone. Bickham Sweet-Escott, a one-time classical scholar turned banker, a member of Section D and an early historian of SOE, described it as 'a large hideous Victorian house'.

During the Victorian period the Wilsheres became enthusiastic collectors of trees from around the world, adding to the large number of native species imported Cypress, Redwood, Wellingtonia, Sweet Gum, Tulip, Japanese Maple and many others. The estate eventually contained almost 600 trees which became an important collection, reputedly the second finest arboretum in England. Unfortunately, many were lost in a serious gale in 1921 and some of their replacements were among the casualties of the Great Storm of 16 October 1987.

In 1934 Gerald Wilshere and a friend opened 'The Frythe Residential Private Hotel'. It boasted central heating, eight bathrooms and fresh fruit and vegetables from the estate kitchen gardens. Among the local amusements listed in its brochure was the Barn Road House which had a large, floodlit swimming pool, dancing, cabaret and tennis courts. Little did they know then that the Barn was to share in the wartime activities of The Frythe. First-floor rooms cost up to five guineas a week including all meals but one paid an additional 6*d* (six old pence) per person for early morning tea. The hotel flourished in some splendour until war was inescapable. Then, around midday on the last Saturday in August 1939, a detachment of soldiers and civilians under the supervision of a 'Man from the Ministry' ascended the long drive to the mansion to advise the thirty or forty staff and residents that they must pack their belongings and be gone by eight o'clock that evening.[2] Despite the protestations of the owner, a First World War veteran who had been captured, repatriated and then badly wounded when back in France, the authorities insisted that they were requisitioning the estate forthwith. War was imminent and the estate was needed immediately, in this case for Section D, the small semi-autonomous and largely unacknowledgeable branch of SIS. The 'Man from the Ministry' was almost certainly George Taylor, a severe man who later became one of the leading lights in SOE. Throughout the winter of 1939–40 the new residents began to establish Station IX's first research group, the Wireless Section. By mid-1941 a number of single-storey, good quality, prefabricated, felt-roofed wooden huts, (typical size 35 ft × 15 ft) extended to the south and housed the rather basically equipped laboratories of the Experimental Section, which had been moved from Station XII in July. The internal layouts were fairly conventional with a hut being partitioned into, for example, two laboratories, a specialist room and two small offices. Central heating from a steam boiler plant was available in winter. The terrace had been excavated to form an explosives pit with a concrete observation bunker with bomb-proof windows. The Wireless Section occupied part of a wing of the mansion. The meadows leading down to the main road were used for trials of non-explosive devices. Some of the bedrooms in the house had been converted into offices, while others provided living accommodation for some officers and secretaries.

The Engineering Section started in a small way with one workshop of 600 sq ft area. As demand increased, an area adjacent to the explosives pit was excavated to provide a large workshop hangar and, nearby, an associated test tank was constructed. The Section finally possessed a Small Mechanisms and Fine Machinery Shop, a Heavy Metal Shop, Light Metal Shop, Electricians' Shop, Carpenters' Shop and a Drawing Office.

Later in 1944, the very primitive laboratory facilities were enhanced by the construction of a few specialist buildings. Among them was the so-called Thermostat Hut, which was of more substantial construction than the others, being brick-built with a corrugated asbestos roof. It was designed to provide a number of constant-temperature environments in which research could proceed into the problem of the time–temperature coefficients of delayed action devices such as the Time Pencil. In addition to two small offices it contained a laboratory, initially equipped with a hydrostatic pressure test apparatus, vacuum and compressed air services and a small refrigerator, which was later converted to simulate the humid conditions of the Far East; an analytical laboratory with soldering and glassblowing facilities and a fume cupboard; and the thermostat room. This contained eight temperature-controlled cabinets which varied in size from 3 ft × 2 ft × 3 ft high to 3 ft 6 in × 5 ft × 7 ft high. Two could only be heated above the temperature of the main room; two had heating and limited cooling; two had cooling only while two provided a range of temperatures from –40°C to +20°C. Thus any conditions from the tropics to the arctic could be simulated. A large amount of space in the room was taken up by the main timing bench. Here, the controlled temperature chambers (thermostats) were linked to six panels, each with six electric clocks and twelve counters counting six-minute intervals (1/10 hour). So in all there were 36 clocks and 72 counters to record the delay times of fuses.[3] The lack of this essential facility had handicapped the work of the Experimental Section until the construction of this building in 1944.

It is today surprising to learn that the security was such that many of those working at The Frythe during those wartime years did not know of the existence of SOE until many years later or that ISRB was part of that organisation.

At the end of the war, while a small Admiralty presence remained working on hydrogen peroxide propellants, The Frythe was leased to Imperial Chemical Industries Ltd, who set up their Butterwick Research Laboratories in the huts used so recently for clandestine sabotage research. A few years later the establishment was expanded with some permanent buildings and they purchased the site, renaming it the Akers Research Laboratories after Sir Wallace Akers, an ICI Director who had worked on the atomic bomb. In the early 1960s ICI sold The Frythe to Unilever Ltd and they subsequently sold it to SmithKline Beecham Ltd, currently known as GlaxoSmithKline.

ASTON HOUSE, STATION XII

Even before the outbreak of war there was recognition of a duplication of effort between MI(R), and Section D. A scheme was drawn up at the highest levels of the Civil Service for their amalgamation.[4] Section D had, by the middle of 1939, two officers conducting experiments with weapons at Bletchley Park. But they were not yet in a position to experiment with and devise techniques for the use of the revolutionary plastic explosive which was still in the development stage at the Royal Arsenal at Woolwich. On the declaration of war this experimental section was increased to seven plus a part-timer. As the Bletchley Park de-coding operation expanded, a search for alternative accommodation for Section D and MI(R) resulted in the move to Aston House in the village of Aston on the south-eastern outskirts of Stevenage in November 1939. It was initially designated Signals Development Branch, Depot No. 4, War Department. Later it was known as Experimental Station 6 (War Department), E.S.6 (W.D.) and, in SOE, as Station XII. It included a Research Laboratory and a Development Section responsible for the placing of orders with outside manufacturers. Later a separate Production Section was formed (see Chapter 13).

Aston House, sometimes referred to as Aston Place, had been built in the seventeenth century and, with its estate, occupied 46 acres close by the church of St Mary. The mansion itself in the Queen Anne style was constructed partly on three levels, while the wings to the west and east were lower, the stable block at the extreme east being on two floors. Included in the central part of the building was an octagonal library. In 1815 the estate, which included a walled garden, belonged to Mr Francis Wishaw, a local land owner, and was occupied by a Mr Edmund Darby, who also rented much of Aston and Aston End from him. Capt W.E.F. O'Brien took over the estate in the latter part of the nineteenth century until, in 1895, F.W. Imbert-Terry became the resident. In 1912 Arthur R. Yeomans bought the estate and it remained in his family until requisitioned by the War Office.[5]

The mansion became the officers' mess. The additional buildings erected to meet wartime demands included one known as 'the factory', a NAAFI canteen, a Nissen-type entertainments hall and many Romney Nissen huts. Aston Park or 'the pleasure grounds' to the west of the mansion became underground explosives stores and testing grounds.

After the end of hostilities and when the disposal of all SOE assets was completed the Ministry of Supply sold the site on 1 February 1947 to the Stevenage Development Corporation, who were embarking on the construction of the New Town at the start of the postwar housing boom. Although the mansion was now suffering from the ravages of dry rot in the lounge and wet rot with worm and beetle in the dining room, the Corporation used it as its headquarters and the wartime buildings as stores, garages and a hostel for labour.

Aston House was eventually demolished in the early sixties. A high-class housing development was built in its place and incorporated by luck or design the wall of the former walled garden. The short road running through this small estate is called Yeomans Lane after the last private owner of the land and the area containing the explosives stores and testing grounds became a golf course.

BRIDE HALL, STATION VI

The Arms Section of SOE was not strictly part of its Research and Development organisation but it has been included here because of the close connections it had with Station IX in the early days of its existence.

One of the first requirements for a clandestine organisation charged with setting up a resistance network in enemy-occupied countries was to find a source of supply of small arms, a task that was none too easy after the humiliation and losses sustained in the fall of France and the evacuation from Dunkirk. Maj Hugh B. Pollard (who had been created a Don by Franco for services to him) was given this responsibility, along with a room at 2 Caxton Street in London from which to discharge it. The room became a small armoury for automatic pistols and machine guns and while Maj Pollard spent much of his time travelling abroad seeking batches of weapons to bring back, Mr E.J. Churchill, a well-known London gunsmith, shared his time between running his business and working voluntarily servicing the weapons procured. As can be imagined, this team of less than two full-time members quickly became overwhelmed with the burgeoning workload and managed to recruit Staff Sergeant Elliot, a gunsmith by profession. Shortly afterwards he was injured in a London air raid and a safer home for the Arms Section was sought. Before 1940 was over, Maj Pollard and Mr Churchill had both left and Lt Col J.N. Tomlinson, RE, took charge of the section and soon organised a move to Station IX. In December the North Road Garage in the village of Welwyn was requisitioned as a section store pending the erection of an armoury hut in the grounds of The Frythe. Some idea of the hard work and early success of this small unit can be gauged from the fact that, in February 1941, a consignment of 20 tons of arms was sent from this garage to Norway.

By this time demand for small arms weapons of all types had increased. Capt E.I. Rowat was appointed London Liaison Officer dealing with the War Office, Air Ministry (for the recovery of weapons from crashed aircraft), the Ministry of Supply, the police and various gunsmiths from whom he purchased weapons, these transactions being known euphemistically as BDPs (back door purchases). The search for weapons was very wide-ranging and given considerable impetus by Sir Norman Kendal, the Assistant Commissioner of Police at Scotland Yard, who later organised at least three appeals to patriotic holders of firearms certificates. It was at this time that the police chief regretted the fact that the British were not a very 'gun-minded' nation. Nevertheless, in response to the appeals and in the course of other searches, the Arms Section started to acquire large numbers of various types of automatic pistols which were not available from Army sources and yet were so essential for SOE's purposes. In January they secured the services of another armourer, Cpl Spice, and as the section became established a steady stream of weapons passed through their hands, every one of them having been serviced by the armourers before being sent on its way to the Continent, Middle East, or the Balkans. Soon, the accommodation at the North Road Garage was overstretched and the stores were moved to the splendid dining room at The Frythe. At the end of May Second Lt Kendal joined the Section and, in July 1941, as the accommodation of one hut and the dining room was clearly inadequate, the Arms Section was moved (lock, stock and barrel) the short distance to the large and rather beautiful, centuries-old barns at Bride Hall near Ayot St Lawrence, which became Station VI.[6]

The Bride Hall estate was owned by a timber magnate, Sir Gerald Lenanton, whose wife wrote historical novels under the name Carola Oman. He had already evacuated to the unlikely safety of the Bristol area together with some of his staff but returned to the handsome red-brick mansion in 1943 to share the accommodation with the few resident officers. Of the three gardeners and four other staff, one gardener together with a housemaid, the cook and the butler remained to look after the new guests.[7] The barn walls were painted with black pitch beneath the deep red-tiled roofs and the walls were lined with tarred brown paper to keep out the draughts. One of the barns became the armoury for repairing and servicing weapons, another was used for the storage of ammunition, bombs, machine guns, etc., while a third eventually became the sleeping quarters for the other ranks, its heating being by two wood-burning stoves whose flues were prevented from setting fire to the massive old timbers by sheets of asbestos fixed all the way up the lofty walls. Sgt Elliott and another 'three striper', however, were blessed with accommodation in no. 2 of the nearby tithe cottages. The Section at this time employed four officers, a secretary and eight men on the armoury staff. It had what was probably a unique collection of foreign firearms of all calibres in addition to a large number of standard small arms. Two firing ranges were created: one in the orchard and the other behind the nearby woods. The officers dined and slept in the comfort of the gracious Hall, originally built in 1602 by a wealthy mariner as a wedding present for his daughter, while the other ranks ate well but in the servants' hall. A hand-cranked petrol pump topped with a one-gallon capacity glass globe was installed outside the workshop to supply the steady flow of service vehicles. Second Lt Paton and Second Lt Richard Wattis (later to star in many comedy films and television series) swelled the officer numbers to six, while additional help was obtained by swearing in the London gunsmiths John Wilkes & Co. At the end of the year Capt Rowat became Officer in Charge.

The Arms Section became involved on the fringes of the development of the silenced version of the Sten gun in the autumn of 1942 but its problems were not resolved until the following year, the first consignment being sent out in June. Capt Rowat left the Section in August 1943 and Second Lt Kendal succeeded him as O/C, while on the secretarial front Miss Halcomb succeeded Miss Bentham.

Although now separate from The Frythe, it is worth recalling that this small unit did amazing work in procuring arms from anywhere they could. The 'Pistol Drive' appeals to holders of firearms certificates netted some 7,000 hand guns in July 1942, 3,000 in September 1943 and an undisclosed number of German automatic pistols early in 1945. An indication of the success of Station VI is evident from the realisation that they procured, serviced and supplied the Country Sections of SOE with 3–5,000 hand guns and ammunition each month. In all, over 100,000 pistols and revolvers of non-standard types were sent to the field. In the lead-up to D-Day, with the need to prepare for the arming of large numbers of Resistance fighters, the Section expanded further. Lt Ramsden joined in April and was replaced in July by Lt Sumpoter. The unused barns were converted into billets. Local pensioners still recall that on VE day the soldiers went down to the party in nearby Wheathamstead but on VJ night they decided to give the local villagers a firework display using any pyrotechnics they could lay their hands on. Unfortunately, one of these flares arced into the night sky to descend on a haystack, setting it alight. Eventually the fire brigade arrived but the results of the subsequent enquiry are not recorded.[8]

THE THATCHED BARN, STATION XV

The Camouflage Section started in a small way at The Frythe in January 1942, took over the Victoria and Albert Museum's larger workshops at 56 Queen's Gate in London the following month and in June spread to a building not far from Elstree film studios which must have been familiar to the Section's head, Elder Wills. This was the Thatched Barn Road House (now replaced by the Elstree Moat House), a sprawling, two-storey, mock-Tudor hotel built in 1933 by a Mrs Merrick to serve motorists on the recently opened Barnet bypass. It was given the designation Station XV. With private motor transport drastically reduced in wartime, it provided a useful site, with public rooms being converted into workshops and bedrooms into accommodation for the staff.[9] The building was attractive in its day and was frequented by film stars from the nearby studios. The Barn was purchased by the Queen's Moat House chain in the mid-1970s and the last vestiges of the original building were demolished in the mid-1980s.

The Camouflage Section retained 56 Queen's Gate (Station XVa) and took over the Demonstration Room in the Natural History Museum in Cromwell Road which became Station XVb, and a house in nearby Trevor Square, off Knightsbridge, which housed another sub-section known as the Photographic and Make-up Section, which became Station XVc.

OUTSTATIONS

Besides the major ISRB (SOE) establishments described above, there were a number of outstations with particular facilities (see Appendix A). Thus the Engineering Section at Station IX had research and testing facilities at Staines and Queen Mary reservoirs, and a unit at Fishguard for the testing of underwater craft. Station XV had a number of outstations with special facilities for forging and the printing of code sheets. Important facilities were made available by the RAF such as the provision for testing supply dropping equipment at Henlow. Many of the production facilities for the Wireless Section were, in the later period, moved to several outstations in North London.

FOUR

ORGANISATION OF RESEARCH AND DEVELOPMENT

At the outbreak of the war the 'art and science of sabotage' had, in its fundamentals, changed very little in centuries. Sabotage and murder by explosive and incendiary methods has a long history. Among many examples from the past one might quote the murder of Darnley in 1566 and the Gunpowder Plot of 1605. In the nineteenth century, cartoons of a sinister-looking agent carrying a plum pudding-like bomb with a dangling fuse characterised the popular image of the revolutionary saboteur. For many centuries the only explosive available for these purposes was gunpowder or one of its modifications. With the development of mining a major body of expertise in the handling of gunpowder for both civilian and military purposes grew up. The situation began to change, however, around the middle of the nineteenth century with the introduction of ammonium nitrate and the invention of the family of nitro-explosives by Nobel and others. These new explosives had extensive civilian uses both in mining and quarrying. In the military sphere explosives for demolition and camouflet* operations were developed and instruction in the military use of explosives for demolition was included in the training of the Royal Engineers. Even before 1940 Section D and MI(R) were beginning to develop new devices which overcame some of the disadvantages of traditional methods of controlling explosions. When they merged in July 1940 they brought together two small groups that had begun to work towards meeting the objectives which had been set for them individually when they were created a couple of years previously. The early designs of time-delays and of pull-, pressure- and anti-

_____

* The undermining of enemy positions by tunnelling and detonating explosives beneath them.

23

disturbance switches had been developed and by 1940 some were becoming part of Army equipment and were described in *The Demolition Handbook Vol. 1*. These developments are racily described by Macrae in *Winston Churchill's Toyshop*.[1] Much of the work had been done by Jefferis's group MI(R)c, backed by Lindemann and Churchill, but Section D had its own unit working along similar lines. There was both collaboration and rivalry between the two groups, but Section D had the important advantage of having direct links with operations in the field – they had a clearly defined clientèle. Their paths, as noted earlier, diverged later in the war as MI(R)c became MD1 and was increasingly involved in large-scale military problems such as clearing minefields and beach obstacles in anticipation of the Allied invasion.

When SOE was formed in June 1940 it thus had at its disposal a number of basic devices, some of which were prototypes undergoing development and yet to reach the production stage. It was clear, however, to the higher echelons of SOE that, for the effective prosecution of the main aims of SOE, more sophisticated equipment, designed specifically for the needs of irregular warfare, would be needed. The following pages outline the organisation that evolved in the pursuit of these objectives, and give a brief account of the scientists and engineers who were involved.

To these ends, the Research, Development and Supply Directorate was set up under Col F.T. Davies, (AD/Z), with the responsibility of ensuring that Resistance workers in the field were supplied with equipment and weapons appropriate to their diverse operational needs. The major objectives of SOE were to undermine the enemy's war economy by disruption of his transport, communications, vital supplies and their production, and through a variety of other means to create a sense of uncertainty among the occupying forces, and to encourage the hopes and aspirations of Resistance groups as D-Day approached. Later in the war it was expected that these activities would assume paramilitary characteristics and in some theatres of war to be associated with guerrilla-type activities.

To achieve these objectives, it was necessary to develop a new range of offensive equipment to enable SOE to play a full part in the war effort. In 1940, as noted above, some of these needs had been foreseen, and some progress had been made in designing several basic devices. It was clear, however, that not only improvement in existing equipment but new ways of attacking the enemy would have to be invented.

It was first necessary to envisage the circumstances under which individual stores would be employed. This required new thinking since these would often differ quite fundamentally from those encountered in conventional warfare. SOE had little previous experience to build upon, although the pre-war studies of Holland and Gubbins provided some guidance. In many areas they had to start virtually with a blank sheet, and had to rely on the imagination and inventiveness of the research personnel to foresee the opportunities and problems associated with this newly developing technology of clandestine warfare. A new organisation was needed within the AD/Z Directorate to ascertain and formulate the operational requirements (ORs) appropriate to unconventional warfare; to determine whether these requirements could be met by existing stores; if not, to initiate research and development programmes to meet these needs. Any resulting stores had to be subjected to rigorous functional and user trials and to be produced to high standards of reliability. At the same time the organisation had to be flexible enough to be able, at short notice, to produce one-off solutions for coup-de-main operations. The fledgling organisation had to be bold and prepared to learn from its mistakes.

To head the science research organisation, Davies sought a scientist who would visualise SOE's needs and gather round him a team of the best minds, skills and knowledge. The organisation had to have a degree of flexibility which would attract original and inventive types – rigidity is often the enemy of lateral thinking. Waiting in the wings was someone who had, back in 1940, some contact with Gubbins's Auxiliary Units. This was Dr (later Professor) D.M. Newitt, who was appointed on 9 January 1941 to the newly created post of Director of Scientific Research, DSR, with responsibility for Stations VI, IX, XII, and XV. His duties were to act as chief adviser on all scientific matters, to initiate and plan research into all mechanical and chemical equipment and to participate in both short- and long-term planning where technical matters were involved.

Dudley Maurice Newitt (1894–1980) had begun his career as an Assistant Chemist at the Ardeer factory of Nobel Explosives. This was interrupted by the First World War when, as a junior officer in the Sikh Regiment, he saw service in the North-West Frontier of India, Mesopotamia and Palestine. He took part in the historic entries into Damascus and Jerusalem. In 1918 he was awarded the Military Cross for his part in the capture of Samaria. On demobilisation he entered the Royal College of Science (later Imperial College, London) to study chemistry. After graduation he embarked on research in chemical engineering and became a leader in the field of high-pressure technology. He was promoted to Reader in 1936 and to Professor in 1946 and was elected to the Royal Society in 1942. Subsequently, after the war he became the first Courtauld Professor of Chemical Engineering at Imperial College and was later President of the Institution of Chemical Engineers. Newitt's tenacity of purpose and resolution were major factors in his leadership of SOE's technical development. His training in chemical engineering and his military experiences in the First World War meant that he was in a good position to make realistic assessments of proposed projects and to curb some of the more fantastic ideas that were propounded from time to time. He was outgoing, clubbable and his good sense and natural kindliness 'tinged with a delicious sense of irony' made him a notable leader. His slightly twisted yet disarmingly friendly smile usually meant that he was about to fire a challenging question to which he expected an equally incisive reply. There were those, it is said, who looked upon him as a typical absent-minded Professor. If that was how he appeared to some, then it was almost certainly a deliberate pose concealing his efficiency. The energy and drive he put into his job gave little support to this view.

On his appointment Newitt joined an embryonic organisation which, as a whole, attracted suspicion and lack of support from SIS, was looked upon as unethical by the Royal Air Force and (not without good reason) unqualified to venture into marine design by the Admiralty. Consequently, SOE was forced to work independently on a series of projects from scratch. It urgently needed specialised items of equipment to carry out its primary tasks but it had little expert knowledge on which to draw so had to set about learning, inventing and developing them itself. The nucleus of the research structure consisted of the small group of engineers and scientists of the Experimental Section at Aston House. Already at The Frythe was a Wireless Section working on radio communication equipment. Since its work was to become closely linked to that of Station IX, it is appropriate to include an account of it in this book (see Chapter 12).

The major areas in which research and development were to be directed included: chemical and physical sciences dealing in the widest sense with the application of special operational devices, explosives, incendiaries and fuses; the engineering of weapons, waterborne craft and vehicles; medical and clothing supplies; camouflage to disguise or conceal the presence of various devices; operational research to ensure that requirements were properly assessed, trials conducted and quality maintained; and means of getting supplies to the Resistance movements.

His group was also charged with maintaining technical links with missions abroad and with UK research resources in Government scientific circles, industrial research organisations and the laboratories of academia.

Newitt set up his HQ at 64 Baker Street with a small staff. He had to build up a team of first-rate scientists and technicians to meet the research and development needs of the rapidly expanding organisation. He looked for recruits beyond the business, banking, civil service and military establishments which had dominated SOE up to that time, eventually gathering some 500 people covering a wide range of skills and experience.

The division of responsibility between the research, development and supply activities of the AD/Z Directorate was loosely defined, partly because of the small number of people involved and overlapping interests. One of Newitt's first tasks was to rationalise the situation by separating the Research and Development functions from the Production and Supply Section. The Experimental Section was therefore transferred in July 1941 from Station XII to Station IX. Here they would have greater freedom from the pressures of production. Station XII was now to concentrate on taking equipment from prototype to full production, while Station IX became the main source of research for SOE.

During 1941–42 the structure of the DSR evolved and for the rest of the war consisted of the following main sections:

- HQ Section at 64 Baker Street was in overall control of the R&D activities.
- Experimental Section at Station IX (shown on organisational charts as Physico-Chemical Section), which was concerned with a wide range of physical and chemical problems.
- Engineering Section, also at Station IX, with sub-sections dealing with weapons and water-borne craft.
- Camouflage Section, initially at Station IX but soon moved to Station XV, was responsible for development of a wide range of materials and methods of concealing sabotage and subversive equipment.
- Operational Research, working mostly from Station IX but also calling on the facilities and personnel of Station XII and HQ, ensured that operational requirements were properly assessed,

trials conducted and quality monitored. It operated through the User Trials Section and later the Air Supply Research Section.

The primary sections of this research structure were broken down into sub-sections, sometimes of only three persons, one of whom was an expert in his field. Newitt knew well that he wouldn't get the best from a rigid organisation so the one he drafted on paper was flexible and had, in reality, very blurred boundaries. There was a good deal of collaboration between different groups, while the flexibility and freedom from unnecessary bureaucratic constraints gave people the opportunity to come up with and develop their own ideas.

HEADQUARTERS SECTION

As well as having overall control of the research and development activities, HQ was also the route through which new ideas and projects were fed into the programme. It therefore had to maintain technical links with Country Sections and Overseas Missions and was involved in operational activities through a Technical Planning Officer (DSR/OP) who worked in association with SOE's Technical Intelligence Section.

In late 1943 the research and development work of SOE came under scrutiny following a reorganisation in its highest ranks. On 9 September 1943 Sir Charles Hambro stood down and Gubbins, newly promoted to Major General, became the head (CD) of SOE. Lt Col Sporborg became the Vice Chief. Within a few months Sporborg had carried out a review of the procedure for research and development in SOE. He decreed that the overall policy of research, priorities of work, and progress of development and production should be overseen by a permanent committee, the HQ Research and Production Committee. It was to be chaired by Col Barry and comprised a group of SOE 'top brass', including Davies and Newitt. At the first meeting on 4 December it was ruled that work at Station IX would henceforth be in accordance with the committee's policy and priorities. To maintain some degree of flexibility over urgent demands, etc., the procedure was, however, not to apply to research, development and production in respect of ad hoc operations. Shortly after, another committee, the HQ Wireless Research and Production Committee, was created, again chaired by Col Barry.

The files do not record the extent to which these Committees affected the work of the DSR Section since they were, to a large extent, concerned with setting priorities for production. However, in anticipation of the likely length of the war, some longer-term projects which were deemed unlikely to reach fruition before the end of hostilities were cancelled. Otherwise, these Committees had no great influence on the day-to-day running of the DSR Section other than stressing the urgency of the work to those who were in any case already committed to their jobs.

Ideas for new projects would have come from any of several sources. Agents returning from the field often identified the need for a means of carrying out a particular operation; the Training Sections were similarly able to pinpoint deficiencies in existing equipment and suggest ways of overcoming them; Country Sections often expressed a wish to be able to tackle specific targets; and, last but not least, ideas flowed regularly from the scientists at Station IX, while Station XV produced a large number of camouflaging devices, some of them bizarre or impracticable. The general public and press from time to time also came up with what they envisaged as 'war winners'. Their contributions had to be considered carefully and assessed in case they contained any practicable new ideas. One senior SOE member, Bickham Sweet-Escott, wrote that, by 1942, suggestions for both equipment and targets were pouring in from the field. Agents needed advice on how best to sabotage dock gates, telephone exchanges and power transformers. They wanted to know how much explosive was needed to destroy a Ju 52 and where best it should be placed. Answers to these pressing questions required research and experiment if the agent was to be successful and escape to fight on. Most of these requests were for methods of using standard explosive charges on particular targets. But where a technique had been developed for attacking a specific type of regular target it was only a short step to designing a device to carry this out more efficiently.

Before starting any major work on a new project it was necessary to have a clearly stated Operational Requirement (OR), including a specification of the range of conditions under which the device would be used. At an early stage proposals were given preliminary consideration at 64 Baker Street before being passed to Station IX, where they formed the subject of discussion at one of the weekly meetings of senior staff chaired by Dr E.G. Cox. If the feasibility of meeting the OR was established then detailed design was put in hand. Development then usually involved a sequence of laboratory tests and design improvements leading to a prototype. After preliminary user trials the device would be passed to Station XII to produce a production prototype and to arrange for mass production. The sequence was monitored in its later stages by the Trials Committee whose role is discussed later.

In assessing a new device a number of important considerations had to be kept in mind. A primary requirement was obviously that it should be technically sound, but it was equally important that it would perform under all likely conditions of use. Many operations had to be carried out at night, often in wet and cold weather and wearing gloves. The heightened nervous tension occasioned by the need to carry out the operation in haste and in secrecy placed extra emphasis on the ease of handling. Moreover, in many cases the agent would not have been fully trained in the use of all devices so that simplicity of operation under adverse conditions was essential. Furthermore, all devices had to incorporate adequate safety features to prevent premature activation which could expose agents to additional hazards over and above those inherent in their task. The greatest attention had to be paid to the avoidance of circumstances in which an agent, already at high risk from the nature of the operation, was let down by the shortcomings of the equipment. It was imperative that the extreme bravery of dedicated operators should not be compromised by technical failure or inadequate safety features.

Although the forefathers of SOE – Holland, Grand and Langley – were military men, when the new organisation was formed its leaders were drawn largely from the City Establishment and their recruitment was mainly through personal acquaintances: when Newitt set up the DSR organisation he sought people with a scientific and technical background which meant turning to the universities and industry as his main source of manpower.

One of the first scientists to join the HQ was Dr (later Colonel) B.K. (Bertie) Blount who had been an early recruit to SOE. Blount was born on 1 April 1907. The family had a military background, his father having been an artillery colonel who was awarded the DSO in the First World War. His mother was the daughter of a major general. He studied organic chemistry at Trinity College, Oxford, where he worked for Sir Robert Robinson on the colouring matter of a particular lichen which only grows on apple trees. He studied for a doctorate at Frankfurt University, and after three years as Dean of St Peter's Hall (later St Peter's College, Oxford) he joined Glaxo as Head of their Chemical Research Laboratory.

Blount was commissioned into the Intelligence Corps in 1939 and soon was seconded to SOE. When Newitt was appointed DSR in 1941 Blount joined his HQ Section as DSR/B. He was in effect Newitt's roving liaison officer and kept in touch with several Sections of SOE. His quiet charm and slightly eccentric manner gave him easy access to new surroundings. He took a realistic view of SOE's activities. He regarded it as part of his job to 'explain to over-enthusiastic officers that they would be better off using traditional methods of killing than the various gadgets that they asked scientists to devise'. This was perhaps a dig at some of the crazy ideas that emerged from Station XV. He was keen that equipment was assessed under realistic conditions and he involved himself among other things in the testing of the waterproof suit enabling parachutists to drop into water. In 1943 he had taken an interest in various user trials but he left it to the newly established Trials Committee to organise them on the ground.

In 1943 Blount was parachuted into Greece to liaise with the various factions to assess the performance of SOE stores and to ascertain whether there were operational requirements which had not been properly appreciated in London. His report, which does not seem to have survived, made good travel reading but added little to knowledge already available from established agents on the spot. In much the same way in 1944 he was infiltrated into remote South-west China. He was able to move toward the coast relatively easily and to report that the Japanese forces were thinly spread. Again he wrote an interesting travelogue but with little important military content. He obviously enjoyed this mission. He did, however, bring back the story (possibly apocryphal) of the agent in China who broke the stem of his favourite pipe. His interpreter offered to take it to the nearest village to get the woodcarver to make a new one. After a few days he returned and proudly presented the new pipe. It had been faithfully reproduced: it was in two pieces with the broken ends carefully copied!

Towards the end of the war Newitt and his group were asked to provide a scientific assessment, under the code name Operation Foxley, of the possible means by which Adolf Hitler might be assassinated, including the use of bacteria and poisons. Blount was sceptical. He commented that 'the possibilities of poisons have been much over-rated by popular belief and popular fiction, both now and in the past'. This did not stop the press writing the headline for his *Times* obituary: 'Scientist who devised a scheme to assassinate Hitler using anthrax'. After the war Blount served on the Allied Control Commission in Germany and was appointed Director of Scientific Intelligence at the Ministry of Defence. He subsequently held a number of high-profile public positions until he retired in 1966 and died, aged 92, in 1999.

Later Newitt was joined at HQ by Lt Col J.W. Munn, RE, who had been with SOE from the beginning, having been Chief Instructor at the Arisaig Training School and later in charge of Massingham, the SOE North African organisation in Algiers. Munn took a particular interest in the user trials and took part in several.

EXPERIMENTAL SECTION

One of the earliest members of Station IX was Colin Meek (DX/1) who was in charge of the Explosives Sub-Section. He had been seconded to Section D early in 1939 from the Research Department at Woolwich Arsenal where he had been involved in the development of plastic explosives which were then just coming into use.

Meek was an experienced explosives expert whose wide knowledge and good sense contributed greatly to the work of the Section. It is unlikely that he was at all concerned that he had not been given leadership of the Experimental Section and had to work with, and to some extent under, two 'outsiders from academia'. The structure of the group was, in any case, very informal and any minor personal problems, if they existed, did not prevent them from forming an enthusiastic, hardworking and happy team.

To strengthen the scientific basis of Station IX Newitt recruited Dr (later Professor and Sir Gordon) E.G. Cox with the symbol DSR/X in January 1942 to take charge of the laboratories at Station IX. Cox, born in 1906, was a First Class Honours graduate in Physics from the University of Bristol, whose interest in X-ray crystallography developed when he worked at the Royal Institution under Sir William Bragg, the 'Father' of X-ray crystallography. He moved to a lectureship in chemistry at the University of Birmingham where he elucidated the crystal structures of several inorganic and organic compounds. He became particularly interested in the crystal structures of explosives. One of the results of the X-ray analysis of a crystal is the so-called electron density map of the molecule which reflects the shape of the molecule. Cox was one of the pioneers of this technique. He was intrigued by the fact that in the recently developed explosive PETN, the four arms of the molecule were arranged in the form of a swastika. He commented that this perhaps symbolised the role of PETN in the fight against Nazism!

Cox had joined the Territorial Army in 1936. Although mobilised at the outbreak of war, he was returned to the University by the end of November and to the University Training Corps. He led an Advisory Group of the Ministry of Supply where he was involved in the problems of explosive production. So his appointment to Station IX was particularly appropriate. Cox, known inevitably as 'Pippin', led the experimental group with tact, humour and good sense. He took a close and critical interest in the full range of problems facing the Station and not infrequently proposed highly original ideas for their solution. Later in the summer of 1944 he went, as a Lieutenant-Colonel, to France as a Technical Staff Officer where he was employed in a succession of liaison meetings with the Underground on V-2 rocket sites and counter sabotage activities. His interrogation of members of the Belgian Resistance Group G revealed valuable evidence on their highly successful sabotage work during the occupation.

After the war, Cox was appointed to the Chair of Crystallography at the University of Leeds. He also continued his interest in explosives including the problem of the initiation of dust explosions by an electrical discharge. He was elected to the Royal Society in 1954, became Secretary of the Agricultural Research Council and was knighted in 1964. He died on 23 January 1996 at the age of 90.

In the autumn of 1942 the scientific strength of Station IX was further increased by the appointment of Dr (later Maj) Douglas Everett who was born in 1916. He had a family military background since his father had been a regular soldier in the Middlesex Regiment and had served in France, Egypt and Northern Ireland and was recalled in 1940 to command a Company of the Pioneer Corps for the duration. Everett had been in the OTC at the University of Reading where some of his left-wing student contemporaries could not understand how he could reconcile being a Corporal in the OTC with his chairmanship of the Student Peace Society.

After gaining a first class degree in Chemistry at Reading University he was a Ramsay Memorial Fellow at Balliol College, Oxford, and studied for his DPhil in the Physical Chemistry Laboratories at Oxford as a member of a team under Professor C.N. Hinshelwood working for the Ministry of Supply on chemical defence with particular reference to respirators and active charcoals. He thus had links with the Chemical Defence Establishment at Porton Down.[2]

Everett's route into SOE followed what had become a familiar pattern using one of the various 'grapevines'. His supervisor at Oxford, Hinshelwood, was approached by Newitt asking whether he knew of someone suitable to 'join him at the War Office'. He suggested Everett, who was called for interview by Newitt at 64 Baker Street in September 1942. At this stage he had little idea of what the job involved. The title Inter-Services Research Bureau was obscure. Over lunch Newitt gave little away and Everett was not told much either about the work he would be doing or about the organisation for which he would be working. Newitt felt strongly that the lessons of the failed Dieppe Raid a few weeks before should be learned and tackled scientifically – a policy which in other hands led to the development of Operational Research as a scientific discipline. Newitt implied that Everett might be required to observe operations in the field. A couple of weeks later, during which Everett would have been positively vetted by MI5, the two lunched again and this time Newitt, accompanied by Davies, outlined a little more clearly the true nature of ISRB and its role as a sabotage organisation. At this stage the initials SOE were not revealed. Everett was told that he would need to go on training courses[3] to acquaint him with the conditions under which subversive operations had to be carried out and to familiarise himself with the range of equipment involved. He would be given the same training as an agent but would not be expected to partake in operations in the field. The objective was to enable him to appreciate, under nearly realistic conditions, the problems encountered by agents and to use this knowledge in assessing the design of new weapons and their employment. Accordingly, Everett was sent on a shortened paramilitary course at Arisaig in the Scottish Highlands. The course included instruction in the use of explosives, weapons and various booby trap devices. Also included was a short paranaval course at Mallaig, which curiously enough never appeared in the accounts of others who attended this course and received only passing reference in Rigden's introduction to *SOE Syllabus*. This part included instruction in the use of Folboats (folding canvas canoes) in the attack on shipping in harbours. A night-time exercise in Mallaig harbour involved placing a limpet mine on the hull of the island steamer using the recently developed limpet placing rod. This was accomplished successfully and quietly. However, on inspection the following night it was found, when the ferry returned from its daily run, that the limpet had been washed away. Clearly there was a need for improved magnets. The exact purpose of the paranaval course was not at all clear. It lasted only a couple of days and involved only small boats. The course was based on a rather fine luxury yacht in the harbour and was run by two individuals who had, it was said, before the war managed one of the high-class Piccadilly nightclubs (thought to be Quaglinos). Life on board was well supported by lobsters and malt whisky. It looked, from the point of view of the student, a very comfortable and easy war job! It is difficult to know how long it went on – there seem to be no references to it in existing SOE records.

There followed the Beaulieu course on propaganda, surveillance, coding and briefing on the German Army and Security Forces. It included a couple of daytime exercises on following and avoiding being followed and on 'casing' and later breaking into one of the other houses in the area. The night-time SS-style interrogation was, he suspected, less dramatic than that to which real aspiring agents were subjected.

Equipped with the knowledge and experience gained on these two courses, Everett was posted to Station IX at The Frythe on 18 November 1942, shortly before his twenty-sixth birthday, when he became Cox's deputy and acquired the symbol DX/14. Later as D/BT he was put in charge of the User Trials Section and also was responsible for the Air Supply Research Section. This involved him in two overseas liaison visits, to the Middle East and the Far East, to assess the performance of equipment in those theatres.

After the war Everett held Fellowships at Oxford, was a Professor of Chemistry at University College, Dundee (University of St Andrews), and later at Bristol. He was elected to the Royal Society in 1980 and retired in 1982.

By the autumn of 1942 the Experimental Section at Station IX consisted of just over a dozen scientific staff together with technicians and secretaries. It was headed by Cox (DSR/X) with his deputy Everett (DX/14).

EXPLOSIVES SUB-SECTION

Meek was in charge of the Section and was concerned with the use of explosives for specific targets. This required detailed information on the target so that the charge could be designed to be placed at the most vulnerable part. In this he was in close contact with Lt Col G.T.T. Rheam, whose Training School (STS 17) at Brickendonbury near Hertford was particularly concerned with industrial sabotage. Meek and his group were responsible for the design and construction of the charges for Operation Gunnerside, the attack on the heavy water plant at Vemork in Norway.

Meek was ably assisted by Douglas A. Barnsley (DX/1a) and Charles Erwood, whom he had brought with him. Barnsley is remembered by some for the useful little Austin Seven car he ran while Erwood, a good photographer, lost a finger when a device exploded in his hand. Capt Charles Critchfield, RE had been a ship's engineer officer before the war, visiting many European ports, and John Collins was in charge of the fuse-testing laboratories at Station IX but was handicapped because they were under-equipped. He subsequently went to the USA on a purchasing mission and did not return to The Frythe. This responsibility was taken over by John T. van Riemsdijk (DX/3), who designed and supervised the work of the Thermostat Hut.

The Explosives Sub-Section was reinforced in 1943 by the arrival of the 32-year-old Dr Gordon (later Sir Frank) Claringbull, a mineralogist and X-ray crystallographer who had been introduced to SOE by Cox. After graduating from Queen Mary College, London, he had been working on explosives for the Ministry of Supply on secondment from his post as Assistant Keeper at the Natural History Museum, where SOE had on the ground floor an extensive secret exhibition of their wares. Initially, Claringbull collaborated with Colin Meek's group, but later in 1944 he moved to Baker Street to work on possible measures against the launching sites of V1 and later V2 missiles. This involved assessing intelligence reports (many of which had been collected by the Poles in Northern France) on the sites themselves and the routes by which they were supplied. Although the Poles had carried out some minor sabotage it is not clear whether SOE had any plans for larger-scale attacks. Claringbull was promoted to the Directorship of the Museum in 1968 and retired in 1976, having been knighted in 1975. He died on 23 November 1990.

INCENDIARIES SUB-SECTION

The Incendiaries Sub-Section, which again was inherited from Section D, was led by Maj O.J. Walker (DX/2) who had been recruited from University College, London. He was joined later by Dr C.H. Bamford who had been working at Cambridge on alkyl boron compounds, some of which were spontaneously combustible when exposed to air. In fact, none of these candidate compounds proved to be useful as incendiary agents. This group was, as described later, concerned with the design of the incendiary for Operation Braddock. Bamford was also a near-professional standard violinist who spent many evenings practising in his office. After the war he joined the newly created Courtauld Research Laboratory at Maidenhead, as did several other ex-SOE people. Subsequently he was appointed Professor of Industrial Chemistry at the University of Liverpool and was elected to the Royal Society in 1964. He died in 1998. Among Walker's younger colleagues was David H. Malan (an Oxford chemist – see how the network operated) who later joined Courtaulds, changed to medicine and became a consultant psychologist at the Tavistock Clinic. Another chemist, David Levi also joined this section working on novel incendiaries.

FUSES AND SMALL
MECHANISMS SUB-SECTION

Small mechanisms were the province of John Cotterill who came from Courtaulds. He was a highly skilled small mechanisms designer whose previous experience had been in the design of spinning machinery. He was a perfectionist and his ability to foresee and avoid problems in transferring a design from a prototype to production made him a particularly valuable member of staff. John T. van Riemsdijk was an engineer who was knowledgeable about continental railways and developed the Imber Railway Switch described in Chapter 8. After leaving SOE in 1946 he enjoyed a period manufacturing clockwork devices before joining the staff of the Science Museum in London, eventually becoming Keeper of Civil and Mechanical Engineering. He was responsible for laying out the National Railway Museum at York and for writing several books on engineering history.

Also attached to this group were L.G. Wilson, B.H. Chibnall and P.T. Trent.

PHYSIOLOGICAL SUB-SECTION

The Physiological Section was headed by Dr Paul Haas (DX/3) who had an assistant, Mr Glascock. Dr Haas had been a Reader in Plant Chemistry at University College, London, and a lecturer in Physics and Chemistry at the Royal Botanic Garden at Kew. He had an encyclopaedic knowledge of plant and medical chemistry. Born in 1871, he was almost totally bald and wore steel-rimmed spectacles. To many he was the archetypal scientist, a forbidding character at first meeting but in fact a mild, soft-spoken and kind person. This hardly matched his role in SOE, where he was deeply concerned with, among other things, drugs and poisons. Younger people stood somewhat in awe of him, partly because of his age and experience but mainly because of his very high scientific and ethical standards. Haas was to become involved with both the chemical toilet and the system for the removal of CO_2 from the Welfreighter.

In 1943 Dr A.G. (Sandy) Ogston was recruited by Everett and became a member of Newitt's group. Ogston in turn brought in Callow. Ogston was a biophysical chemist and a Fellow of Balliol College, Oxford where he also taught medical students. He was a tall, bearded Scot with a lively sense of fun, who had spent the early war years working with Professor R.A. Peters's external Ministry of Supply team seeking treatments to minimise the effects of mustard gas. Several colleagues at the time were used as guinea pigs and many carried scars on their wrists where the proposed treatment had failed. In fact, no satisfactory solution to the problem was found. Ogston's main activity in SOE, besides taking an active part in a number of field trials, was in devising compact ration packs and medical kits, partly for SOE agents but also for the Jedburgh teams – groups of three serving officers to be dropped after D-Day to cooperate with and coordinate the operations of the SOE Resistance groups. The ration packs had been designed to provide a balanced diet, making use of the evolving technology of the food manufacturers in the production of dehydrated concentrated foods. Alternative formulations were developed for use both in arctic and tropical areas. Ogston's lively sense of humour extended to his daily life. He commuted between Oxford and Baker Street by train. In those days railway carriages were divided into compartments, each seating up to eight passengers. Sandy liked to have a compartment to himself and would therefore arrive in good time for his train, find an empty compartment, ensconce himself in it and take out his latest Fair Isle knitting project, the pattern for which he invented himself as he went along. Old ladies peering into the dimly lit compartment and seeing a bearded man knitting did not venture into such an eccentric situation. But Sandy's sense of gallantry would certainly not have allowed such a person to stand in the corridor. Back in Oxford after the war, Sandy was offered and rejected several Chairs but was finally persuaded to accept the post of Professor of Biophysical Chemistry at the Australian National University in Canberra. He returned to Oxford in 1970 as President of Trinity College. He was elected to the Royal Society in 1955 and died in York in 1996.

In his work on dehydrated concentrated foods Ogston sought the collaboration of Lt Col Geoffrey Bourne, an Australian whom he had known in Oxford and who was now in charge of research and development of rations and physiological problems for the SOE forces in South East Asia. Later he had a distinguished academic career in medicine, having been the Nutritional Adviser to the British Military Administration in Malaya, and Vice Chancellor and Professor of Nutrition at St George's University, Grenada, in the West Indies. Ogston, in collaboration with Dr Haas and Bourne, designed a compact medical kit which fitted into a flat cigarette tin. As well as containing basic items, it also had self-inject morphia tubes for use in relieving pain.

Later in 1943 Haas was joined by Dr Ken Callow, an RAF Squadron Leader who had seen service on the North-West Frontier of India but had been posted back to the UK on medical grounds. Callow had graduated from Christ Church College, Oxford, in 1923 with first class honours in Chemistry. He had a short period in industry and then studied for his DPhil on aporphine alkaloids. He joined the National Institute for Medical Research working on vitamin D, which he was one of the first to purify. On the outbreak of war, despite the fact that he was in a 'reserved occupation', he succeeded in persuading the MRC to allow him to join the RAF, where he was trained as an armaments officer. In India he was responsible, with the minimum of equipment, for defusing several 500-lb bombs which had failed to explode. He suffered several attacks of malaria and returned to the UK and to SOE, where he collaborated harmoniously with Haas. One incident in which he was involved must have become widespread knowledge for it was recounted independently by at least Cox and one of the secretaries, Miss Agnes Kinnersley. A small stone jar was found by the Army and suspected of being a booby trap. In view of Callow's experience in defusing bombs it was sent to him. It contained a liquid which was looked upon with suspicion. Callow extracted the liquid and subjected samples to a variety of tests without finding anything noxious in it. He then suggested to a colleague that they should try the 'organoleptic' test. He produced two glasses and expected his colleague to follow him in tasting the suspicious liquid. It turned out to be excellent gin – but it might have been something lethal!

Callow also features in another novel technique derived from his experience in India. When he was serving on the North-West Frontier an isolated outpost telegraphed asking that a supply of eggs be dropped to them. Perhaps this was a joke request but Callow took it seriously. The solution was to put a chicken in a brown paper bag and drop it from a low-flying aircraft. The bag protected the struggling chicken from the effects of the aircraft's slipstream just long enough for it to break out of the bag and flutter to the ground. In 1945 just the same technique was used to get pigeons to the Resistance groups in Belgium. It is not known whether Callow was responsible for this application. Callow later worked at Baker Street on problems of warfare in the tropics: this will be discussed later. After the war, Callow resumed his scientific work, in particular on the synthesis of cortisone. He was elected to the Royal Society in 1958 and died in 1983.

OPERATIONAL RESEARCH AND TRIALS SECTION

Further increase in the staff of Station IX followed in 1943 when Dr Richard Moggridge, another Balliol chemist, joined the Trials Section. As the User Trials commitment increased, he spent an increasing amount of time on this work. After the war he joined the Courtaulds research laboratory at Maidenhead but died suddenly in 1947. Capt George Brown, a chemist from Magdalen College, Oxford, joined the User Trials group in 1943 and played a major part in its activities. Brown had been called up on graduation but soon found the desk job allocated to him too boring and succeeded in getting transferred to 'Special Duties', which meant assignment to SOE. He, too, was trained at Arisaig, Beaulieu and Ringway and had much the same experiences as those described by Everett. In fact, Brown and Everett were the only members of Station IX who had been subjected to the SOE training course. It is unlikely that either of them was ever considered for despatch to the field – if only because neither of them had adequate language skills. He carried out many trials of the Sleeping Beauty submersible canoe and developed the fog signal method of initiating explosions on railway tracks. In 1944 he was seconded to the Services Reconnaissance Department in Melbourne –

the Australian branch of SOE – to work on, among other things, methods of attacking wooden vessels such as Japanese-commandeered Chinese junks. Brown returned to the UK in 1946 to become chemistry master and later Housemaster at Eton College until his retirement in 1964. He wrote several highly successful chemistry text books. His latest book *The Big Bang, a History of Explosives* deals with many topics in which his service with SOE had given him an interest.

Among others who served at Station IX on the experimental side was the Canadian ex-Rhodes Scholar, Gordon Davoud who had run a small extramural group in Oxford working on fundamental problems associated with Time Pencils, of which more later. He spent the latter part of 1944 at Station IX. Another Canadian, Dr Roddy E. Smith joined Station IX in the summer of 1944 but died tragically in a swimming accident in North Cornwall. Two serving officers were added to the team responsible for user trials. The first was Maj Gerry Bryant, RE, MC, an Irishman who had lost a leg when fighting with the Commandos in Syria and had been awarded the Military Cross. As a result he had a deep antipathy toward the French. He was at Station IX as DSR/OPS for much of 1944 and played a valuable and efficient role in the organisation of trials. He retired at the end of 1944 to join the Colonial Service, where he rose to become Colonial Secretary of Barbados and the Administrator of the British Virgin Islands and of St Lucia. He was created CMG and CVO for his work. On his retirement he has played an active role in several public bodies. Maj Stuart Edmondson also spent much of 1944 and 1945 as a member of the Air Supply Research Section (ASRS) where he was responsible for the organisation of several major trials. Much of the administration of the ASRS and links with operational sections was channelled through Baker Street and was in the capable hands of Capt P.A.C. Howlett who also took part in the trials programme.

From the end of 1943 the American Office of Strategic Services (OSS) had a liaison officer at the Frythe. The first was Lt E. Charlton Crocker, often seen resplendent in smartly pressed pink pants and dark green jacket. In April 1944 he was replaced by Lt Bob Daley who was an equally colourful character. During July and August he was joined by Lt S.W. Cutler. Although at the higher levels SOE and OSS did not always see eye to eye, the relationships at the research level were always cordial and the enthusiastic participation of OSS personnel in the trials programme was valuable.

No account of the Research and Development Section's personalities would be complete without mention of a figure who comes and goes in the story. He is Dr F.A. Freeth who had been associated with Section D from the outbreak of War and on their move to Aston House in 1940 had become a full-time member. Freeth was a physical chemist with wide industrial experience. He had been with Brunner, Mond and Company (later to become Imperial Chemical Industries Limited) during the First World War, where he had been concerned with the production of ammonium nitrate, an essential ingredient of many explosives. He was a strong advocate of the close links between fundamental science and industrial processes. He was an ardent admirer of the Dutch school of physical chemistry and in particular their use of the Phase Rule, a somewhat neglected but very important scientific principle. By applying this rule he was able to predict the ideal conditions for the crystallisation of ammonium nitrate from a solution of ammonium sulphate and sodium nitrate and so improve greatly the production of this important chemical. Indeed, he would claim that his work had been a major factor in the maintenance of supplies of explosives in the First World War and hence to the Allied victory. He became Director of the Alkali Division of ICI but a breakdown led him to relinquish this post. It is clear that in the pre-war years he had been in contact with various secret agencies within the Government which led to his association with Section D. His name disappears from the formal SOE papers. However, he continued to have close links with SOE HQ and maintained a liaison rôle across the organisation's technical sections. For some time he lived at The Frythe. He was nominally a supernumery adviser to Newitt but in practice a stimulating influence throughout the whole of Station IX. He will be remembered as an exuberant and compulsive talker with a host of stories. He claimed to have some credit for the discovery of polythene. It was on his initiative that the Dutch techniques of high-pressure chemistry were adopted and developed by ICI, research which provided the technical expertise which led to the discovery of polythene. An indication of his somewhat eccentric character was that he always wore a black skull cap. To those who assumed that he was Jewish he pointed out that its sole purpose was to keep his bald head warm! One of his party tricks was to challenge one to give the value of π. Most of the team could get as far as 3.141 ... but Freeth would continue for another few dozen digits. It is not recorded whether anyone checked the correctness of his response. Always concerned with the dependence of industry on a supply of competent scientists, he was influential in persuading ICI to establish the ICI Fellowship Scheme to enable young scientists whose work had been interrupted by the war to return to academic life.

ENGINEERING SECTION

The Commanding Officer of Station IX and Head of the Engineering Section was John Robert Vernon Dolphin who had been born in 1905 in Chester. After initial schooling at Rhyl, he attended Marlborough College and the United Services College before going on to Loughborough College of Engineering. He was apprenticed as a pupil from January 1928 with the Hydraulic Engineering Company in Chester. Later, as manager at the Austin Hoy Company from 1930–34, he invented the Hoy Double Box Coal Cutter Chain and reputedly demonstrated it personally in coal mines. He joined the Army and was made Lt Colonel when he took command of Station IX. He is best remembered for his development of the small submersibles and the parachutists' mini-motorcycle, and for his attempts to interest the Australian Forces in the former. Between 1946 and 1950 Dolphin was Managing Director of the Corgi Motorcycle Company, where he exploited his experience with the Welbike; Dolphin Industrial Developments Ltd and Hydraulic Developments Ltd. He was then appointed Chief Engineer of the Atomic Weapons Research Establishment at Aldermaston, receiving a CBE in 1956 before spending two years as Engineer-in-Chief at UKAEA. There followed Joint Managing Directorships at Lansing Bagnall Ltd, the fork-lift truck manufacturers, and J.E. Shay Ltd before becoming a Director of TI (Group Services) Ltd from 1964–68. He was credited with a number of inventions including the Harrier Folding Jeep and the Lina-Loda Freight Handling Machine. Dolphin died on 2 May 1973 at the age of 68.

One of the leading engineers at Station IX was John Irving Meldrum, a Liverpudlian born in 1917. At Merchant Taylors School in Crosby he won a scholarship to Liverpool University, where he was awarded the Graduate Scholarship in 1939 and the William Rathbone Medal. In addition to gaining a first class honours BEng in 1939, he also gained a first class honours BSc from London in 1938.

Upon call-up in 1940, Meldrum joined the Royal Engineers at

Shorncliffe in Kent and soon took command of 141 OCTU. He was engaged in bomb disposal work in the Portsmouth area, which included the Isle of Wight. Almost a year later he was promoted to Captain and found himself posted to ISRB in June 1942 as engineering assistant at the engineering experimental establishment. Here he worked on the design, progress and development of midget submarines. Together with Dolphin and Porteous he was credited with the design of the trim valve for these craft.

During the winter of 1944–45 when the Chief Engineer, Col Dolphin, was away he took over and was directly responsible to Newitt for a section of six officers and 194 tradesmen. In March 1945 responsibility for the establishment changed from SOE to the Admiralty and Meldrum became answerable to Commander G.E. Williamson. After the war he joined the No. 2 Laboratory of Courtaulds in Coventry as a research engineer on textile machinery.

Working alongside Meldrum was Hugh Quentin Alleyne Reeves who had been born in Seaford, Sussex in late 1909 and attended Harrow School and Cambridge University, from where he graduated with a second class BA in Engineering in 1931. He joined J.H. Robinson and Co. of Liverpool as an assistant manager and in 1936 moved to Hazlehurst Consulting Engineers as a partner. He soon became joint managing director of the company and was concerned with boiler and electrical generating plant and water services. He was commissioned into the Royal Army Service Corps. Maj Reeves was probably the most prolific of engineering designers at Station IX, being concerned with a variety of projects from the Welrod and Sleeve Gun to the buoyant limpet and sucker device. He finished the war with the rank of lieutenant colonel. Postwar, Reeves became involved with the noise suppression of jet engines and tragically was killed while working on one.

Durward ('Dagwood') W.J. Cruickshank, born 1924, arrived at Station IX in late July 1944 straight from an engineering course at Loughborough. C.P. Snow (who with Julian Huxley and Dr Bronowski starred in the BBC *Brains Trust* programme) travelled round Britain's universities seeking talent for the Allied war effort. One day he interviewed Cruickshank at Loughborough and sent him off to Station IX for further vetting. He worked on the Welfreighter with John Oxford under John Meldrum and celebrated his twenty-first birthday the following spring. He was involved in a great deal of design and testing on the vessel both at The Frythe and at Fishguard before leaving early in 1946 to join Cox's X-ray group at Leeds. He moved to a Chair in Chemistry at the University of Manchester Institute of Science and Technology and was elected to the Royal Society in 1979. Assisting Cruickshank was Meldrum's right-hand man, Eric Porteous, a civilian draughtsman who was also involved occasionally at Fishguard.

FIVE

PHYSICO-CHEMICAL SECTION – SABOTAGE DEVICES AND MATERIALS

In 1941 Churchill appealed to the President of the United States with the words 'Give us the tools and we'll finish the job'. At the same time the Resistance groups in Europe, through their Country Sections in London, were making the same plea to SOE.

Chapter 4 described the structure of the research and development organisation built up by SOE in the early part of the war. The following chapters describe how the tools which were developed fulfilled the operational requirements of those in the field.

The main operational objectives assigned to SOE included the disruption of transport by rail, road and water; attacks on power supplies and communications; the sabotage of major industrial plants; destruction of major stocks of materials; and the spoiling by contamination of vital fuel, food and mineral stocks. Direct attacks on military targets were not generally considered except where SOE could provide specialist materials or expert advice. Its main involvement in paramilitary affairs was through the development of weapons dealt with in Chapter 8.

Some way also had to be found for causing the maximum embarrassment to the German Security Forces by deflecting their attention from military activities by a variety of 'pinprick' diversions of varying severity. By themselves they were usually relatively trivial, but their psychological objective was aimed at undermining the enemy's confidence and at the same time boosting the morale of the general population of occupied countries. However, those planning this kind of sabotage had to tread a cautious path between upsetting the enemy and triggering brutal retaliatory measures. Attention had to be paid to devising equipment for operations which the French called *insaissible*, whose perpetrators could not be readily identified.

Many of the materials described below had applications across several types of target. They are therefore dealt with according to their broad characteristics rather than specific applications.

Station IX had a very wide and flexible remit. In the broadest terms it was responsible for the invention and development of equipment of all kinds covering the various needs of the saboteur in the field. It did not, however, start from a completely blank sheet. As outlined in Chapters 2 and 4, in the years leading up to the creation of SOE in 1940 many of the basic needs for equipment had been foreseen in papers and pamphlets written by Grand, Holland and Gubbins. New devices to meet these needs were being developed by Section D and MI(R). SOE inherited a number of basic devices, some of which were already in production. It is interesting to record that, thanks to the foresight of Section D, when SOE was formed its agents were supplied with commercial-type detonators of German manufacture which had been obtained from South Africa before the outbreak of war.

The work of Station IX and to some extent of Station XII was initially directed to improving many of the existing devices, and they will appear in their improved form in the following pages. A major effort was, however, devoted to the invention, development and production of novel equipment.

To inform SOE sections of the developments being brought to fruition by the R&D Directorate, restricted publication began in November 1943 of a 'Most Secret' quarterly *Technical Review*. This dealt with: new stores and modifications to existing ones; research and wireless notes; camouflage; training and operational topics. The Research Section provided a series of 'Laboratory Contributions'. Copy No. 88 of the first issue and No. 25 of the third issue (May 1944) of this Review have been traced. The latter also contained notes on quality control and technical literature. In the following account, reference is made to some of the material in these issues to supplement information from other sources, including personal recollections.

To keep Operational and Training Sections abreast of developments a Demonstration Room was set up on the ground floor of the Natural History Museum in South Kensington to which senior officers had access. Later this was supplemented by the compilation of the Top Secret 'Descriptive Catalogue of Special

Devices and Supplies' which has recently (2000) been published openly by the Public Record Office under the title *Secret Agent's Handbook of Special Devices*.

EXPLOSIVES

In the early days, SOE depended largely on the currently available military explosives such as gun cotton, Nobel 808 and ammonal but the commercial blasting gelatine packed (by arrangement with the makers, ICI) in continental-type cartridges was also used. Meanwhile, new forms of explosive had been developed in the Research Department at Woolwich. This led to the invention of plastic explosive (PE) prepared by the incorporation of RDX in a suitable softening agent to produce a pale yellow, putty-like material which could be cut and moulded into appropriate shapes. An important property of PE was that it was both more powerful and yet safer than many other explosive materials. In particular, it could not be detonated by a rifle bullet and needed a booster charge (primer) in addition to a detonator to initiate it. Its physical nature meant that it could be dyed to imitate putty or Plasticine and carried in suitably camouflaged containers or cartons. Although it still had a detectable odour it did not, like 808, result in severe headaches. It was safe in storage – unlike compositions containing ammonium nitrate, which tended to cake under humid conditions: breaking up caked explosive was a very hazardous operation. The use of home-made explosives was encouraged by providing agents with recipes for making explosives from relatively easily obtainable ingredients such as potassium chlorate weedkiller and agricultural fertiliser.

The Explosives Section under Colin Meek was to a large extent engaged in examining the use of PE in sabotage operations. Experiments led to an assessment of the appropriate quantities of explosive needed for typical operations on various targets such as metal girders, concrete and wood. Much of this was done in collaboration with Col Rheam's Special Training School 17 at Brickendonbury near Hertford where agents were instructed in demolition techniques based in part on experimental research at Station IX. This led to guidance on the amounts of explosive needed and where it should be placed to achieve the maximum disruption and damage to machinery and industrial plant. Where details of the target had been obtained either by personal reconnaissance by an agent, from stolen drawings or from carefully analysed photographs, then special charges were designed and assembled at Stations IX and XII. Thus the charges for the most successful and most famous SOE operation, Gunnerside, were designed specifically for placement in the most vulnerable locations in the heavy water plant at Rjukan in Norway (see Chapter 15).

SOE, through Stations IX and XII, also designed, assembled and fused the explosive charges carried by HMS *Campbeltown* in the St Nazaire raid of March 1942. There were undoubtedly many other operations in which the Explosives Section played a significant role but no records of them have been located.

Also available were a series of standard made-up charges containing 1½ lb or 3 lb (0.68 or 1.36 kg) of explosive already fitted with primers and Cordtex detonating fuse. More specialised charges such as limpets and clams are described below. In many instances, however, agents made up their own charges based on the instructions given at training schools. This could under certain circumstances involve an unexpected hazard. Homemade charges were usually wrapped in rubberised fabric and sealed using the thick, black adhesive Bostik. As anyone who has tried to make up charges in this way well knows, it was almost impossible to avoid getting excess Bostik on one's hands or clothes. This was difficult to remove completely even with the use of solvents such as benzene or carbon tetrachloride. The resultant odour, which persists for some time, and the presence of traces of Bostik under fingernails, could easily identify a bomb maker.

It is likely that the successful SOE attack by Harry Rée's men on the Peugeot factory at Sochaux in July 1943 depended on the use of charges prepared in accordance with training based on Station IX research, as did the destruction of twenty-two transformers which halted production at the Fives-Lille engineering works in June 1943. These were but two of nearly a hundred attacks on French industrial targets in 1943–44 listed by Foot.[1]

Among the many charges designed at Station IX for specific jobs were adaptations of standard charges for cutting cables and chains below the waterline – these were probably used to cut the cables of the Italian liner *Duchessa d'Aosta* in Operation Postmaster. Charges for scuttling ships, demolishing gun barrels and cutting pipelines were also designed.

The knowledge amassed at Station IX was not kept exclusively for SOE. Officers of the Explosives Section were made available to give advice to the Admiralty, Combined Operations and Auxiliary Forces, particularly on ad hoc operations where there was a specific and specialised target. The long-term research work on such topics as cavity charges, bending and cutting steel members (including rails) by explosives, cutting timber by explosives, and the effect of explosives fired underwater gave valuable scientific information to the entire military. Furthermore, the technical investigations, carried out in what were then described as 'properly designed and equipped laboratories and magazines', into the design of bursters, poured fillings, cast explosives, incendiary explosives, coloured explosives and booby trap devices added significantly to the sum of knowledge on these more specialised subjects.

LIMPET MINES AND CLAMS

Among the most widely used explosive devices were limpet mines and clams. The original limpet mines had been developed by MI(R)c. They were said to have resembled the British steel helmet of the time, no doubt giving rise to the name. They were provided with an array of magnets that allowed the mine to be attached to the side of a ship or other metal target. The SOE Mark II version consisted of a rectangular brass box measuring some 9½ × 5½ × 5½ in containing about 4½ lbs (2 kg) of explosive. The box was fitted with six magnets, three on either side. The sealing cap at one end was provided with a port threaded to take an AC fuse while an anti-disturbance fuse was fitted at the other. To enable the magnets to take up the curvature of the ship's side they were mounted on rubber bushes. The back of the mine was fitted with a bracket which could engage with the end of a folding placing rod (also developed at Station IX) to enable the mine to be attached beyond arm's length. Whereas the first versions were satisfactory against stationary targets (e.g. steel or iron equipment or ships in dock) their adhesion was insufficient to prevent them being washed away when the ship was underway, as Everett observed during his training at Mallaig. Improvements in the magnets were essential and this was Station IX's main contribution. Originally they were the simple horseshoe type, but by modifying the shape it was possible to increase the area of contact. At the same time close liaison was kept through Dr Wilson with Jessops, the Sheffield company which produced the magnets and was active in developing improved magnetic alloys. Over a period of a year or so much stronger magnets were available for use on limpets. These improvements were also incorporated in magnetic holdfasts for attachment to the side of ships. In mid-1943 limpets which were attached to HMS *Titania* remained in place after two days at sea at speeds up to 10½ knots in rough water. Magnetic limpets were used in many operations, the most publicised of which was the 'Cockleshell Heroes' raid at Bordeaux in December 1942. ISRB was responsible for producing 56,000 limpets up to mid-1945.

The clam was a smaller version of the limpet measuring 5¾ × 2¾ × 1½ in and containing half a pound of plastic explosive. This could be used with either a Time Pencil or an L-delay inserted into a pocket in the body of the device. But it could not be used underwater. The clam was easy to conceal and, even when seen, did not attract attention. In fact, the French Section agent Harry Rée reported an incident in which a clam fell from the pocket of a member of his 'Stockbroker' circuit in the presence of a German soldier who handed it back to him! Some 68,000 clams were made under the supervision of Station XII.

MOBILE LIMPETS (WELMINES)

Limpets were originally intended to be attached to shipping targets in dock. However, when close approach to the target was operationally difficult or too dangerous, a need was seen for a limpet which could be propelled towards, and attach itself to, its target, i.e., to act as a miniature torpedo. The main problems in developing these devices required the skills of the Engineering Section which worked on the various types of Welmine described in Chapter 8.

NAIL FIRING DEVICES

Not all target ships (e.g. minelayers and minesweepers in Europe and junks in the Far East) were made of iron, so a requirement arose for methods of attaching Limpets to wooden, or other wet surfaces, and work on this started in December 1943. Four attempts were made to develop a quick-setting cement capable of sticking to wet wood. Only limited success was achieved, and attention was directed towards a nail-firing device. The main disadvantage was that it was noisy so that its use was only practicable where it would be muffled, possibly by the noise in a factory or dockyard, or where silence was not an important factor. Although considerable improvements were made so that it could be used on both non-magnetic sheet metal and wood it was not entirely satisfactory. Among the problems were the very variable results which were obtained with woods of different density. Further development was undertaken by SOE's Far East Research Section (the Services Reconnaissance Department in Australia) where Capt G.I. Brown made a speciality of devising methods of destroying Japanese-commandeered junks.

FUSES AND SMALL MECHANISMS

To set off an explosive it is usually necessary to use a fuse which initiates a detonator which injects a spark or small explosion into the bulk explosive. Historically, use was made of the 'slow burning fuse' which consisted of a thin cord impregnated with potassium nitrate. The modern version is the 'blue touch paper' of domestic fireworks. Over a century ago this was replaced by the Bickford fuse in which gunpowder is wound into a core of twisted hemp and coated with a waterproof material. When initiated at one end by a match, the powder burns at a roughly constant rate of about 1 cm per second until a spurt of flame is ejected at the far end into a detonator which has been inserted into the explosive. Many of the safer explosives also require an additional small intermediate booster charge (or primer) placed into the bulk explosive. The alternative is the electric detonator which is set off by an impulsive current produced by operating an 'exploder' connected to the charge by a wire. The mode of use of explosive charges in sabotage operations depends on the circumstances under which they are to be used. Electric detonators have the advantage that the object of attack (e.g. a train) can be kept under observation and blown up at just the right moment – a technique used, for example, by T.E. Lawrence (of Arabia). The disadvantage is that the operator has to be close to, and in sight of, the target and has to escape from the scene. The Bickford fuse introduces a time delay between lighting it and the explosion and gives the saboteur the opportunity to make a safe getaway. But there is a maximum length of fuse which can conveniently be used, beyond which delayed action devices are needed. Often it is necessary to transmit the explosion from one charge to another. This may be achieved by connecting them by a length of 'detonating or instantaneous fuse' burning at a rate of 88 ft per second. (Cordtex in the UK, Primacord in the USA.)

Broadly speaking, a need existed for two types of switch – those which operated instantaneously for use, for example, in booby traps and those whose action was delayed for a predetermined time. In view of the likely conditions of SOE use, the following principles were laid down for the design of explosives initiating devices.

1) They should incorporate a safety pin of the interlocking type such that it could not be removed if the device was in a dangerous state. In other words, if the device had been accidentally tripped and the striker was prevented from initiating the explosion solely by the safety pin, that pin could not be withdrawn.
2) Where appropriate they should incorporate a suitable arming delay.
3) They should be weatherproof and in some instances waterproof to a specified hydrostatic pressure.
4) They should withstand storage and operation under climatic changes in temperature, pressure and humidity from Arctic to Tropical zones.
5) They should be able to withstand rough handling resulting from air dropping or during operational use.
6) They should be based upon mechanical and not electrical firing.[2]

'BOOBY TRAP' SWITCHES

The main instantaneous switches which were available, or shortly to be available to SOE at the outset, were: (i) the pressure switch, which responded to a weight being placed on its hinged metal plate by releasing a striker to ignite a detonator, (ii) the pull switch intended to be inserted in a trip wire, and (iii) the pressure release switch (or anti-disturbance switch) which operated when the load on the case was released. Minor improvements to these switches were made by Stations IX and XII to increase their reliability and safety, and in some cases they were modified so that they could be incorporated into some of the camouflaged devices produced by Station XV.

Methods of disrupting road transport were high on SOE's agenda. A simple device for disrupting light motor traffic was an adaptation of the medieval 'Calthrop' which would be scattered on roadways or aircraft runways. In this, three sharpened triangular knife edges are welded together to form a tetrahedral unit which, when dropped on a flat surface, always presents at least one sharp point upwards. In addition, the SOE Double-Bladed Dagger Jackknife incorporated a hooked tyre-slashing blade.

For attacking heavier traffic an explosive tyre burster was developed. In this, a ring of explosive surrounded a pressure switch, all within a 2 in diameter container made of two telescopic parts ⅜ in high. A force of 150 lb (68 kg) caused the mechanism to operate. Station XV had great fun incorporating these items in simulated animal droppings appropriate to the country concerned.

The tyre burster also formed the basis for two improvised anti-tank mines described in the *Technical Review No. 1*. The first consisted of a cardboard box filled with PE or 808. The lid pressed on the end of a vertical dowel rod, the end of which rested on a tyre burster on the bottom of the box. This operated at a load of 150 lb (68 kg) and was intended for use against lightly armoured vehicles. A more powerful device containing a much larger charge of PE was contained in a square box, at the four corners of which were placed tyre bursters supporting the lid. This operated under a force of 600 lb (272 kg) – a man could even jump on it safely. After preliminary trials at Station IX on plasticine filled mock-ups, a full-scale trial at Farnborough in the summer of 1943 demonstrated its potential.

RAILWAY SWITCHES

Other devices designed to operate immediately on activation included a modification of the railway 'fog signal' used extensively in civil life in foggy conditions to warn train drivers of a red signal ahead. They operated when crushed by the leading wheels of the locomotive. Since in SOE they were intended to be used to blow up a section of track ahead of the train, the method of use was to employ the fog signal to detonate a length of Cordtex which in turn detonated the main charge some metres in front of the train. For SOE use some modifications were needed to improve the clips which held the device to the rail to avoid the signal being pushed along the track and pulling out the link with the detonating fuse. Various layouts were devised by individual Country Sections to suit local situations and sometimes involved the use of several signals linked together to overcome the possible misfire of a single device.

Alternatively, a rail charge could be set off using a pressure switch under the rail. This had several advantages over the fog signal because it was relatively inconspicuous and easily concealed.

However, a solid base had to be established by clearing away ballast and the gap between the pressure plate and the underside of the rail had to be bridged by an adjustable extension rod. This was a somewhat fiddly job not easily performed in a hurry in the dark. Account had to be taken of the variable deflection of the rail depending on the solidity of the base and the weight of the train. Various modified versions of this switch for railway use were developed and tested. Despite their disadvantages these switches were used extensively in France, especially in the period after D-Day to delay the re-supply of forward German troops. It is recorded that the Resistance achieved over 950 interruptions to the railway system during the single night of 5/6 June 1944.

Other devices which operated instantly on activation included the altimeter switch which could be set to fire when an aircraft reached a predetermined height. There is, however, no reliable record of this having been used operationally. It is argued that the attempt on Hitler's life, when a bomb disguised as two bottles of Cognac was put aboard his plane but failed to detonate, might have been more successful if an altimeter switch had been available to the dissident German officers. A photoelectric switch which responded to the switching on of a light was also developed and tested but was not put into production. The OSS is reputed to have used a similar device to blow up trains as they entered tunnels, thus adding to the effectiveness of the simple charge.[3] A number of anti-disturbance switches were incorporated in camouflaged devices produced at Station XV.

THE IMBER RAILWAY SWITCH

One of the variations of the Railway Switch was the Imber Switch, an ingenious, mechanical device originally conceived by Imber Research and further developed at Station IX, which conducted trials on it at Longmoor in July 1943. Because the Germans were in the habit of searching the track ahead of ammunition trains and other likely targets, there was not much time for saboteurs to lay their traps between the inspection and the arrival of the train. So Imber came up with a pressure switch which could be activated by up to the eighth train to pass over it, which allowed much more time to set it in place. It would not have been too difficult to arrange the explosion on the eighth time the pressure rod was depressed by the deflection of the rail, but this might have been by the eighth axle of the first train. This switch was therefore designed to distinguish between axles and whole trains.

The Imber Switch measured 3 in × 2¼ in × 6 in high when the telescopic actuating rod was extended. Like the basic Railway Switch, it was buried in the ballast and the rod length adjusted until it touched the underside of the rail. Because this switch could be set for any subsequent train up to the eighth, reliable information on the order and contents of trains was essential. When the first axle of a train passed over it the rail movement pushed down the rod, which indexed a ratchet wheel, which, if this was not the target train, would initiate a delay in allowing the rod to return to its former position. This was sufficient to ensure the entire train had passed before the switch reset itself. In early versions this delay was achieved by a dash-pot arrangement. Experimental work revealed that at the high temperatures to be expected in the Far East the dash-pots became unreliable and so a mechanical 'clutter mechanism' was designed for it. This was similar to the escapement in a clock and had the effect of retarding the return of the actuating rod. Linked to the ratchet wheel on a cross-shaft was a disc which had a cutout in its edge. When this cutout came round to the relevant position on the arrival of the target train, a sprung hammer was released to set off a percussion cap on the end of the Cordtex fuse.

An example of this switch is in the National Railway Museum in York.

TIME DELAY SWITCHES

Of major operational importance were switches which could be set to operate after a predetermined time delay. The most accurate were clockwork delays, but these were more expensive to produce and generally not robust enough to withstand rough treatment. Having the disadvantage that their tick could reveal their presence, they were used only on special operations where accuracy of delay was paramount and appropriate means of camouflaging them could be taken. There are frequent references in trials reports and diaries to the 'Eureka' clock. Its exact nature is not known but tests of its robustness were carried out successfully. It may have been simply a carefully designed time delay fuse. Alternatively, it may have been intended for use in conjunction with the Eureka/Rebecca navigational device (see Chapter 11) to arrange for the ground station of this equipment to be switched on at previously arranged times.

Development of this device was probably in the hands of Lt Col H.H. King, a retired officer and keen amateur watchmaker, who worked away unobtrusively in a small office in Station IX. It is not known whether any of his models were ever used in the field but after the war he was given the credit for the ISRB Allways fuse, details of which have not been found.

The need for a simple, inexpensive delay which could be readily produced in thousands was met by two rival models: the Time Pencil and the lead delay. The latter was a product of MD1 and was never widely adopted by SOE, who employed almost exclusively the Time Pencil.

THE TIME PENCIL (SWITCH NO. 10)

The basic concept of the Time Pencil originated in a German device invented in 1916. It was later developed by the Poles and Gubbins brought back a sample from Poland in 1939. It was taken up by Cdr Langley at Section D and further developed and improved through the years. Its final form is shown on p. 8 of the plate section. The striker was held back by a steel wire kept under tension by a strong spring. Its operation depended on the thinning and failure of the wire by a corroding solution contained in a thin glass ampoule which was brought into contact with the wire by crushing the bulb. When the wire broke the striker was released and operated a percussion cap attached either to a short length of Bickford fuse or to a detonating fuse. The rate of corrosion and hence the time delay was controlled by changing the composition of the solution.

In most descriptions of the Time Pencil the solution in the ampoule is said to be 'an acid': but there is evidence that work commissioned by Langley and carried out by Bailey at the British Scientific Instrument Research Association (BSIRA) led him in 1939 to choose an aqueous solution of copper chloride as the most suitable corroding fluid. This acts electrochemically, and is easily demonstrated by dipping a piece of iron in a copper solution when copper is deposited on the surface of the iron and a corresponding amount of iron is dissolved. The time delay was controlled by the concentration of the copper solution or, for longer delays, by the addition of glycerol which, because of its higher viscosity, reduces the rate of corrosion. The glycerol had the advantage of acting as an anti-freeze; but on the other hand the increase in viscosity at lower temperatures led to a considerable increase in the delay time. This feature probably led to claims from the field that Time Pencils did not work under freezing conditions.

Five compositions coded by the colour of the safety strip became standard, covering the nominal ranges of: 10 min – black; 30 min – red; 5½ hr – green; 12 hr – yellow and 24 hr – blue. These timings were dependent on the temperature and the nominal values were stated to refer to 15°C, but even at the same temperature they were found to exhibit undesirable variations in the delay times. Unreliability in the case of the shorter nominal delay times could have devastating effects. For example, in July 1943 an agent complained bitterly that a red Time Pencil with a nominal 30 minutes delay had operated in just three minutes. Such incidents tended to give the Time Pencil a bad reputation among agents. No reliable statistics were available to enable the seriousness of the problem in the field to be quantified but the situation was regarded with great concern and a major programme of research was started urgently at Station IX in March 1943 to try to identify the origin of this variability. To make the experiments statistically significant at least 15 replications were made in each set of experiments. As it was impractical to carry out these tests on actual Time Pencils, they were done on laboratory replica rigs. At first very elementary methods were used to obtain the timings. For shorter times, kitchen alarm clocks were lined up on a shelf and the experimenter had to keep watch and record the time at which each operated. For longer times where it was not very practical to have the experiments kept under observation overnight, the breaking of the wire was arranged to drop a pin into the works of the clock and so record the time at which the wire failed and the clock stopped.

It was typical of the practical problems encountered that, because for some time the laboratory did not possess a refrigerator, it was not possible to test the effect of temperature on these timings! Later, a well-equipped testing laboratory fitted with an array of electric clocks and including constant temperature chambers controlled between −40 and +60°C was set up by van Riemsdijk (see plate section, p. 8). This was used for the routine testing of batches of production pencils.

In all, over 700 experiments were carried out during the summer months of 1943. The statistical analysis was made more tedious by the fact that Station IX did not possess a single calculating machine: use was made from time to time at weekends of a hand-operated Brunsviga machine at Oxford. Among the many factors affecting the delay time was the composition of the corroding solution. The picture which emerged was rather complex and not easily understood. For example, it was found that, contrary to expectations, an increase of concentration of copper chloride led to an increase of the delay time from about 20 minutes to 80 minutes. On the other hand, when copper bromide replaced the chloride, an increase in concentration decreased the delay. Copper nitrate and copper sulphate proved to be much less corrosive, but again, increase in concentration (as with the chloride) lengthened the delay. A wide range of timings could be obtained by using a mixture of copper chloride and copper acetate. To avoid the use of glycerol a series of experiments using n-propyl alcohol instead enabled a wide range of timings from 30 minutes to 15 hours to be achieved.

At this stage the work was beginning to take on the character of a more academic study of corrosion science and further work was carried out on an extramural contract with the Physical Chemistry Laboratory at Oxford under Dr J.G. Davoud, who later joined Station IX. Although it might have been possible at this stage to change the solution composition to take account of the work carried out, production of the pencils would have been interrupted. This would not have been justified as the reproducibility of the results was only marginally better than that of production pencils. The standard deviation of a single result throughout all the laboratory work was about ± 20 per cent, comparable with that for production pencils, i.e. there was a 95 per cent chance of an individual pencil operating within 20 per cent of its nominal value. Statistical analysis gives no information on the likelihood of rogue results arising from one-off factors. In the experimental programme only 5 out of 700 led to a rogue result. An investigation was undertaken to try to identify other factors which might affect the performance. One factor which was identified was the cleanliness of the wire, since traces of grease on the wire as supplied lengthened the time delay. There were also occasions when the wire supplied by the contractor was already starting to rust! Difficulties also arose when a shortage of supplies meant that different sources of wire had to be used. In particular, wire imported from the USA exhibited characteristics different from those of the British material and the solutions had to be varied to take account of this. It was not clear whether in the production process sufficient care was taken to ensure that the tension on the wire was constant, nor whether attention was paid to ensuring that the screw holding the wire was properly tightened. Major failure of the switch to operate correctly could have been caused by one or more of these factors. All of this pointed to the vital importance of rigorous Quality Control (QC) by the manufacturers and by Station XII, and to the need to tighten up the specification. This was done in collaboration with Maj Bedford and Capt Ault at Station XII. In all, some twelve million pencils were produced under the control of Station XII.

SOE was not the only organisation experiencing problems with devices equipped with Time Pencil-type delays, although in one case it was not the delay itself but the firing mechanism which was at fault. The failure of a German version of the device (or a captured SOE one) probably prevented a change in the course of the war. On 13 March 1943 a group of disaffected German officers made an unsuccessful attempt on Hitler's life when he visited the Army Group Centre at Smolensk. Over lunch, Col Henning von Tresckow asked one of Hitler's party if he minded taking two bottles of Cointreau back to headquarters on the return flight, explaining they were part of a bet he had made with another officer. After Hitler had boarded the aircraft the 30-minute delay was crushed to initiate it and the package handed to the aide. The bomb failed to explode, the reason never being fully explained. With astonishing coolness, Tresckow telephoned headquarters to tell them to hold on to the package as there had been a mix-up. Another officer on the daily courier flight retrieved it the next day and substituted a genuine package. On examination it was found that the capsule had broken, the solution had eaten through the wire retaining the firing pin, and the firing pin had struck the percussion cap which seemed to have ignited. But the charge had not exploded. One theory was that the heater in the aircraft's hold had malfunctioned, a not unusual event, and as a result the explosive, which was sensitive to cold, failed to react.[4]

THE AC DELAY

The main disadvantage of the Time Pencil was that it could not be used underwater. A time fuse was therefore needed for use with limpets and other mines. This was met by the AC (acetone cellulose) Delay, which, in its Mark II form, was widely used. The AC Delay Mk II depended on the softening by a mixture of acetone and amyl acetate, followed by the breaking, of a cellulose acetate tension bar holding back a spring-loaded striker. (In the Mk IA, the striker was held back by a plastic washer.) The solvent was contained in a glass ampoule, which could be crushed by a thumbscrew operated through a watertight gland. The delay time depended on the composition of the solvent, and a coloured dye indicated how long the operative had got. The six options were: red – 4½ hrs; orange – 7½ hrs; yellow – 15 hrs; green – 26 hrs; blue – 42 hrs; violet – 5½ days. Again, these were temperature dependent and the above figures referred to 15°C. When assembled, the switch was screwed into the body of the limpet.

Somewhat similar problems to those experienced with the Time Pencils arose with the AC Mk II delay. In those days the precision moulding of plastics was not well controlled. The tension bars were supplied by Halex (of toothbrush fame) and in one early batch of pre-production bars examined at Station IX, out of 100 bars some 30 were misshapen or badly scored and only eight were free from internal strain. Station XII (Maj Bedford and Capt Ault) tightened up the specification and imposed stricter quality control to eliminate these discrepancies. But another problem arose. The delay times were controlled by changing the proportion of amyl acetate in the solution, and these times seemed to depend on the source of the amyl acetate. Savory and Moore, who supplied the ampoules, assured Station IX that their amyl acetate conformed to the appropriate British Standard based on the refractive index, boiling point and density. What was not appreciated until the BSS was examined carefully was that it allowed the amyl acetate to contain up to 20 per cent of butyl acetate! Various batches from different suppliers would contain varying amounts of butyl acetate and hence give varying delay times. Again, the vital importance of a precise specification and adequate quality control was brought home. There were also other important design problems affecting the ease of manufacture. The waterproofing depended on the use of a rubber sealing washer resting on a seating ring. The exact design of the thread and seating proved to be vital and although Station XII were reluctant to change the design, it proved to be necessary. As with the Time Pencil this problem involved close collaboration between Stations IX and XII in tightening the specification and ensuring adequate quality control.

Everett was also concerned with the development of a plastic version of the Time Pencil delayed action fuse. His notebooks include several references to the PTP (presumably the Plastic Time Pencil) and to the despatch to Station XII of working drawings of the switch. They have not been located. There is no indication of the way in which it was intended to work. One speculation is that the wire retaining the spring was looped over a copper pin and that corrosion took place at the contact. Among the timing trials there is an obscure reference to the effect of the 'length of the copper pin'.

For ad hoc operations the section produced a soluble delay, a push/pull combination switch, an air-armed non-removal switch and a time-delay, referred to as the 'Eureka' clock.

It is the variety of devices worked upon but not put into production which gives a clue to the way Newitt's 'Baker Street Boys', as the scientists were sometimes referred to, were thinking about the next series of weapons in the fight against the enemy. These included the pocket hand grenade, the hydrostatic switch, the parachute canopy delay opening switch, the Allways switch, the parachute grapnel for landing, a thermal switch, the magnesium/lead alloy delay, an anti-tank mine activated by vibration, a device for climbing wire rope, an anti-disturbance switch, the sodium alginate relay, an air speed switch, a centrifugal switch, the photo-electric switch, the hydrostatic 'fog signal' switch, a speed switch for limpets, a mechanical altimeter switch for ascent and another for descent, an AC pencil time fuse and the air leak delay (disc time delay).

From time to time there are references to an 'air leak' or 'disc time' delay based on the rate of diffusion of air through a porous disc which was under development at Station IX towards the end of the war. Newitt thought it might be the ultimate answer to the need for a temperature-independent time-delay. No further information has been located in the files. Although Everett was involved, he could not remember any details until a clue was found in a rough free-hand sketch in his notebook covering the period 2 March to 3 April 1945 (see title page). It would appear from this that the main body of the switch was to be divided into two compartments separated by a thin, curved, metal diaphragm (probably of phosphor-bronze) which would 'click' over into one of two positions depending on the pressure difference across the compartments. The diaphragm would carry a firing pin at its centre. One compartment was at atmospheric pressure and the other evacuated and sealed. When the seal was broken air could diffuse through a porous plug (or disc). When the pressure difference approached zero a compressed spring would force the diaphragm to click over and cause the firing pin to strike the percussion cap. Conversion of this basic idea into a practical device would have involved some very precise engineering. It is recalled that among the main problems were those of making porous ceramic plugs with well-defined and reproducible characteristics, and fabricating the metal diaphragm. Everett has a vague recollection that advice on the latter was sought from Negretti and Zambra – a company better known for its barographs. Other difficulties would have included the problem of how to ensure that the device had not leaked in storage: how to devise a safety mechanism. One can speculate that, had the war been prolonged, this basic idea would have been developed into a reliable, largely temperature-independent time delay. Newitt considered it probable that all normal requirements could be met by a single switch of this kind and preliminary laboratory tests suggested that an overall error of less than 12 per cent was possible: but the war ended before the switch could be developed.

Wireless detonation also came under examination at Station IX. In February 1943 a Pole by the name of Sienkiewicz claimed to have invented a device for detonating explosives electrically at long range by means of wireless techniques. Letters passed between 'C', the head of SIS, and 'CD', the head of SOE, in which it was pointed out that the device was similar to, but not as good as, an invention already developed at Station IX. SOE had, in fact, rejected the Pole's device a year previously.[5]

As a result of experience in the field it was recognised that a delay device need not in general be highly accurate – except in the case of short timings, when the accuracy could mean a matter of life or death to the agent – provided that they were 100 per cent reliable under the conditions encountered. The reproducibility of better than ± 20 per cent was regarded as satisfactory provided that the quality control excluded any faulty items. A further precaution was to use Time Pencils in pairs. Early in the war it was thought a saboteur would need time delays of from one day to in excess of six days and Time Pencils had been produced in a range from ten minutes to six days. But in the 1942–44 period the demand had been for shorter timings, very few being over six hours.

As a result of suggestions fed back from the field for a means of firing a number of charges simultaneously without the tiresome and hazardous business of directly linking them with instantaneous fuse, the Station had developed the sympathetic fuse, which responded to the pressure surge from a nearby explosion. Forms for use both in air and underwater were developed.

As an illustration of the diversity of problems and the advantages of a flexible organisation, it is recalled that the amateur clockmaker, the retired Lt Col H.H. King, became concerned with a completely different topic, that of the problems of dropping dogs by parachute. Details of this work have not been found and one can only surmise that his skills were called upon to devise a mechanism to release the dogs from their harnesses once they were safely on the ground.

INCENDIARIES

From the outset, fire-raising was seen as a most effective means of sabotage. Given the right conditions for combustion, which were often simple and not difficult to arrange, the ignition from a single source might wreak enormous destruction. It is not surprising therefore that by the end of 1940 the anticipated requirements for small incendiary bombs and incendiary arrows were one million of each. Among the earlier incendiary devices inherited by SOE were a large incendiary bomb (2 lb, 0.9 kg) and a smaller (2 oz, 56 gm) device, the latter especially suited for use among loose inflammable material. Several of the incendiaries developed by Station IX were based on a mixture of aluminium and iron oxide (Thermite). When ignited with a chlorate initiator this can attain a temperature of 2,400°C. The molten iron so produced had been applied in peacetime in certain welding techniques. In any case it was a very efficient incendiary. Two such devices were available: the 1¾ lb (0.8 kg) Mk II Firepot and the 2½ lb (1.1 kg) Thermite Incendiary.

A number of smaller devices about which little is known and which probably had their origins at Station XV included: Incendiary Cigarettes (popular with the Italians!); Incendiary Ground Nuts, and Cough Mixture Incendiary Material.

Another device about which there is limited information was the Incendiary Arrow. It is said to have resembled a large safety match about 18 in long with a percussion fuse in the head. It could be fired from a bow or catapult with a range of about 50 yards. Although it was ordered in large quantities in late 1940, there is no reliable information on its use in the field.

Among the incendiary devices which appear in SOE archives but which may have been inherited in mid-1941 from Naval scientists is the Deckerette. This was described as a sandwich of raw rubber sheet impregnated with kerosene between two 2-in square celluloid leaves. Each celluloid sheet had a small disc of phosphorus wrapped in cotton attached to its outer side. Phosphorus is, of course, spontaneously flammable in air so the cotton wrapping would have provided only a degree of safety in its handling. This device was looked upon as being suitable for starting conflagrations in crops, forests, timber yards and warehouses.[6]

The project that engaged much of the attention of Walker, Bamford and Wilde was the design of the Pocket Incendiary. It was a small incendiary consisting of a plastic case filled with petroleum gel, and ignited with a 30-min. Time Pencil. It was a conveniently sized device which burned for about four minutes. When proper preparations had been made with respect to secondary fuel, draughts, convection, conduction and radiation this was a very effective device, so much so that larger incendiaries might not be necessary. It was a versatile piece of equipment which, when mounted on an instruction card and dropped in large numbers from the air, provided the basis for Operation Moon (later called 'Braddock'), the full story of which is recounted in Chapter 15. Several million were produced but only about a quarter of a million were actually delivered to the field.

A very simple incendiary device was that known as the Tyesule. It was a gelatine capsule containing 2 oz (57 gm) of a petrol/paraffin mixture. At one end the capsule was coated with a match composition which, when rubbed on a striker board, caused the device to ignite. With this, one had to choose targets carefully, for it did not provide any delay in which to make good an escape.

In confined spaces, where the supply of air was limited, use could be made of the Incendiary Block. About the size of a brick, this consisted of a wax block strapped to a cellulose acetate box containing sodium nitrate which decomposed to provide oxygen to fuel the flames.

In cases where the fuel for the conflagration was enclosed, such as in a fuel tank, a combined explosive–incendiary device was tested. In the case of a diesel oil tank the explosive ruptured the tank after a preset delay and dispersed the oil in a fine mist which was ignited by the simultaneously fired incendiary device.

Meanwhile, the search for alternative incendiary materials was being carried out by Walker, Bamford and their group on an oil/nitrate incendiary and on phosphorus/iodine gel. Other incendiary devices included a Directional Incendiary, a Magnesium Flash Incendiary, a Flash Grenade and a Jet Thermite Bomb as well as a Pocket Smoke Generator. Unfortunately, details of these devices are unavailable; although considerable progress was made, none was put into production. Bamford also conducted research aimed at setting fire to Chinese junks being used by the Japanese. This involved causing a dust explosion of magnesium powder which would be spread onto all the surrounding wooden surfaces and make the fire almost impossible to extinguish. In trials, mock-ups could be burnt to the waterline very rapidly. Interest was shown in this principle being adapted for an air-delivered weapon but the Japanese surrender occurred before work on it was completed.

DESTRUCTION OF DOCUMENTS

The need for a means of destroying documents quickly and completely had long been recognised. This arose when, for example, an embassy had to be vacated at short notice in the face of an invading enemy. There must have been many examples as the Germans advanced across Europe. An equally important and frequent need arose when an agent or a courier was captured in possession of a briefcase containing secret documents, such as coded messages. A first requirement was that the document case could be destroyed rapidly by the agent or be booby-trapped so that if opened subsequently then an incendiary device was activated and destroyed the contents. In this connection it is important to realise that burning of tightly packed sheets, as in a book (please do not try it!), is extremely difficult – very often the edges of each page are singed, leaving the bulk unaffected. This means that sensitive material should not be packed tightly and that adequate incendiary material must be incorporated.

Station XV responded to this need by devising a number of incendiary briefcases and document boxes containing a variety of incendiary materials.[7] In the early days such devices were not always subjected to user trials, and in any case many of them were 'one-off' devices produced to the personal needs of the agent. When later extensive tests were made, a number of shortcomings were found in some of the devices, which proved dangerous even when tested in a user trial. There is one well-documented example of a serious failure in the field recorded by Sweet-Escott. 'Poor David (Smiley) took with him an agent's briefcase, one of the proudest inventions of our devices department in London. It was fitted with a switch which made it explode if the holder were attacked, thereby destroying the secret documents inside. Something went wrong with it when he was in Siam and it blew up, badly damaging his forearm. No doctor could be found there and he had to be flown out.' When he arrived back in India he was still picking maggots out of his arm.[8]

Among the proposed improvements in the efficiency of destroying papers was that of typing on to lightly nitrated paper, or using this inter-leaved with the documents. Tests of this paper showed indeed that when a single sheet was ignited it burned fiercely for a few seconds and left practically no ash. But if more than a few sheets were used, especially if they were packed closely, they tended to detonate. This was demonstrated in a user trial by rolling a sheet into a loose ball, igniting it and then trying to stamp it out. The result was a detonation and a sore foot. It was soon realised, in addition, that this nitrated paper had a short shelf-life – despite requests from time to time it was never produced in quantity although it was listed in the SOE catalogue.

Station IX took up the challenge to make a document case which it was virtually impossible to open without it igniting. It was realised, for example, that, in the simpler versions, examination by X-rays could reveal the nature of the booby trap. If the device was contained in a metal case, then a hacksaw or diamond wheel could be used to open it. Taking all these points into consideration a group at Station IX under Maj Walker and the physicists Wilson and Chibnall set about creating the 'ultimate' document case. This turned out to be a cylindrical metal container some 4 in in diameter and 10 in long, the hinging and opening components being protected by one or more keys or combination locks opened either mechanically or electrically. The documents were to be rolled round a Thermite incendiary charge. To protect against X-ray examination the case was double-walled, the cavity being filled with a paste containing a lead compound (probably lead oxide – although this is speculation); to protect against sectioning, the metal walls were incorporated in an electrical circuit so that a hacksaw blade would short-circuit the two walls and set off a detonator. It is not now known what other precautions were taken, but every attempt was made to ensure that the contents could not be extracted unharmed. The result was a somewhat heavy device which would certainly not be cheap to produce. Nevertheless it was considered that there might be circumstances when transporting extra top-secret material in which the expense was justified.

A good deal of interest was shown by several Government organisations, in particular MI5, where Lord Rothschild was an acknowledged expert on the defusing of sabotage devices and booby traps, having been awarded the George Medal for his work.[9] He visited Station IX several times during the development of the incendiary document case and expressed a strong desire to test his skills on this new challenge.

Everett was deputed to take one of the prototypes to show Rothschild in his office in St James'. This was not entirely simple since, on the appointed day, no transport was available from The Frythe to London. The only way was to flount the law and carry an explosive device by public transport. Everett got a lift to Welwyn Garden City carrying the document case in a brown paper bag. He then took a train to Liverpool Street with the parcel bouncing ominously on the string baggage rack above his head, crossed London by Underground and presented himself to Rothschild. After explaining in detail all the components of the case, Everett cautioned Rothschild strongly against any attempt to open it.

Next morning a phone call came through to say that, alas, the device had operated and that the Thermite charge had burnt a hole in the floor of Rothschild's office! No details were ever revealed as to how the attempted opening had failed. It was no doubt considered unwise to invoke his wrath by advertising his failure. There is no record of more than a few of these devices ever having been made or used in the field.

Summing up the work of the Incendiaries (or Fire Raising) Sub-Section in his immediate postwar appraisal of the Research and Development Section of SOE, Newitt said it had been devoted largely to establishing the fundamental theory of combustion as applied to various categories of targets and to developing time-delay matches (sic). Papers had been written on the theory of fire-raising in warehouses and similar structures, oil tanks, wooden ships and chemical plants. They give an indication of the wide-ranging ideas emanating from the establishment.

SIX

PHYSICO-CHEMICAL AND PHYSIOLOGICAL SECTIONS

hapter 5 dealt with materials needed for major sabotage
operations – explosives and incendiaries, together with the
ancillary components needed for their use. In this chapter
attention is mainly devoted to less violent clandestine activities
designed to erode the enemy's war effort by disrupting his transport
and communications, destroying vital supplies and immobilising
sources of production of key stores. Their impact ranged from
nuisance value, with its associated psychological effects, to large-scale
disruption of services and infrastructure. Also included is an account
of the more subtle work of the Physiological Section.

SABOTAGE OF RAIL TRANSPORT

Much emphasis was placed on the need to interfere with rail transport
and the various ways of doing this by direct explosive attack are dealt
with in the previous chapter. Up to December 1942 there was a veto on
the use of explosives in SOE operations in the Vichy zone of France.
There were, however, other, more ingenious ways of achieving the
same results. Thus, steam locomotives could be put out of action by the
addition to the boiler water feed tank of the foaming agent Vulcastab,
while the addition of 'explosive coal' or 'explosive rats' (provided by
Station XV) to coal tenders not only had a direct effect but also created
an unwillingness on the part of engine drivers to operate their trains.
There is evidence that the introduction of these devices caused a good
deal of consternation and at least had a significant effect on morale.

A technique for which considerable success was claimed involved
the contamination of the axle boxes of freight wagons with an
abrasive grease containing carborundum powder, leading to the

seizure of the bearings. This was one of the first materials to be distributed by SOE in 1941. It was produced and supplied as a dry abrasive powder which could be used in this form or mixed with lubricating oil and was packaged by Camouflage Section to suit the local circumstances.

Evidence for the effectiveness of this treatment was based on somewhat scattered reports from the field which one suspects were often exaggerated. Similar claims were made from time to time that a wide range of additives including fuming nitric acid, sulphuric acid, sand and strong alkali were also effective. It is known that, even in normal peacetime use, 'hot boxes', the overheating and seizure of axles in their bearings, was not unusual, especially with poorly maintained rolling stock. It would have been easy (and tempting!) for agents to attribute such occurrences to their own subversive action. Foot has commented that 'this is the sort of story which resisters like to tell one another to keep their spirits up', or for that matter to report to their Country Sections in London.

It was clearly important for planning purposes to have credible information on the effectiveness of the various proposed treatments, and in January 1943 Station IX was commissioned to carry out experiments to ascertain which, if any, were reliable methods of sabotage. To this end the testing facilities at the Great Western Railway workshops at Swindon were commandeered and experiments were made on a number of continental goods wagons which had been trapped in the UK on the outbreak of war. The bearings on most continental wagons were the plain white metal type lubricated by pad and wick. The exact design depended on the country of origin but according to Tony Brooks, whose 'Pimento' circuit operated widely in the south of France, few could be doctored without removing the cover, whether bolted or loose. It was sometimes possible, using a specially modified grease gun with a flat-nosed pipe attachment, to get the abrasive on to the pad. The details of the trucks used in the experiments cannot be remembered, but at the time they were thought to be a representative sample of those most likely to be encountered. Their axle boxes were treated with a range of contaminants chosen from those which agents claimed to be the most effective. They were then run continuously at 50 mph on test beds for four weeks in February–March 1943. To the dismay and surprise of Station IX (and in particular of Sgt Campbell, who had sat watching the tests day after day waiting for something to happen) not one of the several dozen bearings under test showed any sign of serious overheating after over 5,000 miles. Unfortunately, the report of these trials has not been found, so the details of the tests cannot be checked. Despite the negative results of these trials, it was felt that they were not conclusive and that abrasive powder and grease should continue to be included in the Catalogue of Special Devices and issued to the field.[1]

There is, however, one well-authenticated example of the vital role played by abrasive powder in the weeks following D-Day. The crack 2nd SS Panzer Division (Das Reich) was stationed near Montauban in Southern France. When the nature of the invasion became clear, Das Reich was ordered to proceed to the Normandy front. Actions by SOE so delayed its progress that it did not arrive until D+17. The initial delay was brought about by the sabotage of the axle boxes of the tank rail transporter wagons by members of Brooks's 'Pimento' circuit using abrasive powder. Several accounts of this action have been published but, viewed from a technical angle, they are somewhat ambiguous.

According to Foot, 'when the Division sent for its transporter cars every one of them seized up after loading at Montauban'. This seemed to imply that the abrasive grease had acted while the wagons were at rest and the bearings only seized up when they were moved; while Wilkinson and Astley refer to the 'legendary exploits of two French schoolgirls who sabotaged the axle boxes of the transporter cars and delayed the departure of Das Reich'. This again seems to imply that the seizures occurred before the Division moved off. To clarify the story we are most grateful to Tony Brooks who has provided us with what must be the definitive account of this successful sabotage operation.[2]

The tanks and their transporters were dispersed in villages around the Tarn and Garonne. Their distribution 'all over the place' was established by members of Brooks's team including two girls whose reconnaissance located the wagons. The wheels of these special transporter flats – 'magnificent wagons' as Brooks describes them – ran in Timken roller bearings. The technique adopted was to drain the oil by removing the drain plug and put in dry abrasive powder via the oil filler hole so that the powder got directly onto the rollers or, in some designs of bearing, onto the lubricating pad. One bearing per wagon was treated. When the order to move was given the transporter wagons were assembled with the tanks at Montauban and moved North. After 50–100 km the axle boxes overheated and seized, bringing the train of tanks to a halt. The SS abandoned their transporters and, as described in various accounts, unloaded the tanks and proceeded by road, harassed on their way by successive SOE and Resistance bands.

The effectiveness of abrasive powder in this instance was proved dramatically. It remains to be asked why the Swindon experiments failed to yield positive confirmation of the effectiveness of abrasive powder. Since the report on these trials is no longer available reliance has to be placed on memories. The bearings installed on the freight wagons were almost certainly white metal but it is not known whether they were loaded with ballast. The effect of axle loading was not, it is thought, included in the variables studied; nor can it be remembered whether the oil was completely removed from the boxes. It is probable that the urgency of the test programme did not allow time for a more detailed investigation. An alternative form of abrasive produced by Station IX was as Carborundum Pastilles, but a description and mode of application of them has not been found either. Despite the undoubted success of the use of abrasive powder against Das Reich, there must be some lingering doubt about its general applicability. As Tony Brooks comments, 'We had a few reports of hot axles, but nowhere near the number of boxes attacked. Perhaps its main contribution was its value as a way of keeping chaps busy and it was good for morale.'

SABOTAGE OF U-BOATS

With the Battle of the Atlantic intensifying, the war against the U-boats escalated during 1942. It is not surprising that SOE was asked urgently to address the subject of countering this menace. SOE considered what contributions it could make and a number of projects were developed leading to a technical assessment prepared by Station IX, which was the subject of a report of 26 July 1943. This report has not been found although it is referred to in Laboratory Contributions No. 58 in the *Technical Review*. Direct explosive attack by saboteurs was made almost impossible by the very strict security measures around U-boat pens: as far as is known no successful operations of this kind were carried out. Attention was therefore directed at the U-boat crews. As early as 1941 SOE had introduced Mucuna, an itching powder which, as discussed later, was used successfully to contaminate their underclothing.

Another aspect of the war against the U-boats concerned the

possibility of demoralising the crews by persistently interfering with their normal food supplies. DSR was requested to recommend an adulterant for wine and olive oil to make them unpalatable but not poisonous. At the end of March 1943 DSR replied that wine would be turned sour by exposure to air and the addition of vinegar would spoil it but, as shown later, Haas was working on more effective measures. In 1941 he had been experimenting on the contamination of sardines. His report for DSR was resurrected in 1943 as part of the war against the U-boats. Just how much of this research was put to use in the field is not known.[3]

The most vulnerable equipment of a U-boat was its bank of accumulators, which provided its propulsive and secondary power when submerged. Identification of the locations of works manufacturing accumulators showed that this important industry was well scattered: there was no one area which was at risk from air attack. A study of ways of sabotaging accumulators led to the development of the 'Platinum Pill'. It was envisaged that these might be smuggled aboard and dropped into the accumulators, or added to them during transport from the factory. Before these pills had been fully developed pamphlet CM20 describing them was circulated to Country Sections without proper authorisation and Newitt was incensed that knowledge of this product had been leaked. But it was well known that accumulators are sensitive to the presence of impurities, and that platinum in the form of platinum chloride was particularly deleterious. The action of a soluble platinum compound is to deposit, during the charging/discharging cycle, finely divided platinum black on one or both of the electrodes, thus poisoning the electrode reaction and ruining the battery. As little as one part platinum in ten million increases the local action at the negative plates by 50 per cent. Anything over one part in two million discharges negative plates by 60 per cent or more in a few hours.

By the end of December 1942 DSR wrote that SOE had available tablets of platinum salts each sufficient to deal with about ten litres of battery acid, which was a fairly large cell. It was recommended that the pills be introduced into the distilled water or acid either in the factories or as it was supplied to the submarine bases. By June a new type of pill had been produced in two forms: camouflaged and non-camouflaged. Each pill would deal with 50 litres of acid, the camouflaged type taking 20 minutes to dissolve, the other only four minutes. They were given the name 'Volcase' Platinum (Submarine) Pills.[4] There is a record of these pills being introduced into the batteries of a U-boat at La Pallice and Lord Selborne's quarterly report to Churchill in October 1943 states that submarine batteries at Bordeaux had been dosed with 'pills'.[5]

It was anticipated that agents might want to make their own platinum pills. A project at Station IX investigated ways in which they could be made from items of platinum jewellery donated generously by the public using chemicals which might be stolen from chemical factories or laboratories.

There may have been other examples of U-boat sabotage but evidence is scarce. The same quarterly report to Churchill recorded that 'home made' pellets, whose nature is not known, had been introduced into the engines of two submarines, causing one to return 'on the accumulators' after five hours' sailing. The fate of the second U-boat is unknown. These appear to be examples of an unexplained method of sabotage, as in these cases the foreign material was introduced into the engines rather than the batteries. Had the batteries been doctored, the stricken U-boat would not have been able to return to port on its accumulators. Station IX had, in fact, been working on the sabotage of diesel engines: at least one compound which might have been procurable from a chemical factory was shown to be effective.[6] In this connection, and as an example of the petty problems which faced Station IX from time to time, when a decision was taken to investigate the sabotage of diesel engines it proved exceedingly difficult to acquire an engine on which to experiment. The London Passenger Transport Board (LPTB) was unable to provide an old omnibus engine, nor were approaches to other users any more successful. In the end, undercover visits to various North London scrapyards led to the acquisition of a suitable engine for a few pounds in cash.

Since the chances were slight of getting explosive or incendiary material into a U-boat to damage its electrical and electronic equipment, the alternative was to ensure that supplies of such essential components were curtailed by bombing or sabotaging the factories producing them. This required detailed information on the sources of the various items. The possibility of obtaining this technical information arose from the following circumstances. On 27 August 1941, *U570* surfaced in the North Atlantic unaware that in its periscope's blind spot was a patrolling Hudson aircraft of Coastal Command. After several attacks the U-boat crew appeared on deck showing a white flag (the Captain's dress shirt) and surrendered.[7] They were taken off by the Royal Navy, who towed the U-boat to

Iceland for repairs before moving it to the Holy Loch at Dunoon where it was recommissioned as HMS *Graph* on 29 September 1941. This was the first, and perhaps the only, U-boat captured intact and virtually undamaged. Not only did HMS *Graph* provide valuable information on the technical advances made by the Germans in submarine design, but it enabled SOE to carry out a technical survey of its equipment and to identify its origins. This was carried out by Everett on 14–15 April 1943, his report being incorporated in Station IX's overall assessment of ways of sabotaging U-boats. One interesting fact emerged – a considerable proportion of the sophisticated equipment bore the names and locations of companies such as Braun-Boveri in neutral Switzerland and Sweden. Whether the items were actually manufactured there is not clear, but curtailing their production by bombing was not an option. It is not known what use was made of this technical intelligence in planning the bombing programmes on German industries.

ATTACKS ON ENEMY MORALE

One of SOE's objectives, as part of the Ministry of Economic Warfare (MEW), was to undermine the morale of the enemy, and in particular his armed forces. It is well known that important factors in maintaining morale are physical comfort and adequate nutrition. Ways were sought of making life as unpleasant as possible for certain selected groups. Among these were the crews of U-boats. One of the most effective ways of inflicting persistent discomfort on enemy troops was by the use of Itching Powder (the barbed seeds of the Mucuna plant) and this was one of the first stores to be supplied to agents. It was intended to be dispensed from a talcum powder tin (ex-Station XV) into the clothing of German troops at laundries or clothing factories. In November 1941 the first small consignment was sent to collaborators in Switzerland for use on the clothing and bedding of German troops. Supplies were sent periodically to SOE's representatives in neutral countries and a report of June 1942 states that the powder had been introduced into the clothes of German ships' crews. Another report, referred to earlier, records that it was placed in a consignment of shirts for U-boat crews at Troyes and that at least one U-boat had to return to port because the crew thought they were suffering from severe dermatitis. Lord Selborne's quarterly report to Churchill in July 1943 stated that

7,000 German uniforms had been sprinkled with the chemical. Three months later he claimed that 25,000 U-boat uniforms had been 'treated with itching powder which torments the tender parts of the human anatomy'.[8]

It was not only underclothing and uniforms which were contaminated with this irritant. Norwegian resistance workers experimented with putting it into condoms destined to be used by the occupying German forces. After treatment, re-rolling and re-packing they were sent for distribution mainly in the Trondheim area. No reports on the effectiveness of this piece of sabotage were received until after the capitulation of the German forces when it was revealed that considerable success had been achieved. Hospitals had been frequently called upon to treat the painful irritation. As an added bonus, the condoms had been sold at a good profit to local 'houses of assignation'.[9] What may be seen at first sight as a juvenile prank could, under the right circumstances, become a serious weapon in the Allies' armoury.

Annoyance and frustration among troops in confined spaces – such as U-boats or tanks – can result from the presence of persistent body odours, especially when the source is not obvious. Such circumstances can be exploited by providing agents with capsules of malodorous or noxious liquids. Dr Haas and Col King devised appropriate formulations leading to the S-capsule, which contained a blend of higher fatty acids. Besides being useful in rendering the atmosphere in poorly ventilated spaces – such as bars – unpleasant, they could be used more directly, leading to embarrassing situations and annoyance if an agent could get close enough to a dignitary to discharge some onto his clothing. At about this time, the story circulated at Station IX that von Papen, Hitler's Foreign Minister, was attending a prestigious formal reception in Ankara when an agent succeeded in squirting some S-capsule liquid on to his coat. He made a sudden departure, much to the consternation of his hosts. A similar mixture was incorporated in drags intended to put dogs off the scent of an escaping agent.

It was a short step to consider means of demoralising the German forces by rendering their food supplies unappetising by the clandestine introduction of substances having either offensive smells or tastes. As early as 1941 Haas had been experimenting with the production of bad tastes and smells and laxative action by the tainting of sardines with unpleasant contaminants. His report was resurrected in 1943 when, as part of the anti-U-boat campaign, L/IT approached DSR asking for suggestions for adulterants of wine and olive oil which would make them unpalatable but not poisonous. Apart from allowing the wine to go sour, or adding vinegar, Haas suggested the addition of butyric acid or iso-valeric acid, the latter creating the bonus of an offensive odour which could readily be blamed on accidental infection or abnormal fermentation. Olive oil could be made to taste or smell objectionable by the addition of paraffin oil (kerosene), oil of turpentine or camphor. Croton oil, on the other hand, would be undetectable but could prove fatal if more than a carefully measured small quantity was added.

Dr Haas extended his research into making wine and olive oil unfit for consumption by altering its colour. In May, DSR reported that two dyes had been found. While discolouring white wine was easier, they could turn red wine a deep inky blue with 10 gm/100 litres or a deep green with 30 gm/100 litres.

More drastic effects were to be expected from the use of purgatives which, in Haas's genteel words, caused 'loss of bowel control'. There was a rumour in 1943 that, on the eve of a crucial battle in the Italian campaign, the wine consumed by the Italian High Command had been doped with a mild purgative – phenolphthalein – which by the following morning had a dramatic effect: they lost not only bowel control but also the battle. Whether or not this was true, the story was good for the morale of those working on this mild form of chemical warfare.

Later, Professor J.H. Gaddum, FRS, was consulted and drew attention to a much more powerful group of purgatives. If very small amounts of Carbachol (or Doryl, or Carbamylcholine) which was made in laboratory quantities by Burroughs-Wellcome were mixed with common salt and introduced into the food, it would produce a very powerful evacuation of the bowels. It was claimed that no medical examination or even post mortem could detect the drug. Two other powerful cathartics were also suggested: Isachen and Colocynth, the latter thought to be less detectable by taste if put in beer. A paper entitled 'Evacuation against Evacuation' was prepared, proposing that packets of the chemicals be made up by SOE and distributed with instructions for use. Whether this was ever put into effect is not known.[10]

Among the means of publicly denigrating the enemy occupying forces was the use of graffiti on walls and windows. However, most of the paints then available could be removed without too much difficulty. The need was expressed for a more permanent means of daubing offensive and obscene remarks on shop windows or German vehicle windscreens. Considerable effort was expended, with the help of ICI, in developing an etching formulation of finely ground ammonium bifluoride which would etch glass and be essentially non-removable. Eventually it was possible with the use of gums and dispersing agents to produce a material which could resemble sun pigmentation cream, Nivea face cream or toothpaste. This was provided camouflaged in two forms, either in tins or tubes of a popular shaving or toothpaste packing, neither of which would create any suspicion in a search. To complete the deception, clandestine consultations with a London toiletry firm produced perfumes which were tolerable imitations of the scent of the creams they were meant to simulate. There was, however, a snag. Early in 1943 a consignment of 'toothpaste' was sent to North Africa without instructions. It was issued as genuine toothpaste with devastating effect on both the teeth and morale of some agents – and a furious cable to HQ.

MISCELLANEOUS SABOTAGE MATERIALS

A wide range of equipment and materials was needed to meet the diverse and often bizarre operational concepts being developed at HQ, as well as the immediate requirements of agents in the field.

Since many sabotage operations were carried out at night it was important that members of a team were kept in touch with one another. This was not too difficult in moonlight but less easy on a really dark night. The use of luminous tapes attached to clothing was an obvious solution, but most available luminous materials which were activated by exposure to light faded after a few hours in the dark. The Polish Section came up with a more radical solution by using discs coated with a radioactive paint which retains its luminosity indefinitely. Depending on the size of the disc and the concentration of radioactive paint, they could be clearly seen over a distance of several metres. Did the Poles wish to emphasise the practical application of Madame Curie's discoveries? When samples of these discs were sent to Station IX for test Dr Haas was horrified: the radiation from them was dangerously high and he judged that if left in contact with the skin for a few hours they would produce a severe burn. Geiger counters were not available. He recommended strongly that, because of the danger of putting them into inexperienced hands, they should not be issued, except in very special circumstances; and they should be stored in lead-lined boxes. It would appear, however, that the enthusiasm of Country Sections overcame these concerns and they were duly included in the Catalogue without any warning as to their potential danger and no indication as to how they should be stored. These discs were also considered for use for the location of parachute containers in the dark (see Chapter 11). Again, there was reluctance to do so since they would automatically be acquired by agents unaware of the danger involved in their use.

There was also a desire to provide agents with night glasses especially for use around dusk and in moonlight. Presumably the cost of high-grade binoculars ruled out their general issue and an alternative, less expensive, lightweight binocular fitted with plastic lenses with a magnification of X2 was tested. It certainly helped to pick out dimly-lit objects, but the Technical Review confirmed the view of the Trials Committee that they were not suitable for arduous use because, among other things, of the need to protect the plastic lenses from scratching.

Station IX was also called upon to test a variety of other materials such as soluble paper which enabled messages to be destroyed if the agent was caught. An oft-repeated call from the field was for waterproof clothing. Obviously, it was not acceptable to provide anything manufactured in Britain or identifiable as originating outside occupied Europe. The alternative was to provide agents with a means of waterproofing their own clothing. Discussions with ICI and tests at Station IX led to the development of Dipsanil V, a wax-based emulsion in a formulation which could be applied domestically using only normal kitchen equipment. The burst of enthusiasm for camping and outdoor sports since the war has seen the extensive availability of similar formulations on the domestic market.

Among other requests from agents in the field was one for a purpose-made jacket for carrying special stores during operations. Another was for silent footwear and a plea that SOE be granted special facilities to obtain the necessary rubber, such was the wartime shortage of this precious commodity.

Research was conducted in December 1942 into ways of detecting when envelopes had been opened and resealed or tampered with in other ways. Work was also undertaken on special torches with infra-red filters. Available for issue was a waterproof torch, designed and made at Station XII for use by both SOE and CCO. Despite being an everyday item, the SOE-designed waterproof version (some with a long, conical-shaped lens shade) was not a great success, the chief problem being waterproofing the switch. Another device was an apparatus for distilling volatile spirit from rubber. This was intended to provide fuel for one of the several types of battery charger developed at Station IX; but, since rubber was as scarce as petrol, it was of little use in Europe. In the Far East, however, it was expected to be of some value.

Haas and his group were active in investigating a wide range of problems. He became an expert in the use of secret inks and was presumably responsible for the extensive range of ingredients listed in the SOE Syllabus.

They also produced items of make-up intended for disguise. Some were temporary and some, like Mepacreme, dyed the skin yellowish after 12 doses and a deep brown if continued. Carotene was made from the pigment of carrots, while so-called 'wrinkling cream' did not wrinkle the skin but produced an unhealthy pallor.

PHYSIOLOGICAL SECTION

The Physiological Section took on the bacteriological and toxicological aspects of Professor Newitt's organisation in 1941 and dealt with the clandestine aspects of small-scale chemical and bacteriological warfare. A great deal of their work was to find chemicals and the means of administering them which could enhance an agent's performance and others which would degrade to various degrees that of the enemy. The chemical agents under investigation were classified according to their speed of action and their lethal properties. Slow-acting poisons were required to have a delayed action so that the agent administering it could distance himself from the victim before the effect (which was not necessarily fatal) became apparent. On the other hand, quick-acting poisons should have an immediate effect and in the form of suicide pills lead to the death of the agent before he or she could be interrogated.

From 1942, Station IX had regular informal contact with the Chemical Defence Experimental Station at Porton Down under the 'Kummerbund' project for biological matters and the 'Saccharine' project for chemical matters. A whole range of poisons were subjected to experiments, though they were not necessarily produced in other than laboratory quantities, let alone being issued to agents in the field. Some of the laboratory test samples were prepared by

Imperial College, London and some by Cambridge University, academia being a rich source of scientific expertise.

The 'Saccharine' project resulted in Porton Down supplying SOE with:

Stores A – a lachrymatory substance for use in a tear-gas grenade.

Stores B – a thickened mustard gas in a toothpaste tube for smearing on items that were likely to be handled by the enemy.

Stores C – a smoke and lachrymatory generator.

Among the chemical agents developed at Station IX and available to agents for 'Special Requirements' were the 'A' tablet, 'B' tablet, 'E' capsule, 'K' tablet, Mecodrin tablet and 'L' tablet.

The 'A' tablet was for air sickness and was similar to those commonly available after the war. It was actually in capsule form and the agent was required to take one half an hour before take-off, another fifteen minutes after take-off and then a third an hour after take-off. The maximum dosage was three per flight. The 'B' tablet was Benzedrine, already in use pre-war, and used to stave off tiredness or to give an extra spurt of energy. The maximum dosage was two. The 'E' capsule, actually an ampoule of possibly ether-based solution, was a quick-acting anaesthetic which produced half a minute's unconsciousness half a minute after administration. The 'K' tablet was a Morphia-based sleeping draught to be used offensively. One tablet would put an average-sized man to sleep for four hours. For a large person it was better to use two tablets to be sure. Agents were warned to dissolve the tablets before putting them into a beverage and not to administer them in tea due to the bitter give-away taste the two produced. Eight tablets were a lethal dose.

Mecodrin tablets were amphetamines or 'speed' and were provided on certain operations to give a boost to the agent. Other drugs available included ascorbic acid tablets; caffeine tablets; halazone water-purifying tablets; halibut liver oil capsules; Mepacrine tablets – an anti-protozoal drug which can also be used in the treatment of malaria; morphine hydrochloride for pain relief; and quinine bihydrochloride tablets.

During its lifetime, SOE produced several variations on the 'suicide pill'. Some were tablets which dissolved in the body's natural juices and released their contents. Some contained the active cyanide ingredient within an impervious capsule which had to be bitten, while others acted most rapidly when sucked. In July 1942 'L' tablets were lethal cyanide pills. If sucked, rapid and painless death was said to ensue in 30 seconds. If swallowed death might take up to five minutes. In an actual reported case a convulsive death occurred after an hour and a half, but the victim had been unconscious and incapable of being interrogated, which was the object of this drastic action. C.H. Mackenzie, Director of Delhi Group, advised officers to 'play up to the agents' beliefs and emphasise the potency of the drugs'.[11]

Some suicide tablets were very small, five of them making the diameter of an old penny. They were claimed to act within a minute or two and could be used offensively by being dropped into the victim's drink. Another type had a triple coating of insoluble bedacryl (methyl methacrylate). These could be easily secreted in the mouth until chewed to dispense their poison into the system. It is interesting to note that test tablets were produced containing methylene blue which showed up in the urine if the coating were damaged. These were intended to give the agent confidence in the triple coating. One report tells of Dr Paul Haas and some others deciding to test some cyanide capsules by sleeping with them tucked into their cheeks. This would appear either foolhardy in the extreme or a demonstration of absolute confidence in their product, for if it had been accidentally bitten or had leaked they would not have woken. One Danish group reported that their 'L' tablet was 'very effective', though they didn't specify how they knew this. They also considered them to be somewhat compromising in a search and suggested that they be camouflaged in the form of a button, a good idea, but it is not known if it was ever taken up.[12]

Biological warfare was outlawed by the Geneva Protocol of 1925 to which Britain (but not the USA) was a signatory. But when it was learned in 1936 that Germany was researching in this field a review of the situation was undertaken.

The investigations carried out at the Chemical Defence Experimental Station at Porton Down into the offensive use of biological agents were, it was said, in order to devise countermeasures to any attack upon our troops or this country. These bacteriological agents, by their very nature, took several days to produce their disabling effects and so were totally unsuitable for offensive use in a conventional assault. But they could conceivably be used by saboteurs. One of the most toxic, botulinum toxin 'X' was found to be most effectively introduced through the skin. Infected darts and .22

ammunition contaminated with 'X' were successfully tried on animals. There is evidence of a silenced pistol and ammunition being provided by SOE to Porton Down and one can imagine the trials being carried out using the same means of delivery as in the field. It was also established that a small bomb which had been coated with the organism would provide fragments which remained biologically lethal. Furthermore, Porton investigated the use of this toxin as a poison administered by mouth.[13]

The War Cabinet Bacteriological Warfare Committee was concerned in the early months of the war at the possibility of German agents using bacteriological sabotage in this country and issued warnings and guidelines to police forces throughout the land. An instance of probable, though unproven, sabotage occurred against the French in Africa when it was thought that one ampoule containing tetanus toxin was substituted for an anti-meningococcal vaccine, resulting in the deaths of 43 Africans.[14]

The Government's concern extended to the risk presented by the initiation of epidemics of a range of diseases including bubonic plague, rabies, cholera and typhoid fever, anthrax, psittacosis, tularaemia, pneumonic plague, typhus, yellow fever and foot and mouth disease, the last named not being serious to humans but, as is now known, having the potential for a catastrophic effect on the nation's agricultural industry. On 19 January 1942, Lord Hankey wrote to Gladwyn Jebb at the Ministry of Economic Warfare to say that, in the event of the enemy contravening the international agreements relating to biological warfare, SOE should be in a position to take immediate retaliatory action. As there was unlikely to be much warning, 'the Government should put in hand measures to make our action effective'.[15]

Two stories have grown up over the years concerning the use by SOE of chemical and bacteriological agents. Both are of doubtful veracity. One story alleges that the bomb thrown by SOE-trained agents to assassinate Reinhard Heydrich, the Nazi Reichsprotektor in Prague on 27 May 1942 was poisoned with botulinum toxin 'X'. Heydrich died from infection on 4 June. Again, there is no firm evidence to support this supposition and although records show that Porton Down did indeed provide SOE with two small amounts of toxin 'X', it was not until 10 November and 6 December 1943. What SOE had in mind to use it for is not recorded.[16] Indeed, knowing of the somewhat basic laboratory equipment Station IX had to work with, one wonders what risks were taken in handling such organisms. Modern containment cabinets, or even simple glove-boxes, were not available. But in those days microbiologists relied for safety on meticulous laboratory technique and a certain amount of luck when working with these substances. A scientist would lay out a lint pad soaked in a chlorine-based disinfectant and work above it so that any spillage was mopped up by the pad. But over-energetic use of a pipette could give rise to aerosols and had to be guarded against. It is perhaps an interesting coincidence that in April 1942 a gourd of the rapidly fatal curare poison was procured by British Security Coordination (an umbrella organisation that eventually represented MI5, SIS, SOE, and PWE throughout the Americas) from up-country Venezuelan Indians and forwarded to London. Its destination is not known.[17]

The second story was set around Christmas 1944, when the Head of the German Directorate, Gen Templer, was urgently considering ways of disposing of Hitler (Operation Foxley). Among the assassination methods examined was the use of poisons. Templer seems to have had some doubts but he called upon the AD/Z Directorate to assess the possibility and report. A small committee prepared a research assessment. Blount, Ogston and Haas were almost certainly members and the wording of the report bears the stamp of Blount's views.

Two physiological agents were considered: one, coded as 'W', was ricin,[18] the toxin from castor beans and the other 'N', a bacteriological substance. But according to the story, Blount is said to have proposed the use of substance 'I', thallium acetate. This account is attributed to Dr Paul Fildes, FRS, the Head of the Medical Research Council's Bacteriological Metabolic Unit in the 1930s and leader of the British biological warfare team established at Porton Down in 1940. There is no evidence to corroborate this story of substance 'I', nor is there any indication of how it was intended to administer the toxin.

The reality was that after full consideration of the possible routes set out in detail by Rigden in *Kill the Führer* – by mouth, inhalation, injection or absorption through the skin, Blount's report rejected the use of poisons as impractical. As already indicated in Chapter 4, Blount was sceptical and the report commented, 'There is often a tendency for the non-scientist to be rather bemused by the power of science: this may be flattering to the scientist, but is the enemy of clear-headed thinking.'

The association between Station IX and Porton Down was

formalised on 10 November 1943 when Dr Ogston, representing SOE, met Dr Fildes in his capacity as member of the Biological Warfare (Policy) Panel and agreed that when the clandestine organisation required technical advice on biological warfare matters, Porton would be their sole adviser. SOE was to originate any proposals but it had to be understood that they could give only an outline of the proposed use of a material with no justification nor any guarantee to supply Porton with details of its effectiveness in use. For their part, SOE accepted that there were some uncertainties about the effectiveness of the doses of materials Porton could produce. Inevitably, SOE would have to disclose certain details of their operational plans so that the Biology Section at Porton could establish the quantities of any materials to be used as these were often related, for example, to the body weight of the victim. The section would advise on matters of practicality and the best way of carrying out projects. They, with the expertise and more sophisticated facilities, would be the laboratory undertaking any research and development work needed and they would supply approved materials. This effectively prevented SOE's Physiological Section scientists from becoming directly involved in biological warfare matters with academia or commercial bodies such as the Lister Institute at Elstree in Hertfordshire, which had been engaged on highly sensitive work of this nature since 1940.[19]

In mid-1944 there was concern that the enemy might use biological weapons in a last-ditch attempt to gain the initiative in a war which was now going disastrously wrong for them. Intelligence reports spoke of hangars in occupied Denmark containing thousands of rats and fantastical stories of plans to drop infected ones by parachute. There had already been suspicions that the Japanese might have dropped infectious material on a Chinese town, causing an outbreak of bubonic plague, but the evidence was not conclusive. A memorandum of 16 June 1944 from G.H. Oswald and O.H. Wansborough-Jones of the Inter-Service Sub-Committee on Biological Warfare suggested that definite instructions should be issued to Dr Fildes of Porton Down regarding collaboration with SOE. At the sub-committee's meeting the following month it was decided to invite Gen Gubbins to attend the next meeting to explain SOE's interest in biological warfare in the past and what role, if any, it might have in the future. The minutes of that meeting contain no reference to Gubbins' attendance, nor can any other reference to it be found. Did this mean that SOE had not been involved and therefore had nothing to say? Something must have made Oswald and Wansborough-Jones feel that Fildes was perhaps getting too friendly with SOE. Or was it that now the invasion of the European mainland had started, any proposed clandestine use of biological agents needed even higher grade political clearance?[20]

A publication to which Physiological Section must have made a significant contribution was a little book on how to fake illnesses. Agents or resistance workers who found themselves in danger of being sent to factories engaged on enemy war-work or even perhaps press-ganged into the Forces, needed to know how to convincingly fake an illness to escape from their predicament. This book was also used at a time towards the end of the war when attempts were being made to encourage German forces to desert or to fake illnesses as excuses for avoiding further participation in the conflict. It was, in essence, a Malingerer's Handbook and could be supplied with a kit of substances capable of imitating the symptoms of various debilitating illnesses.

The book gave detailed instructions on how to hoodwink the most sceptical of doctors and obtain a certificate of unfitness to work. Emphasis was placed on the need to adopt the right attitude when visiting the doctor: to make him believe you did not want to be ill, and to display the right symptoms but not to tell him too much. Let him ask the questions and make it easy for him to be convinced of your illness.

The choice of illnesses which could be faked included pains in the back, partial paralysis, pain in the chest, severe digestive trouble, mental blackout, tuberculosis, infectious inflammation of the throat, serious diarrhoea, jaundice and a range of skin diseases. For whichever complaint was selected there was set out full details of how the sufferer could contrive the symptoms. In the case of back pain, for example, a walnut placed under the trouser belt would cause pain and by learning how to move without using the muscle one could give the exact impression of someone suffering from a serious back condition. A diagram showed the position of nerves which could be subjected to pressure overnight to display paralysed limbs the next day. Some illnesses such as inflammation of the throat and diarrhoea required the administration of harmless solutions, sometimes readily available herbs. If it was decided that severe digestive trouble was the illness of choice, one had to be prepared to attend hospital and surreptitiously consume a small amount of dried blood in order to impart the correct colour to one's stools. Confidence was imparted to those who took this route by the writer pointing out that when you were eventually operated upon it would be under a general anaesthetic and you wouldn't feel a thing!

Among the other helpful sections of this excellent little malingerer's bible were instructions on how to remove ink writing to alter a doctor's certificate and how to reproduce an official stamp using potatoes, hard-boiled eggs or kitchen gelatine.[21]

Meanwhile, at HQ, Blount, Ogston and others were concerned with the welfare of agents. They designed ration packs for issue to agents and the three-man Jedburgh teams in Europe, and others specially adapted for use in arctic or tropical conditions. Extensive use was made of concentrated, dried food now being developed by the industry.

This group also designed a compact medical kit which fitted into a flat cigarette tin. Besides ordinary medicaments it also included a small supply of self-inject morphia to counteract pain.

In the spring of 1944, with the invasion of the European mainland imminent, the group's attention turned to the well-being of agents going to the Far East. Sqn Ldr Callow, an organic biochemist, was given the task of preparing advice on personal health for agents going to work in the tropics. With Ogston he wrote a comprehensive paper, Ref. AGO/3903 (R.1837), 'Health and Hygiene in the Tropics', covering everything from diet, clothing and sunburn to the avoidance and treatment of infectious diseases caused by contaminated food or insects. It even included a table showing the intake of water and salt required for heavy, medium or light work during hot or cool days and nights. This became an extensive manual on keeping fit and well in the tropics and many of its warnings and recommendations are now incorporated in the travel guides for tourists to these regions.

In January 1943 the chemical destruction of crops was considered but SOE was told 'on the highest authority' not to pursue this line of research 'at present'. The main difficulties were said to be the then prevailing inadequacy of transport and the shortage of operational personnel, but it is more likely that such action would have denied food to civilians and would therefore have been politically unacceptable. Furthermore, when the planned invasion of Europe did take place, local food supplies would be vital to feed the displaced populace, the captured Axis forces and to supplement the Allied rations. Minutes of the War Cabinet Inter-services Committee on Chemical Warfare dated 18 August 1944 reveal that a substance known only as '1313' could disrupt farming with a dose of only 1 lb per acre, though how it could be applied offensively was not known.

With the widespread spraying of crops not yet developed, the opportunity for secretly substituting this material for a commercial pesticide or fertilizer did not exist. Work was also being carried out on '1414' to establish how persistent was its effect after ploughing and re-sowing. But the time required for building the chemical plants to produce the substances on an adequate scale ruled out the possibility of their use against Germany. This decision was welcomed by Mr J.C.S. Fryer of the Agricultural Research Council, who wanted effort diverted from research into operational use and on to commercial uses.[22] Nevertheless, experimental results were available in March 1943 from work undertaken into the contamination of rice.

SEVEN

CAMOUFLAGE SECTION

Inevitably, camouflage has an important role to play in clandestine organisations whose covert actions have to be concealed from the enemy. In the case of SOE, as Newitt quickly realised, a Camouflage Section would be needed to enable the devices and methods developed at Station IX and produced at Station XII to be deployed effectively for use by agents in the field. In this context the term 'camouflage' had a somewhat different connotation from that normally associated with its military use. It was not to make an object blend with its surroundings but rather to conceal an object either by making it look like something else, or by hiding it in what appeared to be an everyday item.

To establish this component of his organisation, Newitt recruited in November 1941 an Army Camouflage Officer, Capt J. Elder Wills. He was to lead one of SOE's most colourful research and development sections that produced what must have been some of the most exotic gadgets ever used in warfare. His recruitment to run the Camouflage Section was a stroke of genius.

Wills, born in April 1900, was educated at Christ's College and joined the Army. In a short military career he transferred to the Royal Flying Corps (which later became the Royal Air Force), became deaf in one ear and suffered a leg injury as a result of an air crash, before being demobilised in February 1919. After some time at London University and an architectural school he had a short-lived job with a firm of builders, tried his hand as a scenic artist at Drury Lane and even lasted three weeks as an actor. When he obtained the position of display and advertising manager to a firm of wine merchants he achieved some success and for two successive years won the Crawford Trophy, being second at his third attempt. Then followed a career in film-making. From 1926, still in the era of silent films, he was at various times art director, director and producer. The first film he wrote and directed was *Tiger Bay*, released in 1933 but his most successful was the 1935 musical *Song of Freedom* starring Paul Robeson. At the end of this decade he was working for a tiny firm which was eventually to become Hammer Studios.

Wills volunteered for service when war was declared in 1939. But he was disappointed when, at 39 years of age, weighing 18 stones, deaf in one ear and sporting a beard, he was rejected by the RAF and the Royal Navy. When he learned the Army was seeking Camouflage Officers, he shaved off his beard and obtained a commission in the Royal Engineers. He went to France but was brought back just before Dunkirk with a wounded leg. After recovery he set up the Army School of Camouflage and made two training films on the subject. He spent a year camouflaging buildings and aerodromes and making dummy aircraft and tanks from cardboard to deceive the Luftwaffe into believing that Britain was stronger than it really was. In November 1941 Capt Elder Wills joined the ISRB as Camouflage Adviser. He returned to the film industry after the war, working for the Rank Organisation and later at Hammer once again.[1]

In January 1942, Wills opened a small camouflage workshop at Station IX, as The Frythe was designated, assisted by one 'other ranks' (ORs) and a civilian. He was to build up his section with great vigour, eventually, as Lt Col Elder Wills, controlling around 300 people at various stations in most of the main theatres of war. The following month the section took over the Victoria and Albert Museum's larger workshops at 56 Queen's Gate in London and recruited six additional ORs who in the main had been film studio technicians in civilian life. Capt Wills could see the way demands were likely to go and sought out the skills he had been familiar with.

It soon became clear to Wills that requests were likely to become more exotic as SOE expanded and required items commonplace in countries occupied by German, Italian or Japanese forces. Once more he drew upon his pre-war experience and recruited an expert buyer from the film industry who could quickly procure such varied items as 150 rat skins, 100 varieties of coal, stones and logs, a Belgian gas meter, a French mechanic's tools, Polish patent medicines and a German toothbrush. The buyers had to be civilians who could think up plausible cover stories for their often strange purchases.

In June 1942 the group had outgrown its accommodation and was moved to the Thatched Barn road-house not far from Elstree film studios, which must have been familiar to Elder Wills. A small staff was retained at Queen's Gate, which now became Station XVa, for work on the design and fabrication of prototypes and for personal contact with agents. At the Thatched Barn (Station XV) Wills recruited leading stage props experts from the film world and embarked them on an incredibly skilful and original programme of work devising methods of concealing vital stores within mundane items and putting them into large-scale production. In stepping up production care had to be taken of the fundamental tenet of camouflage, that standardisation in the end defeats its own ends. If intelligence from the field indicated that camouflaged stores had been compromised, then alternative designs had to be available as substitutes. Another tenet of camouflage is that attention to detail is essential: Wills's production staff followed this rigorously.

Camouflage techniques were involved right from the moment of arrival of stores in occupied territories, through various stages of their deployment and in their final use. The presence and subsequent distribution of supplies had to be concealed from the enemy. They were usually delivered by air and the first problem was that of ensuring the rapid collection, emptying and hiding of the containers and packages, and the destruction of their parachutes. Where items had to be buried, signs of disturbance of the ground had to be reduced as far as possible. Use could be made of natural materials such as foliage and undergrowth, but these could be supplemented by covering with rubber latex sheets disguised as bark and twigs. Where subsequent storage was in farms and barns it was often desirable that the individual items be camouflaged by concealing them in, or making them look like, common articles appropriate to the region concerned and which would not, therefore, arouse suspicion in a casual search. Likewise, when stores were being transported in cars, carts or lorries to caches or 'safe houses', the nature of the loads being carried had to be disguised as, or hidden among, appropriate merchandise.

DEVICES

The Camouflage Section was thus faced with a plethora of challenges and opportunities which led to the invention of an enormous array of weapons and devices, many of which were displayed in the secret SOE museum (Station XVb) in the Demonstration Room of the Natural History Museum in Cromwell Road, accessible only to senior SOE personnel and selected agents – and, incidentally, to the King and members of his family.

The large number of items which could be fabricated were listed in an illustrated catalogue. It is not thought that all of these were ever produced in great quantity but were made up specifically in response to requests from agents who had probably seen a prototype on a visit to Station XVa or XVb. In many cases where the item concealed an explosive charge and/or a time fuse or switch one suspected that the ingenious 'props man' thought he was devising some dramatic effect for a film to be operated by an experienced stunt man rather than by an agent with little training. As a result inadequate account was often taken of the need for safe operation of the device, a failing fortunately identified during user trials.

Among the early items produced in small numbers by the highly original group at the Queen's Gate workshops were a lipstick holder to conceal a message, a pair of sabots carved from wood but with a false sole which provided access to a cavity filled with plastic explosive (sometimes already fitted with a time delay) and pit props reproduced in plaster concealing 3-in mortar barrels. In another project the glass floats of a fishing net were drilled and filled with a fluorescent substance to act as underwater markers. The small band also made self-exploding tobacco boxes, a grenade disguised as a toothpaste tube, a piece of coal which exploded when struck with a shovel and a Tunny fish concealing a Sten gun outfit.

Among the notable achievements of the designers at Station XV were exploding rats which were intended to be deposited where they would be thrown into boiler fireboxes, causing substantial damage. The Germans' discovery of the plot probably caused greater mayhem among the occupying forces than would have been achieved from the actual damage to the boilers. The tiny explosive 'tyre-bursters' capable of wrecking a car wheel were disguised as local animal droppings – horses in Europe, mules in Italy and camels in North Africa. London Zoo, through the good offices of Julian Huxley (of BBC *Brains Trust* fame), provided an assortment of droppings which were reproduced in plastic, hand-painted, filled with the explosive device and used as booby traps.

Very early in the war the possibility was recognised of disguising a bomb as a lump of coal. Coal was the main fuel for power stations and factory boilers as well as for steam locomotives which were the norm on all surface railways. In the *Brown Book of Devices*, published in late 1939, explosive coal, coke, briquettes, logs, etc. were all considered. (No surviving copies of the *Brown Book of Devices* or the *Sabotage Handbook*, mentioned later, have been traced.) At this stage the actual material was bored out to take an explosive charge, but this method had serious drawbacks in production and experiments took place to devise an alternative. At Station XV RSM Wally Bull, a film studio plasterer, under the direction of Wills, worked with S/Sgt Nunney who perfected the following method for producing fake coal.

The piece of 'coal' was made by moulding it in two halves using Herculite plaster mixed to a creamy consistency to which was added 25 per cent of Dextrine and Black Ebony water dye. Each half-shell was reinforced with scrim. When they were dry the interior of each half was painted with shellac, the explosive was inserted and the two moulded halves were joined together with plaster and secured by metal cleats. The assembled lump was then varnished with shellac and dressed with real coal dust to give the final authentic appearance.

A later development of this device was the use of a GP charge instead of plastic explosive. The GP charge, being in a metal container, permitted the pouring of liquid plaster around it while in the mould. Thus the 'coal' could be cast without a join. About 3½ tons (3563 kg) of this explosive 'coal' was made between 1941 and 1945. It is said that because of the fear that coal supplies had been contaminated by the fake explosive variety, many locomotive drivers in the Balkans refused to operate their trains.

In August 1943 the SOE Council expressed its concern over a German propaganda statement that the Allies were making indiscriminate use of booby-trap devices and exposing children to serious risk. This, of course, was exactly what the Germans were doing with their Butterfly Bombs in East Anglia. SOE now ordered that its disguised explosive devices were to be used only for specific purposes and with reasonable safeguards against their falling into civilian hands.[2]

One of the cleverly made containers used to conceal weapons or explosives was indistinguishable from a standard oil drum. But the top part could be removed and was held in place by an internal bayonet fitting. In case the drum cap was removed in an inspection, beneath it was a narrow, cylindrical liquid container. Anyone looking beneath the screw cap would see liquid and even if they dipped it with a stick, it would be seen to have the same depth as the drum. It was discovered that new oil drums were virtually unobtainable in occupied Europe so these items had also to be artificially aged. An offensive weapon using some of the same techniques was the exploding engineers' oil can. This was a conventional can which had a container fitted beneath the filling hole so that anyone checking to see if it was full could see oil in this small receptacle. The body of the can contained explosive and when the spout was unscrewed a pencil time fuse could be inserted and the spout replaced. This oil can would not look out of place close to a vital piece of enemy machinery. The device had originally been produced in late 1941 by Peter Henry at Station IX and been described in the Shipping section of *The Sabotage Handbook*, but later cans (106 were produced up to December 1944) were made at Station XV by S/Sgt Jones.

The concealment of wireless transmitters was important for a number of reasons. They could be incorporated in domestic sets, cylinder vacuum cleaners, portable gramophones or adding machines. However, wireless operators had, for security reasons, to move their sets every few days to avoid being tracked down by the German locating vans. The standard set was contained in an easily recognisable suitcase, so one of Wills's early jobs was to provide a camouflaged version in which the set was easily portable. He sought out old continental types, which could be copied and made to look old by ingenious processes he devised. Suitcases to accommodate wireless sets were designed for the country of use and were carefully artificially aged so as not to attract attention. This effect was achieved by the highly skilled use of sandpaper and Vaseline by technicians who in civilian life had been employed on creating props for the film industry The process was further enhanced by the simple expedient of having a few ORs play football with the cases in the yard.

To meet other specific requirements, Station XV produced a wide range of 'aged' suitcases and briefcases of designs consistent with those in use in the country in which the agent was to operate. Again, the closest attention to detail was called for. In one early recorded instance an agent was arrested because the lock on the suitcase he was carrying was of a type not used in France.

There was a regular demand for an incendiary briefcase which, if the agent was arrested, could be ignited to destroy its contents; or alternatively, would ignite if an unauthorised attempt was made to open it. A number of detailed designs were developed although, as noted in Chapter 8, the ignition mechanism tended to be unreliable causing malfunction leading to premature operation.

Another job was the concealing of codes, which led Wills to produce a new type of invisible ink which only became visible under infra-red light provided by a torch with a suitable IR filter. Yet another simple and effective device was a sandal for use in the Far

East. Two versions were produced: one to leave the imprint of a bare native foot and the other of a Japanese army boot.

THE TAILORING GROUP

Every agent infiltrated into enemy-held territory had to be kitted out with clothing appropriate to the area in which he or she was working. Even the smallest item had to be reproduced so as not to betray the agent. Immediately before they embarked on their transport, usually a Special Operations aircraft, they were searched in minute detail to ensure they were not inadvertently carrying some giveaway item such as a bus or theatre ticket, a British-made tie, belt, pen or matches. Camouflage Section could not hope to produce with their own labour the huge numbers of articles of clothing called for. They were therefore forced to take into their confidence – to a degree anyway – some commercial firms. One such was a clothing supplier by the name of Loroco Ltd which had workrooms at 19 and 20 Margaret Street, near Oxford Circus in London. Another was Anchor Models Ltd, just around the corner at 14 Great Titchfield Street. Clothing was a particular problem as continental tailoring and stitching was distinctive. Refugees from occupied Europe were given new clothes in exchange for their old ones which were taken by SOE, unpicked and examined in minute detail by a Jewish tailor from Austria by the name of Claudia Pulver. The differences in cut between the European and English tailoring were carefully noted and cardboard patterns produced so that a whole range of items could be produced by the band of seamstresses recruited specially for the work. The employment of refugee tailors and seamstresses producing naturally in their own national styles ensured that they were convincing copies which eventually found their way back to the streets of continental Europe. Attention to detail was absolutely vital. For example, at a time when detachable collars were the norm, the back stud hole on an English collar was vertical whereas on the continental version it was horizontal. This was something which could have been easily noticed by a German interrogator. Another feature which was not to be overlooked was the removal by careful use of a dental drill of the trade name 'Lightning' from the pull of English zip fasteners. And, of course, the foreign labels had to be faithfully reproduced for the new clothes.[3] As one Danish group reported, not having any labels at all

SOE: The Scientific Secrets

was as suspicious to a searcher as having the wrong markings. But, as it happened, British markings in Denmark were commonplace and harmless.[4]

At the peak of SOE operations sixteen agents a day were being fitted out with continental clothing correct down to the smallest detail. A comprehensive range of men's clothing and personal equipment was held in stock, 8,665 articles being issued in one month in 1944 from a stock of 20,040. By June 1944 over 90,000 articles of clothing were being issued during a year. Interestingly, no stock of women's clothing was held because fashion tended to change by district. Female agents had a bespoke service.

It was not only clothes that agents had to be careful about. Another essential task which the skilled technicians at Station XV carried out was the supplying to agents of bicycle tyres identical to the Continental brands. Anyone in the Resistance could have been easily betrayed by being spotted riding a cycle equipped with Dunlop tyres.

MAKE-UP SECTION

It became apparent that greater expertise needed to be devoted to the disguising of agents themselves, in particular those who had fallen under suspicion by the enemy and were returning to the field. This time the film industry's experience was called upon to secure the services of make-up experts. Together with eminent plastic surgeons they proved capable of some remarkable changes in appearance. And, of course, if an agent's appearance was altered, so too had to be the photographs on the identity papers which everyone in occupied territories had to carry. To deal with this aspect of SOE's work, Camouflage Section set up on 1 March 1943 a Photographic and Make-up Section at Nos 2 and 3 Trevor Square off Knightsbridge and designated it Station XVc. Its cover name was MO1(SP) Photographic Department. Between its inception and mid-November 1944 this unit was to photograph 1,620 agents, making an average of 1,700 prints per month. In addition, it provided photographs of 1,784 men for British military passes (an average of 560 prints per month), and an average of 750 photographic enlargements per month for Records Section. Another small but highly skilled unit within the Camouflage Section was the Printing and Art Department. They produced all fake labels and printing matter to complete the efficient concealment of items produced elsewhere in SOE's Research and Development Section. They also provided armlets for invading forces, insignias for foreign uniforms and facilities for the printing of codes on silk.

Camouflage Section could adapt almost any commonplace item either to conceal arms or to become a weapon. A bundle of faggots could conceal a suitcase radio, a Chianti bottle a booby-trap bomb. They held in stock a wide range of foreign boxes, tinned goods and labels covering most European countries and Japan. In 1942 the camouflage section produced over 150 different species of disguised articles. Apart from the variety of items which were camouflaged, the quantity was enormous; at one period over 30 tons/month (30,500 kg/month) of arms and ammunition were being camouflaged for one Country Section alone.

By April 1943 the total complement of personnel producing goods at Station XV was five officers, one civilian, 71 ORs, 38 ATS ORs. At Station XVa, the central London branch, there were two ATS officers, one civilian ranking as an officer, ten male ORs and two ATS ORs.

FORGERY SECTION

While all this chicanery was going on at the Thatched Barn, at Briggens near Roydon in Essex, the home of Lord Aldenham, a highly skilled Forgery Section had been set up. Its origins are interesting. In 1940 Briggens was Polish Training School STS 38 where three of its Polish technicians took over part of the cellars to begin the production of the forged documents needed by their compatriots about to drop back into their homeland. Their lack of experience in the work resulted in a British officer taking over control in February 1941, but he, too, was replaced after two months by a more experienced officer who eventually took control of the entire station. Another officer was appointed to take control in London and to liaise with the Country Sections, for this enterprise was no longer a Polish-only one, the value of a central forgery facility for the whole of SOE having been rapidly recognised. Expansion became necessary and the assistance of Scotland Yard was obtained in the recruitment of a first-class forger of handwriting and signatures. The demands on Station XIV, as Briggens became known, grew as their reputation expanded and soon it was decided that Polish Training School STS38 should leave the premises, allowing the printing works to take over the whole extensive house, appropriately on 1 April 1942. In November that year Lt Col Hazell took charge of the False Document Section from Lt Col Perkins.[5]

Newitt also had a small facility at the Imperial College of Science but the main work was done at Station XIV. Virtually any document one needed to live in occupied countries could be copied and reproduced to a standard that was indistinguishable from the original. Highly skilled technicians, some of them ex-convicts, forged large amounts of currency, travel documents and work permits for agents. How SOE identified people with this talent for forgery is interesting in itself, as is speculation as to how their careers might have developed after the war. Among the forgery schemes dreamed up by SOE and PWE was the dropping of counterfeit ration cards of the type used by the German Services when on leave. In April 1943 Lord Selborne reported to the Prime Minister that 300,000 had been dropped over a number of German cities. 'There is most gratifying evidence in the German Press of the disturbance and confusion caused by this pleasantry,' he said.[6]

In June 1943 the SOE Council discussed the possibility of using microphotography as a means of communication of documents and illustrations. It had been demonstrated that using a high-grade camera with ultra-fine-grain film and the correct technique it was possible to reduce foolscap size documents to a mere ⅛ in square, at which size the images could be easily hidden; for example, under a postage stamp stuck to a letter. It was decided to pursue this activity and arrangements were put in hand to fit out Station XIV with Leica cameras, grainless film and a special typewriter.[7]

Station XIV employed a maximum staff of 50 and produced over 275,000 individual documents in its life.[8]

At various times Camouflage Sections were formed in Italy, Algiers and Cairo. As more effort was devoted to the Far East two were set up in India and another in Australia. In January 1945, as the Allies advanced through Europe, Camouflage Section established a satellite workshop outside Brussels. This was the time when agents were going into Germany, sometimes being despatched from SOE stations in liberated countries. Thus it was expedient to carry out some of the camouflage or disguising work close to their point of departure.

Some of the work of the Camouflage Section has been likened to schoolboy pranks: all of it fulfilled the objective of causing death, destruction and mayhem to the enemy. There is no doubt that the major part of the work enabled agents to move around within occupied territories and to transport vital arms and equipment under the guise of everyday items, a facility without which SOE's task would have been infinitely harder. However the Section will be remembered, its high degree of inspiration, creativity and skill cannot be denied.

EIGHT

ENGINEERING SECTION – WEAPONS

The Engineering Section headed by Maj (later Lt Col) J. Dolphin was formed in 1941 originally to service the laboratories, to design and construct their testing gear and to produce prototypes of fuses and small mechanisms developed in other Sections. This role very soon changed as a result of a series of urgent operational requirements. The Section's functions expanded while some of their work for the Physico-Chemical Section was taken over by a small workshop housing the Fuses and Small Mechanisms Sub-Section.

Besides meeting the needs of the laboratories, the members of the Engineering Section were encouraged to develop their own imaginative projects. Furthermore, this degree of freedom, which recognised the skills of the toolmakers, fine mechanics and technicians, worked wonders for their morale. Many of SOE's requirements were unique and urgent and there were no regular stores in existence to satisfy them. The normal channels of specialist design in the Forces were overloaded, so SOE had to undertake the design and development of a number of novel ideas specifically for its own use. Much information and experience was gained through these projects and in Newitt's postwar view the decision to go it alone was largely justified.

The major areas with which the Engineering Section became involved were new weapons, mainly small arms, and the means for clandestine attacks on waterborne craft including naval vessels. This chapter deals with the development of a range of hand-held weapons, and in particular with their silenced versions. It also includes accounts of the mobile versions of the limpet mine and of the tree spigot mortar for use as an ambush weapon. Work on submersible craft forms the subject matter for the next chapter. A host of other devices were developed by the Engineering Section, though many of them did not go into production. They are listed in Appendix D,[1] and a few of them will be discussed in what follows. From time to time equipment was developed to meet the operational requirements of other Services, such as the expressed need of the Airborne Division for a motorcycle which could be dropped by parachute.

As Station IX grew in size so did the need of the Engineering Section for more space. This was satisfied by the erection of a large carpenters' shop and a sheet metal shop each of some 1,200 sq ft in area. Later hangars were built to give an additional 5,000 sq ft in which to fabricate the first twenty Welman submarines while arrangements were made for their subsequent external production. During the period up to September 1944 the Engineering Section expanded from four staff to 160, and from 600 sq ft of working area to 20,000 sq ft.

WEAPONS

General

The types of weapon needed for clandestine warfare differed fundamentally from those for use by regular troops. While small hand guns such as revolvers and automatic pistols were needed as personal weapons, multishot weapons, particularly for use at close quarters, were essential for operations in which agents might be confronted by superior numbers such as enemy patrols. In general, longer-range weapons were not required, while ease of concealment and reliability were essential requirements. Few such weapons were available in 1940 other than the American Thompson gun (Tommy Gun) developed during the gang warfare in the USA. A number of reasons, including the fact that manufacturing rights were held in the USA, meant that it was not a possible choice for SOE at that time. And the British Sten gun was only just going into large-scale production and in its original form was unreliable, being subject to malfunctions of various kinds.

The Norm Gun

In the early days SOE had a need for a small 9 mm automatic carbine weighing less than 10 lb which would be more compact than the contemporary models of the Sten gun while having superior performance. This requirement was met by the beautifully made, and in some respects novel, Norm gun, which completely fulfilled the specification but was unfortunately too expensive to be put into mass production. This gun was designed by one of Station IX's firearms experts, Eric Norman, remembered by one of the site's guards, Tom Rae, for his amorous black spaniel which became used to a dousing with cold water. Norman is probably the person who modified a .22 inch calibre American Woodsman pistol to operate as a machine pistol. The rate of fire was said to have been so rapid that the magazine was exhausted too quickly. The Norm gun was unusual in that it had two grips as well as a steel skeleton stock which was welded to the base of the rear grip. A long, straight magazine was fitted vertically below the breech and the forward grip was clamped to the end of the barrel. Although the weapon had a somewhat awkward appearance, experts who fired it claimed the grips gave them excellent stability and accuracy. It was the forerunner of the Welgun.

The Welgun

It was thought initially that SOE's requirement for a small 9 mm calibre machine carbine might be met by a modified Sten Mk II and on 16 May 1942 Maj W. Hussey of the Central Small Arms Department, Enfield (CSAD) visited Station IX to discuss that possibility. Time passed and there was no response from Enfield so SOE decided to go ahead and develop a weapon themselves.

Maj Hussey notified SOE on 5 June that Col Gibson did not oppose SOE's proposal to design its own special weapon (to be called the Welgun) and about five weeks later Gibson visited Station IX to examine the prototype the Engineering Section had fabricated to F.T. Bridgeman's design. It was completed and sent to Enfield for assessment on 7 August. As a result of these and other tests a series of modifications took place right up to the time it was submitted to the evaluating agency, the Central Inspectorate of Small Arms (CISA) at Broxbourne, in February 1943. Throughout this period Station IX maintained the closest contact with both Enfield and CISA.

By October 1942 six examples of the Welgun had been produced at Station IX for demonstration to CISA. After final modifications the gun was sent to CSAD for further assessment. It was inspected by the Design Department of the Birmingham Small Arms company (BSA) who considered producing it and submitted an estimate of cost on the basis of an initial production run of 60,000.

By December 1942 the gun had passed its tests at CISA. A further six were being made for final tests by the Ordnance Board. On 1 January 1943 CD wrote personally to the Minister of Production about this alternative to the Sten gun. He explained that with the full knowledge of the Ministry of Supply SOE had built the Welgun which could fire British, American and German ammunition. BSA had examined it, thought well of it and were willing to produce it. 100,000 were needed at a rate of 5,000 per month. Given the authority to commence production, BSA could start delivery in April 1943. In reply, Mr Lyttleton, Minister of Production, said as far as he was aware the Welgun was only then being put through its proof tests and asked for them to be speeded up. Clearly, authority could not be given until all the required tests had been successfully completed on the pre-production models. By February 1943 all examples had passed the CISA acceptance trials. Three were then sent to Pendine in South Wales for Ordnance Board trials and three for trials at the Bisley Wing of the Small Arms School. Gen Worthington and Gen McNaughton requested one gun complete with working drawings for immediate despatch to Canada. They had tested the weapon at Aldershot and were obviously impressed.

A month later three Welguns competed in Ordnance Board design and functioning tests against three Sten Mark IVs. In the final total score the Sten gun beat the Welgun by only one point but the Welgun won the trials regarding accuracy, control, rapid operation, etc. It was beaten by the Sten on operation in arctic conditions, mud and sand tests but the Ordnance Board agreed that greater clearances between moving parts would overcome this. The forward hand grip and balance of the Welgun were recommended for adoption on the Sten and all other folding-stock machine carbines. In April the gun passed the trials at Bisley with comparable marks to the Sten but the particularly advantageous features of the Welgun seem to have been ignored in the report on these tests. Nevertheless, word got around and the Royal Navy and No. 62 Commando wanted to examine examples. In May a report on the tests conducted by the Navy and Royal Marines at Whale Island was sent to Maj Reeves. The gun had been subjected to extensive tests and considerable deliberate abuse but continued to work very well indeed. Commander Young had tested one gun and found it singularly accurate, with a performance above any other tried on the range. The Navy, who had been offered Stens Marks II and III to replace the Lanchester carbines used by their boarding parties, had turned them down and now wondered whether to opt for the Welgun.

In the end, to Station IX's disappointment, the cheaper but less accurate Sten Mk IV was adopted and the Welgun did not go into production.[2] The full reasons for this decision are not revealed in surviving documents. No estimates of the relative costs of the alternative weapons are available, nor whether the differences were sufficient to outweigh the advantages of the Welgun. One may speculate that the final choice was influenced to some degree by envy that a gun developed by an outside body (as SOE was sometimes regarded) with no long-term experience of small arms should have been able to challenge the competence of the gun-making Establishment.

The Welrod

Among the silenced weapons used by SOE agents, the Welrod was a small 9 mm or .32 in calibre hand gun with a very effective built-in silencer which gave it its nickname of the 'bicycle pump'. The stock-cum-magazine of the weapon could be readily detached from the barrel, resulting in two pieces which could easily be concealed. In November 1942 some examples of the four-shot .32 in calibre version made to the requirements of the Chief of Combined Operations (CCO) and Capt Sykes had been manufactured and the numbers required were being assessed. After trials the following month it was decided to manufacture 500 for stock at Station XII.

By March 1943 the Welrod had been redesigned with an improved stock, a replaceable magazine, a spring ejector, a knurled boss to replace the bolt action and reduced trigger pressure. At 12¼ in long, the .32 in calibre model now weighed 35 oz (992 gm). It was easier to operate and a great deal simpler to manufacture and it was hoped to reduce the noise still further. The forward silencer unit of the Welrod, which was an integral part of the weapon and included self-closing rubber baffles at each end, was only slightly shorter than the original five-groove, left-twist, rifled barrel, which was retained. Cocking was by means of a knurled-screw boss at the extreme rear of the gun. A quarter turn of the boss anti-clockwise and withdrawal to its limit admitted another round into the breech; pushing it forward and a quarter turn clockwise readied it for firing. Surrounding the barrel was an outer casing known as the bursting chamber which accepted some of the gases released into the silencer. The 9 mm version was larger at 14⅜ in long and 3 lb 4 oz (1.47 kg) in weight.

In June 1943 the SOE Council considered a campaign of

assassination of selected enemy individuals: German civilian officials rather than soldiers or Quislings. To increase the demoralising effect of the undertaking, warnings were to be given by the posting of death warrants. The Welrod was the ideal weapon for this task and with 600 on order, 100 ready for issue in August, it was decided that 'Execution Month', as it was called, should commence on 1 October.[3] No information has been found as to whether this ever took place.

Another campaign, known as Ratweek, was carried out during the last week of February 1944 by the 'Armada' RF circuit in France. About a dozen Gestapo staff were assassinated.

The Welrod proved to be a very effective silent close-quarters weapon. At least 600 were ordered and, in addition to its use by SOE, there are some unsubstantiated reports that even after SOE's disbandment it was issued on operations in Korea, Malaya, Vietnam and Northern Ireland.[4] In his book *The Secret War for the Falklands* Nigel West describes an incident on HMS *Invincible* during the training of the Special Air Service's 'B' squadron for a covert attack on an Argentine mainland airbase in which the weapons specialist produced a Welrod. In the event the raid was aborted after the party had landed and they had to be exfiltrated covertly through Chile.

The Sleeve Gun ('Welwand')

Also developed was a stick-like, single-shot assassination weapon sometimes known as the Welwand which could be concealed in the sleeve of the coat before dispensing its 'magic'. It was about 12 in long including its suppresser and fired a .22 in bullet.[5] Later a similar but more effective device of .32 in calibre was produced. It was known generally as the Sleeve Gun and was a development of the Welrod and it, too, had a built-in suppresser but, being single-shot, did not eject a tell-tale cartridge case. On the other hand it did not give the opportunity of a second shot. (In their training agents were taught always to try for two shots at a target.) Some said it could be used as a bludgeon but it was hardly big enough for that for it was only 8¾ in long, 1¼ in diameter and weighed 26 oz (737 gm). It was meant to be carried on the end of a lanyard running up the sleeve, round the neck and down to a button on the belt. On unbuttoning the lanyard the pre-loaded gun concealed in the sleeve could be slipped down to be gripped with the thumb on the trigger close to the muzzle. After it had been discharged the gun could be drawn back up the sleeve and out of sight by means of the lanyard. The earlier Mk I model had a rudimentary safety catch which could be released inadvertently. An improved catch was incorporated in the Mk II but, even so, considerable care had to be exercised to avoid shooting oneself in the foot.

At that time there was a carefully organised campaign against prominent traitors and denouncers and certain members of the Gestapo and, in the case of Norway, the HIRD (Quisling's organisation) and the NS Police (Nasjonal Samling, the National Party who collaborated with the Germans). This was kept under strict control by London and was governed by quasi-judicial investigations and proceedings. The execution of such persons demanded careful planning and great patience, not to say considerable courage on the part of the operator of the silenced weapon. One Danish group reported that traitors were usually executed by shooting after having been bundled into a car.[6]

The Silenced Sten Gun

The Sten gun was a simple, inexpensive 9 mm sub-machine gun which proved very popular with both regular and irregular forces. It was designed by R.V. Shepherd and H.J. Turpin at Enfield, their initials giving it its name. It consisted of a barrel with a steel tubular frame stock (wooden on some versions) and a magazine which protruded from the left-hand side. A major feature in its success was its ability to withstand severe contamination with sand, mud and water and still keep firing. It was therefore an almost ideal choice of weapon for resistance fighters. However, it jammed easily and had an alarming tendency to fire and loose off a whole magazine if dropped or jarred accidentally.

Various attempts were made to improve the Sten gun, such as by fitting a bayonet and by replacing the usual stock with a pistol grip. Capt Sykes reported that the latter resulted in a serious loss of accuracy but the bayonet showed some promise. Lt Col Woolrych arranged for trials at Group A, the paramilitary schools in Inverness, and STS 43, Polish Section's establishment at Audley End in Essex.

The Sten's use in clandestine operations was compromised to some extent by its characteristic noise which would be a certain give-away to any searching enemy patrol. A Polish officer, Lt Kulikowski, therefore decided to do something about it and initiated what was eventually the most successful modification to the gun: the silencer. Working closely with Maj Reeves he had designed and produced a prototype silencer for the Sten gun and in August 1942 SOE was asked to visit Broxbourne to test it. While it was quite effective as a noise suppresser, it was disappointing in that it reduced the penetrative power of the bullet. Furthermore, the silencer was too bulky and, when fitted, the weapon would operate only on fully automatic. An officer at the Royal Small Arms Factory at Enfield suggested inserting a washer into the breech end of the barrel (presumably to adjust the travel of the bolt), a simple expedient which proved successful in allowing it to fire single shots again. Reeves developed an alternative method of reducing the noise which overcame the earlier side-effects and this was put into production at Station XII for the use of SOE.

A request was received to redesign the silencer for use with WRA American ammunition. This was done and a prototype was sent to Station XII for testing where it was found that the noise level had been reduced to that of the earlier Mark I silencer. By April 1943 production models of the Mark II silencer for use with American ammunition were being made.

User trials at Station IX on 29 June 1943, reported on 4 July, were impressive enough for Gubbins to approve, after minor alterations, the silencer's adoption as an SOE store.[7]

THE SPIGOT GUN

The Spigot Gun was a means of projecting a high-explosive charge at an unapproachable target. Two versions were designed: the Tree Spigot and the Plate Spigot, but only the former was developed to become a standard stores item. The Tree Spigot Gun was intended either as an ambush weapon operated by an agent using a lanyard; or by a tripwire stretched across the path of the enemy; or as a delayed-action bomb aimed at a static target. The original concept and some of the earlier models seem to derive from before 1940. What little information there is suggests that these early models were highly erratic in behaviour.

Unlike conventional mortars where the bomb is slipped into a close-fitting barrel, in the spigot mortar the missile had a hollow tail which slid over the spigot and contained the propellant charge. The firing pin at the tip of the spigot was released by a wire or could be operated by a modified Time Pencil which replaced the normal striker mechanism. The tail incorporated a silencing device which prevented the hot gases discharging to atmosphere.

The spigot was attached by a ball and socket joint to a large wood screw fitted with a pair of handles to provide the torque to enable it to be screwed into a tree trunk or brickwork. The spigot could be aimed using a primitive removable sight, the joint clamped into position and the bomb slipped over the spigot.

The bomb was toffee-apple shaped, filled with 3 lb (1.36 kg) of 808 explosive and fitted with an impact fuse which was armed automatically by the recoil on firing. The head of the bomb was sealed with a thin metal diaphragm which collapsed on impact to place the explosive in intimate contact with the target.

The detailed design of the gun evolved with time and by October 1942 four complete guns were available for tests, two with folding sights and two with removable sights. Further modifications aimed at stabilising the trajectory continued into 1943: it is not clear why the bomb was not fitted with fins. It was accurate to a range of only 50 yards, beyond which it needed a much larger target (see Chapter 10).

By mid-1943 requests were being submitted by returning agents for anti-tank weapons. The Boys Anti-Tank Rifle was considered too cumbersome; the Army wanted to keep the PIAT anti-tank weapon as a surprise; the American one-man rocket was in the experimental stage; and the breech-loading mortar was still under development. The SOE spigot mortar was just coming into production. It was envisaged that it might be used against stationary tanks brought to a halt by a road block and fired by an operator hidden nearby; against parked tanks using a time delay; against slow-moving tanks using either a trip wire or an operator. Although considerable numbers were despatched to the field, there are few reports of its successful use. (The need for an anti-tank weapon was met later by the Tyreburster/AT mine. See Chapter 5.)

THE WELPEN, WELPIPE, WELWOODBINE AND WELCHEROOT

Once SOE had begun infiltrating agents into enemy-held countries and the Resistance had started their clandestine build-up, experience was obtained of the mode of arrest and interrogation by the Gestapo and other Nazi security organisations. Upon arrest and search an agent would be stripped of any items, such as a penknife, which could be used as a weapon, but there was a reasonable chance that certain personal possessions would be overlooked. If a very small weapon could be concealed as one of these commonplace and innocuous items it might give the captive an opportunity to make a surprise attack on his interrogator and escape. It was with this in mind that work started on a series of miniature disguised weapons.

The Welpen was one of a number of short-range, single-shot, 'last resort' weapons which were developed. Officially known as the '.22 Experimental Firing Device, Hand Held, Welpen' it was first worked on in 1941 and, as its name implied, was disguised to look like a fountain pen of the day. The clip was probably the trigger and the user had to take into account the recoil when it delivered its lethal message. In reality, its small calibre meant that it was unlikely that it could have inflicted more than temporarily disabling injuries to the target, but agents were trained to go all out for maximum damage and were well aware of the vulnerability of, for example, the eyes to even a .22 in calibre bullet. However, incorporating the round and its firing mechanism within the confines of a fountain pen was a delicate job and the appearance of the resulting Welpen, not to say its weight if handled, was not too convincing. Only about 100 were made at Station IX before the project was abandoned in favour of the Enpen, which had been developed in parallel by the Royal Small Arms Factory at Enfield. The 'Auxiliary Firing Device, Hand Held, Enpen Mk I' was produced in quantity in 1944. A similar concept was adopted by the American OSS in the production of their 'Stinger' which was a truly tiny device only 3½ in long and weighing less than half an ounce. It was manufactured with the .22 in round in it and, unlike the Welpen or the Enpen, could not be reloaded.

Another disguised single-shot weapon produced in very small quantities was the Welpipe ('Wel-' from the nearby village of Welwyn), a .22 in calibre pistol featuring a bayonet-catch locking mechanism in the stem of what was ostensibly a smoker's pipe. A few were reputedly issued to OSS agents.

A pistol device designed to look like a cigarette was the Welwoodbine. The Woodbine was a brand of cheap cigarette popular throughout both World Wars. The gun was essentially a 3-in-long by ¼-in-diameter tube containing an inch-long .177-in calibre barrel. The breech chamber was detachable by carefully driving out two tiny cross-pins holding it in place. The device could therefore be reloaded with its hardened steel projectile and the pellet of propellant. To add to the Welwoodbine's authenticity it was rolled within a cigarette paper of a type to reflect the theatre of operations of the agent to whom it was issued.

The Welcheroot was similar to but larger than the Welwoodbine. It was about 4½ in long and made to look like a cigar. It carried a single .22 in short rimfire cartridge activated by a lanyard which became accessible when the end of the 'cigar' was bitten off. Pulling the lanyard released the firing pin. A few of these devices are believed to have been issued to the OSS in 1945.[8] These 'last resort' devices were featured in the exhibition of SOE's equipment at the Natural History Museum and although some were manufactured in small quantities, none was put into mass production.[9]

The Welbike

The tiny folding parachutists' motorbike known as the Welbike was the brainchild of Dolphin. A pre-war racing motor cyclist, Mr Lester, and Ken Taylor (the son of H.L. Taylor, a mechanic to Malcolm Campbell, the one-time land speed record holder) were instrumental in bringing the Welbike to fruition. A towing container and a smoke-laying device were also developed for use with the motorcycle. There has been some debate as to whether SOE or the Airborne Division was first to see a need for such a vehicle. The Airborne Division needed a means of personal transport which they could take with them into battle and this certainly kept the Welbike concept alive. Any ideas that it could have been used seriously by SOE agents in the field were quickly scotched when it was realised that such a vehicle would have immediately attracted the attention of anyone who saw or heard it, assuming petrol to run it had been available. It could, however, be reduced to a remarkably small size and was therefore easily concealed. It weighed only 70 lb (32 kg) and was designed to fit into a standard C-Type parachute container which was 5 ft long and 14 in in diameter. After the war it was redesigned as the Corgi which appeared on British roads in the late 1940s, only to be superseded by the Vespa and Lambretta scooters. The Welbike's 98 cc Villiers engine gave it a range of 90 miles at 30 mph on tarmac roads (it was useless on rough ground) and almost four thousand were produced by the Excelsior Motorcycle Company in Birmingham.[10] The Welbike was not a success on several counts: it was totally unsuitable for clandestine operations and its performance could be realised only on hard, smooth surfaces instead of the tracks and fields favoured by the Resistance and, indeed, the Airborne infantry.

It was said to have been most useful as a bribe to certain influential characters in the Far East. In January 1944 during Operation Remorse to acquire Chinese Nationalist Dollars 'through discreet banking and exchange transactions' – a euphemism for a huge black market racket – two Welbikes were presented to the Governor of Yunnan. He was so impressed that he ordered a further forty.

The Weasel

Station IX also took an interest in winter warfare and, in an effort to assist the Norwegian Section of SOE, a collapsible ski sledge for dropping by parachute was produced and issued for some operations. This interest is said to have led to the development of a tracked vehicle which could manoeuvre on snow and ice and whose engine could start reliably at very low temperatures. It was known as the Weasel and would have been the forerunner of what is now called the snowmobile.[11] Unfortunately, confirmatory British reports, photographs or drawings of this interesting vehicle have not been traced although a similar very successful vehicle also known as the Weasel was produced in great secrecy at about this time by the Studebaker Corporation in the USA. It is, of course, possible that the concept was passed to the Americans for development and manufacture. This American Weasel continued in service with NATO into the 1960s.

WATERBORNE TARGETS

Limpet mines of various types, that is, explosive charges which are stuck on to the target by means of nails or magnets (the use of special adhesives was also explored), were available (see Chapter 5) but the operation of attaching them, particularly to shipping, was considered to be a somewhat hazardous business. It was therefore decided to try to develop an explosive device which found its way to the floating target under its own power and then attached itself before detonating after a set time delay. Whether the 'limpet' aspect of the devices was a later development or was worked on in parallel with the mobile mines project is not clear. A miniature version of the Navy's torpedo seemed a good weapon with which an agent could attack stationary shipping in harbour. To make them stick to the target with a delayed action fuse would give the launcher time to make a getaway. So a series of devices was developed at Station IX and were referred to by the generic name of Mobile Mines.

They were worked on by Dolphin and Sq Ldr T.R. Bird and were rather like a small torpedo which had to run on a straight course for at least 200 yards. It should run at a depth of about three feet without breaking the surface to give away its position to an alert lookout. Speed underway was not particularly important, for saboteurs would not normally attack moving waterborne targets. The original mobile mine was 5 ft long and 7 in in diameter, capable of being delivered in a standard parachute container. It weighed 28 lb in air but the buoyancy of fresh water gave it a weight of just 1 lb (450 gm). It was driven by a small single propeller of 2.6 in diameter driven by an electric motor powered by a battery of accumulators. Control of its depth was achieved by a hydrostatic valve operating a drum-shaped hydroplane at the rear.

The first model was tested at the Admiralty Experimental Works at Haslar near Portsmouth on 12 January 1942 and proved satisfactory in respect of range and depth-keeping but exhibited a tendency to turn to the left. It was thought this was probably due to the torque reaction of the propeller and possibly to a small lack of symmetry in the test unit. It was proposed to correct this by fitting an out-of-balance weight and a small rudder which would be adjusted by trial and error until the model ran straight. Some other small design changes were also suggested.

Eight days later a contingent from Station IX arrived at Haslar with three new models of the mobile mine. After a couple of runs for adjustments, the one incorporating the modifications recommended from the first tests performed well, maintaining a straight course for 250 yards at a depth varying between 1 and 7 feet and at an average speed of almost 3 knots. The other two models, one propelled by twin screws and one incorporating a cylindrical rudder around the propeller, had a pronounced inclination to turn to the left and a much lower speed, so it was decided to concentrate work on the earlier version. Unfortunately, trials with propellers of varying pitch could not be completed on this occasion because the batteries were running down and replacements or recharging could not be achieved in the time available.[12]

Development work continued apace and resulted in a number of tests being conducted at the Vickers Test Tank at St Albans in February. The mobile mines were now smaller than the one tested at Haslar, ranging from 4 ft 6 in to just 18 in long. The longest one ran for 270 yards at about 5 knots, keeping a satisfactory course. A 3-ft-long slim model was hinged at the centre so that it formed a unit just 18 in long for storage. Two 18-in-long cylindrical models were powered by coiled springs and clockwork mechanisms rather than by electric motors with their heavy accumulators. But these had a lower performance, their range being only about 50 yards at 2 knots. Another was 18 in long and 9 ins wide with a body whose shape gave rise to its nickname of 'the Whale'. This one was powered by a small battery and, after modification, achieved a range of about 600 yards at almost 2 knots. Finally, there was the Baby Mobile Mine or Welmine which was also only 18 in long and was driven by an electric motor having a power of just 1/100 bhp. It featured a 2.4 in diameter, two-bladed propeller driven through a 4:1 reduction gearbox which ran at 2,000 rpm. A smaller, direct-driven propeller was recommended for improved efficiency but ISRB were reluctant to adopt this.

Station XII, with its wider production facilities, was already working closely with Station IX on this project and after trials in August 1942 despatched eighteen small mobile mines and had another twelve ready by the following month. Three hulls and all the components of a large mobile mine had also been completed and, with the first in the course of assembly, plans were afoot for delivery at a rate of four per week from early October, rising to six or eight per week. Then the large mines ran into difficulties when four performed unsatisfactorily that same month and Newitt was brought in to investigate. A month later, with modifications completed, ten complete mines were handed over for further trials. As a result of the success achieved with a model carrying a 2 lb (0.9 kg) explosive charge, it was decided to increase the power of the charge to 3 lb (1.36 kg). This was known as the Mark III and in tests in December it met all operational requirements. The next stage in development was to include an anti-disturbance switch. All this development resulted in three reasonably distinct devices.

The Percussion Welmine exploded on impact and, while successful from the point of view of attacking the target, did not give the operator time to escape because it did not incorporate a delayed-action device. It was in many respects similar to a very small torpedo which had to be launched accurately over a relatively short distance. This was clearly a most hazardous activity for a saboteur.

The Magnetic Welmine was a cumbersome device, which did not easily lend itself to clandestine operations and proved to be too difficult to produce in mass quantities. In February 1943 the redesigned Magnetic Welmine Mark III was tested in the water tank at St Albans and fulfilled all the requirements except the crucial adhesion trials. It appeared that in order to meet these criteria the tail would have to be jettisoned in some way.

The Jettison Head Welmine overcame the problem of maintaining attachment against the flow of water past a ship's hull. The device allowed the propelling portion to detach itself and sink after the charge had been firmly attached to the ship thus presenting less area to the water flow. It was April before the adhesion properties had been adequately improved and the prototype model had been given satisfactory trials. Although developed to an acceptable standard it was never put into mass production.

In mid-1942, ISRB was engaged in the development of what is briefly recorded as the 'Sounding Mine'. Without any additional information it is not possible to determine if this was an early attempt at an acoustically initiated mine.

At the same time the Navy had an oscillating mine, one which moved up and down vertically on its own mechanism. They offered this to SOE but no records have been traced to establish if the clandestine organisation ever seriously considered it.

According to a document dated July 1943 an anti-mine-sweeping device had been invented by ISRB. But the Navy already used a similar device and, in any case, developments in mine-laying techniques had tended to nullify their effectiveness.

Among the many devices which could not strictly be called weapons was one which was developed as a result of requests from the field for something with which to damage telephone or telegraph lines. This was the Overhead Wire Cutter. Two types of cutter for use on extra thick wire were designed in November 1942 and the following month a hydraulic version was produced at Station XII. The disruption of German telephone communications was a high priority for the Allies. Without land-lines the enemy was forced to use wireless transmissions, which, as we now know, were being intercepted and decoded at the Government Code and Cipher School at Bletchley Park and provided crucial intelligence. This ingenious device was attached to a weighted string which was thrown over the cables to haul the cocked cutter into a position where the action of the wires entering the jaws caused them to snap closed. It was capable of cutting two hard-drawn copper wires of 2.5 mm diameter or one of slightly heavier gauge.[13]

Rubber, traditionally grown in the Far East, was, of course, in short supply to both sides in the war and so tyres were very valuable and hard to obtain. SOE agents and Resistance fighters were keen to damage enemy tyres and sent back a call for any device which could quickly ruin them. Engineering Section invented the small circular knife which became known as the Tyre Cutter and was put into mass production. Unfortunately, no pictures of this have been found although SOE's double-bladed jackknife incorporated a semi-circular tyre slashing blade. The main device for use against tyres was the Tyre Burster described in Chapter 5.

The Engineers at Station IX certainly lived up to the basic root of their name in working with 'ingenuity'. They were prepared to tackle any task to exercise their skill in inventing and constructing a wide range of items. In addition to the weapons, gadgets, surface and submersible seaborne craft, they also embarked on the design and development of some land-based vehicles.

NINE

ENGINEERING SECTION – SEABORNE CRAFT

In the early months of its existence, SOE was regarded with suspicion by the other Services, including SIS, who were unwilling to give it full support and jealously guarded their facilities for seaborne landings and other means of infiltration for its own agents. From Spring 1943 all clandestine cross-channel operations came under the control of a newly appointed Co-ordinator. As a result, SOE sea operations were not attempted on the North French coast east of the Channel Islands, and for some time there was a complete ban on SOE activities between the Channel Islands and St Nazaire. Nevertheless, with the collaboration of SIS a route was established for the infiltration and escape of individual agents and aircrew but it could not be used for supplies. The only area in Northern Europe to which major supplies were transported by sea was Norway, where fishing boats of the 'Shetland Bus', later supplemented by Submarine Chasers of the US Navy, maintained a link both for agents and stores with the UK. In the Mediterranean also, sea links using local boats such as feluccas and caiques played an important role.

However, there were many marine targets such as docks, blockade runners and enemy warships which could only be reached by sea. Many sabotage operations against stationary marine targets required the agent, or sabotage team, to be transported by surface craft to within range of the target, disembarked to pursue their mission, and then withdrawn. A major effort in the Engineering Section was therefore devoted to exploring various means of completing these operations.

This problem exercised the minds of several organisations. Besides SOE there were several units within the Commando's Special Boat Squadron (SBS) that were working towards the same goal. These included the 1st Special Service Brigade with its Mobile Flotation Unit, and Haslar's Royal Marines Harbour Patrol Detachment. The latter proposed to develop a version of the Italian 'explosive boat' in which a high-speed motor boat, carrying an explosive charge in the bows, was aimed at the target, the pilot being ejected just before impact together with a life-raft with which he might escape or be taken prisoner. Haslar's problem was to develop a small craft which would be able to attack the target and withdraw to a safe distance. This concept, codenamed 'Boom Patrol Boat' (BPB), was developed but the original idea was not finalised. Instead, his plan was to rely on canoes for both the attack and withdrawal. Consequently he was particularly interested in the design of canoes capable of being transported by submarine and in developing tactics for their deployment.

CANOES

The simplest and least sophisticated method of making a silent approach to a target was to use canoes or Folboats (folding canvas canoes) with conventional paddles, either single or double. This was the technique used in December 1942 by the Special Boat Squadron (SBS) of the Commandos in their 'Cockleshell Heroes' attack with limpet mines on German blockade runners in the River Gironde at Bordeaux.[1] Canoes were also used in the limpet attacks on German shipping in Norwegian waters which formed part of the series of 'Vestige' operations mounted jointly by SOE and the Royal Navy under the general direction of the Admiral Commanding the Orkneys and Shetlands (ACOS). For these operations SOE developed the 'Vestige Kayaks' but no description of them has been found. However, paddling could be tiring, especially over long distances, and improved methods of making the final approach were sought.

One alternative was to fit the canoe with outriggers so that it could be rowed in the conventional manner with oars. This method was favoured in some quarters, especially in the Far East, where a simple design that could be fitted easily to a canoe was developed and tested at the Force 136 base at Trincomalee in Ceylon. It was claimed that a greater speed could be attained with less effort than with paddles.

A further possibility was to achieve propulsion using electric motors. A silent, electrically propelled canoe with a flexible drive was developed and put into production. This was the forerunner of the Sleeping

Beauty to be described later. In remote areas it was possible to make the final approach by canoe fitted with an outboard petrol motor, but it was essential that the approach be made as silently as possible and the Engineering Section devoted considerable effort to the silencing of outboard motors but without great success.

The Budig Apparatus

An altogether novel method of propulsion was also investigated. Some time before the war, Ogston had seen in action on the Isis at Oxford a canoe being propelled by a most unusual and somewhat 'Heath Robinson' apparatus. The canoeist appeared to be rowing with the conventional to and fro strokes but no oars appeared above the water. It turned out that the canoe had been fitted out with a device invented by the German aeronautical engineer Friedrich Budig in the 1930s. This made use of the force generated by plunging an aerofoil-shaped wing up and down in the water in a flapping motion. Indeed it relied on the same principle as bird flight, but underwater. Outline details had been published in the journal *The Aeroplane* in December 1935 and illustrated the basic principle and its practical application.[2] The Engineering Section at Station IX was given the task of reproducing this device based on the limited information available. The mechanical problem was that of devising a linkage which converted a to-and-fro rowing action into an up-and-down motion. After a good deal of experimentation, a 'Budig Apparatus' was constructed and subjected to functional trials which were promising. Since the 'wings' did not break water the movement was nearly silent. But it turned out that the design imposed severe stress on some of the components which, during the user trial (see later) at Fishguard, failed. Assessment indicated that although redesign might overcome these shortcomings, this would take some time and the project was shelved and later abandoned.

Attack by Underwater Swimmers

Another procedure, developed and exploited originally by the Italians, for the final stages of approach and attack, was the use of underwater swimmers wearing wet suits and breathing apparatus and carrying explosive charges. They were often dropped from surface craft or a submarine some distance from the target and were usually expected to make their way ashore after the operation, where they were taken care of by local agents. They were called 'Gamma assault frogmen' and often participated in operations with Maiale (or SLCs), piloted torpedoes, whose two drivers were also frogmen. The Maiale were brought to the area of operations on the casing of a conventional submarine. When launched, the two drivers, sitting astride the torpedo, piloted it to the target to which they attached explosive charges with time delays. They then swam to a support vessel or to the shore. This technique was hazardous and casualties among the crew were high. But they carried out a number of attacks around Gibraltar in 1940–41: their greatest success was in severely damaging HMS *Queen Elizabeth* and *Valiant* in Alexandria harbour in December 1941.

The idea of using frogmen for SOE operations (they were already in use by the SBS of the Commandos) was considered and the possibility of dropping swimmers by parachute was assessed. Preliminary experiments carried out by Blount showed that it was a feasible although highly hazardous operation; it is not thought that it was ever used in anger.

The Welbum

In certain circumstances, especially in warmer waters, it was envisaged that explosive charges might be carried by swimmers over considerable distances. The need was foreseen for some auxiliary source of power to enable the limit imposed by human endurance to be exceeded. In 1943 this led the enterprising engineers at Station IX to design and develop a bizarre invention, farcically named the Welbum. This was an electrically driven attachment for swimmers.

The device was intended primarily for use by a parachutist dropped into water, but it could also be used from a Folboat or other small surface craft. It consisted of a streamlined metal container housing an electric motor and batteries and fitted with a propeller. The device, which weighed 60 lb (27 kg) in air and was neutrally buoyant, was fastened by a suitable harness to the swimmer's back.

Under the more prosaic name 'Motorisation of Swimmer', a preliminary model was tested and demonstrated at Station IX in March 1943. Within the limited test facilities available at The Frythe the swimmer was reported to be comfortable and to have acceptable control of the device. It propelled a man silently at 1½ knots but a new model was to raise this to 2½ knots. It was reported that the drag of the waterproof suit was greater than anticipated.

The new model was tested at Staines reservoir where it took an hour and a quarter to cover two miles in fairly rough water and it was estimated that the batteries would have propelled it another quarter of a mile. A lighter case was made to compensate for heavier batteries and future models were forecast to complete an hour's run at 2–3 knots.

Although it had been relatively easy to control in the still water of the Welwyn test tank, in the open water of Staines reservoir the Welbum was much more difficult to handle. George Brown, who conducted the user trial, reported that it was almost impossible to maintain a straight course and to prevent the swimmer from going round in a series of circles, especially when kitted out in the shallow water diving suit. It was, he said, an unpleasant experience made worse by the thick algae and mangy fish in the reservoir.

In June it was reported that tests conducted with the Welbum fastened to a simple paddleboard considerably improved its performance, increasing its range to 5 miles and its speed to 2½ knots. Furthermore, the board used in these trials supported not only a man weighing 184 lb (83 kg) dressed in a waterproof suit, but also eight limpets, a Sten gun and its magazine. The man, it is claimed, suffered no inconvenience from the cold. Station IX was still enthusiastic and plans were afoot to conduct parachute jumps with the Welbum.

At the end of June it was announced that the Welbum could be put into production if there was a demand for it, but then SOE Council decided to hand over the design to the War Office as it was seen to be of more use to the Airborne Forces.[3] Nothing further was heard of this device: a bright idea but perhaps ahead of its time?

It is interesting that the same basic concept resurfaced in December 2001 with an advertisement in a Sunday newspaper for the 'Personal Propeller' for use by snorkellers and scuba divers. Weighing 66 lb (30 kg) it is powered by a battery giving a speed of 2 knots and a duration of 50 minutes after a charging period of 10–12 hours. Whether its handling is an improvement over the Welbum is not known.

Chariots

The German battleship *Tirpitz*, which was lurking in the safety of Trondheim Fjord, remained a serious threat to Allied shipping in the critical period 1941–42. It had to be prevented from breaking out into the Atlantic as had the *Bismarck* in February 1941. This blockade tied up a considerable proportion of the Allied naval forces. A major proposal was to use underwater attack by frogmen, and this led to the development of the Chariot series of piloted torpedoes. They resembled the Italian SLC in that they depended on the use of frogmen carried on the outside of a conventional submarine to within swimming range of the target. The craft were then launched, charges laid and the frogmen withdrew to safety.

The first Chariot operation against the *Tirpitz*, Operation Title, was planned and commanded jointly by Admiral Sir Max Horton, Flag Officer (Submarines) (FO(S)) and Lt Col J.S. Wilson, Head of the Norwegian Section of SOE. Horton had been associated with submarine development since the First World War. As Captain of the 2nd Submarine Flotilla in 1923 he was involved with the 'Devastator' project – a proposal somewhat like the Chariot.[4] Two Chariots were shipped across the Norwegian Sea on board a Norwegian trawler, the *Arthur*, in October 1942. They were then hoisted out and secured beneath the hull of the trawler for the passage up the fjord to the *Tirpitz*. German security checks were passed, thanks to the forged papers provided by SOE, and the *Arthur* was given a permit to enter the security zone around the battleship. Unfortunately, a severe storm caused the Chariots to break loose and sink. The crews, with one exception, made their several ways through SOE-organised escape routes to Sweden.

Subsequently, several operations in the warmer waters of the Mediterranean yielded partially successful results. The failure of some of these operations could be attributed to the exhaustion of the charioteers and the effects of breathing pure oxygen for too long. In the end, the main use of Chariots was for beach reconnaissance. Undoubtedly the lessons learned from experience with Chariots influenced the design of the next generation of underwater equipment.

X-Craft

At the same time, the British X-Craft was being developed. They were essentially midget submarines carrying, in place of torpedoes, two large explosive charges, one on either side of the hull. It was envisaged that they would carry divers who could fix additional charges or cut holes in the protective nets and clear obstacles around a target. For this purpose they were fitted with 'wet and dry' compartments through which a diver could leave and re-enter after completing his task. Since they had a range of 1,300 miles on the surface using a diesel engine, or 85 miles underwater using electrical propulsion, the mother ship did not need to remain in the vicinity but could withdraw to a rendezvous at a safer distance. The X-craft were towed to within reach of the target by a conventional submarine. When close to the target the passage crew of three exchanged places with an operational crew to which was now added a diver.

The first X-Craft were ready for initial trials in March 1942 and they were in production by January 1943. But it was not until September 1943 that, using six X-Craft to mount Operation Source, two were successful in seriously damaging the *Tirpitz*, which put it out of action until the RAF could finish the job. However, the casualties were high and success was only achieved by the courage of the crews. Full accounts of this operation which are available elsewhere emphasise the hazardous nature of underwater warfare.[5]

X-Craft were also used in an attack on Japanese warships at Singapore in July 1945 using one large side-charge and a series of limpet mines fixed by divers. The net cutters were used by the divers to sever the Saigon–Hong Kong and Saigon–Singapore communications cables. Again, the severe stress of working underwater for many hours breathing oxygen left the crews in a state of near-collapse and led to the deaths of two crew members during an operational trial.

The Welman One-man Submarine

The serious threat imposed by the *Tirpitz* had led to widespread concern in the highest military circles, and it is not surprising that SOE, which had provided some back-up for the failed Operation Title, should have given serious thought to its own possible involvement.

Some months earlier, consideration had been given to the use of submarines for the infiltration of agents and stores. The improvement in the availability of aircraft in 1941 led to this idea being left in abeyance. The possible use of submarines was reconsidered later in 1942 in response to the *Tirpitz* problem. Information from the Naval Intelligence Department (NID) and (NDC) was passed to the SOE Technical Planning Section who put forward a proposal to Lt Col Wilson of the Norwegian Section for the use of one-man submarines for an attack on the *Tirpitz*. This proposal was later to form part of the operational plan code-named 'Frodesley'.

Financial sanction for the princely sum of £3,000 enabled work on the first Welman (as the one-man submarine was called) to go ahead in March 1942. The project was taken over by Lt Col Dolphin, the assertive Head of the Engineering Section, who despite his name was more used to designing coal-cutting equipment than submersibles.

The Welman was the largest project to be undertaken by SOE's research and development team. It also happens to be the best documented and yet the least understandable. For an essentially land-based clandestine sabotage organisation to have become involved with midget submarines may seem on the face of it highly unusual until one considers the wide-ranging originality of thought exhibited by the engineers and scientists at Station IX.

The initial suggestion by two Norwegian members of SOE was for a super-silent underwater vessel to be propelled by pedal-power and towing a magnetic 600 lb (272 kg) delayed-action charge. It is interesting to recall that the concept of a pedal-driven underwater craft was not by any means new. In 1776 the American States in revolt used such a craft (the *Turtle*) in an unsuccessful attempt to attack Lord Howe's flagship HMS *Eagle* in New York harbour with a 150 lb (68 kg) charge of gunpowder.

Although the general shape of the hull proposed by the Norwegians was sound and, in fact, was retained in the initial models, the idea of pedal-power was considered impractical and dropped. The towing of the explosive charge presented directional and depth control problems so alternative ways of carrying it were under consideration while the initial craft was being constructed. The hull was made in two parts, an upper and a lower, with a longitudinal weld holding them together. The conning tower was only just wide enough for a man to move through and had a series of portholes intended to give sufficient visibility when surfaced. Inside the hull, the single seat was from an Austin 7 motor car, one of the cheapest popular vehicles of the prewar era, while the novel single rudder and hydroplane control was by means of a joystick, reputedly salvaged from a crashed Spitfire. The do-it-yourself theme was continued with the 2.5 hp electric motor, which was said to have come from a London trolley bus – a double-decked vehicle running on normal tyres but with a spring-loaded electrical pick-up boom contacting overhead wires.

The initial craft was not capable of carrying an explosive charge on its bow as the hull came almost to a point both fore and aft. Later models were 20 ft long with a blunter bow designed to eventually carry a 495 lb (225 kg) warhead. Complete with explosive charge the craft weighed 5,240 lb (2382 kg). Its operating depth was 75 ft and its endurance was ten hrs at 2.5 knots. The electric motor, its sole means of propulsion, was powered by a 40-volt, 180 amp hr capacity battery of accumulators, but this was later increased to 220 amp hr. NiFe accumulators were used as these could be sealed to avoid acid spillage or chlorine poisoning as well as minimising the creation of hydrogen gas pockets with their explosion risk. Initially, the trim when submerged was achieved by the simple expedient of hand-moving a 300 lb (136 kg) sliding weight fore and aft but the difficulty of doing this in the highly confined space was soon apparent and later versions used compensating tanks with trimming by pump. Port and starboard ballast tanks were blown by compressed air but flooded by means of a hand lever.

The crewman, referred to as 'the driver', sat in the cramped cockpit amidships on his car seat wearing a face mask fed from an oxygen cylinder beneath the control panel, with a duration of 10–14 hours. To improve the atmosphere within the very restricted space, there was a tray of Protosorb CO_2 absorption crystals, sufficient to purify the air for ten hours.

The rudder and single hydroplane formed a common unit at the stern operated by a highly innovative single-column control. The pump for the bilges and the trim tanks was foot-operated. A compass, barometer, ammeter, voltmeter and depth gauge made up the control panel. There was no periscope, an omission which was later to be regretted, visual navigation being catered for by fitting the conning tower with six armoured glass ports. Dolphin was not, of course, experienced in the design of submersible craft. Neither was he amenable to even constructive comments about his ideas. When he insisted that the Welman should not have a periscope it might have been because of the severely restricted space beneath the conning tower; or the problem of leakage; or uncertainty as to whether control would be precise enough to maintain periscope depth for a useful length of time; or even on grounds of cost saving. Or perhaps he saw the vessel as a very basic and expendable weapon which in many ways it was. The initial estimate from Davies to the Head of Operations Section, Brig Gubbins, was that it would take six weeks to construct a Welman. The astute Gubbins expressed his misgivings at this optimistic time-scale.

Word of the construction of Welman 1 reached the Admiralty and

Flag Officer (Submarines), FO(S), Admiral Horton expressed an interest and visited Station IX to see things for himself. Horton, an experienced First World War submariner, was obviously impressed because he sent Submarine Officer Lt Cdr Hall on attachment to act as adviser. They were not convinced that it would be a practical vessel but thought it might well give useful experience for the design and construction of other offensive weapons. They were curious about the novel features of this craft, such as the stressed-skin construction and the joystick control for the hydroplanes and rudder, which both reflected aircraft design practice. However, there is a report that certain features were redesigned following the failure of a (fortunately unmanned) Welman at 100 feet during a depth test. It was now planned to carry the explosive charge on the bow of the submarine. This would be equipped with two arrays of powerful magnets to hold it against the steel hull of its target and an anti-handling device to dissuade the enemy from removing it before its time delay had run its course. Work on the tricky problem of exactly how to attach it and release it safely had not yet been resolved. As an alternative to a purely offensive role, consideration was given to converting the casing for the explosive charge into a container for 600 lb (272 kg) of stores to be released when submerged, but this idea was not pursued. Further Admiralty interest was shown by two visits to Station IX by Admiral Renouf, Professor Blackett of Admiralty Scientific Research, 'D/Navy', Commander Simms, and by engineering personnel from the Department of Miscellaneous Weapons and Devices (DMWD) to discuss navigation and fittings. What they thought of this vessel being designed by an Army mechanical engineer is not recorded.

This was the time of the Playfair and Hanbury-Williams report, commissioned by Selborne shortly after his appointment as Minister of Economic Warfare to look into the organisation of SOE and its relationships with other Services. Hanbury-Williams, a director of Courtaulds, was 'one of the ablest business organisers in London' while Playfair was from HM Treasury. They recommended some reorganisation, to which the Head of SOE (CD) readily agreed as he acknowledged that SOE had been set up in haste and had grown rapidly to a size where its original 'family business' methods were no longer sufficient. (Out of a total establishment of 3,226, Station IX accounted for 194, Station XII for 54 and Station VI for 11.) Anthony Eden, the Foreign Secretary, commented that the inquiry had shown there was nothing wrong with SOE that couldn't be put right.[6]

At the invitation of Horton, the SOE's Deputy Director of Scientific Research and DSR/D visited Portsmouth to see other small underwater craft such as the X-Craft and Chariots under construction and to assess their suitability for SOE's purposes. They considered that none would fulfil the requirements for Operation Frodesley and, with the approval of Horton, it was decided by DSR (Newitt) that Station IX should proceed with its own design as a matter of urgency.

He reported that progress was being made in the construction of Welman 1, and a tank model would soon be ready for drag tests. He requested that Horton should attach two naval officers with technical qualifications to the staff of Station IX, and drew attention to the urgent need for additional sheet metal workers and mechanics. It was hoped that depth and trimming tests, and the fitting out would be completed by August 1942. He also raised the question of training of SOE people by FO(S).

On 11 May 1942, six weeks into construction of the first Welman and on the originally estimated date for its completion, Sir Charles Hambro, the new Chief Executive of SOE, expressed doubts to Davies as to the wisdom of his organisation continuing this somewhat specialised work. It was, after all, a project aimed at putting an enemy battleship out of action and had obvious Naval connotations. The Admiralty must surely have had more expertise in the design and construction of sea-going vessels of all types and SOE's embarkation on such a project could be seen as duplication of work being done in the Submarine Service, despite what the Deputy DSR's visit to Portsmouth had revealed. Davies informed Horton of these doubts, raising the question as to whether it was duplication of work being undertaken by the Submarine Service. Gubbins became involved in the question and expressed the opinion that this type of work should indeed more properly be carried out under the control of either the Admiralty or Chiefs of Combined Operations (CCO) rather than the still-struggling SOE. Davies undertook to approach these two organisations to see if they were interested in taking over the project.[7]

Meanwhile, Col G.F. Taylor, later COS at SOE HQ, had circulated a minute on 18 May stating that Gubbins as Director of Operations was the SOE director responsible for deciding the use to which Welmans should be put and who should use them. It was the responsibility of Davies's directorate (i.e. Newitt) to research, develop and produce and Newitt should apply only to Gubbins for direction about the use of the craft and the training of potential crews. Taylor, however, seemed to think that SOE Country Sections, the M/H Section, the Admiralty and/or CCO as appropriate should have a say in matters, but Gubbins made it quite clear that *he* would decide which organisations should use it and *he* would negotiate with the Admiralty or CCO, and Capt Simpson RN should look to *him* for direction in these matters. So it appears that although Gubbins was not particularly keen for SOE to research, design and produce the submarines, believing it should be an Admiralty or CCO matter, he wanted them for SOE and to control their use by his organisation.[8]

Some further discussions must have taken place during which time Nelson had been replaced by Hambro. Less than a week later, on 23 May, in what appears to be an uncharacteristic volte-face, Taylor's understanding was that Gubbins had decided that there was no question of the Welman being used by the Operations Directorate (of SOE) and he therefore questioned whether research and development should continue with SOE on behalf of the Admiralty and CCO. Simpson was charged with finding out the Admiralty's wishes and reporting back to Taylor and Davies while the latter approached the CCO. While all these political issues were being ironed out the first Welman was under urgent construction.

Capt R. Wilson RA visited Station IX on 9 June 1942. He was sent by Maj Courtney, the Officer in Charge of the Special Boat Section, S.S. Bde, and like him, Wilson was thrilled at the prospect of the Welman and hoped to be able to drive one. He had logged 150 days of experience in submarines in the Mediterranean, which seemed to be considered sufficient qualification for appointment as a seconded 'operational adviser' on development of the craft at Station IX.

Completion of the first submarine was achieved by the end of June 1942, just about double the time originally estimated but nevertheless a very creditable performance starting from a blank sheet of paper. The trials which followed in July and August demonstrated that the requirements of the specification had been broadly met. Testing at Station IX took place in a large brick-built tank subsequently used to circulate cooling water around some of ICI's laboratories.

Among the flimsy and fading papers discovered in Everett's files is the following anonymous skit upon the Welman and its inventor. 'Bus' refers to Buswell, 'Mel' to Maj Meldrum, and 'Port' to Porteous. 'John' is, of course, the inventor Dolphin but 'Lloyd' is unidentified.

FRATA MIRACULA

And it came to pass that the people of the land of England were sorely oppressed, being set upon by enemies from without.

And the King spake unto his Councillors, saying Go ye forth into the Wilderness that is called Welwyn and bring unto me one John, that dwelleth there.

For I have seen a vision and dreamed a dream, and it hath been shown to me that this John will save us from the enemies which are beyond the sea and in the waters under the seas.

And the Councillors said unto the King Oh, King, live for ever.

And immediately he lived for ever.

Whereupon they departed thence, to find John in the Wilderness and when they came upon him, they told him that which the King had commanded.

And John said unto them I too have seen a vision and dreamed a dream. For behold, in my dream I saw a Dolphin upon the waters, the like of which has never been seen before. Go and tell the King to build an Ark for his peoples, built in the likeness of the Dolphin of my dreams.

But they spake amongst themselves, saying No man can do this.

Whereupon John the Prophet hurled them forth, and called unto him his three sons, Bus, Mel and Port.

And he spake unto them, drawing in the sand at his feet, saying Thus it shall be made, and thus, and thus. Go ye and do my bidding.

And Bus and Mel went forth, but Port looked about him gloomily and drummed his fingers upon the table.

Now passed a period of many moons, when they did gather together many materials. Steel of the finest lustre did they buy, to the weight of four score oxen, and with it rods of the most brazen brass, one thousand cubits.

And day and night they wrought upon it, and when it was nearly finished, Mel said unto Bus Let there be light therein.

And Bus replied, saying There is light, whereupon Port replaced the fuses.

But John their father chided them, saying Haste, for the day cometh when she shall float beneath the waters, to confound our enemies.

So they fashioned for the Ark a cart of huge dimensions,

and having placed the Ark upon it, they wrapped her in silken cloths, so that no man might see that which had come to pass.

And they departed unto the waters.

Now, when they had arrived there, they placed her upon the surface of the sea, crying What Ho! and that she bumped. And all were of good cheer.

But lo! there was a man named Lloyd who set his heart against them. But it was of no avail, for he was cast into the outer darkness.

Now, about this time, John had disappeared from the Wilderness; no man knew whither.

But, anon, he re-appeared amongst them, saying I have spoken unto the Councillors of the King and have sold the Ark unto them, not once but many times.

And they were greatly cheered by his words.

And so it came to pass that the words of the prophet were fulfilled and a Dolphin floated upon the waters, the like of which had never before been seen.

HERE ENDETH THE FIRST PART OF OUR CHRONICLES.

It appears that the earlier questions of control of the Welman project had been resolved in favour of the Admiralty, for the FO(S) now began a close association with the project. Early in July Horton wrote to Dolphin with a list of twenty trials which he required to be completed satisfactorily before he would consider the craft up to Admiralty standards. In his opinion these should be carried out at the Vickers test tank at St Albans, Horsea in Portsmouth harbour and Port 'D'. On 27 July 1942 Horton told CD that, after useful conversations with two SOE officers, he considered that trials and exercises with the Welman should continue but at Staines reservoir rather than at Horsea. He was sufficiently impressed to order the second vessel to ISRB's (Station IX's cover name) design, the hull of which the Admiralty would pay for and Station IX would fit out. The limited trials so far possible with the original Welman were clearly insufficient to provide a basis for longer-term production decisions. Many more would be necessary before a decision on future development could be taken. But now that the design was more or less settled and with production experience of the first Welman, this second craft was completed in about four weeks.

The trials called for must have proceeded apace for on 12 August

Horton told CD that they had reached the stage when consideration should be given to production matters. He wanted a number of pre-production models built by SOE as a matter of urgency in order to gain detailed experience in production methods and to permit training of operational personnel from the Admiralty, CCO or SOE. Despite Gubbins's decision that Welmans would not be used by the Operations Directorate, Horton was keeping the options open.[9]

Horton, who now seems to have taken charge of the project and was thinking in terms of a production rate of one craft per fortnight up to a minimum of twenty, was told that this would require another building and more machines at Station IX. If large-scale production was decided upon it should, he considered, be under the control of the Admiralty although, he assured SOE, they would need their fullest help in the early stages. He would support their approaches to the Treasury or any other government departments. Mr Hanbury-Williams, the Deputy Chief (D/CD), told Horton that the Minister, Lord Selborne, was very appreciative of all the help the Admiral was giving and CD suggested to Lt Col H. Sporborg, his political assistant, that this correspondence might be mentioned to the Minister, no doubt to illustrate the cooperative nature of the project and to allay any fears of duplication of effort between the Services.

In the following week, on 19 August, CD approached Horton to use his good offices to obtain high priority for the additional buildings at The Frythe. Horton asked the Civil Lord to take the necessary action and a week later told CD that the Civil Lord had told him the Admiralty had supported SOE's application for super-preference. They could hardly have done otherwise since they were placing the orders and impressing the urgency upon Station IX. While all this urgent action was taking place in high places, the second Welman was completed but not early enough for trials to be conducted during the month. Three more were ordered and another twenty were being considered by CCO, who were now interested in this development.

Admiral Mountbatten, who was Head of Combined Operations and something of a law unto himself, took an interest in the Welman. This could only have augured well for the project. Horton's personal interest in the Welman continued and he witnessed trials in Staines reservoir. On 14 September he confirmed to CD that he had told Dolphin that until Admiralty trials had been completed he would not be in a position to recommend the production of more than the three vessels that had already been ordered. Dolphin had informed him that CCO had already ordered twenty-one Welmans. Whether this was a misunderstanding or some far from subtle manoeuvring, Horton had subsequently telephoned CCO and discovered in fact that none had been ordered! Unamused, he told CD that this confusion had better be cleared up. Nevertheless, contract No. CP 8A/70909/42 with the Pressed Steel Company in Oxford was for 153 units, known in the Company for security reasons as 'Floats, sweep, MkIII' (sic), and was dated 28 August 1942. It is suggested that this order could well have been a ploy to reserve production capacity in an already busy factory.

CD's reply to Horton was that he understood Ashbourne and Davies had discussed the future of the submarine but that Horton was anxious to have the production of twenty craft postponed pending further trials to solve some technical problems. Putting back the order had been investigated but there would be difficulty in altering or cancelling certain of the contracts involved. CD presumed Horton still supported the erection of additional workshops, the installation of the machinery and the requisitioning of additional personnel for the pre-production work. CD also understood that CCO had given their requirements through Horton and hoped he would soon inform SOE of their likely commitments.

The saga of negotiation, confusing statements and (one suspects) intrigue was played out in London – while, at Staines reservoir, where steep wooden ramps into the water had been constructed, the second Welman, launched from a heavy wooden trolley, underwent its preliminary trials. Surviving photographs of the Welman show two different models. One, thought to be the prototype with pointed bow and stern, lacks the 'bulges' on each side and the splash-diverter looking like a small snowplough in front of the forward glass port in the conning tower. One picture[10] shows the craft on a trolley with Dolphin in the background, while on the side of the conning tower has been painted an emblem which appears to be of a dolphin within a circle carrying the points of the compass, an apt insignia for a craft designed by someone with such an appropriate name. At that stage it was clearly incapable of having a 495 lb (225 kg) warhead attached to its pointed bow. Other photographs show a vessel with bulges on each side, fixings for the jettisonable keel and a blunter nose to which has been attached diverting bars from the hatch housing. The photographs in SOE's catalogue of stores[11] reveal how the warhead was eventually carried. One view with the warhead removed shows the redesigned bull-nosed bow of the Welman with an annular register on which to locate a mating part of the warhead. In the centre of the register is a single screw fixing to retain the warhead which now had a similar blunt nose to that of its host. The single holding screw passed through a watertight gland to an actuating wheel inside the hull. Consideration was given to fitting the charge with rubber buffers so that the driver could contact the target without making too much noise. The intention was that the driver should bring the bow of the submarine up beneath the bottom of the target until the ten powerful magnets of the charge held it fast with a pull of 1125 lb (510 kg) and a 40 lb (18 kg) positive buoyancy. He would next turn the holding screw fully home to arm the fuse and then turn the wheel in the opposite direction to release himself from the now initiated timed charge.

By the end of October two new workshops had been completed and their machinery installed. The Welman No. 1 had been used by the Commandos for training at Staines while Welman No. 2 had undergone further satisfactory trials. Now that Station IX had a couple of working examples it was anxious to demonstrate its success and accumulate credit among the previously sceptical Services. The captain of HMS *Titania*, a depot ship moored in the Holy Loch in Scotland, and other naval officers were invited to attend a demonstration.

On 9 November 1942 Horton, who had supported with interest the development of the Welman, was posted elsewhere and replaced as FO(S) by Capt Claud G. Barry DSO RN with the acting rank of Rear Admiral. CD wrote a letter regretting the loss of Horton's inspiration and encouragement, no doubt hoping it would nudge the newcomer in the right direction. Welman No. 2 underwent sea trials, although it is not known where, and the construction of Welman No. 3 proceeded.

On the last day of November a meeting took place between representatives of ISRB and Barry to discuss and plan future policy with respect to the Welmans. They saw the possibilities for its use by the Admiralty for attacks on enemy ships in harbour; by CCO principally for beach reconnaissance; and by SOE for miscellaneous requirements. Station IX with their additional workshops were at that time manufacturing or modifying ten Welmans, including the two already undergoing trials. The Admiralty wanted the remaining eight as operational craft. Having earmarked the current production run, the Admiralty told CCO and SOE to submit their requirements through the usual Admiralty channels. It was recommended that The Pressed Steel Company at Cowley in Oxford, used to making motor car body panels in peacetime, continue to fabricate the hulls but if the numbers required increased much more, the question of making expensive press tools would have to be faced.

It was decided that further, more comprehensive trials were to take place at HMS *Varbel*, again in Scotland. The opportunity was taken to propose, at least for the initial eight Admiralty craft, maintenance parties of two EMs, four ERMs, two Stokers and one Officer driver per boat with at least 50 per cent replacements. The training of the crews and maintenance of the submarines were to be the responsibility of the Admiralty, CCO or SOE depending on for whom the units were built. In the light of the Playfair and Hanbury-Williams report of June that year into waste and mismanagement, this seems a surprising duplication of training organisation and effort. ISRB was to be responsible for any developments in the boat's design and Staines reservoir was to continue to be used for training and experimental work by SOE and CCO.

In December the Officer Commanding HMS *Titania*, having witnessed a demonstration of the Welman, wrote a paper comparing the Welman with the Chariot, the existing submersible device which was 'ridden' by a two-man crew called 'charioteers'. The new craft was relatively comfortable and dry for the driver who was also able to take food and drink. He could surface and open the conning tower hatch to relieve any claustrophobia and stale air build-up whereas the charioteer could not get out of his diving suit and Davis Submarine Escape Apparatus (DSEA set). The Welman had a longer range and the possibility was being examined of carrying it to an operation within the casing of a submarine. It could probably resist small depth charges of the type dropped from ships in harbour unless one happened to fall very close. The course of instruction for the Welman was shorter and the care and maintenance simpler than for the chariot with its riders' life-sustaining equipment. Clearly, at this relatively early stage the Welman camp had an enthusiastic supporter.

SOE held a meeting on 10 December at which it was agreed that:

a) Steps should be taken to retain the operational and experimental development of the Welman in the hands of SOE in charge of a special section under Capt Simpson.
b) That Capt Simpson with Lt Col Rowlandson should produce a

memorandum for the Admiralty in which SOE's proposal for this operational development and control should be set out.

c) The closest cooperation with the Admiralty should be maintained at all stages.

Less than seven months after Gubbins had questioned whether research and development of the Welman should continue to be conducted by SOE, positive steps were now being taken to ensure this did in fact happen. Perhaps Gubbins's misgivings had been shown to have been misplaced or maybe the enthusiasm from certain quarters had changed his view. Or could it have been that a further six months of experience in subversive warfare had given him some ideas for its use by SOE?

Davies announced that financial authority had been given for twenty one-man Welmans and a new development, a three-man version. But what was this three-man Welman? A document by T.A. Hussey (DXSR) dated 16 January 1943 states that the three-man Welman was to be used for landing small demolition parties to destroy beach and underwater obstacles prior to an assault.[12] No record or any drawings have been found indicating whether this development was to be physically larger or considerably more cramped and stuffy. If all twenty one-man craft were to be produced at Station IX, yet more workshop space would be needed and this would have a limiting effect on Dolphin's other experimental work, so he would really prefer, say, ten or twelve boats. What was more, it would be necessary for at least three three-man Welmans to be made in SOE's own workshops before constructional difficulties could be ironed out and a final production design could be arrived at.

The eight one-man craft for the Admiralty were to take priority and would take eight weeks to complete, presumably in parallel by eight teams of technicians. Thereafter, one per week would be made for SOE. Estimates gave the cost at that time of producing a Welman in SOE's workshops at Station IX as £800, but if a large order was placed with an outside contractor the cost was likely to be about £1300. With all the initial problems of starting work on a new venture, production by an outside firm would be unlikely to commence for four to five months but after that the rate was estimated to be one per day which seems a wholly unrealistic improvement on earlier estimates and actual production times.

It was then agreed that as five or six of the eight one-man Welmans were required urgently and this would grossly overstretch the facilities at Station IX, an outside order would be placed for a reasonable order of 40 of the craft at a total cost of £50,000. Two additional three-man Welmans would be started as soon as the experimental designs were far enough advanced.

Completing the basic one-man Welman as an operational vessel and bringing it up to a stage where large-scale production would be possible was the first priority of the project at this time. Thereafter the construction of a satisfactory production model of the three-man version was to be pursued. Having available submarines, attention would then be given to production of a device for discharging Welmines (also being developed at Station IX – see Chapter 8) or for releasing numerous magnetic charges without opening the conning tower hatch.

It was, of course, necessary to devise some means of transporting the submarines to the area of any intended operation, for the Welman did not have the range to travel far under its own power. Possible means of transport to an operational area were seen as:

a) The aft compartment of a Sunderland flying boat. (Six Sunderlands were adapted to carry two Chariots each, so why not Welmans?)
b) By Motor Torpedo Boat or SOE's own fast motor boats. It is not clear if these included the American sub-chasers which were used later.
c) By fishing boat or other vessels. Simpson was charged with arranging for trials in the estuary of the Helford River near the Lizard in Cornwall. Gerry Holdsworth, formerly of Section 'D', had set up a small base there in November 1940 from which the 'Helford Flotilla' of SIS and occasionally SOE vessels were busy infiltrating agents into France. From June 1943 the unit was officially known as the Inshore Patrol Flotilla (IPF) and was eventually relegated to a training establishment.[13]

January 1943 saw a certain amount of frustration reflected in reports of slow progress with the Welmans and of CD writing to Barry about the urgency of the project and the labour problems they were experiencing. He asked for a high-level meeting to enable decisions to be made. Welman No. 2 had been refitted at Station IX and sent back to Scotland for further trials. Welman No. 3 underwent a number of trials which included a deep water test and the placing of charges. Welman No. 7 had its preliminary trials in Staines reservoir. Experiments were also carried out with a modified charge and with an emergency release buoy. There had been some concern for the safety of the drivers during trials and training. It is thought that Dolphin considered the risk to be low, but Meldrum made an urgent request to the Experimental Section on 14 January for an Emergency Release Buoy, possibly as a result of a near-fatal incident when a Welman was unable to surface and was not raised for 18 hours. They designed a buoy containing calcium phosphide which, on reaching the surface, admitted water which led to the production of a plume of smoke. It was completed, tested and handed over for fitting to Welman 10 on 3 March.

On 28 January CD took Lord Hankey, the Cabinet Secretary, Mr Clement Jones and Mr Markham of the Ministry of Labour to Station IX to show them its activities, to emphasise to them the urgency of the Welman project and, more importantly to him, the problems they were encountering. They were impressed and promised CD assistance with the labour problem. While SOE's manpower problems were clearly being taken seriously in some quarters, there were some with a wider view who thought in terms of efficiency and who were particularly concerned at the risk of duplication of effort between SOE and branches of the three regular Services. CD, Gubbins, Lt Gen R. Weeks (DCIGS) and Maj Gen Galloway (DSD) met on 12 February to discuss the manpower issue and whether SOE's design and development establishments were overlapping with others, such as Lord Cherwell's protectorate at The Firs near Aylesbury, run by Millis Jefferis and known as Station MD1. Weeks was fairly well satisfied with the explanation given by CD and even approved the existing arrangements for liaison with the other services but, nevertheless, a committee was set up to examine the whole question. The global strength of SOE at that time was 3,352 persons but CD was looking for a figure of 7,000 of all ranks in 1943. There was a need for 180 additional tradesmen, who were hard to find. The policy was to employ personnel who would not be more useful on active service. Hence the establishment included significant numbers of borrowed RAF radio technicians, self-trained ATS girls and some wounded Service personnel.

On the same day, after a discussion with Barry, CD told Davies that he could place an order with the Pressed Steel Company for 120 Welmans. Barry told him he had heard that the CCO had an immediate need for 40 so he was increasing the number to a round 150. 30 were for training; eight for FO(S); 80 for SOE; and 40 for CCO.

Now Dolphin could see the wisdom of placing the large order six months previously. Once again, Gubbins's doubts about the Welman being used by SOE seemed to be receding.

Activity at Station IX at this time was intense. ISRB were constructing about 20 Welmans of which six were now complete and had passed their preliminary trials and four more were due to be launched in the next two weeks. Naval personnel for the Admiralty maintenance crew were being trained with SOE before being posted to HMS *Titania*.

Coincidentally with the urgent work on the submarines themselves, the explosive charge for the nose of the Welmans was presenting some difficulties. Further research into the fusing and initiating of the charge had proved necessary. It will be recalled that fusing the device was achieved by turning the holding screw fully home and releasing it by turning in the opposite direction. If the long screw were to jam after the first operation, the submarine crewman would be faced with the serious problem of not being able to distance himself from the fused charge short of abandoning ship and swimming for it; so the initiating device had to be as near foolproof as possible.

The committee set up the previous month by Weeks met at the War Office on 15 March. Brig F.J. Mitchell was in the chair, the others being Davies, Lt Col Wood of Station XII and Newitt. After what was probably thought to be an unnecessary, and no doubt short, gathering their conclusion was that co-ordination and liaison were complete with all the Services, the Ministry of Production, and the Ministry of Supply with the exception of relations regarding design of weapons and ammunition. One wonders if this exception was born out of frustration with the long series of official tests of the Welgun, the almost universal praise for it, but its eventual rejection. It was to be hoped that future liaison with respect to weapons was, perhaps, of less immediate importance since arms emerging from the fertile design offices of Station IX tended to be of a very non-standard kind (such as the Welrod, then under development) and required in limited quantities.

Towards the end of March there was unanimous agreement to the use of the Welman to lay a special magnetic mine, carried in place of the explosive charge, in narrow waterways such as the Gironde in western France, from which German and Japanese blockade runners were operating, and the Corinth Canal in Greece. It was acknowledged that in some circumstances in such operations the whole craft might have to be abandoned and left as a mine. One of the earliest suggested uses, the landing of agents, was now seen as unlikely due to the particular need for the right conditions of the beach, swell, etc., for success.

Other problems addressed at this time were the limited range of the Welman and finding a suitable means of transporting it to a target area. One ambitious idea considered was to establish a hidden base of operations complete with basic servicing facilities. The possibility of making use of one of the unfrequented bays in the Lofoten Islands off northern Norway was mooted.

On 19 April 1943 Selborne sent one of his enthusiastic letters to Winston Churchill anticipating his interest in photographs of the new one-man submarine which had been evolved (sic) at the SOE workshops. Trials, he said, had been so successful that the Admiralty had ordered 150. He went on to state that certain ideas, new to submarine construction, had been borrowed from the technique of blind flying in aircraft and developed by 'an engineer and a scientist in SOE respectively and appropriately named Dolphin and Newitt'. The technique referred to was the use of a direction-indicating device.

He then described a proposed method of strike against the *Tirpitz* and further boosted the Welman by stating that in a trial it had carried out a successful mock attack on HMS *Howe* during which the submarine had gone 'through and under nets and every other form of anti-submarine protection including all the latest detection apparatus'. In view of other evidence this was almost certainly an over-optimistic and perhaps misleading assessment. Selborne invited the Prime Minister to see the Welman for himself at Staines reservoir. Churchill would have liked to have seen it one day and would perhaps fix something up a little later on. No record has been unearthed that he ever did.[14]

Senior members of the Armed Forces and the Government now addressed the matter of operational policy regarding the use of Welmans. CD suggested they should be used in large numbers, possibly in the Baltic, Black Sea, Adriatic and Danube and their existence should not be revealed by the premature deployment of small numbers of the craft. Introduction of the craft into the Danube to disrupt important river traffic, including the long-time target of Rumania's vital supply of oil to Germany, was clearly an admirable objective but it is not clear how it was proposed to get them into the river. Perhaps they were thinking of entry via the river's delta in the Black Sea. Or perhaps the subsequent experiments with air dropping Welmans were initiated by the problem. The meeting also agreed that SOE's efforts should be concerted with those of the Royal Navy and CCO. There was a clear case for a Combined Operational Committee to study intelligence, select targets, organise training and transport, etc.

The Royal Navy had had representation through much of the development stage in the persons of Lt Jimmy Holmes RN and Lt Basil Maris RNVR who had been attached to Station IX to advise and take part in experiments. They were subsequently to be the two British officers taking part in Operation Barbara. At this point in the spring of 1943 the use of the Welman in the Far East had not been broached but, as will be seen, Admiral Mountbatten and Special Operations Australia were to take an interest in it.

Station IX was instructed to proceed as a matter of urgency with both the Welfreighter (see later) and the two-man Welman (the Mark II; the three-man version appears to have been too ambitious). The two-man version had been requested by Country Sections who envisaged it carrying a passenger in addition to the driver, 600 lb (272 kg) of stores instead of an explosive warhead, and possibly a small petrol engine as outboard propulsion in addition to the electric motor. The overall length would have risen to 25 feet. Newitt estimated that its range could be increased to 60 miles by the provision of 50 per cent more batteries, an improvement considered desirable. He undertook to explore the installation of a petrol engine to increase the surface cruising speed to 5 knots and range to 100 miles. He was asked to follow this up provided it did not delay production of the Welman Mark II, whose prototype was under construction, and the Welfreighter, whose outer skin was now half completed, the design of mechanisms finished and their manufacture in progress. Those addressing the problem of transportation to operational areas now found that the earlier suggestion for air transport of the craft in Sunderland flying boats faced difficulties.

By the end of March 1943 some ten Welmans had been completed and tested. Five were already being used for instructional courses at Staines and at HMS *Titania*. The Emergency Release Buoy had been installed on the most recently completed craft. In a pressure test on the hull of a Welman it had failed at 243 lb/sq.in which is equivalent to a depth of approximately 480 feet, considerably in excess of its operational requirements. This must have been reassuring to both designers and potential crew alike.

At the end of April it was reported that training of Welman personnel and general development would henceforth be vested in the

FO(S). In effect, the Admiralty were now running the project and SOE were merely providing the workshop space and manpower for development work. The petrol motor proposal explored by DSR had been fitted to the two-man Welman Mark II and had given normal runs in the test tank. A towing skid for the Welmans, a structure to give the craft stability when being towed at the higher speeds than it could ever achieve under its own power, had been tested in model form in the tank at St Albans. Research into the mechanical and electrical fuses of the explosive charges was continuing.

Further tests and training were undertaken in April at HMS *Titania* and HMS *Bonaventure*, a depot ship with special facilities for handling midget craft. Welman production had almost reached fourteen, Nos 11 and 12 being completed by the Pressed Steel Company, the former to be sent to America.

Following some correspondence in which the FO(S) expressed the opinion that traditionally superstitious users of submarines would not favour a number thirteen, the Pressed Steel Company was ordered to re-number the thirteenth example (Job No. 6622) as 'Welman 161'.[15]

On 24 May a clearly concerned FO(S) wrote to CD asking if the large order for 150 Welmans ought still to stand. He had read a report on their operational capabilities and noted with some alarm two serious handicaps. Contrary to Selborne's claim, Welmans could not pierce a protective anti-submarine net and the driver's vision at night was very poor. He pointed out that Chariots did not have these problems and queried if the craft could be improved to overcome them. A reply from CD reiterated the good points already made and expressed his strong opinion that the order should stand. Perhaps the improvements which FO(S) sought would be incorporated in the two-man version for no action was taken at this stage. CD, still enthusiastic about the craft, said there would be plenty of lightly defended sea or coastal targets in Norway, the Middle East and the Far East. He argued that if it was finally decided to stop the order for the Welman Mk I, its production slots could be taken over by the Welman Mk II and the Welfreighter, so it made sense to let the order stand for the time being.[16]

By the end of May Nos 11 and 12 had been sent to America and further work had been done on the towing skid to enable the towing speed to be increased. This proved to be an improvement but was unstable above ten knots.

No further work had been done on the two-man Welman Mk II

pending results of further trials. There seem to be no further references to progress on the Welman Mk II, so it is presumed that it was abandoned. At this time the other submersible project, Welfreighter No. 1, had been launched and had completed preliminary trials at Staines.

The exchange of letters with FO(S) in late May concerning the comparison of the Welman and the Chariot had clearly worried CD. In June he wrote to Sporborg, his PPS to SO, saying that he had been disturbed by the FO(S) letter of 24 May. He had decided to read for himself the actual report before commenting. It then appeared to him that the Chariot might be superior in some respects but he felt there was a place for both craft.

As training continued and the day of an actual operation approached, transportation of Welmans and the recruitment of crews were again under consideration. Vice Admiral L.V. Wells, ACOS, understood there was a shortage of volunteers for operations in Norwegian waters but, in his view, the crews should be predominantly British with some suitable Norwegians. In spite of this view, eventually it was decided to fill all six vacancies on the second Welman drivers' course with Norwegians. CD had already said that Lt Sir George Pollock RN (ret'd) should go to Lyness on the Island of Hoy in the Orkneys to lend his experience to Welman attack plans which would, of course, include the transportation issue. Consideration was given to the use of Motor Gun Boats (MGB) with the submarines stowed on deck. The difficulty with towing them was the speed limitation of six to eight knots but with the Director of Navy Contracts (DNC) devising a different skid from SOE's on the lines of a floating dock, it was hoped to be able to tow them at twenty knots.

The suggestion that the Welman might be used for beach-marking work in connection with landing operations led to a decision to equip it with an anchor. Whether this was ever carried out and what form the anchor took has not been determined. The technical details of the carriage of the craft by air were with the Ministry of Aircraft Production who awaited the Air Ministry's instructions to carry out the remaining experiments.

On 4 June 1943 Wells wrote to Rear Admiral E.J.P. Brind that he and Barry had visited Station IX to see for themselves the progress on the Welman and had come away impressed by its possibilities. The craft were costing £700–800 to produce; so, even if each one was abandoned after an attack, they would prove economical compared to a torpedo. At that time they were being produced at a rate of two per week but this was anticipated to improve to one per day. The ACOS therefore wished to have twenty-five Welmans complete with crews for his command by the end of August, plus another ten to replace losses. This was clearly good news for Station IX.[17]

Around this time (June 1943) seventeen inert Welman charges had been made for trial purposes and fifteen live charges were being manufactured to be fitted into the Pressed Steel Company's containers. Fuses Section had devoted considerable time to the fuses and time delays on the Welman explosive charge. A demonstration warhead had been made which included manual safety gear, a detonator placer, an electrical anti-removal switch and a clockwork time fuse. It was approved on 15 June and test units were under construction.

An associated device recently designed and fabricated was the Welman stores container, having seven sections, weighing 120 lb (54 kg) and being ready for user trials. Unfortunately, no description of this unit has been found and one is left to speculate whether this was capable of being floated ashore and how the Station IX engineers had solved the problems of making it watertight.

By the end of June two Welmans needed repairs using the spares stock of internal equipment at HMS *Titania*. The latest craft, No. 17, had been delivered by the Pressed Steel Company on 26 June and was undergoing tests at Station IX.

In July seven officers and men from NORIC (the Norwegian Independent Company) were selected for Welman training and this was started at Gosport Royal Navy Submarine Establishment the following month. This party later proceeded to HMS *Titania* for further instruction and operational training.

The question now arose as to where to set up a formal base to test Welmans in sea conditions as opposed to the relatively calm waters of the Queen Mary reservoir at Staines, where initial testing could still take place. Fishguard in south-west Wales was proposed but concerns were expressed by the Director of Local Defence because it was a search port for traffic to and from Eire and the Iberian peninsula which was known to harbour a considerable pro-German element. The Director of Naval Intelligence did not agree with the proposal, pointing out that Fishguard was not in a Regulated or Protected Area and cranes used to lift the craft into the water would be visible to the public. He suggested a Regulated Area such as the Helford estuary in southern Cornwall but the Head of Military Branch II said this port did not have accommodation and would be becoming busier with cross-channel operations. So the security objections were overruled and the second floor of the Great Western Hotel was taken over for fifteen officers, and existing Naval huts in the area were set aside to accommodate thirty-five men. Others were put in an annexe to the Great Western Hotel.[18]

In August operational plans were developing and the codeword 'Barbara' was allotted to cover Welman missions undertaken in cooperation with ACOS off the coast of Norway. (This codeword seems to have been duplicated as it was also used for an operation to destroy part of the Norwegian railway network.)

In September Lerwick informed London that the first two trained Welman drivers were expected in Shetland, from whence they would set out on their missions, on about the 20th of the month. They wanted to know when Howarth would be available for planning and were told he would be arriving around the 9th to act in a similar capacity for the forthcoming Barbara operations as Sir George Pollock had done for earlier 'Vestige' operations. This meant he would be attached to Maj Sclatter's staff to advise Barbara parties on all Norwegian and SOE matters and to assist in the planning work.

In October a Welman which had been under trials at HMS *Varbel* had received a highly critical report. Smoke laying was possible but was too slow to be of any practical use. Beaching for reconnaissance was hazardous. Not only did it take a long time (twelve hours in all between tides) but the craft tended to fall over on one side which caused the battery acid to spill and the trim to be upset. Firing from the Welman was said to be wildly inaccurate. Since it was not normally equipped with armament this presumably referred to firing a weapon from the open conning tower. Seven hours of operation in the cramped conditions was considered to be too onerous for the normal operator. There was little visibility at night and the crewman was unable to hear at all. The craft was unstable without its jettisonable keel so in an emergency when it was dropped one did not know which way up the craft would arrive at the surface.[19] In the same month degaussing equipment, to protect the vessels from magnetic mines, had been installed at Staines. The three underwater coils each formed a rectangle 350 yards long by 25 yards wide and were wired to a hut on the breakwater.[20]

On 20 November 1943 four Welmans set out on the craft's first operation and what was to be its only contact with the enemy: details are given in Chapter 15. Here we simply note that the operation failed partly through bad luck. All the Welmans were scuttled as planned (although one was recovered by German forces before it sank) but the reports by the three men recovered after Operation Barbara indicate that only Welman 48 exhibited any mechanical defects. This was a leaking propeller shaft gland which eventually led to its abandoning the attack. Trials to confirm the craft's endurance for the operation had revealed a slack propeller shaft bearing, a heavily scored shaft and the propeller boss rubbing on the tube. A complete new propeller shaft assembly was fitted but it appears that the bedding-down of the seal was to take longer than anticipated and leakage into the hull resulted during the operation. Despite this setback production of Welmans continued into 1944.

SOE's executive was strengthened at this time when a new second Vice Chief of SOE was appointed: Mr M.P. Murray from the Air Ministry was to have the designation V/CD.2.

In the first quarter of 1944 Allied forces were gearing up for the invasion of Europe and it must have been obvious that the scope for the use of Welman and similar midget submarines was becoming strictly limited. Not only would resources be demanded at the main theatre of war, but the senior decision makers would have their attention diverted to that area also. It was decided that production was to cease after the manufacture of Welman No. 100. However, No. 88 was being fitted with remote controls, the idea being that the driver would disembark carrying a small air bottle attached to the craft by a light airline before submerging it out of sight. Having reconnoitred the shore he would return to the water's edge, recover the air bottle and resurface the Welman for his getaway. A unit known as the Middle East Raiding Forces were interested and, subject to Naval approval, it was thought that there might be a demand for it.

Those concerned with the transportation of Welmans had turned their radical thinking to the idea of dropping Welmans into water by parachute. For this they were considering a Mark V special craft whose details have not been discovered, one of which was nearing completion and was to be sent to Fishguard for proofing by mid-February 1944. This dropping technique required the development of a release gear to detach the parachutes once the Welman was in the water. The record in the PRO states that 'the stores previously dropped on land would be dropped on water' from which one could deduce that initial trials of the release gear, perhaps with only ballast, had been carried out over land where recovery was assured. Provided the results were satisfactory the experiment would be written up and accompanied by a film illustration for FO(S), COS and any others who might be interested. A satisfactory drop of a dummy Welman (whether this was the Mark V special craft is not known) was made from a Lancaster into the water off the Suffolk coast at Orford Ness on 26 April. The system used four 96-feet diameter parachutes giving it a gentle descent and immersing the craft into the water in a satisfactory manner. One of the parachute releases worked perfectly but the second was rather late in releasing due, it was surmised, to the tight tolerances in the new mechanism. Viewed from a position of comfort and safety over fifty years after the event it is difficult to imagine how it was thought possible, let alone economical, to clandestinely introduce a small submarine beneath four huge parachute canopies. Unless it was intended to drop the submarine close to a mother ship which had the driver on board, the hapless crewman would have to sit in the cold and claustrophobic craft in the bomb bay of a bomber until he heard the doors open and was suddenly falling towards the sea. Welman crews were brave men but such a prospect must have made even them blanch.

When Mountbatten moved from CCO to the Far East, the Welman project lost an influential supporter. Gen Robert Laycock, who took over the post, had no interest in midget submarines and told the Admiralty on 15 February that CCO had no further use for Welmans. Furthermore, Rear Admiral Barry was not keen to find other uses for them. But in the Far East Mountbatten's enthusiasm for the craft was still evident as late as November 1944. A report into the facilities and training system at the Careening Bay Camp at Garden Island in Cockburn Sound near Fremantle, Western Australia states that it was intended to provide a base for ten Welmans and ten Sleeping Beauties. The camp also had a degaussing coil for Welmans.[21] In October the first Welman arrived from England. They had no Welman operations in mind so it was used for preliminary training for the Welfreighter. The Australians found the one-man craft difficult to manage so they later designed a periscope for it, a feature which, ironically, might have reversed the outcome of its only operation.[22]

On 17 April 1944 the order had been given by the Head of M11 that 'production of Welman and associated equipment was to stop forthwith'. The Staines station was to become a Naval establishment, the Admiralty Testing Station, but its Commanding Officer was to be Maj H.Q.A. Reeves, RASC, the acoustics expert and inventor of the Sleeping Beauty. When the war drew to a close the facilities at Staines were taken over by the Ministry of Aircraft Production at the end of August 1945. ISRB had taken over the United Dairies Co. Ltd premises at 487 Western Avenue, Park Royal, London W3 for storage of Welmans, Welfreighters and Sleeping Beauties and its Commanding Officer was Capt A. Lane. On 13 September 1945 the store held 60 Welmans in the process of cannibalisation and nineteen Welfreighters as well as quantities of spare parts. By 6 October they were all gone.[23]

So ended the short operational life of this unusual craft. Conceived and built in the depths of Hertfordshire many miles from the nearest sea, three of them ended up at the bottom of a Norwegian fjord. Sixty days of hard weather in the autumn of 1944 and the fact that Norwegian operations were, in any case, suspended between mid-May and early August because the nights were too light to provide cover, meant that perhaps the Welman was denied the opportunities to demonstrate its potential.

At least six Welmans were delivered to Australia, eventually to be declared surplus to requirements, loaded onto LST 3014 and dumped off Rottnest Island in 1946.

In retrospect several commentators have suggested that the design of the Welman was seriously flawed from the start. However, the records seem to suggest that it was strongly supported by FO(S) in the form of Admiral Sir Max Horton, an experienced submariner who had been involved with conventional submarine design since 1918. He, if anyone, would have been in a position to make a critical assessment of the Welman, but there is no record of his having done so. On the other hand it may well be that criticism of the design was ignored or suppressed – for it is well established that Dolphin was not one to accept and respond willingly to opposing views.

In the 1970s a rusted and encrusted Welman was recovered by HMS *Reclaim* from the seabed in Rothesay Bay off the Isle of Bute and another was recovered from the former training area in Scapa Flow in 1980, the crewmen having apparently escaped. Whether their limited use had any connection with the story that Admiral Mountbatten as Chief of Combined Operations had narrowly escaped drowning while testing one in the Welsh Harp reservoir in north-west London and arrived late and wet for a meeting at Chequers will perhaps never be known. A glass port had failed and it was necessary for him to jettison the heavy keel in order to regain the surface.

However well-meaning the project, it cannot be denied that the design was carried out by a team of enthusiastic amateurs in the environment of a research establishment, albeit in wartime. The first examples were constructed in what was little more than a sheet metal workshop set up in a hangar building. One cannot help feeling that it was the Royal Navy who had the experience of submarine design and operation and closer cooperation between them and SOE in the conceptual stages might have resulted in a more effective weapon. Nevertheless, the craft that went into action showed that SOE had produced a practical vessel.

THE WELFREIGHTER

The Welman had developed initially from ideas for infiltrating agents when other means had been denied to SOE. The provision of stores to agents also faced the same problems in the early years and therefore it was natural that a seaborne means of supply should be considered. While trials on the first two Welman one-man submarines got under way in November 1942, tests started on a quarter-scale model of the Welfreighter in Vickers' experimental tank at St Albans. The Welfreighter is often misleadingly referred to as the Welman's big brother. It was certainly not a two- or three-man version of the midget submarine, with a detachable explosive charge on its nose. As the name implied, it was intended for transport and was designed to carry a ton (1,018 kg) of stores in seven drums on the freight deck close in to a secluded enemy-held shore. On arrival at its destination the drums were to be floated off to the reception committee. The prototype Welfreighter was an incredibly ugly vessel with three rectangular ports facing forward in a raised section near the bow and the remainder of the superstructure sloping down to the rear. The design must have been radically altered because photographs of a model show a much more aesthetically pleasing craft with a conning tower amidships. Subsequently the Welfreighter had quite an elegant hull with a sharp bow and a deck which swept downwards and outwards about a third of the way back. The superstructure appeared rather crude, though no doubt functional, and included rising rails which looked as if they were intended to deflect underwater obstacles above the 'bridge' or 'conning tower', but were in fact exhaust pipes from the diesel engine used for propulsion on the surface. Behind this 'bridge' on early models was a large, box-like feature used during surface trials. The vessel was 37 ft 3 in long, 7 ft 1 in wide and had an operating depth of 50 ft. It weighed 13 tons 5 cwt (13,439 kg) and, powered by a 42 hp Gardiner 4LK diesel engine, could reach a surface speed of

6 knots. On the surface the diesel engine drove a single large propeller but, when submerged, NiFe batteries drove two small propellers. The vessel would normally travel low on the surface where it was reasonably out of view of the casual lookout. On approaching an enemy-held shore or in an emergency, however, it was capable of submerging out of sight. Compressed air cylinders for use when under water were strapped in a well behind the conning tower.

By the end of 1942, further research into the Welfreighter had taken place using the quarter-scale model and the surface performance was promising enough for manufacture of the full-scale keel and keel bracings to take place. The experiments continued but revealed problems and the quarter-scale model had to be redesigned, making it highly stable when towed at 10–15 knots. By February 1943, alongside the one-man submarines, production of a full-scale model of the Welfreighter was under way and purchase of the engine, pumps and controls was proceeding. In March Station IX was being pressed with the urgency of the work to develop the submersibles and had half completed the outer skin of the Welfreighter. A month later satisfactory progress had been made, the motor and shaft having been lined up, but another gearbox was awaited from Messrs Vospers. It was to be 8 May 1943 before the first of these vessels was launched for preliminary trials at Staines.[24]

By June 1943 Welfreighter No. 1 had undergone comprehensive trials at Staines from which information had been obtained for the operational prototype. There were some unsatisfactory features such as insufficient freeboard, lack of comfort and failure of the craft to tow with stability at high speed – 7 knots![25] Photographs of the prototype on test remind one of the half-submerged front end of a London bus. Nevertheless, work on the second Welfreighter was proceeding.

At about this time a few of the engineers gathered at the test tank at Station IX to witness the first floating of one of the Welfreighters. As the water bore its whole weight it showed a very marked list. Colin Meek, who was merely an onlooker and had nothing to do with the submersibles, measured the angle with his eye, noted its width and other features and proceeded with some verbal mental arithmetic, at the end of which he put a foot on the craft and said something like: if you put 700 lb (317 kg) of ballast three feet below my foot, it will come upright. The quiet-mannered Meek proved right and, with the rearrangements of various components, this Welfreighter floated upright.

In the spring of 1944 Lord Selborne was becoming increasingly frustrated with the slow progress of the Welfreighter, which he was anxious to use – if not in the Adriatic, then certainly in the Far East. But the Admiralty were not pleased with having to take responsibility for its seaworthiness and for financing it while SOE were the only organisation showing an operational interest in it. The trials of the prototype had not gone smoothly and many alterations had proved necessary.

Handling of the Welfreighter at sea required some care: more, some would say, than should be expected for a vessel which might be operating under hazardous conditions. When on the surface the ballast and side tanks had to be kept full of air by means of the engine exhaust. Having submerged, the required depth was maintained by adjusting the contents of a compensation tank to achieve the desired buoyancy. To surface from a dive the midship side tanks had first to be filled with air from the compressed air bottles situated behind the conning tower, then upon surfacing the forward main ballast tank was blown by a low pressure blower before the engine was started.

Selborne wrote to A.V. Alexander at the Admiralty on 8 May 1944 complaining that while Welfreighter trials had been 'on the whole satisfactory', the Admiralty wanted more and more modifications. The craft with its crew of two was urgently needed to land two agents and a ton of stores on hostile coasts. The Admiralty expressed the deepest reservations about the working conditions for the crew, especially as there was an intention to operate in the tropics. The allowance of air in the vessel was only one-third of that provided for the crew of the Navy's X-Craft.

The Admiralty agreed to the firm of Oppermans embarking on the construction of six Welfreighters for completion by 1 October. There were tentative plans for a further thirty-four after successful trials on the first batch. It was further agreed that SOE should undertake the development of the Mk III from the end of June. With the war now going in the Allies' favour doubts began to be expressed about whether this could be completed and made operational before the end of the Japanese war.

Political, production and engineering problems continued to beset the Welfreighter. Allegations of financial delays were levelled at the SOE Director of Finance who retorted that 'Production for SOE will need careful scrutiny as to real value'. The Admiralty had second thoughts about the ability of Messrs Oppermans to produce six vessels, so placed a contract with them for only a prototype. Then it was discovered that the Gardiner 4LB diesel engines needed alteration before installation in the hull. In September a proposal was tabled to place an order for thirty-four craft, required as soon as possible after 1 October, with the Letchworth, Hertfordshire firm of Shelvoke and Drewry, whose peace-time activity was the production of municipal waste disposal vehicles, one of which was called the 'Freighter'. A security vetting of the firm noted this as a useful cover story!

Delays continued. On 3 November Lord Selborne wrote to Alexander yet again emphasising the urgent need for the Welfreighter and deploring the constant demands by the Admiralty for modifications. 'If these continued they may lead to the eventual abandonment of the project without an alternative craft being available', he said. Three days later Sir Frederic Wake-Walker, Controller of the Navy, wrote to the First Lord refuting Selborne's insinuations and expressing his concern for the safety of the crew and vessel, which he described as dangerous. He had not seen details and had not therefore been able to carry out calculations so, understandably, he was not prepared to accept responsibility for the vessel's seaworthiness. If, however, SOE wanted to accept the Welfreighter, subject to a number of Admiralty provisos on safety, then there was nothing more to be said.[26] No doubt these provisos would have placed severe restrictions on the limits to which the vessel could be used and would not have been welcomed by SOE.

In a further letter on 9 November 1944, the Controller of the Navy again made the point that the Admiralty had been asked to accept responsibility for a craft which they had not designed and which appeared 'extremely dangerous to operate according to our standards'. He illustrated this point by reporting that when the craft had been taken (presumably on tow) to Port Bannatyne in Scotland for diving trials it had developed a 40° list and later in a towing trial a 90° list! During these trials the upper tanks had been allowed to fill with water, thus upsetting the stability of the craft. To overcome this problem, at least in part, midship side tanks were fitted consisting of low-density wood pieces cased in sheet steel. In his view this was an example of the problems being encountered that had given rise to complaints of the Admiralty constantly wanting further modifications. He strongly proposed that there should be definite limitations placed on the operation of the craft.[27]

At this time six Welfreighters were more or less ready and could be sent to the Far East for training purposes. The remaining thirty-four under construction would have to incorporate the latest modifications. One modification which might have resulted from the limited operational experience with the Welman was the fitting on later models of a fixed height, rotatable Barr and Stroud periscope.

It had been intended to use the Welfreighter to deliver stores to the Albanian partisans on the Adriatic coast but the war ended before they could be deployed. Eight were sent to the Far East to be based at Port Moresby with the intention of towing them part-way to the Malay peninsula, where they would supply guerrillas fighting the Japanese but, again, the war ended before they could be put to this task.

The sea trials of Welfreighters took place at Fishguard and they were not without their hazardous, not to say light-hearted, moments. The following is an account of just such an episode discovered among the faded papers of Everett, who was Chairman of the Trials Committee. (See Chapter 10 on the Operational Research and Trials Section.)

A FISHGUARD COMEDY
Cast in order of appearance:-

Archie	Capt J.R. Abbott, RE
Charlie	Lt E.C.Crocker, O.S.S.
Oscar	J.R.B. Oxford, B.A.
The Gallant Maj (R.N?)	Maj J.G. Bedford, RE
The Phoney Doctor	R.C.G. Moggridge, Ph.D.

Archie, in a canoe fitted with the Budig apparatus, had been joy-riding round the harbour on tow from a Freighter; the fun started when the Freighter came in towards the mole to cast off the tow. She sailed in, serene in her confidence to check her way by reversing with her electrics; alas, they failed to function and she proceeded on to the rocks with a sort of majestic inevitability. She finished well and truly stuck with the tide falling fast, and all that was accomplished by turning engines full on was a slight forward movement followed by frantic protests from the propeller hitting rocks.

Archie departed for the escort vessel a mile or so away, flapping his Budig way across the harbour like an exotic water insect. He enters the story no more, except that being an apt student of Trials Committee methods, he managed to break his machine; but lacking the finesse to which the Trials Committee aspires, he broke it in mid-sea, and had a long and weary paddle back to harbour. There, as a revenge on an unkind fate, he left his canoe tied to the rope from the raft in the swell trap. This in a single stroke cut all communication between raft and shore and was the cause of much fury when the Freighter finally reached harbour.

Meanwhile the seaborne members of the Trials Committee, ever chivalrous, had sailed to the assistance of the Freighter in distress. Charlie and Oscar, in a canoe, had been towing a Wheelwright* laden with the Gallant Major and half a ton of lead; casting off their tow, the exuberant pair started to pull a 15-ton Freighter off the rocks by means of their 1½ horse engine. Charlie in the bows was holding the tow-rope. The canoe twisted out of line. The rope engaged on a recessed portion of the Oscar torso, and in a remarkably short space of time the canoe was inverted and two bodies were in the water. The turn over had something of the smoothness and style of a first-class serve at tennis. Charlie struck out for the Freighter, while Oscar climbed on the still inverted canoe and started to roar with laughter. The shore party was already so convulsed that they had to sit down on boulders to give rain (*sic*) to their mirth.

The merriment was increased by the spectacle of the Gallant Major, nobly paddling to the rescue of all and sundry on one heavily laden Wheelwright. He and Oscar then added to the fun and games by trying to right the canoe from the Wheelwright. Every time they got the canoe nearly vertical, it floated away from them, leaving them the alternatives of dropping the thing, or of diving into the widening gap of water between the two craft. Unfortunately for the onlookers, they succeeded in avoiding the second alternative; but during the third attempt the canoe cut a neat 6" slit in one of the Wheelwright's buoyancy chambers, which flattened with a derisive hiss.

The seaborne forces then abandoned the canoe to its fate, merely taking a rope alleged to be attached to the canoe, and throwing it in the general direction of the shore party. The rope, reached with some difficulty, was found to have little apparent connection with the canoe; its end was, as an act of faith, tied

* A type of inflatable rubber dinghy.

round a large boulder in the hope that it would keep the canoe from drifting out to sea.

The next item was the arrival of the escort vessel, making remarkably foul-mouthed and ineffective attempts to throw a line to the Freighter. The rope was finally passed and the escort started to tow the Freighter out in a line perpendicular to her axis; a process which, it seemed, might well pull the craft over on her side. Certainly Oscar was seen to prefer the safety of the much abused Wheelwright, and Charlie even disembarked on to a submerged rock. All went well, however, and the freighter departed to sea at speed – to the consternation of the shore party, who were suffering from the illusion that an unbroken chain of ropes connected the Freighter, Wheelwright and canoe to the above large boulder.

The party then broke up and its constituent sections proceeded homeward by their several methods. The escort took the Wheelwright in tow, and proceeded at speed; whereupon the Wheelwright, no longer in its best condition, stood on its side and deposited nearly all its lead and miscellaneous stores, some of which were much valued, in the harbour.

The engine and canoe were recovered at low tide, being found connected solely by the throttle cable. The closing act of the Comedy occurred later, while packing the Wheelwright for transport home. The craft had evidently encountered the local sewer, and it succeeded in contaminating both the Gallant Major and the Phoney Doctor. They are both large men, and their size was exaggerated by Ursula suits. As a final tableau one had two gigantic backsides striding towards the sea, intent on the removal from their persons of unwanted matter.

> It seemed no small pity that men of such wit
> Should have covered their hands with so very much -it
> Is hard to find words for the muck that are fit
> For use in this bit of a versified skit:
> Suffice it to say that the stuff we'll call 'it'
> Proved uncommon reluctant to flit, or to quit
> The hands of our couple enough to permit
> Them to feel it quite fitting at table to sit.

In an interesting insight into life at Station IX, a former secretary to Maj John Meldrum RE, Agnes Kinnersley, recalled the uncanny silence as a number of employees squeezed into the vessel for a dive in the test tank. But this was not the last of SOE's undersea adventures.

The Under-Water Glider

One of the most confusing names given to an invention emanating from Station IX must have been that of the 'under-water glider'. The first reference found is in an extract from the diary of Maj H.G. Haslar RM in C.E. Lucas Phillips's book *Cockleshell Heroes*.[28] Haslar notes a meeting on 30 July 1942 with 'Prof Newitt re underwater glider' which Lucas Phillips takes to mean the Sleeping Beauty. First references found in the archives were reports which appeared in October 1942 when it was said that tests with a model of the device had continued satisfactorily. In fact, later that year the Admiralty experimental facilities at Haslar were used to test a number of scale models of ISRB submersibles. By December Short Brothers, the aircraft builders, had started constructing the first full-sized model from drawings supplied by SOE. Forecast for the end of February 1943, then the end of March then, with the hull completed, in April, tests were carried out in three modes: with the craft on the surface, with only the pilot's head above water, and totally submerged. A surface speed of 3 knots was obtained with excellent stability and good handling. It was estimated that a range of six miles might be obtained. With only the pilot's head above water the speed dropped to 2½ knots and stability continued to be good provided that the ballast did not shift its position. Full underwater trials were not conducted at this time as the hydroplane area was thought to be too small.[29]

On 29 May 1943 the Under-Water Glider Mk I was satisfactorily tested at Southsea by the Royal Marines Boom Patrol Defence. They conducted trials of paddling, sailing and motoring, launching directly off the beach into the Channel. The prototype of the Mk II was earmarked for further trials.

The Mk I was taken to Staines where on 5 June it was dived to the bottom where the pilot got out, inspected the bottom of the reservoir, returned to the craft and drove around underwater before surfacing to return to the landing stage.[30] Three days later correspondence between DSR and AD/Z refers to 'the submersible glider (Sleeping Beauty)', which would seem to indicate that it was possibly the forerunner of the Sleeping Beauty which came into its own the following year.[31]

Sadly, subsequent records of the craft have not been found. However, the Imperial War Museum photograph HU 56756 reproduced in the plate section, p. 24, which is said to show a development of the Sleeping Beauty at Vickers' testing tank at St Albans, might offer some clues. This craft is clearly much more sophisticated than the 'Sleeping Beauty' shown in photographs elsewhere; its sleek construction is typical of the work turned out by aircraft firms such as Short Bros; and closer inspection of the photograph shows hydroplanes fore and aft. All this leads one to wonder if this is the second prototype of the underwater glider with improved hydroplane area. Furthermore, Appendix III of Admiralty Experiment Works Report No. 117/42 dated 16 December 1942 on investigations for ISRB shows a sketch of a 9 ft long submersible craft with a shape similar to the one in the photograph.[32]

The Motorized Submersible Canoe (MSC) – Sleeping Beauty

A device invented and developed at Stations IX and XII which was primarily for use by Combined Operations Forces such as the Royal Marine Commandos and the forerunner of the Special Boat Squadron (although, like the other submersibles, it appeared in the SOE catalogue) was the Motorized Submersible Canoe. This intriguing craft was conceived in 1942 and became known as the 'Sleeping Beauty' since its inventor, Maj Quentin Reeves, was seen lying in an early mock-up with his eyes closed as if asleep. It was another illustration of the lateral thinking of the SOE scientists and engineers and their keenness to pursue ideas, even on behalf of other agencies. On 27 May 1943 the design produced for the Chief of Combined Operations showed sufficient promise for Prof Newitt to send details to Col R.H. Barry.[33] It was almost 13 feet long and was powered by a 0.5 hp electric motor giving it a range of 12 sea miles at full speed (4.4 knots) or 40 miles at cruising speed (3.1 knots) in still water. On at least some models the forward storage hatch covers, complete with instrument panel carrying three dials, could be hinged open to the left for loading. The instrumentation consisted of a clock, a compass and a depth gauge. It carried an emergency mast and a lug sail of parachute silk. Some examples were fitted with hydroplanes fore and aft. The canoe would normally travel very low and unobtrusively on the surface but in an emergency it was capable of submerging, the pilot wearing the sinisterly named Sladen Clammy Death suit and using an on-board oxygen system. It could carry at least three 20 lb (9 kg) explosive charges or about twelve limpets and was seen as being eminently suitable for attacking shipping in harbour. Consideration of the device dragged on to the end of the year when Station IX agreed to produce three of the six prototypes required by COHQ, subject to the Admiralty financing their manufacture. It was agreed that SOE might possibly have a demand for some.[34] By the second quarter of 1944 production was carried out under Admiralty instructions by the Fairmile Marine Co. Ltd of Cobham, who sub-contracted the hulls to Messrs Briggs of Dagenham, and trials and training were held at Station VIII (Staines reservoir).

Despite its being manufactured by an outside contractor, the Sleeping Beauty absorbed a considerable amount of the capacity of the Contracts (formerly Production) and Quality Control Departments of Station XII during the period Spring 1944 to Summer 1945. Station XII was entirely responsible for the technical control of the contract and for the inspection and testing of the craft. Great pressure had to be exerted to obtain the craft and their 'J' containers, in which they were transported by mine-laying submarines, in time to meet the requirements of Operation Hornbill. At one time, it was necessary to transfer up to fifteen personnel from the Aston House workshops to Cobham to carry out assembly and inspection work. Acquisition of the oxygen breathing apparatus, the underwater clothing and ancillary equipment also fell to Station XII.

In April 1944, in anticipation of successful trials of the craft, plans were made for the employment of Sleeping Beauties against shipping targets in Norwegian waters and preliminary training of a Norwegian instructor was started at Station IX and at Staines reservoir. An extensive operational exercise which included a simulated night attack on a target vessel took place on Loch Corrie near Oban from 8 to 10 May in the presence of a representative from the Admiralty and proved satisfactory. Another Sleeping Beauty was fitted out and delivered in June.[35] But delivery of the craft was slow and it was not until a number were transferred to the operational base at Lunna in Shetland in August that operational training by the Norwegian crews was able to start. The planned attacks against targets in Norway were codenamed Operation Salamander and were severely hampered by SIS being unwilling to remove their objections to operations in areas of interest to them. On 9 September 1944 two MSCs were landed from sub-chasers (the 110-ft-long, fast, long-range American vessels loaned to SOE) in the

Nordfjord area of Norway to attack shipping in Maaloy in Operation Salamander 2. Having accomplished the difficult preparatory part of the exercise and concealed the equipment, the party was given away by a woman herding cattle on the island and were lucky to escape with their lives. They were recovered by a sub-chaser on 18 September 1944.

In Operation Salamander 5 a party sailed on 13 September 1944 in the fishing vessel *Sylvia* with the intention of introducing an MSC into Trondheim carried under the keel of the ship. At the last moment news was received of arrests of key agents in the operation, so attention focused on the secondary target. The planned base proved unsatisfactory so the party moved to a different location, only to find that excessive phosphorescence in the water prevented any chance of an unseen attack. The party was obliged to scuttle the *Sylvia* but they and the MSCs were recovered by a sub-chaser on 30 September 1944.[36]

In the Far East the India Mission in 1944 ordered twelve Chariots, nine Welmans, twenty-four Welfreighters and forty-eight Sleeping Beauties. In the event, only the Sleeping Beauties were delivered – although there is evidence that a few Welmans and Welfreighters were delivered to Australia at some time. In a raid code-named 'Rimau' it was planned to use fifteen of the craft to make simultaneous attacks on six different areas of Singapore harbour. A junk was captured to transport the Sleeping Beauties to the target area but while anchored in Rhio Straits on 10 October it was challenged by a Malay police launch. The leader, Ivan Lyon, a regular army captain in the Gordon Highlanders who had enjoyed great success with Operation Jaywick when his party destroyed or badly damaged seven Japanese ships in Singapore using conventional canoes and limpet mines, thought that they had been unmasked and ordered the party to open fire. With all the police killed the junk and the Sleeping Beauties were scuttled and the party took to their Folboats to escape. They were relentlessly pursued by the Japanese and were all caught or killed. Those who were taken prisoner were executed a month before the end of hostilities.

As mentioned earlier, the Careening Bay Camp near Fremantle had facilities for Sleeping Beauties which included workshops, a degaussing coil and a testing tank. It is interesting to note that the Sleeping Beauty training regime was much the same as at Staines but with more night work, work on anti-submarine netting and with practical experience of attacks on ships, presumably using dummy limpets.

Over 200 Sleeping Beauties were produced before the order was cancelled after VE-day.

The Sleeping Beauties which were delivered to Australia were dumped off Rottnest Island in 1946, although one was restored and passed into the Western Australia Maritime Museum collection.

TEN

OPERATIONAL RESEARCH AND TRIALS

W hen Newitt was appointed Director of Scientific Research in January 1941 he soon recognised the need for an Operational Research and User Trials Section staffed by scientifically or technologically trained people. In the early days of SOE there had been no organised route by which requirements for equipment and weapons were assessed. Nor did items of equipment have to satisfy any formal performance trials before being adopted as an SOE store and issued to Operational Sections. Many of the devices then available had been developed more or less ad hoc by Section D and MI(R) and had in general been tested for basic functioning under laboratory conditions. However, many of the camouflaged explosive and incendiary devices produced by Station XV (see Chapter 7) had not been critically evaluated. They were often unsafe in the hands of untrained operatives and malfunctioned from time to time. Knowledge of the performance of equipment under operational conditions was largely dependent on reports, both written and oral, from agents in the field or during their debriefing. Since few agents were scientifically or technically trained, their reports tended to be coloured by subjective reactions rather than objective analysis. At an early stage in his thinking Newitt had considered the possibility of including a technically trained observer in actual operations but, for a variety of reasons, this was considered inappropriate for SOE activities.

Newitt set up the Operational Research Section to test equipment before issue to agents and check that it was well-designed, safe and effective in use under the severe conditions – cold, wet, darkness and nervous tension – likely to be experienced by operators in the field. At first this was a small, loosely structured section which called on the facilities of Station IX and its staff. It was headed at HQ by Maj Blount and at Station IX by the Trials Officer Maj Holloway, a member of the Research and Development Section. It was his responsibility to arrange 'field and user trials' of devices produced by Stations IX, XII and XV. There was no rigid ruling that all devices should pass through his hands, nor were the trials procedures and their scope and nature clearly defined.

As the number and variety of explosive and incendiary inventions being produced by Stations IX and XV increased rapidly it became clear that these informal arrangements were inadequate to make certain that the devices concerned worked satisfactorily and were safe in use, packing, transport and storage.

In the period up to August 1943 there had been an increasing awareness that the trials which were undertaken at this time were open to criticism. Their validity could be thrown into doubt by the rather haphazard planning and sometimes relaxed atmosphere under which they were conducted.

One example of a trial of this kind that emphasised the need for properly conducted trials was that of Night Glasses. Baker Street sent Station IX samples of lightweight binoculars fitted with plastic lenses which were being considered as possible equipment for agents. A few days later after dinner in the Mess it was suggested that they might be tried out. It was a reasonably dark night with little moon. The glasses were passed round a group recruited in the bar who were invited to try to identify objects around the garden. No records were kept. Someone commented that no comparison was being made with the Army issue field glasses, so a pair of unspecified binoculars was produced and wholly subjective views were expressed as to the relative merits of the two types. The procedure was carried out with a degree of levity, influenced no doubt by the alcohol consumed earlier. It was clear that no reliable assessment could be made on the basis of these completely unscientific and frivolously conducted tests. Everett was present and decided that this was no way to undertake serious testing, and that a proper trial was needed. So he had made in the workshops four circular white discs some 12 in in diameter on which could be placed black segments of various angles and sizes. Individuals were asked to say at what angles the segments were placed. A properly conducted comparative trial was then carried out and a report submitted to HQ. In the event the lightweight binoculars were found to be inferior. But it was the report of this trial, probably as much as anything, that stimulated the realisation at HQ that there was an urgent need for a properly constituted body to oversee User and Field Trials.

The Trials Sub-Section of the Operational Research Section was set up in August 1943 under the general supervision of Lt Col J.W. Munn (DB) at HQ. It functioned under the newly appointed User Trials Committee which was chaired by Everett (DB/T) and included representatives from Trials Sub-Section, Training Section, Research Section together with the R&D officers directly concerned with the device in question, and a quality control representative from Station XII. From May 1944 the Production Section of Station XII were invited to send a representative as and when it was thought necessary.

The function of the Trials Committee which met every two to four weeks was to oversee trials on all stores under consideration for adoption by SOE. Many of its members, being representatives of other Sections, could not devote their whole time to trials. The Trials Sub-Section was therefore created as a full-time nucleus of the Trials Committee, and its duties were solely concerned with organising and carrying out trials and submitting its findings to the Committee. Opportunities were provided for all those concerned with a device to be apprised of problems arising in its use, and to express their views on its suitability for use by SOE.

The members of the Trials Sub-Section were initially drawn from Station IX and consisted of three officers. Its numbers increased to a maximum of six officers and two or three NCOs in mid-1944. From June 1944 Lt Crocker OSS was attached as liaison officer with the American Office of Strategic Services. At the end of January 1944 Everett took on the extra duties of the Air Supply Research Section (see Chapter 11) charged with the development and testing of equipment for air supply. He remained Chairman of the User Trials Committee, but the responsibilities of organising and running trials devolved on Dr Moggridge.

One of the first actions of the User Trials Committee was to ensure that an appropriate and well-defined Operational Requirement (OR) was drawn up for each new device, against which the resultant product could be tested. The conditions under which equipment was used were severe and these had to be taken fully into account, both in drawing up the OR and in the subsequent testing. In general there were three basic criteria which all equipment had to satisfy: it had to work reliably, had to be safe in operation by the agent, and had to be easy to produce.

It was intended that the testing should cover all SOE stores, that is, those which were to be included as standard production items. Acceptance of a device as a store was now dependent on its passing a series of clearly defined trials. Moreover, the section regarded itself as an advocate of the end user, committed to assessing the safety of stores under circumstances resembling as closely as possible those to be found in the theatre where they were to be used. They wished to understand the effect of field conditions on the performance of the items and the ease or difficulty the agent experienced in their use in darkness, secrecy and haste.

When research on a device was complete a functional performance trial was conducted on a laboratory sample, upon which a decision was made by DSR on whether to proceed to further development. This led to the subjection of a production prototype to more extensive user trials under conditions replicating as closely as possible those likely to be encountered in the field. Acceptance trials to ensure that the production models met the specification were done on samples selected at random from the first production batches and were the responsibility of the QC Section at Station XII.

The trials programmes covered a full range of aspects including tests of general handling, general functioning, safety, rough usage, tropical storage, waterproofing, etc. And they had to be as close as possible to reality. Thus in some trials the ease of manipulation when blindfolded, wearing gloves or under severe weather conditions was tested either by members of the Section or by volunteers. Moreover, operations such as the application or release of a safety catch or clip had to be silent, while reflective metal surfaces were to be avoided.

Special attention was paid to the risk of accidental operation of explosive and incendiary devices. The Trials Committee insisted that designs incorporated a positive safety pin and that it was not possible for the device to operate under rough treatment with the pin in position. Designs and prototypes were scrutinised to ensure that it was not possible for the striker to be retained solely by the safety pin, a circumstance which could prove fatal to a user.

Rough handling tests of generally robust devices were usually in excess of what was expected to be experienced in the field. Thus the AC delay Mk II and the air-armed anti-removal fuse withstood repeated drops from 6 ft on to concrete. On the other hand, fragile devices like the Eureka clock, torches and infra-red lamps were excused the rough handling tests. Tropical storage tests were left to Sqn Ldr Ken Callow, who became an expert in this field. Waterproofing tests were a combination of depth and time of immersion and were generally slightly more severe than the worst possible operational conditions.

It was sometimes difficult to be sure that tests reflected accurately the conditions of actual use. For example, a requirement was identified for an adhesive for attaching an explosive charge to a non-magnetic target where the use of limpets or clams was not possible. Station IX devised a formulation which was successful in sticking a dummy Plasticine charge to wood or metal. But it failed completely when tested using an actual charge of plastic explosive. Fortunately, this shortcoming was identified before the adhesive was accepted as a store. One could imagine the frustration of an agent trying vainly to stick a plastic explosive charge to a locomotive or factory machine with an adhesive which had performed quite satisfactorily with Plasticine.

A somewhat more subtle example of the failure of trials to foresee a difference between the conditions of actual use and those under which the trials had taken place arose in the case of railway demolition. Trials of devices and techniques for destroying railway lines were often carried out at Longmoor in the south of England, where the Army had extensive sections of track and samples of rails used in different European countries. A series of trials were conducted during late December 1943 to establish the appropriate quantity and positioning of explosive charges to cut a French railway line. This happened to coincide with a particularly cold spell of weather when the temperature never rose above freezing. The opportunity was taken of making realistic tests on the ease of fixing charges under such severe conditions. When the instructions resulting from these tests were followed after the D-Day landings it was found that the damage was far less than expected, only the vertical web of the rail being knocked out. What had not been anticipated was that at the temperature of the French summer the ductility of steel was far greater than at $-5°C$: the conditions of the trial did not match those in actual use.

Among some of the more extended trials were those on the Spigot Gun (Tree Spigot Mortar). In its earlier forms it had many shortcomings and no less than nineteen trials were conducted on models which had been successively modified to improve its performance and reliability. The bomb was ballistically unstable. In flight the tail precessed around the direction of flight. It might have been expected that the provision of fins on the tail would correct this, but there is no recollection that this was attempted and the model illustrated in the 'Handbook' had no fins. The removable sight was also difficult to use – the operator had to peer down on to the graticule while adjusting the spigot and making sure that the clamp was not disturbed as the sight was removed. Moreover, it was difficult to ensure that when the bomb was placed on the spigot the spigot did not sag, either because the clamp had not been sufficiently tightened or the screw had not been inserted firmly in the trunk of the tree. In addition, care had to be taken to fix the mortar to a large enough tree so that the aim was not affected by the wind. If the target was lower than the mortar position then in early models the bomb tended to slide off the spigot and appropriate clips had to be fitted to prevent this.

Relatively few tests investigated the effectiveness of the bomb. It was presumed that the bomb with its 3 lb (1.36 kg) of explosive would put out of action lightly armoured vehicles, but no full-scale tests on actual targets were done. Later in the war when fighting was expected to take place in built-up areas, tests were called for on the effect of the spigot bomb on buildings. A series of trials were done on derelict buildings in the East End of London. The bomb was capable of punching a 3–4 ft hole in an external brick wall. A much more spectacular result followed from the projection of the bomb through an open window. The explosion in the room lifted the ceiling and pushed all four walls outwards, leading to complete demolition. It was clear that, provided a fixing could be found for the spigot screw, for example in the joints of a wall, this weapon could have a role to play in fighting in built-up areas. Although a considerable number of spigot mortars were despatched to the field, there seem to be no reliable records of their use.

When firearms were the subject of trials, in addition to accuracy, silencing and penetration tests it was necessary to assess the reliability of the ejection of rounds, freedom from 'double taps' and 'runaways' with automatic weapons, and use with all varieties of ammunition likely to be available to the user with the weapon elevated and depressed. Rough usage tests included contamination with mud and sand and all the time the safety catch had to pass its test. There were no facilities for testing under arctic conditions.

It was not always possible to conduct a fully realistic trial. Thus the best that could be done with the assassination weapon, the Sleeve Gun (see Chapter 8), was for Everett to spend time drinking in the bar with the gun concealed in his jacket sleeve without, he was told, attracting any attention. He then slipped the gun into his hand and fired a round into a conveniently placed sandbag. The silencer was so effective that no-one was aware that the sandbag had been 'murdered'!

In the case of incendiary devices it was difficult to interpret the results of trials in terms of damage to an actual target, a fundamental problem which was never satisfactorily solved. One could test the reliability of the initiating system, the local temperature achieved and the duration of the flame. But the spread of the fire on an actual target was subject to many variables which individual agents had to deal with. In an attempt to study the factors determining the rate of spread of fire, Bamford wrote a theoretical paper, backed up by experiments, drawing attention to the fact (now well established) that the rate of spread of a fire is enhanced if inflammable material is disposed in such a way that radiation from one fire centre augments that from nearby centres.

Explosive devices were tested in the explosives pit that had been excavated below the terraces of The Frythe and fitted with a reinforced concrete observation cabin with blast-proof windows. Problems arose when an explosive invention failed to detonate. Should one seek the source of failure by dismantling the device, which might be in a dangerous state? After one or two scary incidents involving exotic products of Station XV, it was decided as routine to place alongside each device a counter-charge which could be detonated electrically if the item under test failed to explode, but it was no longer possible to identify the cause of the failure. At times such as these one wished that the team had included a quarryman!

Trials of the ISRB Anti-Tank Mine which made use of four Tyre-Bursters were carried out at Farnborough, while a few trials were done at Station XII.

Much of the time of the Trials Section was taken up in testing individual items leading to their classification as (A) needing no or only minor modifications to enable production to proceed, or (B) needing more extensive modifications and retesting before being handed over to Station XII. A further group (C) were judged either to be unsuitable for further development or, if improvements were possible, it was unlikely that they could be made in the anticipated time available. A list of the major items tested by the Trials Section in the twelve-month period October 1943 – October 1944 is given in Table 1. Most trials were carried out in a day, although some required much longer. The pressure under which the Trials Section worked may be judged by the fact that in one twelve-month period it dealt with 78 devices, carried out 159 trials (three a week) and issued 118 reports (two a week).

TABLE 1

Devices Tested by Trials Section.[2]
1/10/43 to 1/10/44

A = no or very minor modifications needed.
B = substantial modifications needed.
C = adverse report – reject.

	Number of trials	Result A, B or C.
Anerometer Mk I	2	C
Ascent fuse	1	C
MD1 Altimeter fuse	2	B
Adhesive for demolition work	2	C
Bicycle pump gun	1	C
Block incendiary Mk I	1	B
Block incendiary Mk II	1	A
Blowpipe	1	C
Bags, paper, damp proof	1	A
Berg submersible dinghy	3	B
Cigarettes, incendiary	1	A
Clams, filled pentolite	1	A
US short time clock fuse	0 (Report only)	A
Clock, Eureka	3	B
Container location device (bell)	3	A
Container, K-Type	2	A
Cordtex initiators	2	A
Cavity link charges	2	A
C-type containers, water tight	2	B
Container, acid dropping	1	A
Carbine, M1, silencer	1	A
AC delay Mk II	3	B
Directional incendiary	1	A
Firefly (US)	2	B
Fountain-pen gun	1	C
Face cream	1	A
GP grenade	1	A
MD1 3.7-in gun	1	A
Holdfast, magnetic	2	B
Infra-red homing devices	3	A
Infra-red receiver case	1	A
Jet thermite bomb	1	C
Modified limpet keeper plate	1	B
Plastic limpet (US)	1	A
Limpet coupling device	1	A
Multiple detonators	1	B
Night glasses	1	A

Nitrated paper	1	B
Anti-removal fuse (water armed)	6	B
Anti-removal fuse (air armed)	6	B
Nail firing device	4	B
Oil/nitrate incendiary	3	B
Parachutists over boots	1	B
Photoelectric cell ('Mole' US)	0	C
Photoelectric switch	1	C
Limpet placing rod	1	A
Pull igniter (US)	1	A
French rail charge	1	B
Extending push rod	5	B
Imber rail switch	6	C
Delay setting pressure switch	2	A
Pyrotechnic delay rail switch	2	B
Type 6 pressure switch, modified	1	A
Seaplane reception lamp	2	C
Silenced Sten	5	B
Sleeve gun Mk I	2	A
Sleeve gun Mk II	2	A
Smoke pistol	2	C
Spike attachment	1	A
Standard charge (2 pellet)	2	A
Speed switch (limpet)	3	C
Silenced outboard motor	3	B
Suction adhesion device	2	C
Sleeping Beauty	2	A
Swim fin Mk II	1	A
Sleeping Beauty limpet	1	A
Telephone cable shorting pliers	1	A
Thermite well charge (US)	2	A
Torch, reception, 5-cell	1	A
Tree spigot	19	A
Tree spigot incendiary ammunition	1	B
Dipsanil V	1	A
Welcase	3	B
Welmine	1	C
Welrod 0.32 in	2	B
Welrod 9 mm	2	B
Wirecutters	1	A
Welbum	1	C

78 devices

Accepted (little or no modification)	(A)	47%
Accepted (considerable modification)	(B)	31%
Rejected	(C)	22%

A high proportion of those in category B were subsequently modified and passed later tests.

Besides testing the wide range of devices listed in Table 1, the Trials Section became involved in a number of more extensive programmes. One of these dealt with the location of stores containers in the dark in collaboration with the Air Supply Research Section and is described in Chapter 11.

In the period from October 1944 to the end of the war the work of the Trials Section continued but on a less strenuous basis, since work on the development of new weapons was phased out. A limited amount of work for the Far East was kept on, mainly concerned with the effects of tropical storage on the efficiency and safety of equipment.

As part of the duties of the Trials Section constant liaison with the inventors was essential to ensure that those devising new equipment were well aware of the circumstances in which it would be used. At the same time the Section had to maintain the highest standards of testing and criticism. The essential function of the Section's work was not calculated to endear them to the designers. Very few inventors enjoy seeing their devices dropped on to concrete, a circumstance which required handling with a good deal of tact.

ELEVEN

OPERATIONAL RESEARCH – THE AIR SUPPLY RESEARCH SECTION

The problems of providing Resistance groups with arms and explosives taxed SOE throughout its existence. Although in the early days stores were landed from fishing and other small boats and submarines, this method became too hazardous for routine use in north-west France and along the English Channel and North Sea coasts. Such methods were, moreover, unpopular with the SIS and the Admiralty who guarded jealously their absolute right to control all seaborne operations. Furthermore, the Royal Air Force was reluctant to spare any of its meagre stock of aircraft for the risky task of dropping agents and stores into occupied Europe, activities which they saw as of lower priority than bombing.

It was only later, in the summer of 1941 that, under pressure from Dalton, the RAF Special Duties Flight of three aircraft was increased to a full squadron. Henceforth, for the bulk of arms and equipment reliance had to be placed on supplies dropped from the air.

AIR DROPPING OF STORES

In the early days of SOE, air dropping of stores was on a limited scale because Resistance groups had not yet been organised in sufficient numbers and the RAF was reluctant to divert even a few of its valuable aircraft for use by SOE. A major effort had therefore to be made to persuade the Air Ministry at the highest level of the importance of the Resistance movements and the need to provide air supply support for their activities. The earlier reluctance to support SOE had doubtless been influenced by the opposition of the Chief of the Air Staff, Lord Portal, who, in a frequently quoted letter, wrote on 1 February 1941 expressing strong ethical objection to the methods employed by SOE: 'The dropping of men (*sic*) dressed in civilian clothes for the purpose of attempting to kill members of the opposing forces is not an operation with which the RAF should be associated.'

But this was before Dresden! And it is significant that he ignored (or perhaps did not know of) the vital role played by women in SOE.

A strong argument in support of SOE activities was based on the cost effectiveness of sabotage operations in comparison with large-scale bombing. Because of the inaccuracy of aerial bombardment with its collateral damage and civilian casualties, the huge cost in aircraft and aircrews of a large bombing raid on an industrial target often bore little relationship to the amount of damage it caused to the enemy's war effort. The same damage to industrial targets could in many instances be inflicted for a fraction of the cost by agents on the ground. Placing small amounts of explosive in exactly the right places in a factory could cause a maximum amount of damage with the minimum harm to the local population.

The classic example of this must be the blackmailing of M. Peugeot, whose car factory was being used to manufacture tank parts for the German Army. Two bombing raids in July 1943 had failed to stop work at the factory and had caused many civilian casualties. The 'Stockbroker' circuit in eastern France was organised by the agent 'César', whose real name was Harry Rée (later to become Headmaster of Watford Boys' Grammar School and Professor of Education at York University). He approached M. Peugeot with the proposition: 'Let my agents in to destroy selected machines or I will arrange for the RAF to attack again with the resultant damage to surrounding areas.' M. Peugeot let them in and the factory was put out of action for three months. Moreover, when replacement machinery arrived from Germany the barges carrying it were sunk in the canal. This and many other similar examples in which production was halted for a few weeks or many months are listed by Foot.[1] No doubt they helped to persuade the RAF of the valuable role that SOE could play in appropriate circumstances. Of course, the relatively small number of SOE agents could not have a decisive impact on German industry, but a succession of smaller operations could play a significant role both physically and psychologically. In the end SOE was successful in obtaining RAF support but this was often given grudgingly and at a lower priority.

In January 1943, with increasing use of air supply, the responsibility for 'coordination of test work' and for 'service trials of special equipment for air and sea supply operations' was placed with

AL/C, the Air Liaison Section of SOE. This involved collaboration between Stations IX, XII and the Training Sections and, from August, with the User Trials Committee. Previously air supply liaison had been carried out by Q-Branch of AL Section (Maj R.H. Buxton followed by Maj J.R. Hare).

In the period up to autumn 1943 the methods of air supply in use involved stores packed in one of two types of metal containers, C-type and H-type, which were carried in and released from the bomb racks of bomber aircraft (see later). They had been designed and produced by the Ministry of Aircraft Production (MAP). Alternatively, stores were packed into wire cages (panniers) and dropped from the side door of a Dakota or through the jump hole in the floor of a Halifax.

From time to time Station IX had been called in by AL Section to undertake development work on a number of topics. These included the design of lightweight containers, waterproofing of containers, development of roller conveyors for despatching from aircraft, reception committee lighting, methods of locating containers in the dark and parachute delay opening devices. In addition, Station IX and DSR HQ personnel were in close contact with the Airborne Forces Experimental Establishments (AFEE) at Sherburn-in-Elmet and Amesbury regarding various other development projects.

Drop testing of new stores to determine their suitability for delivery by air and the introduction of new methods of packing were also carried out by AL Section to meet the requirements of Operational Sections. The rapidly increasing operational commitments of AL Section had, by the autumn of 1943, reduced very considerably the time and care that could be given to drop testing and trial packing and to the compilation of reports on these trials.

The problem was eased in October 1943 when further reorganisation led to the transfer of all problems affecting the transport of stores by air to DSR (Newitt) under AD/Z (Davies). This involved the setting up of the Air Supply Research Section (ASR) as part of D/B Section based at Baker Street under Munn, D/B, but calling upon staff from Station IX as and when necessary. It was headed at first by Holloway until his posting to Force 133 in Cairo in January when Everett took over the headship while continuing his chairmanship of the User Trials Committee, retaining his symbol D/BT. Organisation of User Trials was later passed to Dr R. Moggridge while Everett concentrated on expanding the Air Supply Research Section.[2]

Increasingly, bureaucracy had to be negotiated or short-circuited to avoid the work of the ASR Section being held up. The responsibilities of ASR Section and the procedures to be followed were set out in a formal routine order on 15 November. Under the new arrangements, all requirements for research and for the adoption of items as SOE stores were to be put up to DSR in the first instance. D/B Section was made responsible for field, user and acceptance trials and for liaison with MAP, the Royal Aircraft Establishment (RAE) and Airborne Forces on all questions of air transport, except those which were purely RAF matters. E Section (i.e. Station XII), in conjunction with AL/C, was made primarily responsible for liaison with MAP on questions of supply of air transport equipment. The official channel of approach to Station 61, the Special Parachute Section at Henlow and RAF Operational Squadrons working for SOE was via AL. SOE requirements for development work to be carried out by the Air Ministry were to be considered first by D/Plans, be passed to DSR, then to K/AIR.P who would submit them to the Air Ministry. All applications for drop testing of new or existing stores were to be made in the first place to D/B who was to arrange for such tests to be carried out by the most convenient aircraft available. Dropping and other trials for DSR should be carried out by Station 61 and/or by operational squadrons, arranged by AL. However tedious these routes proved to be, compliance with them had to be endured.

The ongoing developments previously under AL were transferred to ASR. Work on these and other developments are discussed in the following sections.

Information on the use of air supply by SOE was recorded in a series of files under the general heading 'Planning and Supply of Air Dropping Equipment'. Unfortunately, most of these are missing. There is no trace of the fifty or so files with the archive reference numbers 250/2.1 to 250/2.54. However, the Bimonthly Progress Reports of the ASR Section from April 1944 to May 1945 have been traced, together with the 'History of the Air Supply Research Section', written by Everett in August 1945.

To aid in operational planning the ASR Section compiled the 'ISRB Air Supply Handbook' which included tables of wind drift, drop height and wind speed as well as data on parachutes and size of bomb racks in various aircraft. Although produced in limited numbers this was said to have been found of great assistance, not only to SOE but also to the Army Airborne Transport Development Centre. Copies of this handbook were reputed to have been sent to the War Office but none has been found.

General Technical Considerations

The basic requirements of air supply were that stores had to arrive in enemy-occupied territory undamaged and delivered into the right hands at the right time. Since supply operations usually took place at night and the stores included fragile items such as radio sets and the accumulators to power them, the problems were considerable.

The successful outcome of an airdrop depended first on the location and identification of the dropping zone (DZ) and then on the accurate dropping of the stores. Once the DZ had been located the pilot had to fly in at a predetermined height and speed and on a course taking account of wind speed and direction, and the containers had to be released at the appropriate moment over the DZ. Since most operations were carried out in moonlight, the skills demanded of the aircrew were considerable: it was far too easy to run in too low so that the parachutes did not fully develop before the load struck the ground, or to be over-cautious and drop from too great a height, leading to excessive drift in the wind. The requirements were much more stringent if agents were to be dropped at the same time. The design of equipment for such operations involved making a compromise between the parachute size, the weight of the full container and the amount and nature of the packing material. The objective had to be that the container spent as little time as possible in the air, commensurate with an impact velocity which did not damage the contents. The impact speed and hence the amount of packing material required could be reduced by increasing the size of the parachute. But this meant that the loads remained for a longer time in the air, so increasing the wind drift. For a run-in at a height of 500 ft the load was in the air for less than half a minute. Even with a wind speed of 10 mph this meant a drift of 150 yd from the point of release. With container despatches at intervals of half a second, the length of a stick of ten containers dropped from an aircraft flying at 130 mph would be some 300 yd. Moreover, if a number of containers and packages of different weights were despatched on the same run, then to minimise scatter on the ground the parachutes had to be chosen such that the rates of descent of the different loads were roughly equal.

The above considerations determined the choice of the appropriate combination of parachute size, weight of load and packaging requirement for a given operation; in the early days these were reached by trial and error. An explanation of the optimisation of parachute sizes is given in Appendix F.

Choice of Dropping Zones (DZ) and Reception Committee (RC) Procedures

In the early days before organised Resistance groups had been established, agents with W/T sets were dropped 'blind' into areas where there was reason to believe that they could make contact with previously identified friendly nationals who would work with them to set up a local organisation. But time and time again, as records confirm, such drops were made far away from the intended location – sometimes as much as 50 km (32 miles) distant. And often the agents were quickly arrested. It was not until agents with W/T operators were able to make contact with London that Reception Committees at a precisely defined DZ could be arranged.

In choosing a DZ certain minimum requirements had to be satisfied. It was recommended that to allow for variable wind drift, the DZ should be at least 600–800 yards square and preferably in level country. It had to be free from trees and other obstacles for some 200 yards outside its perimeter. It was particularly important that the aircrew were well briefed as to useful landmarks to enable them to come within a few kilometres of the DZ. The choice of dropping point would be influenced not only by the technical requirements but also by operational factors such as the location of enemy units, the availability of members of the reception committee, and of means of transport to accessible concealment or storage sites.

Signalling Devices

Supply operations were normally limited to a period of a week or so on either side of the full moon. The aircrew had therefore to navigate (as in a bombing raid) by dead reckoning backed up by identification of landmarks such as rivers and railways. When the reception committee heard the sound of an approaching aircraft visual contact by means of lights or fires had to be established, and a prearranged procedure followed for the mutual recognition and clear identification of the DZ and aircraft. The detailed methods depended on local circumstances. In remote areas such as the Balkans, where the enemy presence was thinly spread, it was possible to use fires to attract the attention of the aircraft. They were not appropriate in closer country where, even if not observed by the enemy at the time, they left tell-tale evidence of a supply drop. An alternative sometimes recommended where fuel for a fire was not available was to fill a large tin, such as a petrol can cut in half, with soil or sand, wet it thoroughly with petrol or paraffin and set it alight. This had the advantage that it could be extinguished quickly and carried away in the case of emergency. In some cases, especially in the Far East later in the war, signal flares were used. However, in most of Europe more clandestine methods had to be employed.

Light signals to aircraft had to be capable of being seen by aircrew on the lookout but not so obvious that they would attract unwelcome attention on the ground. The more sophisticated signalling lamps such as the Aldis and the Admiralty Automatic Morse Signalling Lamp were not readily available and were in any case somewhat bulky and not easily concealed. Moreover, they were too bright for clandestine use. Reliance had therefore to be placed on simple domestic torches or bicycle lamps which might be available locally or could be dropped from the air. The standard issue SOE torches were modified Ever Ready 2-cell torches of somewhat flimsy construction. The dry cells available at that time were of the now obsolete zinc/carbon variety of relatively low capacity. They were optimistically said to have a lifetime in continuous use of between three and five hours, and a relatively short shelf life. The switches on the torches tended to corrode and were not waterproof. It was soon realised that these torches were not really robust enough for satisfactory use in the field. Several attempts were made to design a waterproof torch which could withstand immersion in two feet of water (e.g. in a ditch). Only moderate success was achieved and difficulty was found in waterproofing the switch – something that would present no problems with today's materials. None was put into production and later a US torch with improved but not perfect properties was adopted. Although the SOE catalogue describes a 'French Torch' as an exact replica of a French make, these were never submitted to a user trial so their performance is not known.

The SOE torches were supplied with a set of coloured filters: red, amber, green and blue to assist in the identification of DZs. Over a period of a few months several trial/training operations were carried out to test the various methods of locating and identifying DZs. In a trial on 5 August 1943, a clear night four days after the full moon, an aircraft flying at 1000 feet was able to pick out visual signals at a range of five miles. Green and red filters were most easily seen while orange and amber were less easily distinguished. These and other trials in conjunction with the Training Sections also compared alternative layouts of reception torches at the DZ.

As time passed more sophisticated methods were being evolved. The Eureka/Rebecca system developed by the Telecommunications Research Establishment (TRE) involved a transmitter (Rebecca) in the aircraft which was tuned to respond to Eureka on the ground at the DZ. This enabled the aircraft to be guided to within a reasonable distance of the DZ when visual contact using torches could be made. There is evidence that this system, although used successfully by Airborne Forces, was less popular with SOE. Among other things, Eureka was heavy, weighing nearly 1 cwt (51 kg), and was difficult to conceal and transport, although the Camouflage Section devised several ways of disguising it.

Meanwhile, as described in Chapter 12, the Radio Communications Division at Station IX had taken up the idea dating from 1940 of developing a short wave radio telephone – the S-phone. This enabled the aircraft not only to home in on the ground station (carried on a pack by the operator), but also to pass verbal messages between them. Despite early technical problems, the S-phone proved to be of immense value in raising the efficiency of air-dropping operations. Whereas in the early days a major cause of failure of an operation was the inability of the aircraft to locate the DZ, this was greatly reduced when homing devices were used. Further developments of the Eureka/Rebecca system and trials of alternative radio beacons and similar American systems were being planned when the war ended. The use of infra-red devices for air/ground signalling were also under active discussion, although nothing more than a few preliminary experiments had been done at Station IX.

As the opportunities for daylight operations increased (especially by the US Air Force), consideration was given to alternative methods of organising daylight receptions. It was found that the American fluorescent ground markers were considerably more effective than the British versions. An alternative method of attracting the attention of aircraft (originally for Air/Sea Rescue use) was the employment of mirror devices, the reference beam of which could be aimed accurately. Two very efficient models were tested. Standard Army smoke generators were found to be useful in indicating wind direction in daylight drops.

PARACHUTES

The development and testing of personal parachutes was in the hands of MAP, SOE having no direct involvement. The standard British parachute (at first the type A, later the type X) was made of silk, 28 ft in diameter, and was designed to give a rate of descent for an average person of around 17 ft per second. SOE as users had good reason to be especially concerned with their reliability. Work was proceeding in the spring of 1943 on improving the reliability of the parachutes, some of which had failed to develop properly. The experimental A-type rig had been abandoned and investigations into the tangling and twisting accidents with the X-type packs had reduced the failure rate which in training had been about one in five thousand drops. Nevertheless, failure of the personal parachute to open was a rare occurrence and often the reason could be identified with causes unrelated to the parachute itself. No overall figures are available for European operations but the French Sections had a total of six fatal parachute casualties – none of which was during training. One in July 1942 resulted from a bad landing at night on rough ground, at least one in January 1944 from being dropped from too low a height, and one from failure to hook up the static line properly. There were only two cases in which it was suspected that the cause was a faulty parachute but a reliable record of the overall failure rate, attributable to equipment failure, has not been found. Several serious but non-fatal accidents were attributed to dropping from too low a height, caused by either poor weather or pilot error.

Supply Dropping Parachutes

Official tests of supply dropping parachutes for MAP were the responsibility of the RAE who arranged for them to be carried out by Sqn Ldr Bunn at Henlow and by AFEE. The parachutes used by SOE for supply dropping were standard cotton C-type of diameter 28 ft and later 22 ft. In general SOE was not directly involved although close liaison was maintained with Sqn Ldr Bunn. In dropping tests which took place at Henlow in June 1943 a comparison was made between cotton and Celanese canopies and the RAE cotton type showed marked superiority.

Drops were usually made from a height of only a few hundred feet to improve the accuracy of targeting the drop zone. This left little time for a parachute to develop and if it encountered adverse conditions in the aircraft's slipstream, a hesitation of only a couple of seconds might mean the difference between the successful delivery of much needed stores and the salvaging of severely damaged goods from a wrecked container. Attention turned to the reliability of parachutes after storage, it being known that a canopy stored in a damp atmosphere, perhaps with the weight of others on top of it, was likely to develop more slowly than a dry, freshly packed one. Thus it was preferable for parachutes to be hung in sheds until required for use. The problem was more acute in tropical climates and considerable effort was made to design a waterproof package for parachutes.

There are no reliable statistics on the parachute failures in supply dropping in Europe, although ASR Section prepared an analysis of failures reported from the field in the last six months of 1944. More detailed records were kept for North African operations, but these do not appear to have been preserved. However, it was claimed by one agent operating out of Massingham, North Africa, that in one area one fifth of the supplies were lost either because the parachute failed or the container burst open in mid-air or on impact. Other isolated examples in which containers burst on impact and the contents caught fire were reported from time to time by British agents. Similarly, the supply dropping in support of the 14th Army in Burma in April 1945 was plagued by parachute failures. On one major operation, among 131 drops there were 50 parachute failures. In many cases, as recounted in Chapter 16, the cause could be traced to failure of those responsible for loading containers onto the aircraft, or to damaged or badly packed parachutes. Rigorous checks on a subsequent operation reduced the failure rate to zero.

Parachutes for High Speed Dropping

The standard speed for dropping loads of up to 300 lb (136 kg) was 130 mph. To enable higher speeds to be used RAE designed a parachute which tests at AFEE showed could be dropped at 250 mph with a load of 350 lb (158 kg), while a load of 500 lb (227 kg) could be dropped at 200 mph. This new parachute, designated Type R, was of shaped gore design with a flying diameter of about 20 ft. (The gore is the section of canopy fabric between rigging lines running from the peripheral hem to the crown.) The rate of descent was practically the same as that of a 28 ft flat chute with a comparable load. This promised SOE the possibility of raising the weight of the standard container to 500 lb (227 kg), subject to packing and dropping trials. Production of this parachute commenced in February 1945 with the expectation of 10,000 being available in two months. However, ASR Section plans to test the new parachute with SOE operational loads were suspended pending the decision whether to deploy this parachute in Europe and in the Far East.

The American G1 Parachute

Problems arose when supplies of British parachutes became critical and American G1 cargo dropping parachutes became available. These differed from British parachutes in that while the British chutes were made of cotton, the US types were of a rather closely woven viscose. The ASR Section was called upon to check these parachutes with SOE containers under SOE dropping conditions. The first tests were carried out at Henlow in May 1944 when four fully loaded containers were dropped from a Whitley aircraft flying at 135 mph. The result was alarming. Two parachutes failed and one container filled with incendiaries caught fire on impact and burned furiously. The firework display was brought under control by the Station Fire Brigade. This was the first trial to be recorded on cine film and demonstrated the value of having a proper record of trials. On examination of the chute it was found that the rigging lines and lift webs were badly torn. The consequent doubts about the suitability of the G1 chute for SOE operations were strenuously opposed by the Americans and led to some strongly worded exchanges. Further trials were carried out in June by both ASR Section and AFDC. In the ASR trials, out of a total of nine drops at 150 mph and with loads of 300 lb (136 kg) two parachutes failed completely while three parachutes were damaged leading to substantial damage to the containers. A failure rate of five out of nine was regarded as unacceptable. Meanwhile, AFDC dropped 48 panniers of 330 lb (150 kg) at the lower speed of 120 mph and had only one failure. The interim conclusion was that these parachutes should be dropped at a maximum speed of 140 mph and loading of 300 lb (136 kg). This was endorsed in September by MAP who, however, reduced the maximum speed to 135 mph. The British results were not accepted by the Americans who proceeded to arrange joint trials with ASR Section. In these the drops were from B24 Liberator bombers and were covered by air-to-air cine film. To ASR Section's consternation the Americans were so confident of their ability to drop accurately that they proposed to drop into the courtyard of historic Howbury House east of Bedford which they had requisitioned; but under pressure from the ASR Section they were persuaded to drop into the adjacent fields. The written report of these trials has not been found and the conditions were not recorded. However, the cine film which has survived confirms that of some dozen drops only one parachute appears to have 'candled'. It was found that for use with British containers some modifications were necessary to enable the chutes to be used with the British static line. ASR Section issued detailed instructions for these modifications and its assembly in November and this was eventually cleared by the Air Ministry in February 1945. Then a few weeks later, for reasons unknown, the Air Ministry ruled that this parachute should not be used with British containers. The sheer number of parachutes required was astonishing. Operations envisaged required a total of 212,000 parachutes between January and April 1944 alone, and up to the end of June a staggering 1,220,000 parachutes were called for. This number would certainly have included those for the three-man Jedburgh teams dropped just after D-Day and for the supply drops to the Maquis after the invasion. Whether they also catered for the Airborne Forces involved in the D-Day drops into France is not clear. This quantity could not be met by ordinary means, even with the help of a parachute factory set up in Cairo to make use of locally produced cotton and of the American manufacturing facilities. To relieve the situation, at least as far as the Far Eastern operations were concerned, hundreds of sewing machines, benches and treadle units were shipped out to India for local labour to manufacture parachutes in hastily created workshops.

CONTAINERS AND PANNIERS

Stores containers and panniers had to meet several criteria. Containers had to be designed to fit into the bomb bay of the aircraft and to be sufficiently robust to withstand the stresses imposed by aircraft manoeuvres and from the impact with the ground. They had to house a parachute at one end and an impact absorbing device at the other. Panniers had to be of a size, shape and weight to enable them to be manhandled around inside the aircraft to the jump hole and their contents so packed as to protect them from impact. During flight they had to be securely anchored to the airframe. Both containers and panniers had to be easily opened and yet secure enough to withstand

PEOPLE AND PLACES

The Frythe at Welwyn in Hertfordshire became the centre of SOE's research and development activity and was known as Station IX.
Author's collection

Prof. D.M. Newitt, FRS, Director of Scientific Research in SOE. *Godfrey Argent Studio, London*

Aston House near Stevenage in Hertfordshire was the officers' mess of Station XII, the production and despatch arm of SOE's R&D effort. *By permission of Des Turner's Aston Village History Collection Trust*

The principal site of the Camouflage Section was at Station XV, the Thatched Barn road-house on the Barnet bypass. *Hertsmere Borough Council*

Bride Hall near Ayot St Lawrence in Hertfordshire. Said to have been given by a wealthy mariner to his daughter as a wedding gift, it became SOE's Station VI and housed the Arms Section. *Author's collection*

A Second World War notice still displayed in one of the Bride Hall barns. *Author's collection*

One of several magnificent old barns at Bride Hall. They housed small-arms workshops, stores and accommodation for armourers. The wartime petrol pump (minus its glass globe) can be seen to the left of the open doors. *Author's collection*

Lt Col John Dolphin, Commandant of Station IX. *By permission of Elizabeth Howard-Turner*

Maj Quentin Reeves and Eric Norman of Engineering Section. *By permission of Elizabeth Howard-Turner*

Research and Development Organisation in the Special Operations Executive.

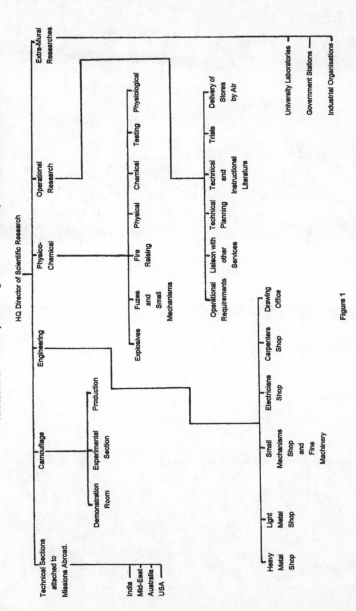

Figure 1

Research and Development Organisation in the Special Operations Executive. *Public Record Office file HS7/27*

Inside a chemical laboratory at Station IX. *By permission of Elizabeth Howard-Turner*

Secretary Heather McReady poses before a danger notice at Station IX. *By permission of Elizabeth Howard-Turner*

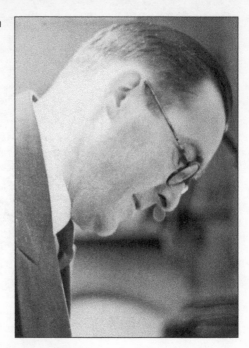

Eric Porteous, Engineering Section draughtsman. *By permission of Elizabeth Howard-Turner*

Major John Meldrum RE of the Engineering Section at Station IX. *By permission of Elizabeth Howard-Turner*

Inside the Thermostat Laboratory where time delays were tested. *By permission of Elizabeth Howard-Turner*

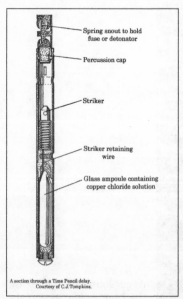

Spring snout to hold
fuse or detonator

Percussion cap

Striker

Striker retaining
wire

Glass ampoule containing
copper chloride solution

A section through a Time Pencil delay.
Courtesy of C.J.Tompkins.

A section through a Time Pencil delay. *C.J. Tompkins*

The Time Pencil, the delay device most commonly used by SOE. *Author's collection*

COMMUNICATIONS

The Type 3 Mk I suitcase set was SOE's first attempt to construct its own wireless. It used obsolete bulky components and weighed 42 lb (19 kg). Its range was 500 miles. *Author's photograph by permission of Royal Signals Museum*

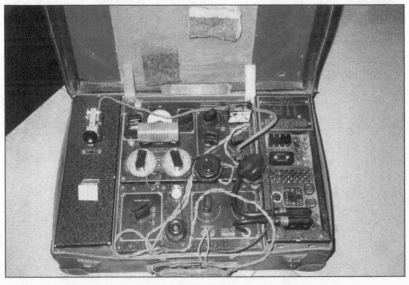

One of the most highly perfected wireless sets made by SOE was the B2 suitcase transceiver made in 1943. It weighed 32 lb (14.5 kg). *Author's photograph by permission of Royal Signals Museum*

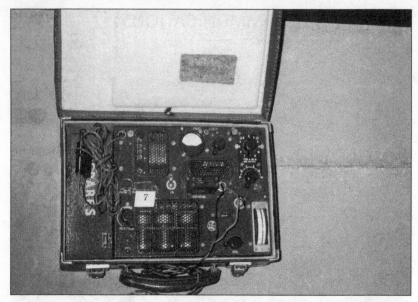

The Type A Mk III suitcase transceiver was the smallest produced during the Second World War. Almost all components were miniaturised giving it a total weight of only 9 lb (4 kg). Its range was in excess of 500 miles. *Author's photograph by permission of Royal Signals Museum*

The MCR 1 receiver was delivered in 2-lb biscuit tins and hence was referred to in France as *Le recepteur biscuit*. Ten thousand were built during the war. *Author's photograph by permission of Royal Signals Museum*

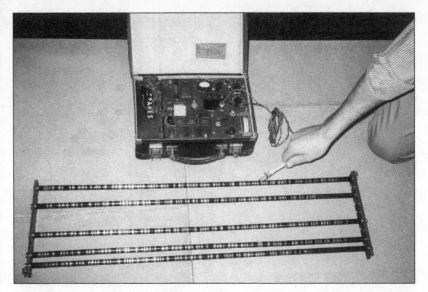

A development towards the rapid transmission of morse messages was this 'Squirt Bar'. The message was set by the arrangement of wide and narrow conducting 'washers' separated by insulators. A contact was stroked down the rods, passing impulses via a Type A Mk III suitcase radio. SOE never used this method in the field, a satisfactory means of 'expanding' the received transmission not being available. *Author's photograph by permission of Royal Signals Museum*

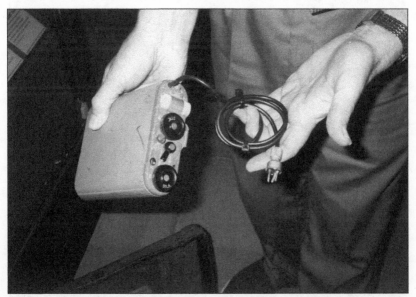

The 51/1 could be carried in the pocket and had a range of about 600 miles. *Author's photograph by permission of Royal Signals Museum*

A conventional bicycle fitted with a generator for charging wireless batteries.
IWM HU56739

A Welbike was fitted with a generator to enable it to charge wireless batteries but its noise and the scarcity of petrol prevented its use in practice. *IWM HU56740*

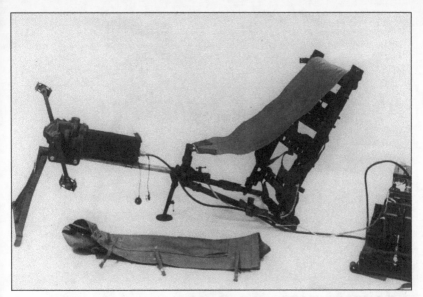

The Type 52/1 pedal-powered wireless battery charger offered a degree of comfort for the operator. *IWM HU56747*

SOE developed a thermal battery charger but no details of its performance have been found. *IWM HU 56746*

A collapsible pedal charger for wireless batteries. This proved difficult to 'ride' without handlebars. *IWM HU56744*

The Welbike with a towing attachment for a mobile delivery container. *DERA*

Sender of message	Forwarding carrier pigeon post	Pigeon reception point	Person receiving message
from _____	at _____ from _____	at _____ from _____	at _____
Pigeon message number	Confirmation of arrival	In the case of message in transit	Useful additions (sketch maps, etc)
at _____ in _____	at _____	at _____ in _____ from _____ to _____	

Absender des Spruches:	Befördernde Brieftaubenstelle:	Empfangende Brieftaubenstelle:	Empfänger des Spruches:
ab:	an: ab:	an: ab:	an:
Taubenspruch Nr. _____ an: _____	Ankunftbestätigung am: _____ in: _____	Bei Durchgangssprüchen an: _____ in: _____ ab: _____ nach: _____	Dienstliche Zusätze (Anlagen usw.)

Hier abtrennen!

Eingetroffen ist dort. Spruch Nr. _____	Es fehlt noch dort. Spruch Nr. _____	Empfangsbestätigung fehlt über hiesigen Spruch Nr. _____	Zahl und Fußringnummern der aufgelassenen Tauben:

S & Z 42

Detach here

Following message arrived	Following message still missing	Confirmation of receipt lacking for message	Quantity and footring numbers of pigeons released
No. _____	No. _____	No. _____	

Pigeon post message form used in Operation *Periwig*.

The translation of this form was kindly made by Lady Cicely Mayhew who translated intercepted German wireless transmissions at Bletchley Park during the War.

Pigeon post message form used in Operation Periwig. The translation of this form was kindly made by Lady Cicely Mayhew who translated intercepted German wireless transmissions at Bletchley Park during the war. *Author's Collection*

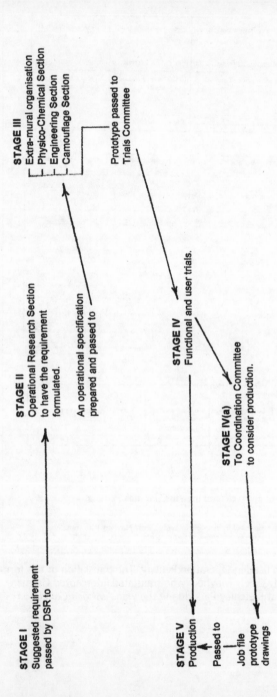

STAGE I
Suggested requirement passed by DSR to

STAGE II
Operational Research Section to have the requirement formulated.

An operational specification prepared and passed to

STAGE III
Extra-mural organisation
Physico-Chemical Section
Engineering Section
Camouflage Section

Prototype passed to Trials Committee

STAGE IV
Functional and user trials.

STAGE IV(a)
To Coordination Committee to consider production.

STAGE V
Production

Passed to
Job file
prototype
drawings

Figure 2

Routing of a suggestion through R&D Section. *Public Record Office file HS7/27*

Courtesy Public Record Office file HS7/27

SUBMERSIBLES

This early Welman is on the ramp from which it was launched at Staines reservoir. At this stage provision of side tanks and attachment for the explosive charge to the bow had not been developed. Note the dolphin emblem on the conning tower. *IWM HU56758*

This photograph of a later Welman at Station IX shows the rudder/hydroplane assembly behind the propeller. *IWM HU56757*

This later Welman has side tanks and a blunter bow to which the warhead was attached by means of the screw in its centre. *IWM HU56763*

Welman with explosive charge alongside a jetty. The magnets for attaching the charge to the target can be seen. *Private collection*

The prototype Welfreighter was an ugly vessel. Here it rests on its launching cradle at Staines reservoir. *IWM HU56786*

Welfreighter No. 4 in Australia. This has been fitted with mid-ship side tanks as a compromise solution to the stability problems. *Private collection*

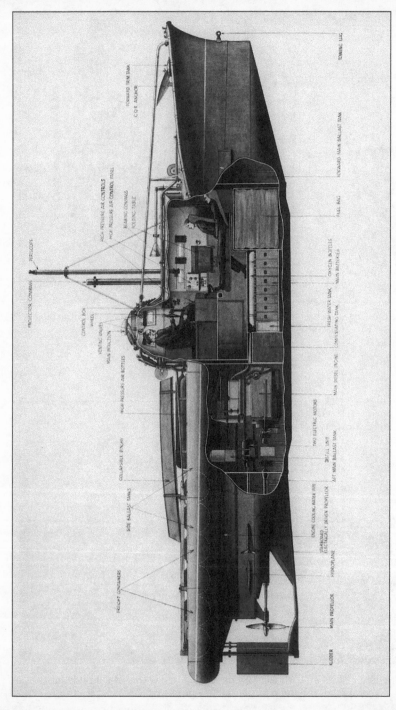

PERISCOPE

PERISCOPE COAMING

HIGH PRESSURE AIR CONTROLS

HIGH PRESSURE AIR CONTROL PANEL

BEARING COAMINGS

FOLDING MAST

FORWARD TRIM TANK

CQR ANCHOR

TOWING EYE

FORWARD MAIN BALLAST TANK

FUEL BAG

OXYGEN BOTTLES

MAIN BATTERIES

FRESH WATER TANK

COMPENSATING TANK

MAIN DIESEL ENGINE

CONTROL BOX

WHEEL

VENTING VALVES

MAIN INDUCTION

HIGH PRESSURE AIR BOTTLES

COLLAPSIBLE DINGHY

SIDE BALLAST TANKS

ENGINE COOLING WATER PIPE

STARBOARD ELECTRICALLY DRIVEN PROPELLOR

TWO ELECTRIC MOTORS

DRILL UNIT

AFT MAIN BALLAST TANK

FREIGHT CONTAINERS

MAIN PROPELLOR

HYDROPLANE

RUDDER

A cutaway drawing of the Welfreighter. *Private collection*

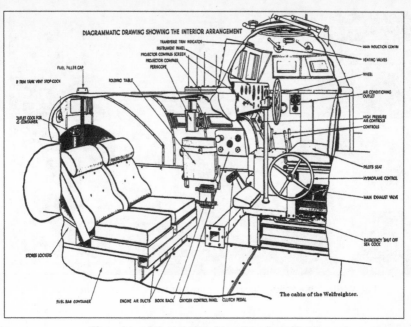

DIAGRAMMATIC DRAWING SHOWING THE INTERIOR ARRANGEMENT

TRANSVERSE TRIM INDICATOR
INSTRUMENT PANEL
PROJECTOR COMPASS SCREEN
PROJECTOR COMPASS
PERISCOPE

MAIN INDUCTION CONTROL
VENTING VALVES
WHEEL
AIR CONDITIONING OUTLET
HIGH PRESSURE AIR CONTROLS
CONTROLS

FUEL FILLER CAP
D TRIM TANK VENT STOP-COCK
FOLDING TABLE

OUTLET COCK FOR Z CONTAINER

PILOTS SEAT
HYDROPLANE CONTROL
MAIN EXHAUST VALVE

STORES LOCKERS

EMERGENCY SHUT OFF SEA COCK

FUEL BAG CONTAINER   ENGINE AIR DUCTS   BOOK RACK   OXYGEN CONTROL PANEL   CLUTCH PEDAL

The cabin of the Welfreighter.

The cabin of the Welfreighter. *Private collection*

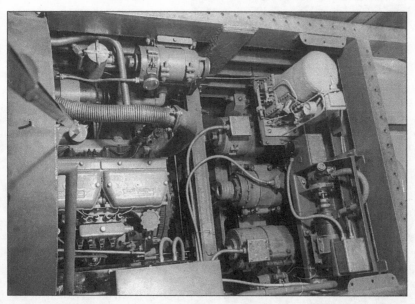

A view of the engine compartment of the Welfreighter. Top right is the water still.
Below are two electric motors for submerged running; between them is the
generator for power and battery charging. At the left is the Gardiner diesel engine.
Private collection

The Welfreighter pilot's view of his instruments. *Private collection*

Looking down on a Welfreighter showing the drums of stores. Sub Lt Ian Ruthven is the officer at the bow. *Courtesy Prof D.W.J. Cruickshank FRS*

Meldrum in the stern of the rowing boat and Cruickshank at the bow conducting stability and torque tests on a Welfreighter at Fishguard following capsizes during towing trials on the Clyde. *Private collection*

D.W.J. Cruickshank taking part in Welfreighter speed trials in Fishguard harbour. *Private collection*

A motorised submersible canoe (MSC), known as a 'Sleeping Beauty', on test at the tank at Station IX. The operator's personal equipment is strapped to the forward casing. *IWM HU56775*

Said to be a development of the 'Sleeping Beauty' at the Vickers testing tank at St Albans, but could this be the 'Underwater Glider'? Note the streamlined construction and the fore and aft hydroplanes. *IWM HU56756*

PONS AND DEVICES

The beautifully made but somewhat unconventional Norm Gun was designed by Eric Norman and was the forerunner of the Welgun. *MoD Pattern Room*

The Welgun ready for firing. *MoD Pattern Room*

The stock of the Welgun folded along the top of the barrel. *MoD Pattern Room*

The 9 mm calibre Welrod (top) and the .32-in version, highly efficient, single-shot, silenced weapons. *MoD Pattern Room*

The silencer for the Sten gun (this version with a wooden stock) was developed at Station IX. *MoD Pattern Room*

Eric Norman probably modified this American 'Woodsman' .22-in pistol into a machine-pistol. It fired so rapidly that it exhausted the magazine too quickly. *MoD Pattern Room*

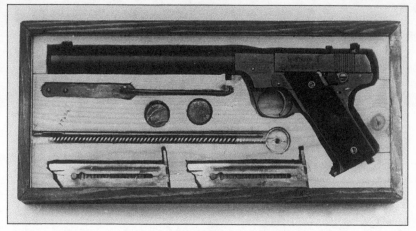

Station IX developed an effective silencer for the American Hi-Standard automatic pistol. *IWM HU56778*

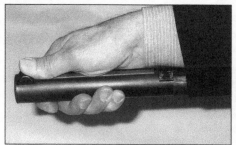

How the Sleeve Gun was fired.
MoD Pattern Room

This flat hand-grenade was developed by Col H.H. King. It did not reach production because it tended to burst rather than fragment when detonated.
MoD Pattern Room

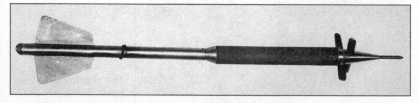

Station IX, in collaboration with Brock's Fireworks at Hemel Hempstead, developed this incendiary arrow which was recovered from The Frythe after the war. It is almost identical to one used by the OSS. *MoD Pattern Room*

The plastic lens binoculars whose testing features in Chapter 10. *Author's collection*

The prototype waterproof torch designed and made at Station IX never overcame leakage problems around the switch. *Author's collection*

The plastic lens binoculars were provided in a folding imitation leather case. *Author's collection*

A display model of the Imber Railway Switch with the sides made of Perspex to reveal the workings. *By permission of David Wright, NRM*

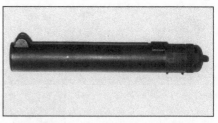

The Sleeve Gun, a silenced .32-in one-shot weapon for concealment prior to use. *Author's collection*

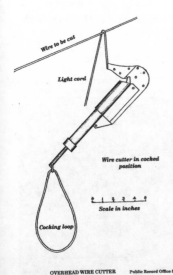

Wire to be cut

Light cord

Wire cutter in cocked position

Cocking loop

Scale in inches

OVERHEAD WIRE CUTTER   Public Record Office file HS7/47

Overhead wire cutter. *Public Record Office file HS7/47*

AIR SUPPLY

Station IX men board a Halifax at Hatfield for free drop trials at Fishguard. Left to right: Cpl Turner, -?-, -?-, Lt Bob Daley (OSS), Maj D. Everett, Stuart Edmondson. *Courtesy Prof D.H. Everett FRS*

'C' type supply containers. *Courtesy Prof D.H. Everett FRS*

These trials of free-dropped stores took place on the rocky foreshore at Fishguard. *Courtesy Prof D.H. Everett FRS*

Linked sacks falling from a Halifax during free dropping trials. *Courtesy Prof D.H. Everett FRS*

A roller conveyor for air supply drops fitted inside a Halifax. Beyond the jump hole alongside the Elsan chemical toilet can be seen a supply pannier with parachute.
Courtesy Prof D.H. Everett FRS

Human Pick-up. A dummy awaits the arrival of the aircraft to snatch it off the ground. *Courtesy Prof D.H. Everett FRS*

CONTAINERS, "H" TYPE

Catalogue No. 15C/170.

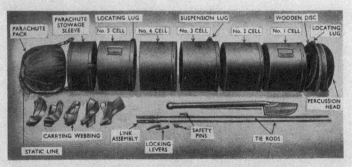

LAYOUT OF CONTAINER COMPONENTS

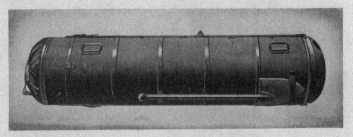

CONTAINER READY FOR ATTACHMENT TO AIRCRAFT

CONTAINERS, "H" TYPE, SPADES

Catalogue No. 15C/229.

DESCRIPTION. The blade of the spade is of metal, into which fits a short wooden handle which terminates in a knob for additional ease in handling. See Figs. 1 and 2 Containers, "H" Type.

METHOD OF USE. The spade is fitted to the clip and bracket provided for that purpose on the Container "H" Type, to which it is locked by a safety pin passing through the bracket. Detachment is easy, and the spade is for use in digging a hole for the burial of the unwanted components of the container, the parachute and any other redundant equipment.

DIMENSIONS. Length 8′ 1″. Greatest width 8′.　　　　**WEIGHT.** 3 lbs.

PACKING AND SPECIAL NOTES. Must be preserved from contact with sea water.

'H' type supply container. *Public Record Office HS7/28*

dropping into the slipstream of the aircraft. Furthermore, they had to be readily removable from the landing site by the minimum of people. The two main types of containers introduced in the early days were the C-type and the H-type.

The C-Type Container

The C-type container adopted by the Airborne Forces consisted of two strengthened sheet metal half-cylinders hinged together along their whole length. The hinged doors were held closed by three quick release catches which were themselves prevented from premature opening by split pins. The container was 5 ft 8 in long and 15 in in diameter and could accommodate either long items such as rifles or Bren guns, or be fitted with three smaller cylinders (15 in diameter by 19 in long) to hold smaller items. These were metal drums fitted with simple quick release lids bedding on to rubber rings and had two carrying handles. Externally, one end of the main container formed a cowling to accommodate the parachute while at the other was an impact absorbing head. In earlier models this was a pad of Sorbo rubber but later it consisted of a metal dome containing a few large cut-outs designed to assist its collapse and hence to absorb the energy of impact. The container was carried in the 500 lb (227 kg) or universal bomb rack by a single suspension lug. In packing the container, care had to be taken to adjust the centre of gravity to within a few inches of a fixed distance from the suspension lug.

They could contain a load of up to 220 lb (100 kg) of stores giving a total weight of 330 lb (150 kg) and were fitted with carrying handles but needed several men to transport them any distance. The preferred drill was to remove the internal cells to give smaller loads for transportation from the DZ and to bury the container and parachute. Alternatively, Reception Committees often arranged for the availability of farm carts or lorries to enable the containers to be removed from the DZ to hidden storage as quickly as possible. Burying or hiding containers was often a problem: to this end at least one container in a drop included a trenching tool.

The H-Type Container

A Polish captain, concerned about the difficulty of burying C-type containers in the hard soil of his country, invented a revised design which became known as the H-type container. It was made up of five interlocking cells held together by long rods with locking levers and safety pins. When these rods were withdrawn each cell could be handled on its own and was therefore easier to remove from the landing site and to conceal. It was two inches shorter than its predecessor, had a payload of 235 lb (107 kg) with the same gross weight of 330 lb (150 kg) and was fitted with straps for ease of handling on landing. One disadvantage was that it could not carry long items. It was, however, capable of delivering a consignment of petrol and oil in three fitted Jerry cans and external clips enabled a trenching tool to be fitted. With the Polish officer supervising the development, the H-type containers were produced by the South Metropolitan Gas Company.[3]

Panniers

Metal containers were not the only means used for packing and delivering stores. A pannier had been developed consisting of a frame of spring steel wire to which was fitted a mild steel lattice. The pannier was in two parts with one fitting snugly inside the other to form a fully enclosed box shape. Each half was covered with khaki canvas duck. For ease of storage and, more importantly, opening in the field, the side frames could be hinged down until the whole assembly was flat. Four sizes were provided ranging from 22 × 16 × 16 in (560 × 410 × 410 mm) to 29 × 18 × 13 in (740 × 460 × 330 mm) and to protect the contents some were fitted with a coil spring shock-absorbing panel in the base. Normal packing materials used were hairlock panels and layers of Koran fibre needled on canvas.[4]

Packing of both containers and panniers was an important job. When carried out properly the load could be very secure, as illustrated by the fact that of a consignment of 200 bottles of printer's ink sent to France, not one was cracked.[5]

Panniers had to be dropped through the jump hole of a Halifax which was 40 in in diameter. To achieve a reasonable accuracy and despatch rate a weight limit of 120 lb (54.4 kg) was imposed for all packages. Under certain conditions this could be increased to 140 lb (63.5 kg) but a second despatcher had to be included in the crew.

Although in the case of containers a compromise parachute size of 22 ft had been agreed upon in late 1943, the parachutes used with the panniers varied with their weight. The recommended chute sizes for use with panniers of different weights are given in Appendix F.

Because of the very limited storage space available in the fuselage of a bomber, the Halifax could carry only six packages; the Stirling MkV ten packages; and the American B24 Liberator twelve packages.[6]

Improvements in the handling of panniers could be achieved by the use of a roller conveyor but, as detailed later, these were not fully operational in Europe before the war ended.

PACKING TRIALS AND DROP TESTING

Of primary importance was the need to ensure that loads dropped by parachute were not damaged on impact. Thus the development of methods of packing containers and panniers assumed a high priority. It is relevant to recall that in those days packaging techniques were in their infancy. None of the modern methods involving the use of bubble-packs, expanded polystyrene and vacuum forming was available and reliance had to be placed on various hessian and coconut fibre-based materials such as rubberised Koran and Hairlock. A highly desirable property of a packing material is that it should absorb energy when deformed. Highly elastic material such as Sorbo rubber, though at first sight ideal, had the disadvantage that it absorbed little energy so that rebound could cause as much damage as the original shock. An additional problem arose when, for logistical reasons, it was necessary for containers to carry a mixed load of explosives, ammunition, detonators and fuses. Great care had to be taken to ensure the compatibility of the contents by stipulating that sensitive items were not to be packed in close proximity. This led to the specification of a large number of 'standard loads', for each of which an appropriate packaging was devised and drop tested.

Early drop testing was carried out from a tethered barrage balloon at Cardington. As the pressure of work built up the facilities at Cardington became overloaded and the simpler method of dropping from a given height on a gantry onto a concrete slab was adopted. These tests were carried out at Henlow and Station IX. The choice of height was based on earlier experiments on the effects of dropping with different parachutes, supported by the theoretical considerations outlined in Appendix F. The effect of dropping a container weighing 330 lb (150 kg) on a 22 ft parachute was thus simulated by dropping from 12 feet, which gives an impact speed of 8.3 m per sec or 27 ft per sec. Panniers were dropped from 5 feet to take account of the lower speed of 17 ft per sec with which they impacted the ground.

In addition Country Sections had a wide variety of special needs which taxed the ingenuity of the packers. Particular problems arose when camouflaged items were involved. Thus W/T sets and S-phones, besides being included in standard packs, were often concealed in metal drums or similar common commercial boxes. Among other unusual loads which were packed and tested successfully were Mk I Folding Canoes, a printing machine, battery chargers and their steam generators, and medical kits.

But there were failures from time to time. Occasionally containers burst open and scattered their contents; this was attributed to failure of the locking devices arising either from a manufacturing fault or from the neglect of the packer to ensure that the safety pins were correctly inserted. On other occasions pilots of stores-dropping aircraft expressed concern that some containers were catching fire or even exploding during their descent. No conclusive evidence for the cause of this was established. Containers would have carried explosives, incendiaries and ammunition but the detonating devices should have been packed separately and insulated from the shock accompanying the development of the canopy. It was known that it was possible for one particular fuse, the PR5, to be activated by strong vibration and these failures could probably have been caused by premature activation resulting from inadequate packing.

A general guide to parachute packaging was prepared in collaboration with Sqn Ldr Bunn at Henlow and circulated to Missions and Packing Stations but no copy has survived.

Lightweight Containers

The ASR Section was concerned with the development and testing of several other containers.

Early in 1943 at about the time that preparations for the Second Front accelerated, metal H- and C-type containers became scarce and attempts were made to develop an alternative lightweight container. A papier-maché version known as the ISRB Lightweight Container was designed and tested. Production prototypes were demonstrated to Country Sections in July 1943 and specifications and working drawings were prepared for it to be put into production if the shortage of metal containers continued. At the same time the Army issued a War Office specification for a lightweight container having a higher payload than currently available to Airborne Forces, but it had to be collapsible for ease of transport and storage. The ISRB container did not meet the latter condition. The RAE designed the Y-type container in a strong canvas material to meet this specification. A similar US Plastic Container (Navy Type A.10) was made of cloth impregnated with cellulose acetate. It weighed only 50 lb but was designed, apparently, for external carriage and needed modifications to fit British bomb racks.

In the event the supply of metal containers improved and work on lightweight containers ceased late in 1944.

Waterproof Containers

It was realised early that it would be a great advantage if containers were waterproofed so that heavy rain or landing in ditches or streams would not harm the contents. The requested operational requirements varied from being unaffected by severe weather conditions, such as in a monsoon, to remaining watertight after immersion in water. Containers were often used to store materials for long periods, so watertightness was an important requirement. In March 1943 attempts were made to provide tight sealing of both C-type cells and H-type containers. Experiments started at Station IX to find a suitable design of sealing ring, but this proved a difficult problem. In particular, any distortion of the metal caused by the landing or the impact with the water surface would destroy the sealing. In earlier models the rubber used for sealing did not stand up to tropical storage conditions and various components rusted easily, making the catches difficult to operate. By April 1944 prototypes had been tested with moderate success but further modifications were needed to ensure that the sealing rings remained correctly aligned after dropping. Even so, it could still not be guaranteed that H-cells remained fully watertight after dropping. Finalisation of design details and production was handed over to MAP early in 1945 and urgent action was being taken to get the modified containers available for the next moon period in March/April. But by now the main use was likely to be in the Far East. A partial solution was afforded by providing waterproof liners for the cells.

The K-Type Container

A much more rigorous Operational Requirement came originally from the Danish Section and led to the development of the K-type container. The basic concept was that watertight containers would be dropped at night into fishing areas at sea or in lakes. They would sink but would be recovered later by fishermen going about their normal business. The requirement was thus for a robust container which could be dropped into water, sink to the bottom and remain watertight. After a suitable delay it would release a buoy attached to a coloured float of the kind used locally. The container would have a ballast weight sufficient to overcome its buoyancy but which could be detached by pulling on the line attached to the buoy. The container would then float to the surface and be hauled aboard a fishing boat without attracting attention.

There were a number of technical problems to be overcome and ASR Section worked closely with RAE, MAP and the manufacturers on the detailed design. It was basically a cylinder of about the same dimensions as conventional containers, closed at one end while the other was fitted with a watertight lid which could be opened and closed easily. Attached to the base of the cylinder by a release catch was a solid block heavy enough to sink the container. The release catch could be activated by a sharp tug on the float line, releasing the ballast block and allowing the container to come to the surface. To avoid detection the parachute was to be weighted so that it remained submerged but was attached to the container so that it too could be recovered.

Among the problems to be solved was the design of a reliable closure for the lid which would not be distorted by the impact with the water, which implied in turn that the container had to be strongly constructed. The mechanical action of the release catch had to be robust and reliable. The delay switch releasing the float was developed from the very early water-activated switches which had been developed by MI(R) and Section D already in use for other purposes. The delay in releasing the float was to allay any suspicion that an aircraft flying over was dropping stores: delay times of between one and three days were requested. Preliminary testing of the individual components was carried out at Station IX and by the end of April 1944 six containers were ready for User Trials which were carried out in May and June.

The final dropping trial took place 2½ miles offshore from Troon in Ayrshire. For this a somewhat aged Wellington bomber was borrowed from Prestwick (arranged courtesy of AL Section). Everett acted as despatcher while other members of the Section observed from below. It was a stormy night and the first take-off was aborted when the cockpit canopy blew open. On the second attempt the four containers were dropped successfully at two-second intervals on a straight course down the Firth of Clyde. The parachutes were observed to open correctly.

The following morning a party went out on a borrowed launch to recover the containers. Three bright red floats were soon identified and a dinghy was launched to test the ease with which the containers could be manhandled over the stern of the boat. A ciné record of this was made but does not seem to have survived. The sea was moderate and no difficulty was experienced in the recovery. All three containers remained watertight. However, despite an extended search the fourth buoy was never found so its container, filled with explosives and incendiaries, lies somewhere on the sea bed. Although the loss was notified to the Admiralty, no attempt, as far as is known, was ever made to locate it.

Meanwhile, production was delayed in part by the fight to get priority for the supply of material for the special 14 ft parachute which was also needed for the RAF's Fragmentation Bomb. By December fourteen containers were ready for operational use.

The first operational drop was over Denmark but was subject to delays due to bad weather and the fact that the proposed DZ was covered by thick ice, a circumstance not envisaged in the OR. It was eventually carried out on 28 February 1945. The reception committee was greatly impressed by the increased security imparted by the technique. The Germans were unfamiliar with this kind of supply drop and had they seen an aircraft would probably have thought it was laying mines in coastal waters. But to allay any suspicions the reception committee left retrieval of the containers for two days. When they did bring the stores to the surface they were in good order but they identified three problems: the container lid was difficult to remove, the container was difficult to unload and the buoys were too conspicuous. The original OR specified that the floats should be coloured to match those used by fishing boats in the area of the DZ. However, it was pointed out after the first drop that the appearance of a large number of buoys overnight might raise suspicions and that it would be preferable to have some of them camouflaged, as ducks for example; but not so well camouflaged as to make them difficult to see. Moreover, a delay of 48–72 hours before they were released to the surface would give a longer time for any suspicions to die down. As the war was coming to an end, the last drop – with a scatter of only 150 m – was made on 23 April near Lendrup harbour between the Logstor area and Livo Island in northern Denmark. Retrieval was delayed for 5 days, but the contents had remained dry.[7]

There still remained an operational requirement for the K-type containers for the Far East. The lid was redesigned to increase its strength and to make it easier to open and close. Special attention was given to improving the tropicalisation – in particular to protect the float cable from corrosion. Samples were sent to India and Australia during April, but it is not known whether they were used operationally.

ROLLER CONVEYORS FOR
PACKAGE DESPATCH

The speed and efficiency of despatching packages from an aircraft was vital for successful supply drops. It takes several seconds to manhandle a heavy pannier through a hole in the floor and if the aim is to place, say, half a dozen in the same field from an aircraft flying at perhaps 120 mph, the speed of handling is of paramount importance. The use of a twin-track conveyor to despatch through the side door of a Dakota had become an established technique in the Middle East. The use of the same method of despatch through the jump hole of a Halifax was considered. Station IX designed, and Station XII made, a prototype which was tested successfully from a Halifax at Tempsford on 8 June 1943 and so impressed Grp Capt Batchelor that he recommended its general use. A number of defects were, however, identified and early the following year the conveyor situation for SOE aircraft was reviewed by the ASR Section. It was considered that, although the Halifax conveyor was defective in many respects, with minor modifications it would meet the current requirements for this aircraft. It could also be used with the Liberator either through the jump hole or rear hatch. At this time Stirling bombers, modified for paratroop operation – the Mk IV – became available and although the Halifax conveyor could be used for this aircraft, much greater utilisation of space could be achieved by redesigning it. An operational requirement envisaged that it could carry and despatch twenty 100 lb (45 kg) packages. These conveyors were designed by Shorts, who had built the original aircraft, and tested in collaboration with AFEE in November 1944. The trials were in general very satisfactory but minor problems remained. The ease of moving standard packages within the fuselage needed improvement, and the lashing techniques to prevent movement of the packages in flight had to be designed to facilitate loading and rapid unleashing before the drop. Of major importance now was to evolve an efficient despatching drill. To this end a Stirling fuselage was installed at Station IX. After some experimentation a basic drill was established for demonstration to various interested parties. There followed a full flying demonstration of the conveyor procedure. It was then proposed that a fully loaded conveyor be the subject of final trials but in the event they were held up because of a technical dispute over the effect on the centre of gravity of the aircraft as it despatched its load. A trial was scheduled for 29 April 1945 but no report of this has been found: it probably never took place.

Dropping from the Mosquito

The use of the Mosquito intruder aircraft for supply dropping was under active consideration early in 1944. The bomb racks of the aircraft were not large enough to accommodate any standard containers, but individual cells from the C-type could be adapted specially to fit the existing bomb racks and clearance for their use was obtained. However, the requirement lapsed for European operations, though it was said to be needed in the Far East. The possibility of replacing the long-range wing fuel tanks by supply containers was actively considered. A container having the same shape and dimensions as the wing tank was fabricated in plywood, using the same techniques as those used for the aircraft itself. Prototypes were tested both in drop tests from a balloon and in stressing trials at RAE. An aircraft drop test awaited the availability of an aircraft. In typical SOE style means were found of circumventing this obstacle. It so happened that the Canadian Air Force Mosquito squadron at Ford in Sussex was commanded by Grp Capt Paul Davoud, elder brother of Gordon Davoud at Station IX. Some brotherly collusion then enabled the wing container to be tested successfully in June. However, for some reason production of these containers seems not to have gone ahead.

DETECTION OF CONTAINERS IN THE DARK

It was inevitable that in dropping containers into a relatively small area at night, inaccuracies of the drop or unexpected wind conditions would lead to a scattering of the containers on the ground. The problem of locating them quickly became of major importance. A reception party had no desire to spend hours searching the countryside knowing full well that the noise of the aircraft would have alerted enemy forces.

Concern had already been expressed in late 1942 at the number of parachute containers which had been lost to the enemy because they could not be quickly located in the dark. Station IX was asked to look into the problem urgently. Work towards the solution engaged the Experimental Section continuously from December 1942 to near the end of the war. It was initially an SOE problem since conventional airborne parachute operations were expected to take place mainly in daylight, although later it became an Airborne Forces requirement. The early trials of alternative devices were carried out by Station IX, though later the User Trials Section and the ASR Section played a major role. Five possible solutions were considered: reflective or luminous discs; a 'birdcall' whistle operated by compressed air; electric bells; supersonic devices; and a luminous cloud. Reports of early experiments with bells indicated that they could be heard at 350 yards and this gave encouragement for further work.

Initial experiments with luminous discs in December showed that on a dark night a 2 in diameter metal disc coated with radioactive paint was visible at a distance of 100 yd and detectable at 150 yd. This was better than the Country Sections had asked for so smaller discs which were visible at 25–50 yd were experimented with. The following month a small quantity of 1 in diameter metal discs which could be seen at 25–50 yd were supplied for trials in the field and in February 1943, 100 belts of luminous discs were supplied for operational purposes. The belts of luminous discs had been tested in Operations Rose and Tulip in March but their success or otherwise is not recorded. What is recorded, however, (see Chapter 6) is the concern of Station IX that the highly radioactive luminous paint was harmful to health if a person was in close contact with it for any length of time. Moreover, flakes of paint could get into the air and become caught in the clothing and be breathed in as dust. It was ruled that the discs should be stored in a lead-lined box and not assembled onto the parachute containers until just prior to loading onto the aircraft. Station IX supplied four radioactive discs per belt and 140 metal plates for use on packages.[8]

Comparative trials of the whistle, bell and luminous cloud devices were held on a fine clear night with brilliant starlight but no moon on 26 January 1943 with a group of observers from Station IX. In each case the detecting devices were effective at distances up to 300 yd, although with the whistle and bell the directional discrimination fell off with increasing distance.

The third device created a blue-green cloud of chemiluminescent droplets by the mixing at an atomiser nozzle of two solutions, operated by compressed carbon dioxide (CO_2). Two versions based on different solution concentrations were developed. In each case the detection device was set off by an inertia switch responding to the impact of the container on landing. In spite of, or perhaps because of, the earlier work on luminous discs, a device based on electric lighting was not considered at this stage since it would not be seen if a container fell behind a hedge or in a ditch. The luminous clouds, using different reagent concentrations were between five and ten feet high, the smaller intense cloud being visible at more than 350 yards. The lifetime of this cloud depended on the size of the CO_2 cylinder and the volume of the reagent solutions. It was extended by operating through a modified Horstman gas clock, on for 4 seconds and off for 10 seconds. The containers for the reagents had sufficient for 20–30 minutes operation, although there was a tendency for the nozzle of the CO_2 bottle to freeze up before this time. Development of the luminous cloud device continued through February and March.

Various modified means of operation were tried. The use of only one solution was possible by replacing the hypochlorite solution with a tube of activated charcoal saturated with chlorine gas which was displaced by the CO_2 stream. Morale among the scientists working on the problem ran high and a note made on 2 March commented 'most of our troubles are over'. But this was not so. Even though the device could be fitted into the chute compartment of the container, it was not easy to ensure that the cloud was released in a vertical direction; mounting the device in gimbals was a possible solution.

At about this time it became clear that a container location device was also an operational requirement for the Army and Airborne Forces, and that there might be a demand for possibly several hundred. It was realised that while the luminous cloud device might be a viable solution for supplying SOE agents with four to six containers per drop, the problems of manufacture on a large scale, and of filling the apparatus with fresh chemicals, made this impractical for major operations. Moreover, it was likely to be an expensive item. At this stage, further development was dropped and attention directed to the bell device and to a revised interest in a lighting device.

SOE was not the only organisation concerned with container location. In particular, the Airborne Forces Research Establishment produced a device which on impact ejected three or four spring-loaded telescopic arms each tipped with an electric light. In some trials of this device at Station IX a number of mechanical problems leading to malfunction were identified. And it did not solve the problem of containers falling into a ditch or behind a hedge. Despite this, Station IX was asked by the Ministry of Supply to develop both the bell and lighting devices.

A programme of top urgency was mounted in the week 26–31 July to prepare six prototype bell devices for daylight dropping trials in the afternoon of 5 August. These were carried out at Tempsford using sand-filled containers. The devices operated satisfactorily, although some minor modifications were indicated. Because of the wind and background aerodrome noises the audible range of the bells was only 20–30 yd. Two of the bells were barely audible because on impact the containers had burst and the bells were immersed in sand. That night the trial was moved to farmland near Aylesbury and was combined with trials of reception committee torches. Two more bell devices were dropped. One operated correctly and in the presence of a light wind and little background noise the bell was clearly audible at 150 yd, and just heard at 230 yd. It was judged that at 200 yd it was unlikely to attract unwelcome attention. The other bell rang for a few minutes and stopped. The simple explanation was that the screw holding the hammer had not been fully tightened. The team had devoted another long working day to this problem: they had left Station IX at 10.00 hours and returned after the trials at 03.00 the following morning.

In a further ground trial on the night of 9 August five bell devices were scattered over a distance of 250 yd. A party of five ORs located all the bells in 3½ minutes, a very satisfactory result. The following three weeks were taken up converting the prototype bell devices into pre-production models in collaboration with Station XII and the South Metropolitan Gas Co. who were to undertake the manufacture. Meanwhile the development of the lighting device was held up because the contractor (Bulgin) could not get quick delivery of the necessary switches and bulb holders. To get clearance for these they had to submit a written application to the Inter-Services Communication Committee (no connection with ISRB), which incurred frustrating delay.

The Ministry of Supply Committee on Airborne Requirements met on 1 September with representatives of many interested parties.

Widely varying estimates of the needs for container detection devices were bandied about. The internal SOE estimates for 2,200 bell devices and 5,000 lighting devices were trumped by an Army request for 80,000 by the end of 1944. A request was made for the revival of the whistle device, and for consideration of a clockwork version of the bell device. No more work was recommended on radio and supersonic devices, while ARDE's work on infra-red (IR) methods was to be continued up to the production stage.

Further progress towards the production of the bell device was pursued by Maj Bedford and Capt Ault at Station XII. But it was not until May/June 1944 that it was reported that successful acceptance trials had been carried out on the first pilot production models. Full production models were to incorporate a much more robust bell and use only one battery. Meanwhile, tropical tests had shown that (without the battery) the device stood up well to these conditions. It is not known how many bell devices were produced.

The manufacture of one whistle detection device was undertaken by the Walter Kidde Company in America. When the first sample appeared at Station IX it was plainly grossly over-engineered, with heavy brass cylinders, and was very expensive to produce. J.T. van Riemsdijk, a member of the Fuses and Fine Mechanisms Section, offered to redesign it and produced a device which relied on a capillary tube for the prolongation of the whistle. An order for 37,000 of them was placed with a firm who, unfortunately, made them without the capillary. Hence when they were activated they gave one loud shriek, followed by silence.[9]

There seems to be little information on the use of container detection devices in the field. After D-Day in the Maquis areas an agent said that 'they had little difficulty in locating containers' as they could 'provide plenty of men as lookouts for ½ to ¾ mile from the dropping grounds. They were extremely useful (sic) particularly when the parachutage was done by the Americans!' These drops were massive and in daylight. It is not known to what extent location devices were used in other theatres of the Second World War.

Records of work on supersonic methods of detection have not been located though research was being undertaken in February 1943 and field trials to establish the effective range of supersonic signals were carried out the following month.[10]

HIGH-ALTITUDE DELAYED DROPPING

While the ability to drop supplies by parachute from heights up to 1500 ft were advantageous in many situations in north-west Europe, the real and urgent need to be able to drop from much higher arose with operations to Poland. It is ironic that the Poles, whose Home Army could make greatest use of sabotage materials and weapons were, in fact, the most difficult to supply. The main problem was that a supply drop to Poland involved a 12–14 hour flight over enemy occupied territory during darkness. The crew of the aircraft would not be at their best after a long cold flight which, to avoid the enemy anti-aircraft fire, had been at an altitude of at least 10,000 ft. They then had a very short time to locate the designated DZ, descend to 500 ft, make their drop and climb back to a safe height for the return journey. Because the aircraft was operating at the extreme limits of its range, the drop would have to proceed faultlessly if the vital fuel needed for the return flight was not to be used up. It was inevitable that under these conditions the payload of stores would be only a fraction of that carried on a shorter sortie in north-west Europe: six or seven tons of fuel were needed to deliver one ton of stores to Poland.

In 1941 the only aircraft available for Polish operations were two long-range Whitley bombers with a range of 850 miles crewed by Poles of 138 Squadron. Later two Halifaxes, with a range of 100 miles more than the Whitley, were made available; three B24 Liberators with a further 100 miles range were added in October 1943. Up to April 1942 only nine successful operations had been made to Poland carrying 48 men but a negligible amount of stores. Later 62 sorties – 41 of them successful – carrying 119 men and 23 tons of stores were flown with the loss of two aircraft. During the summer months the short nights precluded any operations. When they resumed in September 1942 enemy defences had been strengthened and the failure of sorties and the loss of aircraft increased alarmingly. In September twenty-two sorties were flown with the loss of six aircraft – four out of eleven on one night alone. At this point the flight route was changed to a more northerly route over the North Sea, Southern Denmark and the Baltic to reduce the time spent over hostile areas. But this reduced even further the areas of Poland to which drops were possible. It was then decided that, now that much of Italy had been freed by the Allies, the base for Polish operations could be moved to Monopoly, near Bari in Southern Italy.

This took place between November 1943 and January 1944. By this time the need for a means of dropping stores accurately from a high altitude became a high priority. This would not only reduce the risk of interception and of attack by ground fire during flight but would avoid the extra fuel consumption involved in descending to drop the load and climb again. The need for high-altitude dropping thus emanated mainly from the Middle East and the first successful devices were developed for SOE (Force 133) by Maj G.N. Sanderson RAOC in Cairo. The urgency was heightened by the figures in the period April–July 1944 when out of 315 sorties, only 174 succeeded and eight aircraft were lost. A failure rate of 45 per cent was totally unacceptable and demands for the High Altitude Delayed Dropping Apparatus (HADDA) development intensified.

Full details of the original Middle East (ME) device are not known. It appears that it depended on the ignition of a length of Bickford fuse upon the container's release from the bomb bay which, after a chosen time calculated to bring the container to the desired height, initiated a switch to release the parachute. Following the preliminary development of the Middle East HADDA, further work in the UK was initiated by SOE early in 1944.

The problem resolved into two main factors. A means was needed either to delay the parachute opening for a given time or until the container reached a predetermined height. Moreover the ballistic inconsistency and indeterminacy of a tumbling container made the aiming of the drop difficult. Unlike a bomb which has fins to stabilise it in its flight and give a reasonably predictable trajectory, a standard container had no such features and its trajectory was difficult to predict. Furthermore, it could reach a velocity far in excess of that specified for the deployment of the parachute. It was, therefore, necessary to use a small parachute to stabilise the fall in the first part of the trajectory and to reduce the terminal velocity to an acceptable level. The main parachute had then to be strong enough to withstand the shock of opening, otherwise the result would be a bursting of the canopy and total destruction of the container and its contents. In some cases the long flight at high altitude to the DZ resulted in iced-up parachute packs which failed to open. The Stirling seemed particularly vulnerable to this problem.

Preliminary experiments were carried out by ASR Section but it soon became apparent that the technical requirements were of a magnitude that meant that further development work could not be undertaken with the limited resources available to this group.

Consequently, from April 1944 the main work on this project was handed over to RAE, although at all stages the ASR Section kept in close touch with its progress, including the planning and observation of trials at Farnborough. It acted, in effect, as a coordinating body between SOE as the client and RAE.

Three main lines of development were pursued. Trials of a Quilter delay opening mechanism (which had originally been designed for delaying the opening of personal parachutes) modified to increase the delay time to 30 seconds showed that it was unsuitable for use with containers. Secondly, it was proposed to modify the Middle East delay opening device to overcome problems which had arisen in the original design. Finally, the use of the American M111 altimeter fuse was to be tested. An assessment by RAE indicated that a container fitted with a stabilising parachute and an M111 fuse set to release the main parachute at a nominal height of 900 feet above the DZ would probably give sufficient accuracy; however, ASR Section felt that release at 600 feet would be preferable. A 35-second mechanical clockwork delay was also considered but in the form available was deemed to be unacceptable. In RAE's view the Middle East device was also insufficiently accurate. One suspected that this was because it looked too much like a do-it-yourself job, which it was, and did not have the professional touch to which RAE devices would be expected to conform. In fact, SOE continued independently with the improvement of the Middle East device.

From April 1944 onwards pleas from the Polish Section became increasingly urgent. In the period April–July, 318 sorties had been mounted of which 174, or 55 per cent, were successful in dropping 114 men and 219 tons (222,500 kg) of stores: a tiny fraction of what would be required to supply the needs of the Polish Home Army. The situation was aggravated by the refusal of the USSR to allow aircraft to land and refuel at Russian bases in reconquered areas. Although by June trials of the RAE device incorporating the M111 fuse were underway, progress was slow. Among other things RAE's other major commitments meant that it was difficult to get flying time for testing at Farnborough. But time was getting short as the Russians advanced towards Warsaw. The Poles were desperate to liberate their city from the Germans ahead of the Russians. For a short time the hazards of air supply to Poland from the Middle East were judged to be too high. On one sortie fifteen aircraft set out, four were lost and two crashed on landing. Operations were suspended for one or two weeks. By the time of the Warsaw uprising on

15 August the final trials of the RAE device were almost complete. It is not clear to what extent the Middle East device was used in this period but it was reported later that in a series of sorties from Italy some 40 per cent of the devices failed. This gave added urgency to attempts to improve the Middle East device. The ignition system was redesigned and a short length of instantaneous fuse was added to boost the parachute release mechanism. Progress was slow with the RAE device. The main problem was with icing of the mechanism at high altitudes and in one trial one out of three main parachutes failed to open at the assigned height.

Neither device was in a state to use operationally during the crucial period in August/September. In an operation on 13/14 August 54 sorties were launched from Italy. Twenty-three succeeded but eleven aircraft were lost, mainly brought down by fire from the ground as they swept in at low level to make a drop, and many aircraft were seriously damaged: it was in this period that the need for HADDA was most cruelly felt. At one stage after a sortie in which half the aircraft were lost only two or three serviceable supply dropping aircraft remained in Italy. In an attempt to relieve the situation the US Air Force reached an agreement with the Russians which allowed them on 10/11 September to send 110 B17 Fortresses to drop stores from 15,000 ft with the loss of only one aircraft. However, with the great spread due to wind drift from more than fifteen times the normal height of a stores drop, only 30 per cent of the containers were recovered. The feelings of desperation and anguish felt by the Poles in London reacted strongly on members of the ASR Section who were helpless to influence the RAE programme. It was not until the end of September that the RAE trials were completed and 500 devices were about to be despatched. But Warsaw fell on 2 October and the operational need for HADDA in that sphere ceased.

Nevertheless, interest in the high-altitude technique continued, especially in the Far East and with Airborne Forces. SOE continued independently to work on the development of the Middle East device to improve the ignition system and to waterproof it adequately for use under tropical conditions. By February 1945 the RAE device was in full production and was being issued. However, further tests showed that there were still problems of icing which it was proposed could be overcome by the use of an anti-freeze grease. And the static line broke on a number of occasions and failed to withdraw the arming device. Snags also arose in the fitting of the device in the

Stirling aircraft. Some further trials were to be held to assess the use of a modified Mark IX bomb sight for aiming the containers. This work was in hand when the war in Europe ended. The work of ASR Section was summarised in two reports, Nos. 19 and 20, but these do not appear to have survived. Further development was handed over to RAE and Airborne Forces when the ASR Section on HADDA was disbanded in August 1945.

Free-Dropping of Stores

The possibility of dispensing with the use of parachutes was considered seriously early in 1944 when the supply of parachutes gave cause for concern. The ASR Section was given the urgent task of examining the feasibility of free-dropping stores and ammunition. The central problem was that of upgrading the methods of packing to ensure minimum damage on impact at speeds much higher than those experienced when a parachute was used. It was soon established that even with improved packing the free-dropping of C- or H-type containers was impossible. Moreover, it was clear that free-dropping would be feasible only with a limited range of more robust stores and equipment, and that the weight of each package would have to be limited.

Preliminary trials were carried out in December 1943 by dropping from a height of six feet onto concrete. When these proved promising, further tests were carried out on 26 May 1944 from a tethered balloon at Henlow. Drops were made from 3,000 ft onto grass. In these trials the simplest and most readily available packing materials were used. It was found possible to free-drop without damage ammunition and Sten guns firmly wrapped in blankets and enclosed in a mailbag or flour sack. It was thought possible that if the packages were designed to fall in a predetermined manner, then most of the packing material could be placed round the area of impact, with an overall saving of material. To achieve this the packages were fitted with a vane-type drogue which controlled the fall and impact satisfactorily. However, difficulties were seen in obtaining adequate supplies of these drogues. The use of improvised 'flour sack' drogues was investigated. These were made by inserting a wire ring into the mouth of the sack and linking this to the package with four rigging lines. These gave good results, not only because they controlled the direction of impact but also because the gyration or 'spinning leaf' effect reduced the speed of fall. With this technique 9 mm ammunition wrapped in blankets and Sten guns packed in corrugated paper and Koran fibre were dropped successfully from heights up to 3,000 ft from a balloon, and from aircraft flying at 135 mph and an altitude of 200 ft. An alternative was to use standard ammunition boxes fitted with a crash head and with a drogue to control the angle of impact. Drops from the balloon were promising but the ballistics of the load were erratic when dropped from an aircraft.

Furthermore, in these and other trials the presence of the drogue tended to interfere with the handling of the loads in the aircraft. Further development of the use of crash-heads was handed over to AFDC, while simpler methods of improving the packaging were pursued by ASR Section. This led to the specification of the methods of packing of seven standard loads including besides ammunition, Sten guns and grenades, blankets, battledress, boots, shirts, and socks. Standard food packs included dehydrated rations, flour, 50 lb (22.7 kg) sacks of rice each containing one tin of corned beef, baked beans, milk, sardines and margarine. For reasons not apparent, no satisfactory means was found of dropping packs of .303 ammunition. No attempts were made to free-drop explosives or incendiary devices. The free-dropping of liquids raised some problems. The simplest method developed by AFDC was to place a liquid-proof bag of water or petrol inside a larger bag. A 5-gal. rubberised skin bag for use with an outer canvas bag was approved for use in Europe but doubts about the ageing of the components under tropical conditions meant that it was not acceptable in the Far East. The free-dropping of clothing and similar items by themselves was considered wasteful since they were better used to protect more vulnerable items.

Attention was also given to the despatching techniques. In conjunction with the RAE at Farnborough it was shown that a good concentration of sacks could be obtained by linking them together with webbing in strings of four (sausages) and dropping through the despatch hole. With an appropriate aiming technique the whole load of 64 sacks (1½ tons or 1527 kg) from a Halifax could be dropped accurately. In two separate sorties dropped from 1500 ft and 200 ft all the sacks fell within a circle of 75 yd radius. But it was possible to drop only eight sacks on each run in, so that eight runs, taking 30 minutes, were necessary to drop the full load. These figures could, no doubt, have been improved by the use of roller conveyors.

Since it was anticipated that the free-dropping of supplies might be needed to the Maquis areas of South-west France, it was important to check that the methods developed for dropping on grass or farmland were equally applicable for dropping onto rough and potentially rocky terrain. It was thus important to test the packings against more severe conditions.

It was decided to simulate these conditions by dropping onto a rocky hillside near Fishguard where SOE already had a base (Station IXc). This trial, carried out in conjunction with the Radio Communications Division (RCD), would also provide the opportunity to test their procedures for using the S-phone to indicate the release point over the dropping zone. It was also the first occasion on which direct verbal contact between the aircraft and the ground was monitored using the recently developed magnetic wire recorder, the forerunner of the tape-recorder.

The aircraft to be used was the RCD Halifax based at Hatfield. Incidentally, this was said to have been one of the six pre-production models of this aircraft and had been used extensively by RCD in their trials of homing systems using Eureka/Rebecca, S-phone and other devices.

On the morning of Saturday 3 June 1944 one party of the ASR Section had travelled to Fishguard by road while another group assembled at Hatfield and loaded the aircraft with the test packages. It was a brilliantly fine summer morning, so it was a little puzzling that the take-off was delayed. After some time the pilot, a Handley Page civilian test pilot, announced that he had been trying unsuccessfully to file a flight plan but had been unable to get through to Flight Control: his phone calls had been unanswered. He remarked jokingly that as it was Saturday morning the staff must be having a lie-in. He decided that even without flight clearance he would proceed with the trial. The flight was uneventful and a succession of packages – some linked like sausages – were despatched successfully through the jump hole. At the conclusion of the trial a course was set for home. However, very soon one of the engines caught fire and was shut down. So they limped back on three engines.

On approaching Oxfordshire flying at a few thousand feet, those on board had a magnificent view of the peaceful, rolling, checkered countryside basking in the warm afternoon sun. This sight, now familiar to anyone who has travelled by air, was an experience not often enjoyed by many outside the airborne units of the armed forces. But superimposed on this peaceful scene there soon appeared the airfields of Kemble, Fairford and Brize Norton. And here was an amazing sight. Laid out on all the airfields were close-packed herringbone formations of gliders. Very soon the pilot's radio began to crackle. What was a limping Halifax doing in this airspace on an unscheduled flight over operational airfields and with a civilian pilot? A fighter came up to investigate and buzzed the Halifax. Presumably the pilot was able to satisfy ground control and the Halifax was allowed to fly on to Hatfield. No doubt the pilot had a severe dressing down for ignoring the need to file his flight plan. What no-one in the aircraft appreciated was that what they had seen was the glider armada preparing for D-Day. On Monday morning it was clear that, unbeknown to the ASR Section team, they had been privy to the last preparations for D-Day. It was no wonder that their flight had caused so much consternation on the ground. As it turned out this was the last flight of the RCD Halifax, which was deemed unairworthy and was disposed of.[11]

Examination of the packages which had been dropped confirmed that, by and large, the free-drop packing had been satisfactory. The main casualty was a package of six .38 revolvers which had been issued by Station VI on a 'test to destruction' basis. Five of them were unserviceable but the sixth was undamaged. It became something of an embarrassment since there seemed to be no mechanism for returning an item which was listed as destroyed. A night-time free drop was held up by weather and lack of aircraft, but eventually a successful drop using a Stirling aircraft was made on 19 October. Meanwhile, RAE, on the basis of air-to-air ciné films, had cleared the free drop technique for packages of between 30 and 50 lb (13.6 and 22.7 kg) and recommended the use of linked packages.

Free drop research had occupied a high proportion of the time and effort of the ASR Section and had been carried out in close liaison with the Airborne Forces. A healthy rivalry existed between the two groups of workers to the benefit of the overall programme. In the event, by the time the free drop technique became operational the parachute problem had eased and the US Air Force was dropping supplies in daylight to the Maquis areas. The free-dropping technique was therefore not used in north-west Europe but was applied to some extent in the Mediterranean and Far East theatres.

The pioneering work of ASR Section was not wasted. Free drops were used by Air Despatch for the delivery of medical supplies and food to the starving people of Holland in the months after their liberation. And since then free-dropping has been one of the main ways in which humanitarian aid has been delivered throughout the world. But curiously, the linking of packages to prevent their dispersal does not seem to have been widely adopted.

Pigeon Containers

At various stages during the war homing pigeons were used to send messages from the field, especially in north-west Europe. But the problem was that of delivering to agents pigeons which had been kept in lofts at Tempsford. At first a standard British pigeon-dropping container was used. But early in 1944 the Belgian Section reported that in an extensive series of operations a large number of pigeons had been killed or incapacitated in the drop. Considerable effort was devoted, in collaboration with Henlow, to design a suitable container incorporating a device to delay the opening of the parachute. This was tested for use from the practice bomb racks of the Mosquito. Successful drops using live pigeons were carried out.

It was said that, in fact, no container was necessary and that, using the technique adopted by Callow in India (Chapter 4) a pigeon packed in a brown paper bag and dropped through the jump hole had time to break out of the bag and flutter down!

Man-dropping Container

Early in 1944 the ASR Section was involved in a feasibility study, in collaboration with MAP, of a man-carrying container to enable an agent to be dropped from the bomb bay of an aircraft not fitted with a jump hole. Difficulties were foreseen in accommodating such a container in existing aircraft. There were other problems and, although regular contact was maintained with MAP, it appears that this scheme was not pursued. However, it was reported that the Germans were working on a much more ambitious project to design a container for three men and their equipment. This was a huge container 9 ft long and 6 ft in diameter dropped on four parachutes. Presumably it was to be carried outside the aircraft. The SAS expressed interest in developing a similar, improved, design but there is no record of this ever being completed.

Dropping of Dogs

For some reason which is not clear, a suggestion was made that dogs should be dropped by air. At first sight it is difficult to see what advantage a dog might be to an agent since it would be another mouth to feed, might inadvertently give away its master or mistress to a search party and generally was an extra liability. But the clue lies in a comment by the Army School of Dogs who in April 1943 were asked by Col H.H. King at Station IX to meet with Flt Lt Bunn for discussions on the subject. The School suggested that any trial drops should perhaps be done with less valuable mongrel dogs rather than Huskies. We know that Station IX devised a collapsible ski-sledge for dropping by parachute for ad hoc operations and it seems likely that the dogs were seen as a useful adjunct to this in attacks on targets in sub-arctic regions such as parts of Norway. When one realises that this was a couple of months after the highly successful Gunnerside operation against the heavy water plant at Rjuken when the escaping attackers skied for many exhausting miles across snow-bound wastes to reach neutral Sweden, the possibility of dog-sledge transport must have been very attractive.

A number of German Shepherd dogs were dropped with the British Airborne Forces. Their acute hearing enabled them to give advance warning of incoming artillery rounds and they were also capable in some circumstances of sniffing out landmines. When not engaged in these tasks they were used for guard duties.

Glider Snatch Pick-up

In the first quarter of 1944 another, somewhat dubious, method of delivering stores was proposed. Maj R.F. Turner wrote to Brig Mockler-Ferryman, Director of London Group of SOE, advocating the use of gliders for the silent and possibly more accurate delivery of supplies. The gliders then available were designed for carrying troops or even a light tank and had to be towed by a twin-engined C47 Dakota aircraft or the much larger four-engined Halifax or Stirling bombers. Without troops the gliders could certainly have carried a substantial payload of arms and equipment but landing sites would have had to meet much more stringent criteria than those for parachuted supplies. Turner also saw the possibility of later pick-up of the glider if devices then under consideration could be developed sufficiently. The idea had several glaring disadvantages, chief of which were the cost, the depositing of another supernumary in enemy-occupied territory and the difficulty of transporting and hiding the glider till pick-up time.

The pick-up device then under consideration was originally intended for use with messages. Two masts were erected between which was strung a taut rope. Attached to this was a nylon rope fixed to a bag containing the items to be picked up. Torches would be laid out in a predetermined formation to guide the aircraft which would be trailing a rigid pole with a hook on the end. Capt Tice reported on a demonstration of the system at Station 61 on 26 July 1943 which must have shown some promise for a Lysander was modified for this work by 9 August. In fact, the system had already been used by Army Cooperation Command in the North Africa Campaign. But snatching up a message in a bag is a far cry from picking up a glider. To pick up a glider the 'snatching' aircraft must fly in extremely low, precluding the proximity of any trees or similar features which could afford cover for the waiting glider. Although the Americans developed a system for use with the C47 Dakota aircraft, it was not used widely and the SOE scheme appears not to have been pursued. When sporting gliding resumed after the war, the 'snatch pick-up' type of launch was strictly forbidden.

Human Pick-up

In 1944 SOE showed an interest in a technique developed at Wright Field in the USA for picking up a person from the ground by an aircraft flying overhead. A film of the trials in the USA using live sheep was shown at the War Office and reported upon by Everett. Despite an anticipated acceleration force of 10g and a 10 per cent casualty rate these trials had been completely successful, except for the loss of one sheep which had been strangled by its harness.[12] Sacks and packages had also been picked up, but this was, in effect, an extension of the established Army Cooperation Command technique for picking up messages with a Lysander equipped with a trailing hook.

The person to be picked up was positioned in a suitable harness on the ground between two poles about 25 feet high. A long rope ran in a loop through the harness and across the tops of the poles. The aircraft – in the film a US twin-engined Stinson although an Avro Anson was also modified for this work – was fitted with a trailing hook and a means of winding into the aircraft the person snatched off the ground.

SOE subsequently arranged some trials using two human volunteers; an expert US parachute jumper and a British Commando Officer, Capt Lee-Warner. To get them used to the sensation they were first trailed behind the pick-up plane at a speed of 165 mph. For the actual pick-up the man would sit on the ground in his harness facing the oncoming aircraft and leaning back with his knees up to his chest.

The aircraft would approach at 135 mph and had to climb away at 45 degrees immediately after the man was hooked to ensure he didn't swing downwards after the initial acceleration and strike the ground or some obstruction. A recommendation was for the aircraft to have a safety device to cut the cord instead of hooking it should the run-in be found to be too low.

The man experienced a maximum G-force of 4.7 and accelerated to a speed faster than that of the aircraft, due, no doubt, to the elasticity of the shock absorbing devices. He was not wound in to the aircraft until he had stabilised on the trailing rope. Surprisingly, Capt Lee-Warner likened the discomfort to no worse than the jerk experienced when making a bad gear change on a motor cycle.

It was concluded that the pilot of the pick-up plane had to be 100 per cent accurate in speed, height and course of his run up and 100 per cent accurate in the timing of his climb after the snatch. Too early and the hook could miss the rope; too late and the man could be dragged along the ground. The sudden drag of the pick-up would tend to slow the plane, so the pilot had to be sure he had sufficient speed and power to avoid stalling as he entered the climb. It was further recommended that all parties have a knowledge of the equipment and that it should be used only in favourable weather. No records have been found of this technique being used during the Second World War although it was subsequently developed using C130 Hercules aircraft to pluck persons from the sea.

With the invasion of the European mainland only a few months away, the availability of aircraft for personnel and stores drops became critical. 138 and 161 Squadrons at Tempsford were assigned to drops on northern and north-western Europe but were equipped with only 23 Halifax aircraft, just sufficient to maintain an adequate number of drops to SOE's existing circuits but certainly insufficient when the significant operational requirements of the Jedburgh teams was taken into account. Assistance was to come from the Americans who operated B24 Liberators for OSS in a similar manner from what they termed the 'Carpetbagger' base at RAF Harrington in Northamptonshire.

Despite the problems of air supply and the consequent occasional failure, there is no doubt that this route was the only way of maintaining supplies to the large number of Resistance groups in occupied territories. Improvements in the methods and equipment made it possible to increase the rate of supply from 1.5 tons (1527 kg) in 1941 to 28 tons (28,450 kg) in January/March 1943 and 277 tons (281,500 kg) in October/December 1943.

TWELVE

THE WIRELESS SECTION

A n essential need of any secret organisation operating overseas is a clandestine means of communicating with its headquarters. In the mid-twentieth century diplomats had the 'diplomatic bag', generally agreed to be inviolable but not to be used for belligerent purposes. Embassies had their fixed wireless transceivers. But these facilities would not be available in time of war when embassies closed and friendly but neutral countries were unwilling to compromise their status by taking over the regular communications role. The normal postal mail service was, of course, nowhere near secure enough to be used for messages of national importance. What was needed was a rapid and secure (from interference by other parties) means of two-way communication.

Coded wireless transmissions in morse code had been established between the wars by SIS. The wireless sets provided then lacked three essential features for wartime clandestine use: range, portability and ease of concealment.

As the threat of war loomed SIS, which was using the 1936 vintage Mk XV wireless sets in their heavy wooden cases – by later standards huge – engaged a technical consultant in January 1939 to look into the requirements and availability of effective wireless communications. Shortly after, a small laboratory was set up at Bletchley Park where SIS, in the guise of the Government Code and Cipher School (GC&CS), had had its wireless headquarters since 1938. This unit was staffed by Capt (later Lt Col) E. Schroter MIEE, Royal Signals and two assistants. On the outbreak of war this embryonic section was moved to the newly requisitioned mansion at The Frythe. Hence the earliest wartime work carried out at The Frythe, even before SOE was set up in July 1940, included the development of means of clandestine communications.

Although the Wireless Section was one of the first (with part of Section D) to establish itself at Welwyn, it is rarely included in the overall picture of events at Station IX and, indeed, has never been found on an organisational chart of SOE's Research and Development Section. This can be explained at least in part by the fact that in the early days of SOE, even after Section D had been absorbed into it, the new organisation was dependent for its signals work on Section VIII of SIS. This dependence extended to the provision of the unsatisfactory Mk XV wireless sets.

So when Prof Newitt was appointed Director of Scientific Research at the beginning of 1941 his remit did not include the Wireless Section which remained under the Chief Signals Officer. In due course SOE became independent of SIS, establishing its own receiving stations at Grendon Underwood and Poundon near Bicester. As recorded here, the Radio Communications Division as it came to be known, moved away from Station IX in the middle of the war and was split between accommodation at a number of factories mainly to the north of London. Theirs was a vital contribution to the operation of SOE and its research and development work should be included here.

The Wireless Section, or RCD, carried out a great deal of research and development work on the wireless transceivers (instruments which can both transmit and receive signals) – and also on navigational aids to assist pilots in locating drop zones and on devices for the recharging of the power sources for agents' sets. These power sources (accumulators) were normally similar to the car batteries of the day – heavily constructed of glass. To be recharged they required an input of electrical current for several hours; a suitable mains electrical supply was rarely available in the remoter areas of SOE's theatres of operations.

THE 'S'-PHONE

One of the earliest projects of the Wireless Section was conceived in the Western Highlands of Scotland. A Royal Signals instructor, Sgt (later Maj) R.C. Bryant, was working at Loch Ailart under Maj (later Col) F.T. Davies using a small microwave radio-telephone (R/T) set for operation in hilly country, where considerable line-of-sight ranges were possible between hilltops. It occurred to Davies that this form of wireless would be ideally suited for ground-to-air communication with aircraft. Trials were arranged at Renfrew airfield near Glasgow in October 1940 under Capt (later Col) J.W. Munn, RA and were sufficiently promising for the development of the idea to be given to the small research team at what was now SOE's Station IX. This was the start of development of the highly successful 'S' phone which eventually enabled a reception committee to 'talk down' an incoming Lysander or Hudson aircraft delivering and picking up agents in occupied territory.

The S-Phone was a development of an ultra-high-frequency portable R/T which both civilians and the military had been working on before the war. It came in two parts: the bulky section in the aircraft or ship and the other part being self-contained and carried easily by the operator on webbing braces on his body. Shoulder straps held the set with its directional aerial in front on the chest while a waistbelt held seven canvas pouches: five containing miniature batteries, the others being storage for earphones, microphone, aerial and vibrator power pack. The set transmitted over 337 megacycles and received on 380 megacycles but no switching was required between reception and voice transmission, a very significant advantage for the aircraft reception work SOE had in mind. The power output was only 0.1 to 0.2 watts so the range of communication was limited to about forty miles if an aircraft was at 10,000 feet and about six miles when it was down to 500 feet. Interception by the enemy was hardly possible on the ground. The microphone was shielded so that voice communication was very clear, it being possible to recognise an operator's voice and hence sometimes to check on the security of the reception committee, but nothing could be heard alongside the user.

A story has it that during a visit to Station IX, Brig Orde Wingate, the Chindit leader who fought the Japanese in Burma so successfully using unorthodox techniques, is reputed to have heard German being spoken from within a shrubbery. He drew a knife and approached stealthily, thinking enemy agents might have somehow infiltrated the guarded site. He pounced on a man in a trench speaking into a radio before handing him over to a guard who recognised the man as a member of staff who was conducting tests with the 'S'-phone by talking to a colleague in another slit trench in the language common to Hungarian and Norwegian operators.

Even if the principle of this instrument had been originally designed by another agency for other purposes, it was certainly developed and modified to great effect at Station IX. The S-phone proved to be of immense value to the reception committees attempting to guide aircraft to landing fields under a full, or nearly full, moon. One disadvantage of the set was that it was difficult to conceal and impossible to pass off as anything else during a spot check by the Germans.

REBECCA/EUREKA

Another navigational aid was the mobile Rebecca/Eureka radar device invented by the Telecommunications Research Establishment (TRE), a much bulkier apparatus than the S-phone. Rebecca was the airborne component permanently fixed in the aircraft; Eureka was in essence a radar beacon which was set up in the DZ and was coded to respond only to a prearranged signal from Rebecca which would contact it initially when some 70 miles away. With proper use an aircraft could be guided to within 200 yards of its DZ. Both the ground beacon and the airborne portion were fitted with self-destruct devices should unauthorised examination be attempted.

The use of Rebecca/Eureka for clandestine landings was not popular among resisters due to the bulk of the equipment. Eureka weighed almost 112 lb (50 kg), was barely portable and impossible to conceal adequately. The Special Duties Squadrons of the RAF, however, recognised its value to them and tried unsuccessfully to persuade reception committees to simplify the operation by the use of the Eureka grid. The device was, however, used extensively in British and US airborne landings in 1944–45.

By September 1941 the Wireless Section was commanded by Maj H. Pickard and had expanded in response to demand to an establishment of 40 persons, some working on the ground set of the 'S' phone, while others were exploring the problems of wireless communication between agents on the European mainland and receiving stations in England. It has to be realised that at this time there was no proprietary commercial or service equipment available to communicate 150–800 miles round the clock and throughout the year, which was what SOE needed. SOE Signals were still frustratingly under the control of SIS, who provided wireless sets such as the Mk XV. By the end of 1941 it was clear that this presented serious problems. Not only was the older organisation able to read the other's traffic, but it also controlled the numbers and types of wireless sets sent to SOE's agents. Efforts to separate the two signals operations had been initiated by SOE before Col G. Ozanne was appointed Chief Signals Officer in February 1942 and started looking to the future. The following month the Chief of the Secret Service (CSS) unexpectedly agreed to SOE's independence but it was not until June that its first wireless station at Grendon Underwood near Bicester began to transmit. Now SOE was in a position to design and develop its own wireless sets in the small section at Station IX.

It is perhaps worth dwelling for a moment on the sets allocated to SOE by SIS up to the time of their separation.

The Mark XV Wireless Set

Even before the outbreak of hostilities SIS depended for its wireless communications with its agents on the Mk XV set which consisted of a separate transmitter and receiver, each bulky, heavy and far from ideal for a clandestine operation. The two-valve transmitter in its varnished plywood case and its three-valve receiver were of similar size and weighed 45 lb (20 kg). Carrying these items without drawing attention to them was clearly no joke. But at least their 20 watts power output was more than adequate. The transmitter covered frequencies from 3.5 to 16 megacycles in three bands and included a power pack for use with either a domestic mains supply or a six-volt battery, the latter being contained in a heavy metal box. The morse key was built into the face of the unit. Its associated receiver covered three to thirteen megacycles in one waveband and had a fine-tuning dial with a frequency range of 200 kilocycles on either side of the frequency displayed on the main dial.

The Paraset

SIS next provided a few Parasets, relatively simple and compact transceivers housed in steel boxes. The transceiver weighed only 3½ lb (1.6 kg) and the power pack 7 lb (3.2 kg). The receiver covered 3–7.6 megacycles in one waveband while the transmitter had two wavebands covering 3.3–4.5 and 4.5–7.6 megacycles. The power output was about five watts. The sets suffered from a number of shortcomings, not least of which was the ability to interfere with any other wireless set within a hundred yards radius, a fault which did not endear them to agents in built-up areas where they could attract the attention of German listening detectors.

STAFFING THE SECTION

One may wonder how such a small, obscure and secretive establishment recruited the highly skilled personnel necessary to staff its laboratories and workshops. The answer seems to be that word got around, in the case of John Brown among officers concerned with wireless communications. His imaginative skills became apparent early in his military career and spawned a number of extremely successful wireless sets. One of the longest-serving and most talented radio technicians to work at Station IX, Sec Lt (later Maj) John Isaac Brown had lived in the Finsbury Park district of London and from the age of eleven was interested in anything electrical. He subscribed to *Wireless World* (price 4*d*) and learned enough to take over a kit-built wireless set which a friend had failed to make operational, check through it methodically, find the fault and make it work. When he left school he took his wireless set to the firm of Scott-Sessions in Muswell Hill seeking a job. This firm made custom built wireless sets and were sufficiently impressed to take him on as a junior apprentice. Here he was encouraged to ask questions while in the evenings he attended the Regent Street Polytechnic and Northern Polytechnic colleges to further his theoretical technical education.

John Brown became interested in aircraft and flying so, when war was declared it seemed natural for him to apply to join the Royal Air Force. But his wireless firm was classed as carrying out essential work so he was held there in a reserved occupation. Eventually he was called up but to the Royal Signals where the powers that be considered (probably correctly) his skills to be more appropriate. At Catterick he was made an instructor and then one day was told he was being transferred to the War Office. In July 1941 he reported to 55 Broadway to be interviewed by the then Sqn Ldr Frank Pile, instructed about matters of security and, as a second lieutenant, given a travel warrant to 'a place called The Frythe'. His wartime career was thenceforth almost exclusively in the Wireless Section, later to be called the Radio Communications Division.

On his arrival in July 1941 the major expansion of Station IX had not taken place but even so Brown immediately got the impression that what was going on there seemed like way-out science fiction. On the drive was what appeared to be a searchlight. Over dinner with a Maj Schroter, who sported a patch over one eye and was known locally as 'dead-eye Dick', he was told it was a device to beam supersonic sound across no-man's land to drive the enemy mad! Maj Schroter might have known what the device was but it is most unlikely that his explanation to the young second lieutenant was anything but imaginative fiction.

Brown was put to work with a Capt Rickard, given a large, standard-issue Civil Service briefcase complete with the embossed letters 'OHMS' and told to build in it a radio with a range of several hundred miles. He could make full use of the workshop which occupied the conservatory of the mansion. This workshop was staffed by around half a dozen instrument makers and precision tool makers who could work very quickly to a high standard from the most basic of sketches. What was as important was that they were able, and indeed encouraged, to provide their own feedback and ideas about problems they encountered or could foresee. A sketch left with this team on the way to lunch was sometimes turned into hardware and waiting by the time Brown had finished his meal.

One task he was presented with was to see if an ordinary superhet broadcast receiver could be used as a transmitter. He designed a plug-in box which allowed the set to transmit morse code on crystal-controlled short wave frequencies. In September 1941 he was asked to make six of these sets which were called 'L-sets'. He worked on various other projects for people including R.J. Cook of the former D-Section who was dealing with scrambling, coding and remote radio-controlled devices and Capt Bert Lane, whose work on the airborne part of the 'S'-phone was furthered by the use of a Wellington bomber at De Havilland's nearby Hatfield airfield.

From the end of September 1941 many more people arrived at Station IX and it became a 24-hour operation. It was normal to work a 16-hour day, seven days a week. Along with many others, Brown slept in the comfort of the mansion. The increasing tempo of the war was reflected in the urgency attached to everything and the positive response it received. In October, when the numbers of laboratory staff alone had risen to twenty-five, they responded rapidly and produced twelve complete radio sets suitably installed in cases for hurried delivery to the Middle East.

In the late spring of 1942 Brown was asked how quickly could he make a transceiver for communicating with the continent of Europe: it was required in days rather than weeks. This was the period when SOE gained its independence from SIS and work on its own wireless sets could start in earnest. His idea was to adapt a type HE army back-pack set with a range of only a few miles. He had the help of supply liaison officers such as Capt Ward who, brandishing the appropriate piece of official paper, scoured the country to requisition anything needed for this vital work. Brown had only to ask and it would appear very quickly. In August 1942 after a week of hectic work the wireless set was rebuilt to operate on limited frequencies from mains or dry batteries with a range of up to 400 miles and was designated the Type A Mk 1.

The Type A Mk II Suitcase Wireless Set

SOE saw the need for agents to carry their wireless sets, sometimes in great haste, by hand or on bicycles without attracting attention. It therefore conceived the idea of the suitcase set, a wireless transceiver built specifically to fit in an ordinary-looking continental suitcase. The suitcases were produced and 'aged' by Col Wills's Camouflage Section at Station XV, but the 'works' were made at Station IX. The first of these was the Type A Mk I whose valves proved fragile and which was quickly improved as the Mk II. The set comprised three metal boxes each measuring 11 in × 4 in × 3 in, with space at the end for storage of the headset, morse key, spares, etc. The left-hand box contained the receiver, the middle one the transmitter and the right-hand box contained the power pack which provided the choice of either an external 100–240 volt mains supply or a 6 volt car battery. The set operated in two wave bands; 3–4.5 megacycles and 6–9 megacycles, had a power output of 5 watts and the whole case weighed 20 lb (9 kg). Just one prototype was produced before Marconi came to assess it for production in November 1941. Inevitably, there was then a demand for a more powerful set, the Type B, with a range of 1,500 miles and a wider frequency selection. The urgency attached to this project secured the sole use of four of F.J. 'Freddie' Moore's technicians who, according to the history of the section written at the end of the war, 'performed yeoman service'. After a colleague had designed and added a power-pack and it had been fitted into a suitcase, made by the Camouflage Section and suitably aged by being used as a football in the courtyard, it was sent to Pye at Cambridge for production. The drawing office then had to convert the freehand sketches upon which the prototype had been built, into production drawings. The Type B, which had twice the power and versatility of the Type A, had been made in less than a month and by the end of January 1942 three complete Type B Mk I sets had come off the production line. The Type B was later used in the capture of a German general in Crete and in Operation Gunnerside which destroyed the Norwegian heavy water plant and denied Hitler atomic power. The sets also saw service in Singapore and Yugoslavia.

By now 100 of the 'S'-phone ground sets had been produced but the airborne part of the system was proving more problematical. It was also around this time that the laboratory designed and developed an instrument known as the Telephone Interceptor Unit for tapping telephone lines without having to cut them. Their ingenuity extended to a cleverly coded, microwave-operated relay which was successfully demonstrated but did not attract any interest. Their minds were then set the task of devising a vibrator-operated unit for an HT supply to replace the dry battery power for the 'S'-phone, which had proved impractical. Following this Brown was given a free hand to design a smaller Type A Mk II. He made just one prototype before Marconi came to assess it for production in May 1942.

The Wireless Section continued to expand and in January 1942 had a total strength of sixty under the now promoted Lt Col Pickard. It was clearly time for some serious attention to be given to its organisation and it was decided to form four sections: Headquarters, the Radio Research and Development Laboratory, a Supplies Section and a Production Unit. The Radio Research and Development Laboratory was led by Professor A.H. Wilson FRS, a Cambridge mathematics don later to become a director of Courtaulds, and had separate specialists dealing with short-wave apparatus, microwave equipment, laboratory instruments, a model shop, and there were also staff for field trials. The Production Unit was staffed by twenty-five people who were not at this stage required to produce more than small batches of equipment.

The Type B Mk II Suitcase Wireless Set (B2)

Because of the great urgency attached to its design, the Type B Mk I had been a large and heavy collection of various standard components. Now came a demand for the Mk II – a lighter, more robust set. This one was designed completely from scratch and all components were made in the workshops. Col Tommy Davies, known in Baker Street as one of SOE's 'hard men', had set a deadline and to meet it the team worked non-stop for 36 hours, finishing it at the end of February 1942. Such was the urgency for this set that Brown worked through the night of 4 March testing it with people standing by to give any help needed. A Lt Myshrall had a car to rush two sets to a port in the West Country where a ship waited to take them to Cairo. As it happened, the ship became delayed in Malta and when the island's wireless telegraphy station was put out of action by enemy bombing, the powerful Type B Mk IIs were used as a temporary replacement. Technically this was the 3 Mk II but it was usually known as the 'B2' and with the Type A Mk II was the most popular wireless set for SOE's operators in the field from 1943 onwards. It incorporated a feature whereby at the throw of a single switch power could be transferred from the mains to an in-built, 6-volt battery. This was ideal for thwarting Gestapo searchers as they switched off the power to buildings and listened for the transmissions they were monitoring to stop, thus narrowing their search. Such was the importance of the work that it was only after Brown had seen the sets despatched that he was told his wife had given birth to a baby girl and he was granted leave to go and see them both. Soon he was back at The Frythe to work on the instruction books which were essential to any piece of service equipment and to look into the design of a hand generator and a pedal-powered generator for charging the accumulators which powered the wireless sets.

The adaptors for converting a normal receiver into a transmitter were developed further until the Converted Broadcast Receiver was produced. This was a normal domestic continental-pattern wireless set which had been made to serve as a short-wave transmitter. On the face of it, such a set had a great future with SOE in occupied territories but nothing more was heard of the concept. More successful was the miniature broadcast receiver designed by a Norwegian Air Force officer, Lt (later Capt) W. Simonsen. One of these was carried by Maj Everett, who was able to receive the BBC World Service in India and Ceylon. Easy to conceal, this was intended to permit the nationals of occupied countries to listen to the morale-boosting broadcasts and coded messages of the BBC.

In the early summer of 1942 the Wireless Section's strength had risen to sixty-seven, their accommodation being in hastily erected army huts among the trees and rhododendrons of the grounds around The Frythe. More space was urgently needed, as indeed it was for other sections at Station IX. So available factory space was sought and eventually in mid-June the Production Unit moved to the Bontex Knitting Mills on the North Circular Road near Wembley. The Headquarters and Supplies Sections followed a month later and this establishment became known as Station VIIa. The Section seems to have chosen this time to change its title to Radio Communications Division.

The thirty laboratory staff remaining at Station IX were directed by Prof Wilson who was assisted by Dr N.L. Yates-Fish, a physicist, serving as a consultant. A number of small specialist groups evolved to cover short-wave equipment, microwave equipment for aircraft, microwave equipment for ground use, field and air trials, laboratory and test instruments, photographic records and publications, and technical liaison. Then there were the Drawing Office, Model Shop and Stores. Each group comprised on average three persons, two of whom were experts in their fields.

The feedback from agents in the field called for a much smaller and lighter set which could be delivered in a parachute container more easily, carried around with less effort and, most importantly, could be more readily concealed. America had produced the miniature Loctel valves which Brown now incorporated into his draft design, which was passed over to Marconi and became the standard Type A Mk III set. Ill-informed comparisons by Operational Sections between the Type A Mk II and the Type B Mk I sets sparked controversy. What they did not realise was that the requirements to which the designer had to work were different for each set. Brown had fulfilled the requirements, so criticism of RCD was somewhat unfair. It might have been this episode which resulted in Pye of Cambridge being asked in August 1942 to develop Brown's Type A Mk III into a smaller and lighter set than its predecessor but without any loss in performance. In the event the development was a success.

The Type A Mark III Suitcase Wireless Set

This development was smaller and lighter than the B2 and was considered by some to be one of the best sets for SOE's use, being not only the smallest transceiver produced in the Second World War but a product of extremely good miniaturised design and workmanship. It was contained within a small suitcase measuring only 13 in × 9 in × 4 in and an accessories box, the whole set weighing only 9 lb (4 kg). It covered 3.2–9.0 megacycles in two wavebands and produced an output of 5 watts which limited its reliable range to 500 miles.

Under the intense wartime pressures agents sometimes encountered differences of opinion with laboratory staff when they asked for totally impractical features to be incorporated into their sets. Operational Sections came to be regarded as 'absolutely impractical' while the technical staff of RCD were looked upon by them as 'amateurs'. In many ways the entire set-up of Station IX was amateurish. A collection of sharp brains had been plucked from their normal peacetime occupations and set to work on problems in areas which many had never before entered. Such were the demands of SOE that it would have been foolhardy to place research and development contracts with established professional firms of experts, even if they possessed the capacity to indulge in the kind of unconventional activities engaged upon at Station IX.

As it was, a Liaison Group within RCD exchanged ideas with other organisations such as the Telecommunications Research Establishment, the Royal Aircraft Establishment Radio Section, the Signals Radio Development Establishment, Admiralty Signals and with manufacturers of radar equipment.

Brown had the occasional break from the problems of wirelesses, including some electrical work on the Welman one-man submarine, some test runs on the Welbike and some Sten gun firing on the range. At about this time in February 1943 there is evidence but no details of another interesting development, for an order was placed with Creed and Co. Ltd of Telegraph House, Croydon for the production of twenty-four 'semi-automatic morse transmitters'. What these were and whether they had any connection with the high-speed or 'squirt' morse transmission apparatus is not known.[2]

In 1943 the Chief Signals Officer in charge of SOE communications, Brig Nicholls, Royal Signals, who had succeeded Ozanne, visited Station IX and held a meeting in the ante-room where, over drinks on his account, he outlined the need for a successor to the Type B Mk II. And he needed thousands of them. The wireless had to be small, light, robust, capable of operating on any mains voltage – AC or DC – and, above all, it was, of course, very urgent.

In April 1943 concern was expressed at the lack of wireless sets. While the supply of 'A' sets was adequate, there was a chronic shortage of 'B' sets. It was decided that none should go to CCO unless the specific operation for which it was needed was important enough to justify the diversion.

TABLE 2

	April	May	June	July
Demand for 'B' sets	163	163	99	100
Estimated delivery	100	150	50	100

The Miniature Communications Receiver, MCR 1

The leader of the laboratory, Prof A.H. Wilson, received a Laboratory Development Order dated 11 April 1943 for the development of a Miniature Communications Receiver Mk I to the specification agreed. Brown was given the job and moved out of Hut 4 into another with two assistants who had been relieved of all other duties. Capt Ward, the supply liaison officer, was briefed to get anything the team needed. The job had super-priority. Ideas were soon developed into a prototype, all the time considering that this had to be a set suitable for mass production. The packaging of the set was to be a readily disguisable tin. The Philco company at Perivale in north-west London, under the brothers Marcel and Pierre Vaufrouarde, were awarded a contract for 10,000 sets. Brown spent the summer of 1943 sorting out production design problems until in August pilot production started with Sgt Maj Fred Stallworthy, Royal Artillery, taking over liaison work with the manufacturers.

The Miniature Communications Receiver Mk I or MCR1 was, as its name implied, both small and only a receiver. It weighed only 2 lb and was sent out in a Huntley & Palmer's biscuit tin measuring 8½ in × 2 in × 3½ in. *Le recepteur biscuit*, as the French named the set, was soon being produced at the rate of 500 per week and was later to be used in the Far East where the ability to seal the container proved essential in the high humidity.

High Speed Morse Transmissions – 'Squirt' transmissions

On 5 May 1943 the Communications Committee (Technical) had explained to it by someone whose name was not recorded, the principle of the 'squirt' transmitter. This has to be viewed in the light of the great danger agents' wireless operators were exposed to during their periods of transmission. German direction-finding equipment was being improved all the time and the only counter-measures available to operators were to alternate between several wireless sets in different locations and to keep transmissions as short as practical. Around fifteen minutes was considered acceptable; twenty minutes and the risk of detection was increasing rapidly. The 'squirt', or high-speed morse transmitter, was a means of compressing the normal fifteen-minute message into a period of only a few seconds, thereby denying the Germans the time to locate the source. A week after the meeting, Laboratory Development Order No.

140 instructed Mr W.A. Beatty, the deputy to Mr G.A. Willis, who had succeeded Prof Wilson when the latter joined Tube Alloys to work on the atomic bomb, to 'build equipment for a high-speed morse transmitter'. The other part of the problem, the receiver, was to be explored in parallel as a high-speed morse recording system. Beatty left ISRB towards the end of the year and the work passed to his chief assistant, Mr D.J. Spooner. Eric Slater, recruited to ISRB in 1943 from REME to work in the operational research and test groups under Maj Brown, confirms that a device was indeed completed and was capable of transmitting short messages. It was described as a rod on which were a number of brass and insulating cylindrical spacers. By adjusting the length of a brass piece (for example one piece for a morse 'dot' and two for a 'dash') and by doubling the insulators between morse letters, one could simulate a simple message. Some means had to be devised of making this arrangement provide electrical impulses through a transmitter. As a result of a successful trial of a 'squirt' transmitter between Scotland and Station 54 (a Signals Station at Fawley Court, Henley-on-Thames), which was about the same distance as from central France to the SOE receiving station at Grendon near Bicester, it was decided by the Communications Committee (Technical) to order 500 sets of agents' 'squirt' equipment. But sadly this was premature for the equipment was too bulky and a technique for receiving and de-coding the high-speed signals had not been perfected. The development order was eventually cancelled on 20 April 1944. Despite claims in some published works, SOE never issued this intriguing invention to the field except, that is, as a known non-functioning device with the turned German agent Kick in the curious case of Operation Periwig (see Chapter 15).[3]

In *Jacqueline, Pioneer Heroine of the Resistance*, reference is made to a necklace which could be strung with large and small beads in an order that would transmit, when stroked, a pre-selected message at 600 words a minute. Reception was said to be by an American wire recording machine. The author of this book sought to obtain further details from her sources in France but, alas, they had all died.[4]

There is some evidence that a German wireless link existed between Sweden and Norway which used high-speed morse tape transmitters. These had been built on German orders in Danish factories which had been commandeered. With the help of Danish engineers units were obtained and passed to Royal Signals officers working with SOE.[5] The Danes were said to have a 'natural aptitude' for wireless telegraphy matters which might have accounted for the report of a 'squirt' test from Stockholm in June 1944.[6]

Further evidence of the Danes' expertise in this field is quoted by M.R.D. Foot in *Resistance* (p. 276). One of SOE's leading organisers in that country was the Chief Engineer of Bang & Olufsen, Lorens Arne Duus Hansen, whose position gave him access to worldwide technical information as well as many contacts throughout Europe. In the spring of 1943 he completed the third version of a transceiver the size of a Copenhagen telephone directory; much more compact, more powerful and lighter than the British sets in use. Moreover, it used many domestic radio parts so spares were much less of a problem. In August Hansen persuaded SOE to let him supply radio equipment to the Danish Resistance and eventually built around sixty 'telephone book' sets.

At some point, the date is not clear, London asked Hansen if it was possible to transmit morse at high speed. He constructed an electrically driven device in which a paper strip which had been perforated with holes corresponding to the morse message was 'read' by an automatic key and transmitted at seven times the best conventional rate. The signals were recorded in England on wax discs and then played back at a slower, readable speed. The system was used in a limited way in Copenhagen and Jutland. The Gestapo is said to have ignored the rapid transmissions for some weeks on the basis that they hadn't such equipment of their own and it must be too sophisticated for the Danish Resistance.

Another ingenious invention of Hansen's was a means of remote-controlled transmission via the telephone system. Although this was very safe for the operator, it was impossible to change crystals if reception proved poor and it was used to only a very limited extent.[7]

Further evidence that SOE was actively considering 'squirt' transmissions lies in the fact that in the summer of 1944 Station 53b reported that 'Silk Blue has commenced high-speed transmission in the neighbourhood of 100 words per minute and we have successfully received three transmissions covering some thirty messages by this means.'[8]

Meanwhile, Jones was continuing work to improve the 'S'-phone. Air-to-ground trials took place on Newmarket Heath and a simulated reception committee under Bovill would gather in the pitch black of a field near Luton to home-in the aircraft and receive a stick of containers from a Halifax based at Hatfield aerodrome. Less hazardous trials took place at Fishguard using a French fishing boat which had been modified for SOE use. Considerable difficulties were being experienced at this time with the development of the Homing 'S'-phone. In June 1943 Wng Cdr J.C. Corby had been led to believe it was almost ready and was anxious to make use of it. He wrote a letter of complaint to Col Davies and was no doubt advised to be a little more patient.

In 1943 planning was in hand for the invasion of Europe and for offensive action in the Far East. Soon Jedburgh teams of three men were being trained for infiltration into German-occupied territories to organise and prepare Resistance groups for action after the Allies landed on D-Day. It was essential that they had good wireless communications. Various modifications to the Type B Mk II were carried out at their behest. A steam-driven battery charger was also constructed. The tropicalisation of the set needed improving to reduce the ingress of dampness and subsequent rapid mould growth on components, and so Brown designed and built test cabins to simulate Far Eastern conditions in the laboratory.

In the second half of 1943 demand on all departments at Station IX was increasing as the prospect of the 'Second Front', i.e. the invasion of Europe, came closer. Recognition of the importance of signals was its elevation to a Directorate under Brig F.W. Nicholls, who also became a member of SOE Council in September. He was thus responsible for the whole signals organisation including research and supply. Alongside the very real problem of securing suitably qualified and skilled staff to meet these needs, there was also the question of accommodation. What, if any, attention was paid to planning the layout of the hastily erected huts and hangars at The Frythe is not known. The general disposition appears to have been to the south and south-east of the mansion, perhaps to take advantage of the screening afforded by the trees and rhododendrons, perhaps to avoid encroachment on traditional facilities such as the kitchen garden and the Head Gardener's cottage. Whatever it was, the decision seems to have been taken that further expansion of the work of Station IX had to be catered for elsewhere.

The Radio Communications Division had already moved its Headquarters, Production Unit and Supplies Section to Wembley in June of the previous year, leaving only the Laboratory at Welwyn. Then expansion of Supplies Section called for a further move of this group which now numbered 70. In February 1943, under Maj E.J. Kennedy, it transferred to more commodious premises, complete with packaging and despatching facilities, at the Yeast-Vite factory (Station

VIIb) at the northern corner of King George's Avenue and Whippendell Road in Watford. RCD as a whole had expanded from 60 to 320 persons in one year and now all that was left of them at their original home were the 50 in the Laboratory.

Whether the dispersal of the sections was a deliberate policy to avoid keeping all its radio eggs in one basket or was forced upon SOE by sheer lack of suitable accommodation in one place, we shall probably never know. Communication and liaison between the sections must have been difficult for they were now many miles apart. Further dispersal occurred when the Microwave Section of the Production Unit outgrew its premises and found a new home a short distance away in Park Royal. Here it installed Bakelite moulding presses, the press tools for them being made in the factory.

Autumn 1943 saw the last of the original wartime occupiers of The Frythe leave in mid-October when the RCD Laboratory moved to Allensor's Joinery Works (Station VIIc) in King George's Avenue, Watford, just a stone's throw from the Supplies Section. Shortly after this move Maj W. Glendinning succeeded Mr G.W. Willis as head of the Laboratory.

The maintenance of wireless communications with covert agents had always been dogged by the problem of providing a reliable power supply for the sets. One could not guarantee to operate in an area with a notional electrical mains supply, let alone a reliable one. The batteries of the day on the other hand, were fragile in delivery by parachute, needed maintenance with acid and were bulky and heavy to carry around. SOE's experts therefore addressed the problem by designing a series of battery chargers and generators powered by various means from human hand to fire (see later section). Brown's next project was to be one which incorporated a pedal-powered generator in lieu of batteries.

The Type B Mark III Transceiver

At the end of 1943 Brown was asked to produce the Type B Mk III and work started seriously in 1944. This was to work on both CW (morse) and R/T (radio telephone), be positively buoyant, man-carried, capable of operating for several months at a time in the jungle, be fully tropicalised, have die-cast aluminium cases and be hermetically sealed. It would be delivered with a pedal generator in place of troublesome batteries. The whole of 1944 was spent on this project. The pedal generator gearbox was produced by Rotol Ltd, the airscrew company, Hoover made the special generator and Marconi and Radio Gramophone Developments (RGD) were given contracts for the wireless sets. The first models were produced in early 1945 but not more than 500 were completed before the end of the war when the Type B Mk III was handed over to Marconi. The very demanding specification for the Far East requirements had come from Col J.A.C. Knot. In retrospect, all these requirements might not have been necessary and a lower specification could have resulted in it being in service at an earlier date.

So now the Radio Communications Division was dispersed with the Production Unit (Station VIIa) at Wembley and the Supplies Section (Station VIIb) and Laboratory (Station VIIc) at Watford. Dormitory and messing facilities for many civilian and service personnel from The Frythe were provided at Gorhambury House near St Albans which was designated Station XI and was under the command of Maj H.F. Riach. These facilities applied no less to the now scattered RCD. Maj Brown was sharing accommodation with Capt Mats Jenson of the Norwegian Army when they discovered that in the cellars beneath was a clandestine radio station named 'Buttercup' used for transmitting black propaganda to Germany. ORs housed at Gorhambury House were billeted in converted stables which were destroyed by fire on 29 January 1944. Thereafter a small camp of six Nissen huts was provided close to the stables. These were fully occupied by men from Stations VIIb and VIIc below the rank of sergeant. Civilians, sergeants and higher ranks were billeted in the house itself, where there were also some female secretaries from Station IX. But the majority of staff from Stations VIIb and VIIc were housed in civilian billets, where the householder had the advantage of a little more money and another ration book to manipulate. SOE's base stations at Grendon (Station 53), between Aylesbury and Bicester, and later at nearby Poundon (Station 53b) consisted of 125 acres of aerials and many FANYs listening round the clock. As traffic built up it was realised that SOE didn't have enough channels to cope with it. The Post Office Research Establishment at Dollis Hill in north west London came up with the wideband amplifier which was highly directional and could receive up to forty low-powered transmissions. Brown was asked to design small drive units for the wide band amplifiers.

The 51/1 Transmitter

Towards the end of the war SOE produced the 51/1 transmitter measuring 4½ in × 1½ in × 5¾ in, small enough to be carried in an agent's pocket. It weighed only 1¼ lb (567 gm) complete with its battery. It could also be powered by 110–240 volt mains supplies and had a coverage of 3–10.5 megacycles on two wavebands. The power output was 4 watts which enabled the set to send astonishingly clear messages over distances up to 600 miles.

Brown was given the assistance of Dr Yates-Fish, who worked on aerials, and Flt Lt Jack Stowery, on a rest from the field. They soon learned that signals being received were so strong that less powerful, and therefore even smaller, sets could be used. Brown drafted the design for a truly pocket-sized set and Yates-Fish and Stowery finished it as Types 50/11 and 50/31 designs. A small number were made but in the spring of 1945 it was too late in the war to enter serious production. Some of the special components which Brown had incorporated into his sets appeared in postwar designs by the Government Communications Research Establishment (GCRE) at Elstree, and the Diplomatic Service and SAS used his wireless sets as late as the Sixties. His vital work over, Brown was posted back to the Royal Signals at Catterick and subsequently given a draft to Italy.

Miniaturisation of wireless equipment was not restricted to the Allies. The German wireless detector vans with their roof-mounted rotatable aerials were easily recognised by Resistance lookouts, who could pass on the appropriate warnings. The vans were later replaced by converted saloon cars, in France frequently the ubiquitous black Citroën. The equipment was subsequently developed to the stage where the German searcher had it hidden beneath his clothing with an indicator strapped to his wrist. Wireless operators and their guards subsequently kept a lookout for fat men who constantly looked at their wrist watches!

There was no doubt that SOE pulled together a great deal of technical talent, a match perhaps for the bravery of those in the Country Sections. Recruiting was done largely on the 'old boys' network', one eminent officer, scientist or engineer being asked if he knew of anyone suitable for such and such a job. As with other Sections, RCD's recruitment procedure meant that anyone recommended in this way was often too deeply involved before they realised exactly what organisation they had entered. John Brown of the Wireless Section had never heard of SOE until 1944, three years after he started work for them! Security was very good. Newcomers were told that whatever they needed to know to do their jobs, they would be told. Any questions were to be addressed to their immediate boss. Hence, if anyone had been noticed to be asking questions of others, they would come under suspicion – but there were few, if any. John Brown was particularly careful what he said when he attended meetings in London, a task for which he was allocated a motorcycle as his personal transport.

For the lower ranks, when there was a lull in the general tempo of activity they could be put on other duties such as firing off silenced Sten guns on the range to test for wear on the components. Eric Slater was once sent to Baker Street to install a hidden microphone in a room to be used for the interrogation of a North African woman agent suspected of betrayal. He did not, of course, ever know the outcome.

BATTERY CHARGERS AND GENERATORS

As briefly mentioned earlier, the scientists and engineers also considered the peripheral needs of the agents by designing radio battery chargers driven by hand, pedal, petrol, mains power and steam. The latter was devised at Station VIIc, based on a small steam engine with a drum boiler, and is reputed to have worked well. There was even a thermal-powered charger, based on an American design, which consisted of a 9 in diameter metal chimney standing 18 in high on three feet. Around the chimney were hundreds of thermo-couples which, when a fire was lit within the chimney, were supposed to generate electricity. As far as the Norwegian section, for example, was concerned the steam generator was most popular despite its weight of 80 lb and the problem of the dispersal of its smoke. The petrol version was good where this fuel could be obtained, but it was very noisy and therefore dangerous to operate under clandestine conditions.

There were at least three pedal-powered generators, some of which were developed in the Model Shop at Station VIIc. One was a simple device which was clamped on to the rear forks of a standard bicycle. The chain was lengthened to run over the additional sprocket on the generator. When in use the bicycle was supported on its rear stand and the operator would pedal as required. Another version consisted of a foldable triangulated tube support with a bicycle saddle on the top, a set of pedals near the bottom and a chain driving the generator which was beneath the saddle. Without any handlebars or other means of steadying oneself while pedalling, this would have quickly become a tiresome and awkward exercise. A more sophisticated model, the type 52/1, was a development of a model captured from Italian Forces. This had a metal tube frame supporting a canvas seat from which extended a tube carrying a set of pedals incorporated in a generator. Although the operator's semi-supine position looked quite comfortable, he still had to expend considerable energy in pedalling to drive the generator. A hand-powered generator produced for the Jedburgh parties took the form of a box with a cranking handle on one end, supported on three legs. Both the hand- and the pedal-operated generators were unpopular, being very laborious to use for any length of time, while the mains trickle chargers were useful as long as there was a mains supply available. The preferred accumulators were 6 volt, 80 amp/hr car types which had the drawback of being heavy and prone, not surprisingly, to damage when included in a parachute supply drop.

It is interesting to see the estimates of wireless sets required for the year 1945 and their costs. (To find the equivalent cost in 2001 multiply by 23.) SOE had found it necessary to provide each agent as far as possible with three wireless sets hidden in a local circuit and used in turn to avoid detection by the increasingly diligent German detection teams. To allow for other mishaps, SOE had to budget for nine sets to keep each operator in contact with London.

TABLE 3

3,900	Suitcase sets Type A Mk III with spares	£158,370
		(£40 12s 0d each)
21,600	Midget Communications Receivers with spares	£259,200
		(£12 0s 0d each)
6,755	Suitcase sets Type B Mk III with spares	£323,380
		(£47 17s 5d each)

In addition, the programme included 1,600 steam-powered battery chargers and 1,725 pedal-powered generators.

Marconi's Parsons Green factory supplying A II sets was wiped out by enemy action in spring 1944 and gave rise to concern about how to maintain delivery to the field. The other Marconi factory at Hackbridge was producing the A III transceiver but its production was also threatened by the loss of key staff to the forces as the invasion of Europe approached.[9]

Flying bomb activity in 1944 caused a loss of production from the Production Unit at Station VIIa in Wembley. It was therefore moved out of range of the land-launched missiles and established at Kay's Garage in Bristol Street, Birmingham (Station VIId) in August.

As the war ran towards its close so activity in the Laboratory diminished. In the last month of 1944 the staff of Station VIIc fell from 113 to 85. After VE Day SOE's European activities began shutting down but there was still demand for the Far East Theatre and in August Maj Reg Vince, the Officer in Charge at the Yeast-Vite Factory at Watford gave the following breakdown of the estimate of cost for a B III transceiver:

TABLE 4

Receivers from RGD	£110
Gearbox from S.E. Opperman	£15
Pedal generator from Dayton Cycles	£14
Generator MAP from Hoover	£8
Smoothing equipment from Philco	£10
TOTAL	£157

After VJ Day the run-down became rapid. Maj Vince, as Chief Supplies Officer, spent a day cancelling orders to suppliers, stopping half a million pounds' worth between breakfast and lunchtime. Parties were organised to collect all unfinished work, materials and drawings from contractors and take it to the SOE stores. Station VIIb at the Yeast-Vite Factory closed on 10 January 1946, the remaining assets being transferred to Station XII at Stevenage. Brown was transferred from Station VIIc also to Station XII where he was resident for a while with a laboratory in a Nissen hut. His assistants were posted away and before long his equipment was loaded into trucks to be taken away and dumped down a disused mineshaft. He packed all his papers into a filing cabinet but most eventually went to the destructor. Personnel in RCD as a whole had reached a peak of 740 at 30 June 1944. From October 1945 closure was set in train, being finally completed on 11 January 1946.

THIRTEEN

ORGANISATION OF SUPPLY AND PRODUCTION

The development of new items of equipment started typically with an original idea or requirement and consideration of how it might be exploited in the work of SOE. This was followed by research, development, trials and finally production. In the previous chapters an account has been given of the evolution of a wide range of devices and equipment. In this chapter we summarise the way in which such projects were taken from the production prototype to mass production.

Upon the declaration of war the small experimental group of Section D at Bletchley Park expanded and soon sought a new home away from the increasingly busy de-coding operation. The home they found in November 1939 was Aston House on the outskirts of Stevenage. The mansion was converted into an officers' mess and the 46 acres of the estate provided ample room for expansion (see Chapter 3).

In the closing weeks of 1939 Dr Drane was appointed Commandant of Section, Station XII, which used the cover name of Signals Development Branch, Depot No. 4, War Office. Mr E. Norman and Dr F.A. Freeth joined on a permanent basis in early 1940, the latter, somewhat entertaining scientist having come from the Research Division of Imperial Chemical Industries at Northwich in Cheshire with the reputation for having solved the explosive supply problem in the First World War. Capt E. Ramsey Green (D/D2), Mr D.A. Barnsley (D/X1a), Capt O.J. Walker (D/X2) were appointed and shortly afterwards Lt C.V. Clarke (D/DP) joined the section. During 1940 Capt F. Davis (D/DS) was appointed Stores Officer.

At first the work at Aston House was organised on the basis of two Sections; D/D (engineering and small mechanisms) and D/X (laboratory work on explosive and incendiary devices, chemical and physical problems) and included a research laboratory and a development section. The latter was also responsible for placing orders with outside contractors. Financial control had not been given a great deal of thought and in the early days the Station existed virtually on a day-to-day basis, sometimes being overdrawn on a reimbursable account from Headquarters in Baker Street.

Command of the Station passed to Capt (later Lt Col) L.J.C. Wood, RE and later the name was changed to War Department, Aston and then on 12 May 1941 it was officially given the cover name Experimental Station 6 (War Department) or ES6 (W.D.). SOE, however, continued to refer to it as Station XII. Leslie John Cardew Wood was 16 years old when the First World War started. He had been educated for five years at Dulwich College, for two years by a private tutor in France and for a total of four years at the City and Guilds College, interrupted by military service as a Lt Tech in the Royal Flying Corps. After the war when he had finished his studies he spent seven years with the Greaves Cotton Company in Bombay working on refrigeration and water purification plant before returning to England to become manager and later director of Bell's Asbestos Company at Slough. Here he worked on research into and development of applications for uses of asbestos and was the joint holder of a number of patents. On the outbreak of the Second World War Wood was commissioned into the Royal Engineers where, from 1939 to 1943, he was responsible for building up and commanding Experimental Station 6 (WD) at Aston House, Stevenage. In 1943 he was posted to India where he became Director of the Special Forces Development Centre and Colonel 'Q' of Force 136 until 1944.

Early in 1941 a considerable further expansion in personnel took place and it was soon clear that even greater expansion of the workplaces would be necessary as well as increased staff accommodation. At this time various schemes for reorganising the research and development organisation were under consideration. Following the appointment of Newitt as Director of Scientific Research in July 1941 the research side of the establishment (D/X) under Colin Meek, the explosives expert, together with some of the development work of D/D, was moved to Station IX at The Frythe where some additional temporary buildings had been erected, and where they would be freed from the pressures of production. Here they joined the Wireless Section which had been at The Frythe since 1939. Station XII was then reorganised to handle design, production, testing, stores and administration.

The Design Department consisted of a drawing office and a development workshop staffed by civilians under Capt (later Maj) E. Ramsay Green RE. Their responsibility was to take the sketches and prototypes of devices originating from Station IX and work them into proper engineering drawings which could be passed to an outside contractor for bulk production. Prototypes made in a research workshop would often be fabricated or machined without attention being paid to the economies of quantity production. Designers with a knowledge of production engineering would therefore introduce the subtle changes necessary without detriment to the effectiveness of the device. This department also had to find contractors with the necessary qualities to manufacture the items and place the initial contracts with them.

An increasing number of devices and a greater volume of production made it necessary to form a separate Production Section under Mr W.H.B. Billinghurst, who was to control all outside contracts by placing and progressing all orders and inspecting work at the manufacturer's premises. The Testing Laboratory, which carried out routine testing, assisted the Production Section in their inspection role. In December 1941 Capt (later Maj) W. Morland Fox, RE took over the Section.

From June 1940 the Stores Section had started to assemble mixed parcels of stores for the Auxiliary Units intended to wage guerrilla warfare should the Germans invade Britain. In February 1941 the first large order for 1,000 cases was placed.

The organisation of both the Stores and the Administration Sections was at this time very basic with neither a stores accounting system nor qualified orderly room staff for the administration of military personnel.

Explosive and incendiary stores, some in an unreliable state, together with more general stores were kept in small buildings in a confined area close to the mansion. The regulations governing the safe storage of explosives had not been implemented when a serious fire took hold in the early hours of 4 January 1942. The more dangerous stores were not involved and the damage was localised but it resulted in surplus stores being moved to Fawley Court (Signals Section's establishment at Henley-on-Thames) and a few 'Elephant Shelters' being obtained to improve segregation.

At the beginning of 1942 plans were made for a further substantial expansion of the facilities at Station XII. General stores, incendiary and explosive storage, accommodation for explosive filling and a light engineering workshop were completed early in 1943 and there followed a proportional increase in staff. In roughly the same period improvements were made with the financial organisation of the Station when Mr (later Sir) George Turner of the Ministry of Supply and the Master General of Ordnance Finance Department, War Office (MGOF(a)) met and began to pay contractors' invoices from their funds. In addition, arrangements were made for small bills up to £5 in value to be paid directly.

The Stores Section came under increasing pressure in terms of quantities and urgency as they found it impossible to obtain the relatively small quantities of materials at the short notice demanded by the operational sections. It became apparent that a major contributory factor was the lack of any forward planning. The problem was discussed with the user groups and MGOF(a). As a result estimates of requirements for six months ahead were prepared. The increased flow of new prototype devices from Stations IX and XV led in turn to overloading of the Design Department in their task of preparing manufacturing drawings. In a transfer of functions the Production Department took on the task of finding manufacturers and liaising with Station IX on devices moving towards production. Coincidentally, problems were experienced with the inspection function and the somewhat risky procedure of delegating it to individuals at the contractors' works did not prove successful and was abandoned.

The arrival of RAOC personnel in 1942 under Capt (later Maj) D.S. Duke introduced a modified (for the special requirements of SOE) normal ordnance procedure for stores accounts. Attempts were made to comply with the Magazine Regulations and official classifications were obtained from the Explosive Storage and Transport Committee for all SOE devices. Every device now carried in its shipping classification a generic title, explosive group and storage and stowage class. Even at the height of a world war, bureaucracy had to be complied with. In July the storage problem was eased by the allocation of a considerable amount of space at 84 Command AD at Sandy in Bedfordshire.

Over this period the social character of Station XII changed steadily as the majority of new staff were RAOC, REME or RE officers. This increasingly military atmosphere was in contrast to that at Station IX where most of the experimental staff were civilians.

In 1942, SOE and CCO personnel began a series of operations involving detailed planning and 'tailor-made' stores. Targets were very precise and carefully researched and to obtain the best results the stores had to be specific to these targets. Because of the large number of special charges and initiators produced for this campaign, towards the end of the year a splinter group of the Testing Laboratory called Operational Supplies was formed with the purpose of designing and supplying stores for ad hoc operations. The Testing Laboratory was then freed to carry out its inspection work.

Operational Supplies Section was under the direction of the Technical Operational Planning Committee chaired by Lt Col J.L. Bliss. On this committee were represented Stations IX and XII, the operating section of SOE or other force involved (for work was also done, for example, for CCO), the training section and the 'G' staff. Thus the special stores for ad hoc operations were produced almost exclusively at this Station, where close control could be exercised by teams under Maj C.S. Munro and later Maj D.W. Pond. An enlarged workshop complete with its own raw material and tool stores was erected in September and staffed by REME personnel under Maj C.F. Moore.

As the stores became more varied it became apparent that large quantities were being ordered to inadequate descriptions. This eventually gave rise to the formation in December 1942 of the Quality Control Department which was responsible for the preparation of specifications of stores and inspection duties, under Capt (later Maj) J.G. Bedford. The original intention had been to have inspection carried out by in-house staff but it soon became apparent that it would not be possible to recruit and train sufficient numbers. The Central Inspection Agency (CIA) took on the task but with the proviso that Station XII had also to be satisfied, a condition which lead to many disputes with manufacturers. Large numbers of finished parts, components and sub-assemblies, manufactured both internally and by outside contractors, were stored for issue to others for assembly into finished devices.

Early in 1943 Bliss was given another task: Co-ordinating Officer between Research and Production Departments, where liaison had tended to be somewhat fragmented and greater formalisation was seen to be necessary. He therefore set up Co-ordination Meetings at which Stations IX and XII were both represented and these continued for the rest of the war. A further improvement in liaison developed when, in a reciprocal move, Station XII in the person of Capt Bedford was represented on the Station IX Trials Committee.

By the summer of 1943, with increasing deliveries of air-dropped stores to the Resistance in Europe, shortages once again caused serious problems. Headquarters therefore carried out longer-term forecasting of its needs and gave estimates up to the end of 1944, refining these as the war situation developed. Maj R. Gardiner, REME took over the Production Department in the summer of 1943 on the posting of Morland Fox to the USA.

Headquarters turned its attention to the allocation of priorities for the available stocks of stores. It was clearly unreasonable to expect the Stores Section at Station XII to know whose application carried the most importance so an Allocations Committee was set up to meet once a month to allocate the available stocks of stores among the various applicants. The new longer-term estimates included quantities of stores not previously dealt with and raised questions about the contracts needed to meet them. For all contracts over £1,000 value it was decided to set up running contracts through the Ministry of Supply instead of using Local Purchase Orders. This was welcomed by the Finance Department, whose accounting arrangements had not kept pace with the increase in activity, giving rise to delays and mistakes. The change provided only a brief respite however as the problems then showed themselves with the large increase in invoices for raw materials used by the increasingly busy workshops.

In November 1943 Wood was posted to India and Bliss took over command. By January 1944 the production organisation was tackling large runs of high-quality items for various sections of SOE. Capstan runs of 10,000 pieces were not uncommon and the sheet metal shop produced 50,000 boxes of various types in a year. All the production tools were designed and made at Station XII in what was, in effect, its own toolroom. In September 1944 Capt (later Maj) E.C. Kelly was appointed officer-in-charge.

As preparations for D-Day got under way, orders for special demolition stores for use by raiding parties diminished drastically and Operational Supplies Department became increasingly involved in the production of items which the overloaded ordnance factories could not handle. Station XII produced 87,000 1½ lb (0.7 kg) standard charges in ten months and 5,000 rail charges in three months. Half a dozen soldiers from Station XII were sent to the Royal Ordnance Factory at Elstow to use their facilities to pour 25/75 pentolite explosive into MD1 clams, limpets, MSC charges, spigot bomb heads and a variety of special purpose charges.

An indication of the somewhat hand-to-mouth organisation of wartime ventures such as Station XII is shown by the fact that it was not until the end of 1943 that the electrical problems of the site were taken seriously. Throughout the war extensions and the addition of machinery had been carried out in a piecemeal manner without consideration for the effect on the site as a whole. Almost inevitably, a time came when the unbalanced load across the three-phase electrical system became a serious problem and further examination revealed some parts of the system to be unsafe. A separate small section was therefore set up under Capt J.N. Barnett RE to take responsibility for all electrical installations throughout the Station. This was later extended to include the main boilers whose heating system had so far suffered similar neglect. Early in 1944 the sub-station capacity was increased to 400 KVA. A year later a 1,000 amp plating plant was added to the electrical loading.

The departure of Ramsay Green for the USA in April 1944 precipitated an organisational change. The Design Department closed, the drawing office and design function being absorbed by Quality Control and the toolroom and prototype shop by the Workshops. This was claimed to make the Workshops more flexible and able to tackle all development work. The transfer of the drawing office to Quality Control tightened up procedures and ensured that a master drawing could not be altered without the approval of all concerned, including the Trials Committee. Inspection procedures were also made more formal and a system of filing for technical correspondence, drawings, specifications, etc., was at last introduced.

Belatedly, in June 1944 a new accounting system was introduced into the Finance Department by Capt (later Maj) F.J.G. Roberts. The double-entry ledger accounts proved of immediate benefit and even permitted the resolution of disputes outstanding since the early days of the Station. By the end of the summer of 1944 building work at the Station was completed. A new Entertainments Hall, Civilian Restaurant, Routine Test Laboratory, Explosive Packing Shed and an enlarged NAAFI were brought into use. With clear confidence in the future, a piece of land was set aside for the controlled disposal of unwanted stocks of explosive.

The increased attention to the war in the Far East once again raised the problems of tropical packing for stores. Research had been going on at both Station XII and Station IX and, of course, elsewhere in the services. As a result of this work it was decided to redesign nearly all packings and the Carpenters Shop was set up on a semi-production basis to facilitate the change.

Some original development work was done in collaboration with the Arc Manufacturing Company on the welding of polyvinyl chloride (PVC) sheets using high frequency electric current – a technique which became widely adopted after the war.

SOE was very aware of the consequences of the enemy adopting a scorched earth policy as it withdrew from occupied countries and had made preparations with Resistance groups to counter this threat. Special devices had been designed and Station XII had the task of producing, packing and despatching these for infiltration into Scandinavia.

After the end of the war in Europe contracts for orders for the Far East continued but attention turned to the problems of closing SOE Stations and disposing of the surplus stores. Station VIII at Queen Mary reservoir, Staines and Station 61 were wound up. After the end of all hostilities all orders were cancelled and staff reductions began.

The final task which fell to Station XII was to hold for disposal the remnants of Stations VI, XV, VII, IX, XVII and the Exhibition Room at the Natural History Museum in South Kensington.[1]

FOURTEEN

SUPPLY, FINANCE AND MANPOWER PROBLEMS

SUPPLIES SECTION

For the sake of completeness it is perhaps worth mentioning briefly the facilities which worked to procure the many hundreds of different items required by SOE for its day-to-day operation and in particular to permit the original research work to proceed in a time of severe general shortages of materials. Any organisation which is regularly equipping hundreds of personnel and despatching them overseas must eventually have a need for a supply department to locate and procure items as and when required and to keep account of the prices paid for that inevitable future reckoning. When the organisation itself is producing hardware, or having it made by commercial firms, the need is greater and extends to a stores system with adequate means of stock, financial and security controls.

SOE set up its Supply Section (or E Section) in December 1940 under Sqn Ldr (later Wg Cdr) Pyle who was given the symbol E. He and his secretary Miss Rheinhold worked alone for a couple of months setting up a system to cover signals, all stores provided by SOE, the Army, Air Force and Navy, shipping, control of Stations VI, IX and XII and the photographic section. Shortly after, its work also embraced the coding and deciphering sections. Early 1941 saw the arrival of Lt (later Cmdr) E.A. Milne RNVR (symbol E1) and Mrs Hemmings who was to become his secretary. Then Mr (later Maj) Dansey joined to assist Pyle with the codes and cipher work.

It very soon became apparent that the supplies dropped by parachute to the relatively few agents operating in the field at this time required more than casual assembly and packing. If they were to survive the drop some considerable thought and care must be given to the way the package or container was put together and protected. In

April 1941 a Mr H.L. Boley was recruited to become a special packer for urgent operations. So the Supply Section began its growth.

SOE's main need was to procure relatively small numbers of items of specialised equipment notwithstanding the millions of Time Pencils and hundreds of thousands of small arms it handled by the end of the conflict. Military stores were drawn through the War Office and on a much smaller scale from the Admiralty and Air Ministry. Where items had to be manufactured and special production runs were required there was usually sufficient goodwill to ensure adequate priority was given for the small quantities involved.

The handling of stores was centralised at certain specific points. The military equipment depot was at Knoll School, Camberley. The Arms Section, as we have seen, was at Bride Hall near Ayot St Lawrence, not far from Station IX. The Motor Transport Section with its own repair depot was at the North Road Garage at Welwyn. These facilities represented a fairly normal organisation and one which grew eventually to a total of twenty-eight persons made up of a G1, two G2s, two G3s, six junior officers, seven secretaries, three statistical clerks, two registry clerks, four other ranks and one packer. This work expanded rapidly and led to the establishment of several Packing Stations. E Section was responsible for the procurement of all stores for SOE except wireless stores, transport, stationery and camouflage.[1]

FINANCE

Of all the aspects of SOE, the one which prompted most sudden amnesia or invoked the Official Secrets Act most readily was the question of finance. When one considers the organisation was responsible for large amounts of high-quality forgeries of all kinds, it is not surprising that there was a reluctance to publish details of the financial management of its activities. By the very nature of the operation, a secret organisation, creating and issuing large sums of cash, and all in the frenzy of a vicious worldwide conflict, it was not unexpected to find the accounting procedures were not as tidy and watertight as one would expect from a peacetime endeavour. Many, if not most, of SOE's senior players, true to their calling, took these secrets to the grave.

From time to time attempts were made through the House of Commons to identify the source of SOE's funds. In 1941 the Minister of Information was asked whether certain named individuals (including Hambro and Sporborg) were in the pay of his Ministry and whether they paid income tax. His simple answer was that 'these gentlemen were not employed by him'. The question should have been put to the Minister of Economic Warfare! The following year a similar question concerning members of a leading firm of London lawyers was put to the Foreign Minister: he too could answer honestly that the costs of none of them was borne by the Foreign Office. Sweet-Escott seems to indicate that these might have been put-up questions to throw the nosey politicians off the scent.[2] It was only much later that it emerged that SOE drew its funds from a secret fund administered by 'C', the Head of the equally secret organisation, SIS (now MI6). It is relevant that when Everett first joined SOE in October 1942 he was paid weekly in crisp new £5 notes: a month or two later the system changed and income tax was deducted!

One of the aspects reported upon in the Playfair and Hanbury-Williams Report of 18 June 1942 was the apparently casual way in which, when SOE provided stores for other services, most usually for CCO, they were not repaid. The reason was shown to be that SOE received a great deal of help from Service Departments free of charge: all service issues, all material obtained through the Ministry of Supply, the buildings at Station XII and the pay of all the ORs on its establishment. So when Stations IX and XII increased their facilities to supply CCO the extra cost to SOE was restricted to the overheads at The Frythe, the pay of any additional officers and a few miscellaneous purchases. Playfair and Hanbury-Williams recognised that to set up a bureaucratic procedure for mutual repayment would have unnecessarily burdened SOE and strained its security, so it was left as it was.[3]

The only times money is mentioned in the files pertaining to The Frythe is in connection with a few monthly statements of 'devices paid for', the development of the Welman one-man submarine, and suitcase radios. But in the History of E Section – the Supplies Section in Baker Street – which in the early days, at least, exercised some control over Stations VI, IX and XII, there is the following enlightening text written immediately after the cessation of hostilities:

> CD made arrangements with various services to the effect that SOE demands should be met without any questions being asked as to why they were required and that everything should be written off and thereby save any form of accounting for the stores by this organisation. This proved more than valuable to

this organisation as releases were made without query by all three services until the time came when our demands were such that they seriously conflicted with the service requirements generally.[4]

Records of financial matters are sparse and give only the slightest flavour of the sums of money spent at Station IX and its associated establishments. For example between 26 July and 26 August 1942 the value of devices paid for under a sanction known as MGOF(a) (see Chapter 13), as opposed to the free issue of stores, was £59,093, bringing the total for the year 1942 to £368,085 (about £8.5m in present-day terms). Corresponding figures for the month 25 September to 25 October 1942 were £39,032 and £466,129. These figures probably represent the value of devices despatched from Station XII and not the research and development costs.

In the spring of 1942, £3,000 was sanctioned for the Welman project, equivalent to £69,000 at 2002 prices. At the end of that year the cost of producing a Welman in the workshops at The Frythe was given as £800 (£18,500 in 2002 terms) but if a large enough order was to be placed with a commercial firm it was estimated to be £1,300 (£30,000 in 2002 terms).

Nowadays the economical way to produce an item is to have it made in large numbers by a commercial firm which is geared-up and experienced in that type of work and which has been selected on the basis of competitive tendering. During wartime, however, short cuts were constantly having to be taken, commercial controls were often being eroded in the interests of national necessity and, with enormous pressures on key industries, the choice of contractor could be severely limited. Station IX had neither the facilities nor staff to enter upon large-scale production so the hull of the Welman was handed over to the Pressed Steel Company, producers in peacetime of motor car bodies, and the Welfreighter to Shelvoke and Drewery, makers of dust carts.

In 1945 the Type A Mk III suitcase wireless sets with spares cost around £40 each, which equates to over £900 at 2002 prices. The Type B Mark III at £47 was equivalent to £1,100 and the Midget Communications Receiver at £12 would have cost around £270 in 2002. Once again as we have seen, design and development work was initiated at Station IX and quantity production was handed over to experienced large-scale production firms like Marconi and Philco.

The cost of SOE's activities as a whole was for many years one of their most closely guarded secrets and in spite of all the inevitable doubt about their accounting methods the astonishing fact remains that at the bottom line it actually showed a profit, and a huge one at that. Grp Capt J.F. Venner, the Director of Finance and Administration, came up with a final account showing a profit of £23m. This incredible sum can be explained almost entirely by Walter Fletcher's astounding monetary dealings in Nationalist China.

Fletcher was a physically very large man, half-Central European, who lived on the margin of merchanting and smuggling. He persuaded Dalton and then Mackenzie to let him try to smuggle rubber out of the Japanese-occupied Dutch East Indies for which he was given a Treasury credit of £100,000, one fifth of what he had asked for. After two years, during which he moved from the Dutch East Indies to French Indo-China, he had not produced any rubber. He managed to persuade both SOE and the Treasury to let him try mainland China where SOE was forbidden to operate. Fletcher claimed to be merely making friends with Chinese magnates, their wives and mistresses, all of whom had a liking for the expensive things of life. He arranged for de Beers to put up diamonds and for Swiss firms to supply thousands of the finest watches for which SOE paid in sterling, and which were smuggled out through France by agents thinking they were handling aircraft gunsights. Both the diamonds and the watches were sold in China at hugely inflated prices, netting SOE around £77m. In *SOE in the Far East*, Charles Cruikshank describes this as 'the biggest currency black market in history'. And all with full Treasury approval!

MANPOWER

The Welman project had highlighted the need for many more highly skilled technical workers. Satisfying the demand for workers was an ongoing problem for all sectors of both civilian and military life. Men of military age had been called up to the armed forces unless they were in a 'reserved occupation': a job which was vital to the nation's well-being, such as a farmer or a coal miner. Women had taken over many of the less skilled jobs in engineering, munitions and, of course, on the farms with the Women's Land Army. They had also taken on some highly skilled work such as ferrying aircraft (anything from a Tiger Moth biplane to a Lancaster bomber) in the Air Transport Auxiliary (ATA). The women of the First Aid Nursing Yeomanry

(FANY) mounted round-the-clock watch at SOE radio stations receiving morse messages from agents and provided drivers for SOE officers on duty.

Places like Station IX needed many technicians to work on wireless sets, weapons, special devices and equipment. Devices which were under development needed to be fabricated from scratch, tried out, modified, tried again and altered yet again. The very nature of the process required intelligent appreciation from highly skilled precision technicians and machinists who could maintain a rapport with the scientific inventors of the gadgetry. But Station IX was not the only establishment with a shortage of these skills and competition in recruiting became evident. Officers could be recruited from the Services, industry, government research departments and universities. It was much more difficult to obtain good development engineers and design draughtsmen and the Drawing Office at Station IX was never staffed to keep pace with the engineering shops. Fortunately the best technicians, toolmakers and fine machinists could fabricate from sketches and verbal instructions. The recruitment of toolmakers to an establishment such as Station IX may seem somewhat out of place. A toolmaker is a person who can, by using precision machines such as lathes, milling machines, shapers and grinders, make a complicated device to facilitate mass production of an item. The fabrication of the prototypes of many of the one-off devices dreamt up by SOE's scientists and engineers required the same skills and machinery as the precision devices (or 'tools') for mass production in industry.

There was a general disregard among many of the government ministries for the importance of subversive activities. This attitude tended to force SOE into taking matters into their own hands and attempting to develop devices of all sorts, some of which, with hindsight, were clearly outside their field of competence. The submersibles, the spigot gun and the Welmine were all examples upon which much effort was expended but which might have been far more successful had they been designed and developed by a larger and more experienced arm of one of the three main Armed Forces. This lack of support for clandestine subversive forces resulted in some service departments being indifferent towards SOE, an example being in the manpower crisis for technicians. There was one notable exception in Sir George Turner of the Ministry of Supply, who appreciated subversion and helped SOE.

In December 1942, at the height of the development of the

Welman one-man submarine, F.T. Davies, the Director of Services, minuted CD bemoaning the problems of recruiting technicians and retaining them in the face of tempting offers from better recognised departments when the workload was on the increase. CD passed the grumble to Lord Selborne, the Minister of Economic Warfare, suggesting he should get the Minister of Production to inform the Minister of Labour that ISRB should be protected against poachers. No doubt the Minister of Labour was inundated with similar requests from many organisations both civilian and military, who considered their work to be of the utmost importance to the nation.

FIFTEEN

SPECIAL OPERATIONS INVOLVING R&D SECTION

The Research and Development Section of SOE was concerned in the main with scientific work which would show benefits for the Allied cause over a wide range of operations in various theatres of war. Thus the tyrebursters, various switches, wireless sets, motorised submersible canoes and all the other inventions were planned to be used throughout the area of conflict wherever they were appropriate. There were other, rarer occasions when devices were produced for ad hoc operations where circumstances dictated that they needed to be manufactured specifically for particular targets. While there were many such operations, there were a few which, because of their importance or sheer scale, deserve special mention here. As will be apparent, the scientific approach is not restricted to the laboratory bench: it is equally applicable beneath the sea or in dropping objects from high altitude.

OPERATION BRADDOCK (FORMERLY THE 'MOON' PROJECT)

On 27 May 1942 Churchill sent a personal minute to the Minister of Economic Warfare, Lord Selborne, saying: 'I commend to your notice a recent book by John Steinbeck, *The Moon is Down*, published this year by Viking Press of New York. In addition to being a well-written story, it stresses, I think quite rightly, the importance of providing the conquered nations with simple weapons such as sticks of dynamite which could be easily concealed and are easy in operation.'[1]

Several copies of the book were purchased and distributed to ministers and the sentiments within it became the basis for what was initially called the 'Moon' project (but was later renamed Operation

Braddock). Ideas crystallised and the plan for the 'Moon' project, which was reduced to two schemes, was submitted to the Chiefs of Staff on 28 September 1942.

Scheme I was to deliver by parachute 50,000 small packages of arms, explosives and incendiaries broadcast to nationals of whichever country was to be invaded by the Allies, but not until the invasion had occurred. Scheme II was to deliver by floating down on instruction cards large quantities of simple incendiary devices to foreign workers and disaffected nationals inside Germany. The deliveries were to start as soon as the devices were ready and aircraft were available.

Sanction for an initial 1,000,000 incendiaries was given and trials of the device were carried out on 9 January 1943. The Station IX device consisted of a small incendiary filled with petroleum gel and ignited by a Time Pencil fuse with a 30-minute delay. It would burn for four minutes and reach a temperature of 2000°C. The instructions were printed in English, German, Russian, French, Polish and Czech to reach a wide readership among the hundreds of thousands of forced labourers in Germany. Trials of the parachute qualities of the instruction cards were carried out from the tower of Birmingham University. Lord Selborne, who was also SOE's minister, was very keen on the project and the Prime Minister gave his tentative approval for Scheme II. With half a million incendiaries due to be ready by mid-April and a further half million by mid-May, an additional three million devices were sanctioned on 8 February. An interesting and typically devious proposal was for the dropping of large numbers of the instruction cards rolled into little balls as if thrown away by potential saboteurs who had read the instructions and hidden the incendiaries. The problem of how best to drop the devices was addressed and it was considered that low-level drops were too dangerous, while high-level drops would result in too great a spread of the devices on the ground. The latter was thought, on balance, to be the more acceptable.

Between October 1942 and January 1943 a certain Capt Bannister was experimenting with incendiary devices he had invented, suspended from beneath small balloons. These were to be released in favourable weather conditions from eastern England in the somewhat naïve anticipation that the fire-raising part would be released, presumably after a set time delay, over an enemy target. Even with the best weather forecasts of those days, the unpredictability of the wind strengths and directions at various heights made such a venture a forlorn hope. Nevertheless, Bannister submitted his proposal. When Col Davies,

SOE's Director of Research, Development and Supply, heard of this he was somewhat alarmed and considered it dangerous. He said Bannister must not be allowed to drop them as they could forewarn the enemy and spoil project 'Moon'.[2]

Some experiments were carried out on the achieved spread at ground level from drops at height. With parachutes designed to give a rate of descent of 30 ft per second with the packages envisaged for Scheme I, a satisfactory spread was achieved from 20,000 ft at a speed of 200 mph. If this was not considered satisfactory it was suggested the drop be made from only 5,000 ft.

The final form of the incendiary, which was designed by the leader of the Incendiary Section, Maj O.J. Walker and Dr C.H. Bamford, an ex-Cambridge chemist, was 6 in long by 1½ in by ⅜ in and it was estimated that 720 of them would, on average, replace each bomb which would otherwise be dropped. The production rate of incendiaries began to present a problem. The anticipated rate of 500,000 per month was found to be impossible to achieve, so 300,000 per month had to be accepted. It was proposed to drop 250,000 in the spring over north-west Germany, where there was much forced foreign labour and which was relatively easy to reach, followed by 100,000 in different parts of Germany every fortnight.

By May 1943 the project had been renamed Operation Braddock, though there were signs of a diminution of enthusiasm with queries being raised about whether to continue with production of the devices. In September, Scheme I was finally abandoned.

At the end of August an impatient CD wrote to Lord Selborne suggesting that Braddock II should be used over Italy as soon as possible after the British invasion but in a reply from AD/S.1 his proposal was turned down. Italy would get out of the war as soon as it could, said the memo, and the incendiaries should be kept for Germany.[3]

Lord Selborne, still anxious to set Operation Braddock in action, wrote to the Prime Minister on 4 October 1943 arguing that there were an estimated 7,700,000 prisoners of war and forced workers propping up German industry and that among these would be plenty of potentially welcoming recipients of the devices. If only 1 per cent of the 2,500,000 incendiaries then available were picked up and used, 25,000 fires would break out in Germany and a high percentage of them would be of some importance. But Churchill had to choose his moment to take the Americans along with him and he judged this was not the right time.[4]

In the second quarter of 1944, with almost four million incendiaries for Scheme II manufactured, production was stopped. It was calculated that it would require 400 heavy bomber sorties to deliver them, a demand that was sure to meet with resistance from the RAF if it was seen as merely alarming the Germans and perhaps igniting some fires in prominent Nazi establishments. It was decided that Braddock II was to be used only inside Germany and not in enemy-occupied countries. Furthermore, its use should be delayed until conditions had loosened the Gestapo's hold and workers were desperate due to the continued and increasingly severe privations as the Allied armies advanced across Europe. The Minister did not feel competent to judge when this situation was likely to come about.[5]

With the invasion of Europe imminent Churchill wrote to Lord Selborne to say that he could not bother Gen Eisenhower with this matter at the present.

Selborne tried yet again on 24 July 1944. News of the 'trouble in Germany', by which he was probably referring to the 20 July assassination attempt on Hitler and to some rioting in various parts of the country, although being suppressed by the Nazis, seemed to augur well for a start to the operation. He suggested a preliminary shower of half a million Braddocks (as the incendiaries came to be known) on the Ruhr, which was the centre of German Communism and contained many foreign workers. He noted that the PWE (Political Warfare Executive) would need several hours' warning to lay on instructions to finders of Braddocks. Churchill struck through the word 'several' and substituted 7 in his red ink.[6]

Churchill's hesitation was in part due to his concern that the enemy would wreak retribution against prisoners of war, but the very next day Selborne tried to allay his fears by quoting the Geneva Convention which seemed a pretty weak argument when one considers the Nazis' record of contraventions of the Convention. Selborne also had intelligence that the Germans were already nervous about the large number of foreign forced workers in their midst.

With almost four million incendiaries waiting to be dropped and production of them at a standstill, Gen Ismay's frustration at the lack of action led him to suggest to Churchill on 28 July that he remind Eisenhower of the existence of the weapons and the plan to use them.

Braddock II was started on a very small scale and SHAEF was pleased with the results. The US Air Force dropped 250,000 devices on 25 September 1944 in daylight despite the Deputy Chief of Air Staff and Gen Spatz claiming night drops would be better. The Nazis were irritated and puzzled and went to the trouble of distributing warnings throughout Germany. Although there were no reports of actual arson attacks, a modest success was claimed by the disruption caused and Gubbins lent the project some token support, advising Selborne that SHAEF was still considering a large-scale drop. Further efforts by Selborne in November 1944 to inject urgency into the operation met with a 'the present is not the time' reply, which exasperated him still further.

Time slipped by till 8 March 1945, when Churchill's friend and scientific adviser, Lord Cherwell, exhorted him to use the weapon. But now Gen Ismay was having second thoughts and expressed his worries that Braddocks might fall near prisoners of war, prompting reprisals. For the same reason air supply drops near PoW camps were vetoed by SHAEF. Another concern was that they might get into the hands of the German Wehrwolf organisation which was forming groups to infiltrate Allied lines.

Operation Braddock finally ground to a halt on 18 March 1945 when Churchill wrote across the minute in red ink 'No action'.[7]

OPERATION BARBARA

Throughout 1943 planning had been taking place for the initial operation using SOE's first venture into the field of small submersible craft, the one-man Welman. Vessels had been prepared and crews had undergone rigorous training at bases in Scotland, terminating at Lunna Voe in the Shetland Islands, as close to Norway as one could get. To transport them to the target area SOE had applied for the supply of three American sub-chasers, but in case this request was turned down they had an option on some motor torpedo boats in the north of Scotland. The ideas for transporting the mini-subs in Sunderland flying boats or within the casings of conventional submarines had proved either impractical or inopportune. Much to SOE's satisfaction, their application for sub-chasers from the USA had been approved and three were due to be delivered by the first week in October, complete with three American crews until Norwegian Navy Independent Unit (NNIU) members could be fully trained in their use. When they arrived the boats were described as wooden, stoutly built and beautifully fitted out,[8] and there were sixty NNIU ratings waiting to be trained in crewing them. But when the time arrived it was not these fast boats that were to be used in the Welman's initiation.

At last the Welman was to see action. The operation against targets in the Bergen area in German occupied Norway was given the codename 'Barbara' and was planned in great detail by Lt Cdr A.C. Halliday RN. Thirteen pages of handwritten Operational Orders were drawn up and included equipment to be taken, tidal details, speeds and courses to steer. This information was supplemented by air reconnaissance photographs and maps of the region. On 14 November nine men signed the orders to confirm that they had read and understood them. The nine were Lt J. Holmes RN, Lt B. Maris RNVR, Lt C.A. Johnsen and Sgt B. Pedersen who were the nominated team, with A. Cole, J. Lee, R. Hobson, A. McIntyre and J. Rowley as back-up.

On 20 November 1943 Operation Barbara, (also mistakenly referred to in some documents as Operation Guidance which was, in fact, an X-craft mission), set off with the two Norwegians, Johnsen in Welman W45 and Pedersen in W46, while the Royal Navy officers Maris and Holmes piloted W47 and W48. The Welmans were transported in davits by motor torpedo boats *MTB 625* and *MTB 635* from Lunna Voe to the entrance to Solviksund near Bergen to attack shipping and the Laksevaag floating dock in Bergen harbour.

The plan was for Welmans W45 and W46 to attack shipping at Puddefjord and the Dokkeskjaer Quay while W47 and W48 tackled the floating dock. After the attacks the Welmans were to make for the deep water at Dyrsviken where they were to be scuttled and their crews were to swim ashore and be picked up by MTB at Hindenaesfjord 48 hours later. In case this location proved unusable, an alternative of Sordalen was given.

After the Welmans were launched from the MTBs they made their way to the small, allegedly uninhabited, island of Hjelteholmen close to Bergen from where the party was to wait till nightfall. On this journey Maris ran on to a rock and had to climb out to push the boat off. However, throughout the 21 November the island was visited by a number of local fishermen, some of whom entered into conversation with the party. Johnsen claimed to know and trust the fishermen so they decided to continue with their plan. After waiting for an inbound convoy to pass the four Welmans began their run-in to the targets at 18.45, leaving fifteen minutes between each departure.

Pederson, who had taken part in the limpeting of the *Nordfarht*[9] with its cargo of pyrites at Orkla was piloting the leading craft. Drizzle and patchy fog made visibility difficult and when he spotted a small boat heading for him, he dived. After fifteen minutes underwater, by which time he estimated he should be inside the German watchboats, he surfaced but found he had to open the hatch and stand up. Some accounts state that he encountered a net and was forced to surface. Only 50 yards away was a patrolling German minesweeper *NB59*, which immediately caught him in its searchlight and started firing with its 20 mm gun. Before he had time to dive again, the Welman was hit, so Pederson flooded it in the hope of sending it to the bottom of the fjord. The Germans now approached in a rubber dinghy, which he was forced to jump into. He had reckoned that, had he managed to submerge, the area would have been depth-charged with the likelihood of disabling the other three Welmans.

Meanwhile, Welman W48 with Holmes in control was found to be leaking through the stern gland and had to return for repairs. On his second attempt in the early hours the craft continued to leak, and Holmes was also aware that the harbour defences were on high alert, with many small craft searching with lights. He therefore sank his Welman and returned to wait on the island. Maris in W47 became lost in all the searchlight activity and abandoned his Welman near Bratholm while Johnsen in W45, having run aground and pushed the craft back to sea, eventually scuttled his at Vidnes. It was only by good fortune that the three officers escaped after sinking their craft and swimming ashore. They were eventually recovered by MTB two and a half months later after several unsuccessful attempts – but Pederson found himself a prisoner of war and, what is more, his Welman did not sink fast enough to prevent the Germans retrieving it.

MTB 626 was due to sail to the pre-arranged pick-up point for survivors of the Barbara I raid but, with *MTB 686*, was destroyed in a petrol explosion and fire following the accidental discharge of an Oerlikon gun on *MTB 686* while refuelling at Lerwick on 22 November. *MTB 686* lost four of her crew and *MTB 626* lost one. Bad weather delayed further attempts. The sub-chaser *Hessa* sailed on 13 December to the rendezvous at Hindenaesfjord but the three men were not found, having already left the area. A message was received that they were still waiting at Sordalen on 28 January 1944 but bad weather again hampered the rescue. The three, two British and one Norwegian, were finally picked up on the night of 5/6 February 1944 by *MTB 653*.[10]

On their eventual return the three men were able to confirm that the only mechanical defect which had befallen them was the leaking propeller shaft seal on W48. Initial concerns about the effectiveness of the Direction Indicating devices fitted had not been realised.

The Welman that had fallen into the hands of the Kriegsmarine was studied in depth as the Germans were at that time interested in midget submarines. They produced the one-man Biber submarine which had certain similar features to the British craft.

A second proposed Barbara operation was a Welman attack against an anchorage at Askevold. Agents were put ashore on local islands but encountered difficulties and had to be picked up and returned to Shetland. An advance party for Barbara III was landed from a MTB in the Bremanger area on 5 February 1944, the night the survivors from Barbara I were rescued, and prepared to receive two Welmans for an attack on Gulenfjord. The Welmans sailed on 13 February, presumably on the deck of a MTB or sub-chaser but were forced back by bad weather. The raid was postponed till early March in the hope that the atrocious weather period would be past.

A little later, agent Antrum Green was landed in the Syvdefjord area to prepare for another Welman raid, Barbara IV, on enemy shipping. He reported that shipping directions and convoy anchorages were continually being changed, which made planning such a raid impossible. No further Welman attacks were attempted, and so ended the short career of this novel craft.

OPERATION GUNNERSIDE

The late 1930s saw an upsurge of work on atomic physics, and with it the realisation that it might be possible to release the enormous energy associated with the atomic nucleus, either in a controlled fashion or in an explosion. The basic step, nuclear fission, was discovered by the German physicist Otto Hahn early in 1939. Research in the following months opened up the possibility of the creation of an atomic bomb. This was both rapidly appreciated by the physicists involved and sensationalised by the press. Attempts to suppress publication of the scientific work failed. An important step in the production of fissionable material involved the use of large quantities of deuterium oxide ('heavy water') whose production was slow and required considerable amounts of electrical energy. In early 1940 only limited amounts of heavy water were available in the USA and UK and the only major production facility was the Norsk Hydro hydrolysis plant at Rjukan in the Vemork region of Norway.

Norway was well aware of the strategic value of its stock of heavy water and refused to export any to Germany in 1939. With their invasion by Germany imminent, they sent their entire stock to France from where it is believed to have been shipped to the USA. With the invasion of Norway in April 1940, the heavy water plant fell into the hands of the Germans who immediately ordered an increase in production. German scientists from the Wehrwirtshaftstab were looking for 4,500–5,000 kg per year. Although Hitler was eventually to place his faith in the V1 Flying Bomb and the V2 ballistic rocket, by 1942 interest in the prospect of developing an atomic bomb (or at least a nuclear reactor) was growing and so the occupiers demanded a further increase in output.

At about this time the Department of Scientific and Industrial Research, the body coordinating the research effort in various industries throughout the United Kingdom, approached SOE for information regarding supplies of heavy water going to Germany. Where exactly was it going to and for what was it being used? It soon appeared that the Germans might be in a race to produce an atomic weapon, a prospect which, even at that stage of limited knowledge, caused great consternation in the War Cabinet.

What they did not know was that the German scientists' calculations showed that they could not hope to produce sufficient uranium 235 to construct a bomb within the likely duration of the war. So they were working towards a nuclear reactor to produce power. Fortunately for the Allies, the Germans had made an error in their calculations: had they discovered it the outcome might have been different.[11]

Production of heavy water required a specialised plant and was a slow process. It was therefore thought best to deny the materials to the Germans by attacking its source. Rather than bombing the plant with the risk of collateral damage and casualties, putting the electricity supply to a large part of the country out of action, and perhaps not destroying the real target, a Combined Operations attack of some strength was considered.

In July 1942 the Deputy Secretary to the War Cabinet Office approached the Chief of Staff of the Chief of Combined Operations suggesting that Rjukan be attacked as intelligence showed it to be a target of the highest priority. By September a plan had been drawn up for an advance party of SOE agents to act as a reception committee and guides for the main attacking force of airborne troops. The advance group, code-named 'Swallow', of four men from the Norwegian Independent Company landed 30 km north-west of the target in mid-October and had established the vital W/T link the following month. Their up-to-date intelligence indicated that a recent Commando attack on a power station in the general area had resulted in greatly increased enemy security in the Vemork area.

In an audacious move, the Norwegian manager of the works was brought out to England via Stockholm to provide vital detailed information about the plant, as a result of which it was decided that destruction of the High Concentration Plant, situated in a part of the complex relatively safe from aerial bombardment, must be achieved. With this information SOE made a mock-up of the plant to be attacked at one of its training schools while Colin Meek and Charles Critchfield at Station IX designed and prepared the explosive charges required for the job.[12]

On 19 November 1942 the airborne assault force Freshman took off from Skippen airfield near Wick in two aircraft, each towing a glider. In bad weather one aircraft and both gliders crashed around 200 km from the target. All the survivors were shot on Hitler's orders. The Swallow party had been ready with landing lights and had even heard one of the planes on their Eureka set. They were ordered to leave the area and be ready for the next moon period. The objective of Operation Freshman was now known to the enemy, who further increased the garrison in the area as well as arresting a number of local Norwegians they thought likely to help the Allies. It was therefore decided to make a second attempt using a group of six Norwegians (code-name 'Gunnerside') specially trained by SOE with valuable assistance in a consultative capacity given by Prof (later Capt) L. Tronstad, who was attached to the Norwegian Armed Forces.

The December, January and February moon periods were plagued by bad weather which prevented flights. Due to an alert, a last-minute change in dropping zone on the night of 16/17 February meant that the Gunnerside party was dropped onto the frozen Bjarnesfjord, some 30 km from the reception committee. The two parties met six days later and had to carry the charges, provisions, arms, etc., over 60 km across severe country in very bad weather to attack the target on the night of 27/28 February 1943.

In what was admitted by the Germans to have been an extremely well executed operation, the factory was entered, the High Concentration Plant penetrated, the charges were placed on the special cells and as a result four month's stock of heavy water was destroyed; and all without a shot being fired. One member of the Gunnerside team stayed behind with the Swallow party while the other five skied 400 km to Sweden and safety.

The Germans repaired the plant by August and improved security to a point which precluded another ground attack. However, a strong force of US bombers attacked the power station in November and although the High Concentration Plant was virtually unscathed, the power station on which it depended was so severely damaged that heavy water production was abandoned. In January 1944 reports were received that the plant was to be dismantled and sent to Germany. The following month the Swallow party reported that the remaining stocks of heavy water were to be moved to Germany via the ferryboat *Hydro* on Lake Tinnsjo. An SOE group code-named 'Chaffinch' sent two men who, with nine local helpers, planned to sink the vessel. The Germans anticipated an attack to destroy the precious cargo and employed SS troops, two patrolling aircraft and special guards on the railway from Rjukan to the ferry quay at Mel. But in a fatal error they omitted to place guards on the *Hydro* itself.

The Chaffinch agent slipped on board and into the bilges where he placed 8.4 kg of 808 explosive in the bilge water alongside the keel at the bow of the ferryboat. He selected that end so that the boat would sink bow first, thus raising the propeller and rudder out of the water, making it impossible to steer to the lakeside for beaching. The previously prepared charges included in this instance his own time delays made from two alarm clocks with, for reliability's sake, two independent ignition circuits. The clocks and batteries were attached to stringers and the alarms were set for 10.45. It was vital that the boat sink at a previously selected deep part of the lake and so the timing of the explosion had to be accurate. Hence the use of the clockwork delays rather than Time Pencils or L-delays.

The two wagons containing the heavy water were loaded onto the *Hydro* which left at 09.00 for its journey down the long, narrow lake, by which time the Chaffinch agents were well on their way to Jondal, Oslo and safety in neutral Sweden. At about 11.00 on 21 February 1944 the charge exploded. The boat tipped steeply down, the wagons ran forward along the deck and into the lake, and within four minutes 14,485 litres of heavy water were lost for ever.[13]

OPERATION PERIWIG

Perhaps Maj Everett's most bizarre enquiry, and one which stretches the concept of research within SOE to the limit, was made early in 1945 in connection with Operation Periwig which was concerned with 'Methods of Breaking the German Will to Resist'.[14] It was a deception plan to convince the Nazis that there were Resistance groups throughout Germany about to rise up against them. A continuing feature of Government policy since 1940 had been based on the mistaken belief that an *effective* anti-Nazi faction existed in Germany. There had, indeed, been scattered cells of resistance to Hitler ever since he came to power in 1933. It was known that there were German resistance groups on the Austrian–Yugoslav border and throughout Germany a large number of bands of youths were organised into anti-Hitler Youth groups similar to the *Edelweiss Piraten* and Catholic youth groups.[15] But major organised anti-Nazi action was hindered by the church's Lutheran tradition of deference to authority and the military's deep-rooted tradition of loyalty and professional ethic.

Nevertheless, for years SOE's German Section had maintained most secret contact, through its representative in Switzerland, with a railway workers' organisation which had carried out some administrative and physical sabotage to rolling stock in Basle marshalling yards. In the end it was left to the Army but several attempts on Hitler's life, terminating in the plot of 20 July 1944, failed to remove him and resulted in very many innocent deaths. This July attempt on Hitler's life could have been the catalyst that resulted in the setting up of a joint SOE/PWE (Political Warfare Executive) project to revisit the question of anti-Nazi resistance inside Germany. The event revived the hope that an internal revolt might succeed in overthrowing the Nazi regime.

However, Lt Col R.H. Thornley, AD/X1 in the German Directorate and an expert on the German situation, carried out a realistic assessment and formed the conclusion that there was no hope of raising an organisation sufficiently powerful to overthrow the Nazi rulers. Gubbins, with typically 'blue-sky' ideas, argued that if a genuine movement did not exist then SOE should invent an entirely fictitious Resistance Movement in the Reich by the use of 'black' radio transmissions and other convincing deception techniques and convince the German Security Service, and through them the military machine and the German public, that it was a real threat. This would put maximum strain on the Gestapo, leading to the development in Germany of a lack of confidence and a feeling of insecurity, increased general suspicion and doubt, and eventually to the breakdown of the security system. Plans to divert and confuse the German Security service had appeared early in the war. One such was

Plan 'Stiff', proposed by SIS in 1941, which was to parachute into Germany a wireless set, instructions and codes to give the impression that an agent had been dropped but had abandoned his task. It was hoped that the Germans would undertake a search for the missing agent and would play back the set, thus providing information on their techniques of deception. According to Masterman 'practical difficulties' prevented this plan from being executed although it was revived in various forms on subsequent occasions.[16] Some aspects will be seen to bear a resemblance to parts of Gubbins' SOE operation Periwig.

Operation Periwig, one aspect of which has been highlighted by Leo Marks (*Between Silk and Cyanide*, 1998), has excited interest not only in the popular press but in several histories of SOE (e.g. *Gubbins and SOE* by Wilkinson and Astley, 1993; *Secret Agent* by David Stafford, 2000; *The Secret History of SOE* by W. Mackenzie, 2000). Several features of the story have remained unclear and in the view of Stafford 'until historians have thoroughly mined the records, the truth may never be known'. It is now becoming possible to draw together the available evidence based mainly on the recently released Public Record Office files. Additional detail of the involvement of the Air Supply Research Section comes from the personal recollections of Everett, the Head of the Section, together with his contemporary notebooks which have survived. Bearing in mind that more information may still be waiting to be unearthed in files which have not yet been consulted, this account must still be provisional.

Deception techniques, aimed at confusing the enemy by feeding misinformation to its planners, have been a feature of secret warfare from earliest times. The widely publicised example of a successful deception in the Second World War was Operation Mincemeat in which a corpse dressed as a Royal Marines Officer was washed ashore in Spain carrying plans suggesting that the forthcoming invasion would take place in the Eastern Mediterranean rather than in Sicily. A major programme of deception was also a prelude to Overlord. In both these cases the objectives were to give the enemy false information on the location of future military operations. On the other hand, political warfare had the psychological aim of creating confusion among the German people and sowing doubts about the outcome of the war.

The German Section (X) of SOE had placed a great deal of emphasis on 'black propaganda' that included the extensive distribution by air drops of forged ration books, clothes coupons and travel passes. These operations were successful in confusing and annoying the local civilian authorities. They were backed up by 'white propaganda' which was largely factual and designed to convince the German people of the Allies' eventual victory. But these operations were seen as being organised and executed by forces outside Germany. They had to contend with the determination and resilience of the general population – just as the British population responded to German air raids and the broadcasts of 'Lord Haw Haw'. A far greater effect on the determination of the Germans would be achieved if the acts of sabotage and subversion were seen to emerge from inside Germany.

Gubbins's initial plan to create a fictitious German Resistance movement was developed in the late summer of 1944 but received little support from Thornley, the then Head of the German Section, while it was strongly opposed by the Foreign Office. The latter were concerned in particular about the impact such an intervention would have on Anglo-Soviet relations since it would be impossible to explain a venture of this kind to the Kremlin, for whom the concept of 'German Resistance' had an altogether different connotation. As in so many other SOE projects the SIS had serious doubts about any overt SOE operations which they saw as creating dangers for their own agents who operated covertly. To succeed, the operation had to appear to be initiated by groups inside Germany and could not be attributed to the Allies, although help from them should be a response to requests from within Germany. In developing the plan and to maintain its credibility, care had to be taken to dissociate it from overall Allied planning.

Gubbins reorganised Section X on 30 October 1944, transferred its responsibility to a newly formed German Directorate (AD/X) and in early November offered its Headship to an old friend, Gen Gerald Templer, who was recovering from a broken back sustained in his staff car when, as Commander of the 6th Armoured Division leading the advance towards Florence in August of that year, he was struck by a wheel from a 15 cwt truck which had been blown up alongside him by a landmine. He was most enthusiastic at the idea of Operation Periwig. Templer, who was later to head the Control Commission in Germany, take on the guerrillas in Malaya and end his career as Chief of Imperial General Staff, is remembered by some for his 'Mephistophelean countenance' which struck terror into young officers, although he was also described as 'kindly', 'welcoming' and 'ready to put them in the picture'.[17] He had a reputation for unorthodoxy and a prodigious command of bad language. He was said by Sporborg to have arrived in SOE on 22 November like a breath of fresh air. Here was a man likely to push the boundaries of war conduct to the very limits to achieve his objective.

Templer pursued Periwig vigorously. Planning by a joint SOE/PWE Section started on 12 November. A detailed plan was submitted on 20 November to the 'Will to Resist Committee', chaired by Sir Robert Bruce Lockhart of the Political Intelligence Department. While the plan was under consideration, Templer took action to prepare for the operation by briefing Marks and Everett. Marks's highly colourful account of his first encounter with the General is given in *Between Silk and Cyanide*.

One afternoon in late December 1944 Everett, unaware of the political background, was summoned from his office in 64 Baker Street to the offices of the German Directorate in Berkeley Court above Baker Street station. There he met Gen Templer together with James Joll, one of his staff officers, later to become a Fellow of New College, Oxford and a Professor at the London School of Economics. Everett, a mere Major, was shown into Templer's office to receive a crisp and precise briefing from the man who had a reputation of having a dubious vocabulary. He explained that it was proposed to drop into Germany an agent carrying in his briefcase incriminating evidence linking members of the German High Command with a plot to overthrow the Nazi regime. For this to be effective it was necessary to ensure that the papers fell into the hands of the German Secret Service and for this the agent had to be found dead, his parachute having failed to open. Templer's brief to Everett (it sounded like an order) was to devise a way of tampering with the parachute so that it was certain to fail without leaving any traces of the cause so that it would appear to have been an accident. Once the importance of the papers was realised, the Germans, always suspicious of a plant, would undoubtedly examine the parachute and the agent's injuries. It was therefore of the greatest importance that the cause of the parachute failure could not be readily identified. If there were signs that the parachute had been tampered with the plan would lose all credibility. Templer revealed that the agent would be a captured German spy, now a prisoner of war, who had offered to help the Allied cause by becoming a double agent and returning to Germany. He would be carrying the latest W/T set and other convincing 'proof' of his role as an agent meeting up with a resistance organisation. That he was being ordered to participate in a planned murder was not lost on Everett, but Templer brushed aside the ethical implications by stressing that the agent had already betrayed as many British agents as he had Germans. The urgency of the matter was impressed on Everett who was ordered to provide an answer as soon as possible.

To seek advice and collaboration, Everett visited the Parachute Training School (STS 51) at Ringway, near Manchester. Since he could not reveal the reason for his enquiries he had to invent a cover story – using to the best of his ability the training he had received at Beaulieu. He said that there had been one or two unexplained parachute failures in some recent SOE operations and there had been some suspicions that the parachutes might have been tampered with. Since such genuine failures were rare he had, in the absence of specific examples, some difficulty in maintaining his story. It was stressed that it would be difficult to tamper with a parachute since agents either packed their own or supervised the packing: they were responsible for their own safety. Thus if a way of sabotaging a parachute were devised, it would be difficult to conceal this without arousing the suspicions of the agent. Nevertheless, a series of trials over several days failed to find a method of inducing a parachute failure without leaving evidence of the cause. Everett returned to London and reported his findings to Templer in mid-January 1945. He said that the only way of ensuring the agent's death would be to collude with the RAF and arrange either that the despatcher detached the parachute's static line immediately before the drop or that the pilot be briefed to drop from a dangerously low level. In either case the RAF would be implicated in the murder. At this point Templer interrupted to say that Everett need not proceed further with the investigation since the operation had been vetoed by the Prisoners of War Branch of the War Office on the grounds that it contravened the Geneva Protocol on treatment of PoWs. As is now known, the SOE plan for Periwig was in fact vetoed by the SIS on 13 January, though not apparently for the above reason.

The above account is in broad agreement with that told by Marks in his book with the exception that he, as Head of the Codes and Cypher Section, had been briefed to prepare code books to be dropped with the agent in the expectation that on their discovery the Germans would set up radio traffic thinking they were in touch with a subversive group. It seems that Templer did not discuss the use of incriminating evidence in his briefing of Marks. The agent was to be delivered by parachute but Templer said parachuting was a dangerous business and the agent would be dead before he reached the ground. Marks was given the task of briefing the agent, whose name was given as Schiller, on the use of codes and to convince him of the genuine nature of his mission. Marks heard nothing more from the General until, shortly before he left SOE in the middle of March, Templer told him, 'Your friend has had a fatal accident', which Marks took to mean that the operation had taken place successfully.[18]

It turns out that, unknown to Everett and presumably to Templer, similar experiments had been carried out some months earlier (probably in June) by Angus Fyffe of the Security Section. He, too, had been given the task of defining means by which a parachute could be tampered with in such a way that a malfunction was inevitable, but without leaving any trace of the cause of the failure. His experiments appear to have been more extensive than those carried out by Everett but came to the same conclusion. No written record of Fyffe's work seems to exist, nor is it clear who commissioned his experiments. There is no evidence linking it with a Periwig-type operation. In passing, it is interesting to discover that Terry O'Brien of the RAF in India carried out independently a series of tests for a similar operation in which a corpse dressed as an Indian Army Officer was to be dropped in Burma using a faulty parachute. He, too, found that it was not possible to ensure a failure without tampering with the harness. (*The Moonlight War* by Terry O'Brien). The conclusion that it is extremely difficult to cause a parachute to malfunction was supported by Oberst-Leutnant von der Heydte, the German commander who led the airborne invasion of Crete and then commanded the disastrous air drop in the Ardennes offensive in December 1944 when he was taken prisoner. By now thoroughly disillusioned, the officer was interrogated by Everett on 12 February 1945 in an effort to obtain information about an aluminium device found after the drop but during the conversation they also discussed parachute failures. Von der Heydte said he had compared British and German parachutes and found little in their performance to distinguish between them. To reassure his troops he had personally demonstrated that even if the parachute was bundled into its bag without proper folding, it still opened satisfactorily.

The plan submitted to the 'Will to Resist Committee' on 20 November had met with opposition from SIS who objected to certain of the methods by which it was hoped to 'sell' the operation to the Germans. The original document held in the Public Records Office has many paragraphs struck through in red pencil. Templer was abroad around the New Year and came back to find that no progress had been made with Periwig due, he told Marks, to 'a political dispute'. It was typical of the 'need to know' regime which prevailed in SOE that Marks and Everett never formally met, or even knew of one another's existence, although they must have passed in the corridor or met in the lift.

When SIS imposed a veto on the Periwig plan (on 13 January), Templer told Everett to drop his 'failed parachute' experiments. The reasons for the veto are not spelled out in the files and no mention is made of objections from the War Office. One can assume that SIS's main objections arose from the fear that Periwig would lead to a tightening up of German security and thus endanger SIS sources and hinder the establishment of new ones. The situation emphasised again the clear incompatibility of the basic philosophies of SOE and SIS.

Templer wrote to Bruce Lockhart on 19 January setting out the particular aspects of the plan to which SIS objected – these were essentially those paragraphs in the original plan which had been scored through in red pencil. He commented that if the veto were sustained then this would seriously affect the implementation of the plan. The features of the plan to which SIS took objection were listed under four headings. The first concerned the use of agents. Two proposals were made. It was suggested in the first that agents should be introduced with a genuine mission and a genuine belief in the existence of a German Resistance Movement (this in case of capture). Such agents would either be parachuted or infiltrated. This presumably meant that the agent was to be so convinced of the reality of the Resistance Movement that he would attempt to convince his captors of its existence. But this would depend on his being captured together with the material he carried. Presumably the agent would not voluntarily give himself up, so this scenario would depend upon his capture. If he were not captured then he would seek to establish contact with dissident groups.

A second, more controversial, plan was to arrange for the discovery of dead agents carrying documents. Such agents would either be 'shot while attempting to cross the lines or killed by parachute failure'. It was in pursuit of this latter objective that Marks and Everett had become involved. Their briefings had differed only in the details of the documents to be carried by the dead agent. In Marks' version these would be codes printed on silk, while Everett was told that the agent would be carrying documents involving members of the German High Command in a plot to undermine the Army. Some later documents indicate that a possible target would be von Rundstedt, the German commander in the West who had been sacked by Hitler and replaced by Kesselring when he opposed Hitler's ruling that the German Army should not retreat across the Rhine. In any case, this plan depended for its success on the certainty that the agent would be killed in the drop.

The second major component of the plan was to simulate extensive air supply activity by dropping containers and packages containing 'instructions, pamphlets, arms and sabotage materials, etc., with suitable evidence of the organisation and with reference to BBC phrases and briefing'. Separate distributions of pamphlets were envisaged. Further activities designed to mislead would include aircraft 'in suspicious flying including circling and signals to the ground'. One could hardly have expected this last to be supported by the RAF who in genuine supply drops had strict orders not to remain in the vicinity of the drop for more than ten minutes.

Radio deception was to be enhanced by W/T material consisting of self-operating and self-destroying transmitters: these might be disguised as 'People's Radios'. Other W/T material would be dropped which would be discovered and linked up with the supposed subversive organisation. Finally, there was a somewhat vague suggestion that German refugees in the UK and important German prisoners of war should be involved.

It is not difficult to guess why these proposals were vetoed by SIS who, as always, were against any activities likely to endanger their own agents, but their detailed objections do not seem to have been spelled out in hard copy. It is not known whether they raised any ethical objections to the proposed operation which involved the murder of a PoW, albeit a spy who had escaped the hangman's noose. It is now clear, however, that Templer's plan did not have unqualified support even within the German Directorate. Many years after the war James Joll confided to David Stafford, the historian, that he had been involved in a plan to drop an agent to his death with a faulty parachute. He had found this ethically repulsive and he had made strenuous efforts for several weeks to ensure that the plan was dropped. He would have welcomed Everett's conclusion that the 'faulty parachute plan' was technically impracticable. One may speculate that, armed with this evidence, Joll may have been able to persuade Templer to drop the idea. In any case, this particular aspect is neither mentioned nor hinted at in any of the later Periwig files.

In his letter to Bruce Lockhart, Templer proposed that he should 'comeback on SIS and ask them to review their objections in the light of the situation at that time'. The veto also included an embargo on drops within 25 miles of Allied PoW camps to avoid retaliations, and certain other sensitive ground features, with the result that virtually the whole of Germany was sterilised. Furthermore, Bomber Command was reluctant to undertake operations further north than 51 deg. nor further east than 12 deg. After consultation with Bruce Lockhart, Templer agreed to revise the plan to satisfy SIS and to arrange for the revised version to be submitted to SHAEF. According to Templer, this was done on 19 January, but no details of the revision have been traced.

Templer was clearly impatient to get things moving quickly. To this end he proposed to assemble forthwith a Periwig Committee pending the receipt of the reply from SHAEF, so that they could get on straightaway with putting the scheme into operation in its early stages: 'this could do no possible harm and will get things going'. The new committee, with a permanent committee room in Templer's office, was to meet twice weekly for three to four hours. It would consist of an SOE chairman (Tommy Davies AD/Z), an SOE member (Sqn Ldr Potter) together with representatives of PWE and SIS. Its first meeting took place at 10 a.m. on Monday, 22 January. At this meeting it was confirmed that Periwig would be run by AD/X. A draft Directive to SOE representatives abroad was considered (to be destroyed after reading!) and SOE representatives were invited to suggest actions relating to 'the right means and the right victims'. It is not recorded how many responses came from this invitation, but a memorandum was received from HS/F in Barcelona on 23 February. This suggested that as an alternative to air drops, papers should be infiltrated using existing 'C' contacts in Lufthansa, Spanish couriers and German subjects kidnapped and sent home to be conscripted. In the event time was too short to make use of these routes. Shortly after, the Spanish Section (H) indicated that it was closing down its Periwig activities.

The Periwig Committee proceeded to discuss ways of implementing the revised project as soon as the embargo was lifted. It was proposed that agents, believing the German Resistance was genuine, should be arrested by police in neutral countries and interrogated to provide appropriate information which could then be passed to German Security. Agents in both Germany and neutral countries should establish contacts with genuine organisations such as the *Edelweiss Piraten* (the anti-Nazi youth group dating from the

1930s) and link with successful phoney organisations such as the Red Circle Escape Club. They should induce firms in neutral countries and their Military Attachés to believe in a Resistance. By arranging for some of the Periwig operations to fail it should be possible to convince the Germans that the Resistance really did exist. Warnings should be passed to Nazi leaders through neutral channels. This should be backed up by simulation of W/T traffic from within Germany to genuine W/T operators in neutral and occupied territories.

At their fifth meeting on 12 February the Periwig Committee resolved that SOE should take up with Bomber Command the question of the dropping techniques to be employed in getting false information to the enemy. Consequently a joint SOE/PWE meeting was called on 14 February. Everett, as Head of the Air Supply Research Section, attended. Also present was Sqn Ldr Potter and representatives of the Air Liaison Section (AL) and of PWE. No formal minutes of this meeting were issued but Everett took notes which are still extant. The agenda followed broadly the previously proposed format. No mention was made of the use of agents. High on the agenda was the question of the feasibility of dropping briefcases. It seems that Bomber Command were unhappy with dropping from the jump hole since the briefcase might be caught in the slipstream and strike the tail of the aircraft. Would it be better to release it from the bomb bay? These matters were to be taken up by the Air Supply Research Section with Bomber Command, BDU via AL, and AD/G. The equipment needed for the dropping of dummy stores was discussed. The possibility of dropping from Mosquito bombers was proposed. Smaller containers, both 12 in and 16 in in diameter, could be dropped from the bomb rack, while the use of wing containers replacing the long-range fuel tanks had been under development. It was estimated that up to 100 containers and 50 packages would be needed. Other items to be dropped included empty parachutes, empty containers, empty packages, small arms simulators, booby-trapped food tins, all intended to suggest that these were being despatched to resistance groups. It was also proposed that transmitters disguised as People's Radios should be designed and a specification was drawn up. They were to be battery-operated, crystal-controlled and arranged to be switched on by static line. After an arming time of thirty minutes they would transmit for three 7-minute periods each day for seven to ten days, after which they would self-destruct. They would be fitted with an anti-disturbance switch. Thirty sets would be required and

Radio Section was, optimistically, asked to produce a prototype within a fortnight! Finally, the meeting reviewed the use of pigeons both for genuine communication and to act as decoys. In particular, it was concerned about the performance of self-opening pigeon boxes for air dropping. Progress was to be reviewed at a meeting at Station IX on 16 March.

The following day, 15 February, the SIS ban was lifted and SOE was allowed 'qualified operational freedom'. This seemed to imply that SOE was now free to pursue its original plans, although the meaning of 'qualified' was never spelt out. In fact the previous embargo had had little effect since from the end of November to 21 February the bad weather had meant that the RAF had suspended all operations. On 26 February it was reported that the various tests had been carried out successfully by the ASR Section, although there seems to have been no further news of the self-destroying transmitter.

It was now possible for SOE to start its dropping programme and several operations were carried out during the next few weeks. All the drops were 'blind' drops. Since the resistance movement was in reality fictitious, the agent could not be encouraged to think he would be met by a reception committee. The first was 'Pathino' on 21 February which dropped near Marburg a container which carried a complete set of German uniform (of a sergeant) with documents, maps and 1 lb (0.45 kg) of food; a second drop, 'Pathino 2', on the same sortie was made at a different DZ (drop zone). The same night 'Postbox 1' dropped a package of W/T parts with spares, messages and operating instructions near Giessen. 'Postbox 2' carried a similar load the same night but to a different DZ. 'Pettifog' was a drop of carrier pigeons with instructions in German for using them. The objective was to lead the Germans to believe that pigeons were being used to send messages back to England. This was done by including 'duds', i.e. birds which would not home back to England. The pigeons were dropped in special containers and were fitted with leg message containers and message forms. It was hoped that they would home to German lofts and be reported to the authorities. During April some 330 birds which had been kept in lofts at Tempsford for several weeks were dropped. Of these nine homed in the UK and two in France. Five had messages written in German, but provided no information of value. One is reputed to have thanked the senders as the returning bird's brother had been very tasty, and asked for more to be sent!

'Preference 1' and '2' were drops of black propaganda, forged ration cards and an S-phone. Operation Opinion on 24 February delivered four containers of ammunition, four containers of incendiaries, two containers of explosives and one container of food. This was by far the largest consignment of material sent under Periwig. A few days later, the committee at its meeting on 8 March expressed the view that unless the number of operations could be increased substantially the aim of overtaxing the German Security Services could not be achieved. Fourteen stores containers were packed and ready to go during the March/April moon period. They contained a wide variety of stores and devices. Among those listed were booby traps, firearms simulators, explosive coal, explosive logs and rats, empty containers, empty parachutes both open and folded, pin tail bombs, tins of German food, explosive ration tins, women's clothing, and German cigarettes. A further operation 'Impinge' was attempted on 9 March but failed and was repeated successfully on 13 March when a container of incendiaries was dropped. One other operation, denoted as '1.2' in the minutes of the committee, but possibly called 'Aktentasche' took place in March. In this a German briefcase was dropped on a railway station during a low-level air attack. The date is not recorded in the report but was later found to be on the night of 12/13 March, on the last opportunity before the SHAEF ban. The briefcase contained some normal business documents but also an incriminating paper suggesting clandestine operations in a large industrial concern. Other Periwig operations recorded in the committee minutes but not otherwise identified included W6, a Periwig plant; 1.5 described as a 'successful Periwig plant' (possibly via Sweden); W.3 and P.3.

At this stage (12 March) Davies wrote to Templer 'the original concept of Periwig could not now be realised as a result of new limitations' and the need was now to confine itself to 'small nuisance operations through neutral countries' which were unlikely to produce any appreciable feeling of apprehension among either the German Security or the people. Weekly meetings of the committee were not now felt necessary and they were abandoned. Two further operations, 'Princess' and 'Phonotype', had been planned to deliver black radio and W/T simulators but were abandoned.

On 13 March SHAEF banned all further supply drops. Templer left SOE a few days later.

The original SOE plan included the use of agents either infiltrated through the lines or found dead following parachute failure. Although this was vetoed on 13 January, it was reinstated on 15 February. There is no further reference to such operations in the minutes of the Periwig Committee, although the minutes of the third meeting are missing. However, agents were infiltrated from SPU22, which was a holding camp originally for Poles but also used by other nationals waiting infiltration. It soon became, in effect, the advanced Headquarters of SOE. In January 1945, following a liaison visit from Lt Col Wills from Station XV, a small camouflage workshop was set up at SPU22 to service SPU47 and other units. Consideration was given to the use of German nationals (Bonzos) for short-term intelligence work. On 8 March four Bonzos arrived from London and were accommodated at a house in Revogne. Four were infiltrated on 14 April to Koblenz and another to Bremen on 21 April. All returned safely. It seems likely that the 'dozen agents' referred to by Wilkinson as having been infiltrated (and survived) were in fact SPU22 operations mainly for intelligence purposes and not specifically Periwig operations.

The most fully documented SOE operations involving the dropping of agents by parachute into Germany were those carried out in April 1945. Presumably the SHAEF ban applied only to stores drops and not to agent drops. As far as is known no agents were parachuted in earlier than this. On 2 April Gerhardt Bienecke (alias Breuer, alias 'Preacher') and Leonhardt Kick (alias Kauffmann, alias 'Plaintiff') were flown on operation 'Polacca/Polder' from Earl's Colne in a Halifax and dropped near Wildeshausen in the Bremen area. Kick had been through a shortened paramilitary course at STS19, followed by six days at Group B together with two parachute jumps from STS51. He was given both military and civilian cover and addresses to contact in the Bremen region. It is interesting to find that Kick was instructed to use a 'squirt' transmitter. According to the 'History of the Radio Communications Division' in the Public Record Office work on squirt transmitters did not progress far and the devices never went into the field. One can speculate whether Kick was told to use a squirt transmitter (SOE knowing they did not have the means of picking up the signals in England) so that if he was captured the Germans would realise why they had not been able to detect his transmission and therefore be further persuaded of the genuineness of his mission. But his Type B MkII W/T set was lost in the drop. He gave himself up to the Allies in August. Bienecke was dropped with a leg-bag and took codes (camouflaged in a tin of toffees), crystals and a signals plan. He was dropped in German uniform and planned to link up with an important agent in the Berlin area. The final destination of his material was a certain Dr

Eggan. He was recovered from the Russian Zone in August 1945. On 18 April (operation 'Periscope') a Hudson flown from Tempsford dropped two agents to the west of Chiemsee. They were Otto Heinrich (alias Hoffman, alias 'Hawker') and Franz Lengnik (alias Lange, alias 'Lawyer'). Because of the shortness of time they had only a brief course at STS19. The courses at Beaulieu and STS51 were omitted. They were to contact an organisation and to instruct them in the preparation of landing grounds. They attempted to carry out their mission but failed and gave themselves up to the Allies in May 1945. A fifth agent, Kurt Tietiz (alias Fatkow, alias 'Tinker'), started training on 21 April but in view of the progress of the war was returned to the PoW cage on 4 May.[19] The original plan was for at least a dozen agents a month to be dropped, but partly because of lack of time and also the small number of volunteers among PoWs only four were dropped.

There remains the question as to whether SOE ever carried out the proposed operation in which an agent carrying documents would be killed as a result of a deliberately arranged parachute failure. The technical evidence suggests strongly that this was impracticable. But was some other means found to achieve the same result without involving the crew of the aircraft? It is tempting to speculate that the dropping of an agent from a low-flying aircraft might have been carried out under the cover of a low-level air attack. One such attack is recorded on a German railway station between Holzmunden and Stahtoldende during which a briefcase was in fact dropped (Operation I.2 or 'Acktentasche'). Was an agent also dropped? The briefcase was recovered by the Germans but there is no evidence of either a body or a parachute having been found. The operation took place on the night of 12/13 March, i.e. shortly before Templer left SOE. So he could have passed on the news to Marks as he was leaving. However, this scenario can be rejected if, as seems highly probable, the air attack was carried out by Mosquito aircraft which did not have a jump hole. Nor is there any record of these aircraft being modified for the dropping of personnel. Moreover, it is unlikely that a much slower Halifax could have mingled with the rest of the formation. So it would be of considerable interest to discover if any record of this exists in RAF files.

Yet another sinister possibility emerges. If Marks reported accurately Templer's comment that 'the agent would be dead before he reached the ground', then did Templer have an alternative to parachute failure in mind? Was the agent to be killed in the aircraft before the drop by one of the unarmed combat techniques taught at STS 41? After all, a broken neck could well be the result of a rough parachute landing.

It is interesting that the agents Bienecke and Kick had both been briefed in coding, and Kick had been instructed in W/T work (but lost his wireless set in the drop). And Bienecke had codes, crystals and signals plans. So they could have been candidates for Marks's Schiller. But they were not dropped until 2 April and they both survived. Two further clues in Schiller's identity jigsaw have come to light: the minutes of the 'W' Board of the Security Services' Twenty Committee (the body which so successfully ran captured enemy spies whom they had 'turned' to work for the Allies) for 15 March 1945 reveal that Capt (possibly Cdr) Cohen, an SIS member, had suggested that agent 'Teapot' might be used for plan Periwig and the Committee saw no objection to this. 'Teapot' was a triple-cross who had started working for SIS in January 1943 using both W/T and personal contacts.[20] Marks makes the point that Schiller was a first class W/T operator and had worked for SIS. The second fact that might be relevant is that the PWE Periwig Report No. 7 up to 26 March comments that Operation W.5, the possible use of a high-grade P/W, had been cancelled owing to security objections.[21]

Unless further searching of files at the PRO sheds light on possibly as many as thirteen unidentified Periwig operations (assuming the last discovered number to be the end of the sequence and the numbering to be continuous), it seems highly unlikely that the murder of a PoW ever took place. But as Marks commented in a TV interview with Everett, 'Templer would have made sure that he had covered his tracks'.

In the event, Periwig, although initially hailed in some quarters as an imaginative plan, was judged to have failed in its main objective, i.e. to persuade the Germans of the existence of an active and dangerous resistance movement in the Reich. It is clear that the various obstacles placed in its way by SIS and other agencies so delayed its full implementation that it was too late to have any significant influence on the final stages of the war.

It is perhaps pertinent, in hindsight, to question the validity of the original concept upon which Periwig was based. Its success depended both on the use of agents and on the provision of arms and equipment apparently for the use of a movement which did not actually exist. The deception was to be heightened by arranging for the discovery of dead agents carrying documents incriminating influential Germans. These agents were either to have been 'shot while attempting to cross the lines' or killed by 'parachute failure'. Even had a method been found for ensuring parachute failure, the plan would have been faulted. While the discovery of one agent killed in an accident might not arouse suspicion, a second or third similar incident would undoubtedly lead to the revelation of a major deception plan – especially in the knowledge that such failures were rare. Even if the operation were to be limited to one agent then the contents of the briefcase would have to be sharply targeted on influential members of the Nazi regime. In fact, it appears that only one briefcase was dropped (without an agent) and although the contents appeared to reveal the existence of a subversive movement in a large German company, it would be unlikely to strike at the heart of the German establishment. Similar arguments would apply if a number of agents were shot while trying to cross the lines. But Templer's plans envisaged not one but many infiltrations – at one stage he hoped for a dozen a month.

In the same way dropping of empty containers and packages would be difficult to achieve without revealing them as part of a deception plan. It was perhaps not realised at the planning stage that to release an empty container safely from an aircraft it would have to be ballasted with sand. Assuming that there was not to be a reception committee on the ground to empty the sand, then this ploy would not carry any conviction. All the recorded Periwig supply drops were in fact 'blind drops' of containers filled with arms and equipment. So the concept of using empty containers was apparently not pursued. The proposals to drop other items such as dummy radios, etc. were overtaken by events.

Although Templer was undoubtedly a hard man, and perhaps to some even ruthless, there is one incident which gives a different impression of him. Just before Christmas 1944 it was revealed that certain Norwegians were planning to deliver to SS headquarters in Oslo a 6-ft diameter traditional Christmas wreath, ostensibly from Quisling's movement, the HIRD. The wreath was to be lavishly decorated with lights and greenery concealed within which would be a ring of plastic explosive detonated by a fuse in one of the candles. Norwegian Resistance welcomed this plan to wreak death and destruction upon their hated enemy but in London German Section did not support it. Templer showed some common humanitarianism and managed to veto the plan as being 'contrary to the Christmas spirit'.[22]

SIXTEEN

TECHNICAL LIAISON

GENERAL

One of the main responsibilities of the DSR under Newitt was to establish and to maintain contact with Country and Overseas Missions on technical matters concerning the supply and use of equipment, and to ensure that their needs and complaints were referred to the appropriate Sections at Stations IX and XII. Initially the main concern was with Country Sections based in London, but as other Groups and Missions were established overseas it became increasingly important to ensure that their technical problems were brought to the attention of HQ. Conversely, it was important that Country Sections should be kept aware of the results of ongoing research and of its potential applications in their particular areas. This was in part achieved through the regular secret *Technical Bulletins*. It is not easy to say how effective they were, nor how widely these and other documents were distributed. There were occasional complaints that they did not reach those who could make best use of them. In part this may have been because the flow of information between users and providers was subject to security factors based on the 'need to know' principle. This security ethos also tended to mean that full details on the performance of equipment in the field were not always passed on from Country Sections to DSR. Moreover, few agents were technically trained and their reports, when available, often lacked the detail which would have been valuable to DSR in enabling performance to be assessed. Direct contact with agents was rarely possible (again perhaps for security reasons) and their debriefing reports were not often made available to DSR. In the early days these shortcomings were dealt with by Blount who had a roving commission to follow up enquiries and complaints with the Sections and to draw the attention of Station IX or Station XII to any matters needing immediate attention.

Another major task of DSR was to establish contacts with other Government establishments and to seek out new developments which might have applications to the work of SOE. This involved the creation of close links and joint research with RAE, AFDC and CCO covering developments in explosives, small arms and parachutage. Members of DSR sat on a number of Government committees such as the Incendiary Projectiles Committee, and were invited to observe some of the major trials and demonstrations at Aldershot and on Salisbury Plain. Thus AFDC were involved in the problem of the location of containers, while the Engineering Section was in regular touch with the Admiralty with regard to the Welman and other seagoing craft. Among the projects which were developed in collaboration with RAE were the K-type container, the Mosquito wing container, and HADDA. Conversely, the products of SOE's research groups were made available to the relevant Services such as the Commandos, Airborne Forces and the Navy. Any impression that these links indicated an overlap of effort between the organisations was scotched by the Playfair and Hanbury-Williams enquiry which concluded that the operational requirements of the various interested parties were sufficiently different to justify parallel research programmes. Nevertheless, the importance of close liaison was emphasised. As a result, frequent exchange visits were made by appropriate staff.

The DSR Directorate was also the link with academia. Among those whose advice was sought from time to time were Professors Alex (later Lord) Todd; C.N. (later Sir Cyril) Hinshelwood; R.W. Norrish; M.B. Donald; and Sir Charles Darwin.

OVERSEAS LIAISON

SOE maintained contact throughout the world from Algiers to Cape Town and Darwin to Washington often by tiny missions, but in some cases with larger groups or regional organisations. Surviving organisational charts show the steady expansion of activities which took place as the war developed: in spring 1941 there was contact with just three countries outside Europe; in summer 1942 there were four, and by spring 1944 there were five. As far as DSR was concerned the main objective of overseas liaison was to assess the opinions of overseas sections and their criticisms concerning the suitability of equipment and its performance under local conditions.

Overseas Missions

Among the more important overseas missions were Massingham, based in Algiers and dealing with the western Mediterranean, and the Cairo Group (Force 133) concerned with Italy and the Balkans which moved to Bari in southern Italy when the area was in Allied hands. Air supply to the Balkans was directed from Bari where some facilities existed for conducting air supply trials. Station XV had a depot in Cairo headed by the well-known London stage illusionist, Jasper Maskelyne, whose treasure chest exhibited some of the more exotic products of the Thatched Barn.

The Indian Group (Delhi Mission, Force 136) had its headquarters at Meerut near Delhi and some research and other facilities at Kirkee near Poona (Special Forces Development Centre SFDC) and in Calcutta. In 1944 its HQ was moved to Kandy in Ceylon where Admiral Mountbatten had his Supreme Headquarters.

Problems relating to the South-West Pacific Area were initially dealt with by the Inter-Allied Services Department (ISD) based at Melbourne, Australia. When this was liquidated in February 1943 it was replaced by the Services Reconnaissance Department (SRD). One of its research units, the Mount Martha Research Station (MMRS), set up in March 1944 was intended to fulfil the combined functions of Stations IX, XII and XV in the UK. However, the Australian organisation worked independently of DSR in developing a number of SOE devices for use in the very different conditions encountered in the Pacific area. These included Folboats and canoes, demolition and general equipment, and special camouflage projects. Informal links with DSR were maintained by the interchange of personnel. In particular, Capt G.I. Brown from Station IX spent several months attached to SRD.[1]

The effectiveness of the liaison with Missions depended largely on the exchange of information. The mechanisms for this were often inefficient, and suffered the same problems experienced between Country Sections and DSR. They were mitigated by personal visits from members of DSR staff. Thus Blount was despatched to the Balkans in 1943 to ascertain the situation there. Without his report little is known about the outcome of his visit. He made a later visit to SW China to investigate the possibilities for supplying secret Chinese groups with materials to use against the Japanese. Again, no record of his trip has been located.

Middle East

In October 1944 Everett was sent to tour the Middle East Missions in North Africa, Cairo and Southern Italy to collect information on the whole area of Air Supply. Among his concerns was the delivery and performance of supply dropping parachutes. These were being manufactured in Cairo 'sweat shops' from Egyptian cotton, extensive use being made of child labour in the form of small boys of perhaps eight to ten years of age. At Bari and Monopoly, where the parachutes were packed and stored, emphasis was placed on the importance of hanging parachutes in well-ventilated sheds. It was said that parachutes packed in humid conditions developed slowly, a possible cause of some reported failures. Everett's stay in Bari was also concerned with details of the internal organisation of supply flights with Dakotas operating to an airfield on the Adriatic coast. A proposed flight to demonstrate such an operation was eventually cancelled after a week of bad weather.

India and Ceylon

A major and more extensive visit by Everett to India and Ceylon occupied March–May 1945. By now the emphasis of operations was in the Far East so that one of the objectives of his visit was to assess the performance and applications of SOE stores under tropical conditions and in the operational circumstances existing in this theatre. On arrival in Kandy, Everett was briefed by Brig Anstey and his staff on the fundamental operational differences between the Far East and the European theatres. In the first place there were no major industrial complexes in Burma, Malaysia, Siam or the East Indies so sabotage operations were much more like guerrilla attacks on selected targets.

COMMUNICATIONS

Among the most important targets were the Japanese supply lines which were being used to distribute supplies mainly by rail and river from ports to operational areas. There is no evidence that the Japanese supplied their troops by air. Attacks on road transport had to be planned so that they did not lead to prolonged disruption of the advancing British troops. Mining of roads was specifically to be avoided although felling of trees across roads to hinder Japanese withdrawal was encouraged. This could be done using explosive charges either placed as 'necklaces' around the tree or inserted into holes drilled into the trunk. Standard SOE devices were being used in attacks on railways; on the whole they were readily adaptable to local conditions and performed satisfactorily. But there was a short supply of extension rods for use with pressure switches. Important trains were sometimes protected by a pilot engine sent ahead to detonate any previously laid device. Here the use of the Imber switch which allowed a predetermined number of trains to pass before being actuated would have overcome this problem, but it is not known whether any of these devices were sent to Force 136, let alone used. In many areas the main communications were by river so attacks on river craft were a high priority but the general opinion of those concerned was that no really effective weapons were available. The main types of vessel in use were river steamers of metal construction; 'Paddy Gigs', flat-bottomed wooden boats using oars or sails; barges; and a wide variety of country craft. It was difficult to smuggle explosives aboard the larger vessels since security was tight. Proposals for the inclusion of parcels of explosive in sacks of rice were considered unrealistic. Another possibility under discussion was the use of fireships in ports and harbours. To be effective this was only practicable where the density of ships was high and there were few places where this seemed to be likely. Attacks on river shipping from the banks faced a number of problems. Many rivers were more than 400 yd wide with low banks and mud flats extending to a small stream in the centre. It would sometimes be possible to choose bends in the river where the main channel came close to the bank, but the choice of weapon to be used was limited. The two-inch mortar, GP grenades, the PIAT and the Tree Spigot had all been considered but none was regarded as entirely suitable. In any case, heavier weapons were often ruled out by the nature of the terrain and it was important to be able to attack a moving target with as little time as possible for preparation. River targets were often the subject of daylight attacks from the air by the RAF so that increasingly river traffic moved by night. River ambushes could be carried out in darkness illuminated by 15-minute flares floated downstream or by parachute flares. Attacks on shipyards were not generally regarded as of great value and the use of the nailgun for the attachment of charges to wooden targets had not been widely tested.

W/T EQUIPMENT

In addition to attacks on communications, a major role of guerrilla groups was the collection of local intelligence and its transmission to field commanders. The provision of reliable W/T equipment was therefore essential and much of Everett's time was taken up with discussions on the problems of the functioning of radio equipment under tropical conditions. The main concern was the effect of humidity and high temperature on the components. On the whole most sets stood up well to these conditions but some components failed through corrosion, and it was worrying that on occasion equipment was already unserviceable on arrival from the UK. The most widely used set was the BII, but agents complained about its weight. Although when in its carrying case it was reasonably waterproof, the rubber gaskets which sealed it perished rapidly. If it did become wet in high humidity, then a few hours in front of a fire seemed to restore it to normal. A feature not initially recognised in the UK was that under certain circumstances the morse key could develop a high voltage and give the operator an electric shock. In the Type A Mark III this was overcome by adding a Bakelite protective cover. The MCR (Miniature Communications Receiver) was generally regarded as satisfactory although difficulties were often experienced in setting the voltages, partly because the meters tended to stick, while some of the resistors had a short life.

Since mains supplies of electricity were not generally available reliance had to be placed on means of recharging the batteries. There were a number of solutions. Hand generators (usually operated by local recruits) took some four hours to charge a battery. It was hard work and the fibre gear drive tended to strip. On continuous working, fresh gears were needed almost every day and spares were hard to get. The pedal generator was also tedious in use. The saddle was too high so that, without modification, it could not be used by diminutive natives whose legs were too short to reach the pedals. In addition, the lack of handlebars meant that the operator had to balance on the saddle while the feet tended to be chafed by contact with the moving parts of the drive mechanism. They were not at all popular. The steam generator also had its drawbacks. A pressure of at least 40 lb/in^2 was needed to get four amps, so that it took most of a day to recharge a 40AH accumulator. It was noisy in operation but the use of a silencer reduced its output by 20 per cent. It could be used with various fuels. When operated on oil it used ½ gallon a fortnight. But it too had problems with maintenance. The rubber gasket had a very short life and only four spares were provided.

The 'S'-phone had been requested from the UK but it was not clear how many had been received. One report said that three out of four had vibrators which were unserviceable on arrival. Knowledge of the 'S'-phone's capabilities was lacking and Bovill's report on it had not been distributed (nor can a copy be found now). This was only one example of poor communications encountered. Lack of instruction manuals was a general complaint. Capt Ellis handled the distribution of technical literature but the mechanism became confused on his transfer from Kandy to Poona.

AIR SUPPLY: PACKAGES AND CONTAINERS

The Packing Station and Air Despatch Airfield for Force 136 operations into Burma were located at Jessore, some 50 miles NE of Calcutta (now in Bangladesh). The Packing Station (and its main storage area) was on one side of the airfield and was responsible for the packing of both containers and panniers for despatch by a squadron of Liberators and Dakotas whose base was on the other side of the airfield. The packed containers and panniers were loaded ('bombed up') on to the aircraft by personnel of an armament detachment.

On arrival at Jessore on 4 April Everett was surprised to see that ammunition boxes and other munitions were stored in the open under scorching sun and subject to temperatures of up to 135°F and frequent heavy rain. Similarly, packed containers and panniers were stacked in the open. A casual glance showed that under these conditions of high humidity exposed metal was already showing signs of rust. In particular, many of the No. 77 phosphorus grenades were seen to be badly pitted. About noon on that day it was reported that one of the AP8 panniers had begun to emit smoke. It soon became apparent that a No. 77 grenade had burst open and set fire to other contents of the package. Very soon a number of adjacent packages were also affected by the fire which began to spread. After carefully separating and opening the packages, some 600 grenades found to be unsafe were thrown into a nearby rubbish pit which emitted a huge pall of smoke. But the cloud of smoke was mistaken by those in the Operations Room for a crashed aircraft. Very soon the furious Station Commander appeared at high speed in a jeep and proceeded to give Everett a dressing down for not seeking formal permission before taking action. He was soon pacified when it was pointed out that had not swift action been taken the whole dump, which included a substantial amount of explosive might have gone up. Maj Goodall RASC who came up from Calcutta to oversee the clearing up.

When this incident was over Everett began his task of inspecting the methods being used to pack stores for dropping. The contents of each type of package were identified by a serial code. It was found that in general the packing methods were satisfactory although detonators were not always packed securely and kept well away from other sensitive stores. Where possible stores were packed in their original boxes and surrounded with one or two inches of Koran. Some inadequate packaging was identified. A number of Type-C containers were so badly packed that the contents rattled around when they were handled. Particular attention was paid to the type of webbing harness used for panniers. Whenever possible this was arranged so that the package landed on its base. In all some two dozen package types were examined and, where appropriate, recommendations were made to bring the packing up to the standards established by Station IX. Particular attention was paid to the packing of W/T material which in general was more subject to damage than most other equipment. Typically, panniers were packed in two layers. The bottom layer was protected by a layer of cotton waste and contained spares for a BII set and two empty 6v 40AH accumulators. On the top layer was a BII set on a layer of Koran and two bottles of acid for the accumulators. Since there was a tendency for acid to leak, the bottles were contained in a box filled with whiting and well wrapped in Hairlock. All spaces were filled with packing material. One important finding was that Koran wrapping should not be used in contact with tins since it led to corrosion.

AIR SUPPLY: PARACHUTES

The most urgent problem being encountered at this time was the alarming failure rate of supply-dropping parachutes. This was particularly serious since in the early part of April the 14th Army under General Slim was pressing down the Sitang Valley towards Rangoon and was almost entirely dependent on air supply to maintain its momentum. There was already concern at Kandy at reports of a substantial loss of valuable equipment caused by parachute failure and Everett was asked to investigate. The problem was more serious than expected. Everett examined a series of reports from aircrew during recent operations and was deeply concerned that in one short period, out of 131 loads dropped, on at least 50 occasions the parachutes had failed to open. Something was obviously very seriously wrong. To identify this deplorable state of affairs he decided that he would inspect personally all the containers and packages loaded on to the aircraft in preparation for delivery on the next sortie. He spent the whole day working in the intolerably hot and humid atmosphere of the bomb bays and by evening he had inspected all but a few of the loaded aircraft. His findings were devastating. The loading had clearly been carried out carelessly and in a high proportion of instances the parachutes were doomed to fail. The most frequent and inexcusable fault was the complete absence of a static line, or when present it had not been attached to the breaking tie in the aircraft. In some instances string had been used to lengthen the static line. On one Liberator all the chutes had been loaded upside down so that it was difficult to withdraw the release pin. In a number of cases the safety pins on C-type containers had been removed while at least one C-type was damaged and unserviceable. Of more than 24 aircraft inspected only three or four were judged to have been loaded neatly and correctly. All these faults were rectified.

There were no reported parachute failures on this sortie.

This appalling state of affairs could only be symptomatic of a serious failure to train, supervise and inspect the work of the loaders. While there was said to be an acute shortage of staff and the working conditions were stressful, this was no excuse for such laxity which could seriously affect operations in the field. Following his visit to Jessore, Everett wrote a critical report on the problems of air supply in the Far East. In this he made a number of recommendations. In particular he stressed the urgency of appointing an officer with the responsibility for the inspection of parachutes both before issue for operations and after 'bombing up'. It is thought that in subsequent operations the failure rate was much reduced although in Operation Bison on 21 April one arms container exploded in the air and the failure rate of parachutes was 5 per cent. Some internal modifications to the Liberators such as the fitting of more robust strong points in the aircraft and the provision of snap hooks and safety pins were recommended.

By the time Everett returned to Baker Street the war in Europe had ended and hostilities in the Far East would have just three months to run before the atomic bombs were dropped and Japan surrendered.

SEVENTEEN

OVERALL ASSESSMENT

The centre of SOE's research and development effort was amid the magnificent Victorian arboreal collection at The Frythe. Working here for the Inter Services Research Bureau was for many an enjoyable and stimulating experience. Not only was the rural location in deepest Hertfordshire pleasant and safe from the nightly attention of the Luftwaffe, but the accommodation and catering for Service personnel was superior to that in most military establishments. The large number of highly intelligent specialists from industry and academia formed a select establishment which generated and regenerated its own morale and enthusiasm while the security surrounding the work served to impress on staff its importance to the war effort. The scientists were able to engross themselves in their sometimes highly original work knowing it was contributing to Allied successes. At the same time the engineering and technical staff had an intensely interesting range of novel problems to solve.

The Armed Forces, the Civil Service, industry and academia had been scoured for recruits into ISRB. Many of the senior scientists and engineers engaged were experts in their fields, though totally inexperienced in the work they were to be faced with. Those engaged by the Research and Development Section, whether based at Headquarters, Station VII, IX, XII, XV, temporarily posted to one of the subsidiary locations such as Staines Reservoir or Fishguard, or working on a joint project with other organisations like the RAE or the AFRE, were a dedicated, hard-working band. The work they were engaged on was usually of a generally offensive nature and therefore contained more than an element of danger, be it with a weapon, an explosive device, a new type of submersible or a technique for dropping containers from low-flying aircraft. Nevertheless, no records of serious accidents have been found or recalled by those former serving members interviewed for this work.

The size of the R&D effort grew as SOE became more established and successful. A War Office establishment document showed that the stations featured in this account of ISRB employed over 2100 personnel in June 1944, made up of the following numbers:

TABLE 5[1]

Establishments of R&D Stations

Station No.	Soldiers		ATS		Non-Military		Total
	Officers	O/R	Officers	O/R	Officers	O/R	
VII	30	352	1	181	21	184	769
IX	15	231	2	–	42	138	428
XII	3	394	3	163	12	89	698
XV	9	139	2	49	6	14	219
Total							2114

In the period when ISRB was expanding, recruitment and retention of skilled technicians against poaching by other Service organisations was a serious problem. It is interesting to note that as other demands allowed, the Engineering Section was permitted to develop some devices of its own. It would be fascinating to know what they came up with and whether they were put into production. As an illustration of the expansion which took place at The Frythe, by 1944 the Engineering Section staff alone had increased from four to 160 and the workshops had expanded by over 30 times their original area.[2]

There was no doubt that Station IX was busy. SOE as a whole was busy. A large Country Section such as 'F' (France) sent over 400 agents into the field and there were around fifteen country sections. During 1942 SOE establishments dealt with an average of an operation every week, mostly concentrated in the weeks immediately before and after the full moon. This entailed one or more technical conferences, preparation of stores, preparation of mock-ups for training, visits to other technical establishments for information, trials, etc. Operations covered anything from the smallest drop to large raids such as that on St Nazaire. Senior officers at The Frythe had to be available to partake in these preparations if needed.

More than once during Station IX's existence SOE suffered criticism from other Services envious of the degree of independence it enjoyed. In 1943 there appears to have been concern that relations with other establishments might not be all they should be and that therefore some duplication of effort was likely to be taking place. In response to implied criticisms, a report by the Director of Scientific Research dated 29 June 1943 stated that the assistance of other Service departments had been sought and as far as was known, no work was being done at Station IX which could appropriately be done elsewhere and he was not aware of any overlap. As a sign of his commitment earlier long term projects were suspended.

SOE maintained some rooms at the Natural History Museum in London where they displayed the special stores available through them. At the end of the war this became an exhibition advertising (to a selected few from Whitehall and the Military) their achievements. Some of the statistics displayed at this exhibition give some idea of just how much assistance was given to Resistance movements and which weapons were the most sought after.

TABLE 6

ISRB production up to June 1945

Clams	68,000	Limpets	56,000
Railway charges	48,000	Standard charges	79,000
S B Charges	900	General purpose charges	316,300

Shipped to European groups and missions

Sten Gun	600,000	Rounds of Sten ammunition	387,000,000
Revolvers	320,000	Rounds for revolvers	19,000,000
Time pencil fuses	9,000,000	Limpets	36,000
Tyre bursters	630,000	Tons of food	8,000

Incendiaries sent to the field up to June 1945

| Tyesules | 200,000 | Pocket incendiaries | 800,000 |
| Fire pots | 300,000 | ML flares | 200,000 |

For the scientists and engineers there, the atmosphere in the Research Section was one of dedicated hard work and the organisation of the work possessed a curious flexibility which fostered creativity. Typically, many of the staff worked at least a twelve- to sixteen-hour day for a twelve- or thirteen-day fortnight, with weekend leave every three or four weeks. Not only was the Victorian work ethic not dead but the desperate need to defeat the enemy was deeply felt. Those working at The Frythe felt uplifted and motivated by being in the company of others equally devoted to their work. This atmosphere, in the words of John Brown of the Wireless Section 'drove the whole engine'.

Evenings when they were not working were spent by many of the scientists in the handsome drawing room, mostly quietly with devotees of chess and *The Times* crossword setting the tone. Occasionally, however, there was a lighter atmosphere. There were one or two boisterous characters, among them the huge 6 ft 4 in Norwegian, Air Force Capt W. Simonsen from the Wireless Section, whose infectious laugh lightened any atmosphere.

In the smoking room, adjacent to the dining room, was a rarely played organ of the type that had a hydraulic blowing engine in the cellar; when it was being played an assistant was required to control the water. John T. van Riemsdijk occasionally played the organ when he was duty officer at weekends and an employee by the name of George Hill, described as a sort of butler, carried out the cellar duties. 'Play 'ard, sir,' he would exhort the organist, 'or the cellar will get flooded.'[3]

The lives of the scientists and engineers were not without their lighter moments. It did not take much of an excuse to throw a party, the occasional one getting a little out of hand, such as the occasion when the organ in the smoking room was dismantled by a somewhat over-enthusiastic group of inebriated officers in order to confirm some theory about the effect of blowing down an organ pipe. The resultant noise was, it is reported, less than musical and there was some doubt as to whether the pipes were replaced in their original positions. The commandant was not amused.[4]

Sometimes attempts were made to conduct serious scientific business in the alcoholic haze of a party, even a small one. It was on such an occasion when somewhat dubious judgements were being passed on the effectiveness of an experimental pair of plastic-lensed binoculars for use at night when one of the less inebriated suddenly realised that this was no way of arriving at a considered scientific conclusion. The episode gave rise to a properly constituted and formal Trials Section.

Security was concentrated most strictly at the point of work. Information was passed on a 'need to know' basis. Leaving papers unattended on one's desk was strictly forbidden and regular security patrols checked at lunchtime and at night that laboratories, offices and particularly filing cabinets were securely locked. There was a military guard at the main gate and generally a pass was required, but there does not seem to have been a perimeter security fence – the grounds and gardens had nothing more than conventional hedges and fences. As far as the local population was concerned the name Inter-Services Research Bureau was sufficient to explain the comings and goings of the various uniforms and vehicles, and the flashes and bangs which emanated from the nearby woods and fields. To those working in the laboratories however, it was possible to glean something of what was going on in other sections from snippets of overheard conversation in the mess. Even so, the term SOE was unknown to many until after the war had ended.

At the end of hostilities Newitt was called upon to produce from an analysis of operations the basic requirements of a saboteur. In his paper 'The Organisation of Research and Development to Meet the Requirements of Subversive Warfare' he maintains these basic requirements would be satisfied by:

a) A silenced small arm for personal protection or dealing with guards and sentries at night.
b) Two standard demolition sets consisting of a high explosive charge with means of attachment to the target, time delay initiator, means of linking two or more charges and suitable for use in air and under water respectively.
c) Ancillary devices such as anti-removal, pull, pressure and release switches.
d) A standard fire-raising set consisting of a pocket incendiary with a time delay initiator and the means of linking two or more units.[5]

Thus the fundamental equipment of a saboteur was fairly straightforward: but the means of making it more reliable, simpler and easier to use under adverse conditions and more unobtrusive had exercised the minds of the researchers throughout the war years.

There were some long-term benefits from academic studies undertaken on behalf of SOE by some of the country's leading seats of learning. Cambridge University carried out an investigation into the properties of spontaneously inflammable metal-alkyl derivatives; the Imperial College of Science in London produced a new type of explosive having a high oxygen content and great stability to shock;

and the University of Oxford undertook an examination of the properties of certain chemical and physical systems with a view to developing a time delay with negligible temperature coefficient. All three projects were said by Newitt to have 'produced most interesting and worthwhile results'.

The most plentiful devices issued to the field were Station IX's various incendiaries. But how did Station XV's booby-trap exotica, highlighted in recent years in the popular press, come to be developed? For one thing, their design must have provided a certain 'light relief' to the scientists. During relatively quieter times between the difficult jobs of great urgency, they must have reverted to schoolboy mischievousness which was all in the cause of undermining the morale of Hitler's military machine. The booby-traps disguised as rats, Chianti bottles, Balinese carvings, bicycle pumps, lumps of coal and a host of other everyday items could have been included in a parachute container of stores almost as a make-weight, their use being opportunistic. There is no doubt that Station IX was not in the least shy about these apparently juvenile devices. After all, they worked and inflicted various degrees of harm and, more particularly, wider alarm on the enemy so it was right that they should appear in the catalogue of devices available and later in their exhibition at the Natural History Museum. In a twist to the theme of disguised devices, it was discovered that the 20 July 1944 plot by German officers which very nearly killed Hitler was carried out using a bomb 'disguised' as a brief case. Purely by chance, for SOE played no part in this assassination attempt, the plastic explosive and the timing device came from SOE stores which had fallen into the Abwehr's hands two years earlier and been put aside by one of the plotters to await a suitable opportunity to use it.

It would be pointless to attempt to list the most effective devices developed by SOE, for their stores had a great variety of purposes and were used under many different circumstances. The relatively sophisticated inventions and techniques, while being technically interesting, might not have caused as much mayhem to the enemy or encouragement to the Resistance as some more prosaic ones. It is interesting to note in Table 6 that, apart from small arms ammunition and Time Pencil delays, incendiaries formed the greatest quantity of items sent to the field: confirmation perhaps of the soundness of the concept of Operation Braddock.

Sadly, at the end of the war SOE stations were encouraged to destroy their records and a mysterious fire in the Baker Street headquarters destroyed many of their papers before the organisation was disbanded in January 1946. The secrecy surrounding SOE has been lifted only slowly over the last fifty years and even at the end of the millennium, a few files still remain to be released into the public domain. Many of the details of the ingenious and perhaps exotic inventions thought up at Stations IX, XII and XV are lost forever.

Wartime Britain was subject to severe rationing and frustrating controls on most aspects of life. Amidst the thousands of pages of wartime and immediately postwar documents sifted through for this record of SOE's research and development achievements was a light-hearted item which some erstwhile archivist had seen fit to keep for posterity in the Public Record Office. It illustrates the lengths one had to go to in wartime in order to procure something a little different to eat on that special occasion.

STATION XII'S CHRISTMAS PORKER, 1943

The Camp Commandant wrote to the OC Station XII that it had at last been possible to obtain a licence to kill a pig for Christmas for the Officers' Mess. The Camp Commandant had first been referred to the Hertford Rural District Food Office, then to the Agricultural Officer, ECD, then to the Herts and Bucks Area Bacon Officer, then to the Command Catering Officer and lastly to the Agricultural Officer, Eastern Command.

The pig had been slaughtered at 11.00 hours on 11 December. Before the slaughter took place, however, the Hitchin Bacon Factory had telephoned to say the pig had arrived but they must refuse to kill it as the licence only permitted this to be done in the area of the camp. After ringing the War Office, at Command's instructions, special permission was obtained, following a call to the Ministry of Food, Colwyn Bay, from the County Pig Allocation Officer who had finally endorsed the licence and declared that everything was in order.[6]

EIGHTEEN

EPILOGUE

With the advantage of hindsight, doubt has been expressed by some about the worth of special forces such as the SOE. Many commentators cite the deep animosity between SOE and SIS, almost open warfare in some Country Sections but tolerably cooperative in others, as a reason for costly failures. Malcolm Muggeridge wrote: 'Though SOE and SIS were nominally on the same side in the war, they were generally speaking more abhorrent to one another than the Abwehr was to either of them.'[1] There are great difficulties in a democracy in setting up a properly organised subversive department within government, even in the relative calm of peacetime. In the alarm and confusion that existed in Britain in the early years of the Second World War it is not surprising that there was just not time to look into this in sufficient depth. Decisions had to be made and if some Whitehall departments felt aggrieved with them that was unfortunate but a fact of life at the time. It was doubly unfortunate that they led to an unfriendly relationship between SOE and several other departments which lasted throughout the conflict.

There were also other problems. After the war Newitt wrote a paper entitled 'The Organisation of Research and Development to Meet the Requirements of Subversive Warfare' in which he made the point that in a new form of warfare with no past history to draw upon there were bound to be conflicts of opinion as to the kind of equipment required. Such a condition existed in SOE at the outset, much energy being expended in developing types of devices and equipment which proved not to be viable in the operational context.[2]

There are some who say the success of Operation Gunnerside to deny the Nazis a supply of heavy water was in itself sufficient justification for the setting up of SOE. But as history unfolds with the release of previously secret records, it has a habit of changing opinions. In his 1998 book *The Big Bang* George Brown, himself a one-time scientist with SOE, maintains that the Germans had never seriously set out on the long path to make an atomic bomb, even though they were well aware of the possibilities. It is clear, however, from the transcripts of clandestinely recorded conversations of ten incarcerated German scientists after the Nazi capitulation that they were working towards a nuclear reactor. But why go on seeking atomic power, which was an equally long-term project, if not to develop the capability of making an atomic bomb? The German work had been seriously hampered by the stoppage of heavy water from Vemork.[3]

At the outbreak of the war the ordinary Englishman would not have taken kindly to some of the more extreme actions to be perpetrated by SOE. But after Dunkirk it was the realisation of the brutal totality of the Second World War which precipitated a 'by all possible means' approach and the formation of SOE; and the 'means' did not exclude some of the 'dirty tricks' developed at Stations IX, XII and XV. At least these 'dirty tricks' were aimed at the enemy's occupying forces, and if not at specific targets then at its military machine. Unfortunately there were collateral casualties among non-combatants but SOE and the Resistance were not deliberately scattering their anti-personnel devices indiscriminately among civilian populations.

There might have been some duplication of effort between the scientists at The Frythe and those at other secret establishments such as The Firs. There was, in fact, an exchange of information and, no doubt, ideas between these two Stations and later they specialised to a degree. Nevertheless, such apparent duplication was looked into from time to time by powerful men and in any case it is possible that this rivalry inspired greater inventiveness. But above all, SOE was able, because of establishments like The Frythe with their relentless inventive spirit, to put into the hands of its agents the means of doing their job. And by supplying Resistance groups they maintained the morale of those wishing to free their countries of the enemy.

As Nazi collapse became inevitable SOE work turned towards destroying the German Will to Resist and the prevention of damage to the civilian infrastructure by withdrawing armies. Operation Periwig, a somewhat fantastical idea of SOE's Chief, was hindered by SIS and SHAEF embargoes until it was too late to contribute to the outcome, unlike the organisation's anti-scorching preparations. The Germans in Norway, for example, became aware of the extent of the preparations by the SOE-inspired Home Forces (Milorg) to minimize the effect of an enemy scorched-earth policy during any retreat. Nevertheless, they were still astonished at the number, equipment and armament of the

Resistance fighters who appeared as though by magic on the day of surrender. The Allied commander-in-chief Norway attributed at least 30 per cent of the peaceful capitulation of the German garrison of 300,000 men to the activity and strength of the Home Forces.

The careers of the major players in the Research and Development Section resumed in due course after the end of hostilities, seven returning to academia and eventual election as Fellows of the Royal Society, the highest scientific accolade. Dolphin's development of the Welbike, known as the Corgi, was eclipsed by the Italian Vespa and Lambretta scooters which, ironically, had been produced as something for the unemployed Italian workforce to do while that country's war-torn national infrastructure was being rebuilt. He later became Chief Engineer at the Atomic Weapons Research Establishment.

The wartime innovation of The Frythe seemed not to have deserted it with the demise of SOE in 1946. In the early 1960s ICI was in the process of selling the site to Unilever and during this period of joint occupancy by the two companies the Unilever bulldozers unearthed caches of hastily buried ammunition, switches and detonators. Then the Army was called in to deal with some unexploded hand grenades which rolled out of a hedgerow. One was deemed to be too unstable to take away. These were the days before the Health and Safety at Work Act and the problem was solved quickly and without fuss. A Warrant Officer and the ICI Engineer-in-Charge[4] carried the grenade to the nearby Homer's Wood where, in an echo of the wartime spirit of the place, plastic explosive was placed on top, the fuse was lit and it was blown up.

M.R.D. Foot has argued that the Resistance had invincible strength in moral terms.[5] It was in backing up this moral strength that SOE's supplies were so important; and it was the scientific and engineering effort behind the design and development of these stores which made them possible at all.

POSTSCRIPT

Three weeks before the typescript of this book was completed, Douglas Everett died suddenly. We both believed passionately that a record of SOE's scientific work should be made while there were still a few players alive to contribute to it. The contribution he made to the project by injecting first-hand knowledge gleaned from long hours of consulting his wartime notebooks has been invaluable.

Fredric Boyce

RESEARCH AND DEVELOPMENT ESTABLISHMENTS

Station VI	Arms Section	Bride Hall near Ayot St Lawrence, Hertfordshire.
Station VIIa	Wireless Section Production	The Bontex Knitting Mills in Beresford Avenue, Wembley.
Station VIIb	Wireless Section Packing and despatch	The Yeast-Vite factory in Whippendell Road, Watford.
Station VIIc	Wireless Section Research	Allensor's joinery factory in King George's Avenue, Watford.
Station VIId	Wireless Section Production	Kay's garage, Bristol Street, Birmingham
Station VIII	Engineering Section	Queen Mary Reservoir, Staines.
Station IX	Research	The Frythe, Welwyn, Hertfordshire.
Station IX a	Submersibles work at Staines reservoir	PO Box 1, Ashford, Middlesex.
Station IXc	Submersibles work at Fishguard Bay	The Fishguard Bay Hotel, Goodwick, Pembrokeshire.
Station XI	Accommodation	Gorhambury House near St Albans, Hertfordshire.
Station XII	Production, packaging and despatch	Aston House near Stevenage, Hertfordshire.
Station XIV	Forgery Section	Briggens, near Royden, Essex.
Station XV	Camouflage Section	The Thatched Barn road house on the Barnet bypass at Borehamwood.
Station XVa	Camouflage Section	56 Queen's Gate, London SW7

Station XVb	Camouflage Section	The Demonstration Room at the Natural History Museum in London.
Station XVc	Camouflage Section Photography and Make-up	Trevor Square, Knightsbridge.
Station XVII	Explosive trials	Brickendonbury, Hertford.
Station ?	Unknown	The Spartan factory on the North Circular Road near Wembley.

APPENDIX B

INVENTORS OF DEVICES PRODUCED BY SOE RESEARCH SECTION

Towards the end of the war an attempt was made to give inventors credit for the devices they had created. The following is the list drawn up at that time.[1]

Device	Inventor
Improvements in or relating to hand tools	H.W. Moore
Welbike	Lt Col J.R.V. Dolphin
Device for photographic reproduction of documents of microscopic size without a microscope.	Capt T.B. Waddicor
Reinforced paper container	Maj V.E. Holloway
Welgun	F.T. Bridgeman
Welrod	Maj H.Q.A. Reeves
Sten gun silencer	Maj H.Q.A. Reeves
Radio active night sights	Maj H.Q.A. Reeves
Sleeping Beauty	Maj H.Q.A. Reeves
Sleeve gun	Maj H.Q.A. Reeves
Motorisation of swimmer (Welbum)	Maj H.Q.A. Reeves
Roller conveyor	Maj H.Q.A. Reeves
Silencer for Welrod and sleeve gun	Maj H.Q.A. Reeves
Bell device for location of containers	Messrs L.G. Wilson, P.T. Trent, B.H. Chibnall
Welcase	Messrs L.G. Wilson, P.T. Trent, B.H. Chibnall
Welman	Lt Col J.R.V. Dolphin
Time Pencil	Cdr A.G. Langley RN
AC delay	Maj C.R. Bailey, Capt M.B. Donald, Mr R.S. Potter
Anti-removal switch (air armed)	Mr E. Cotterill
Anti-removal switch (water armed)	Mr E. Cotterill
Limpet speed switch	Maj C.V. Clarke, Mr E. Cotterill

Pigeon delay switch	Mr E. Cotterill
Overhead wire cutters	Messrs S.F. Beech, C.J. Sutton
Trim valve	Maj J.I. Meldrum, Mr E. Porteous
	Lt Col J.R.V. Dolphin
Folding seat for Welfreighter	Lt Col J.R.V. Dolphin, Mr G.H. Clarke
Collapsible dinghy	Mr H. Harradine, Lt Col J.R.V. Dolphin
Nail firing device	Mr E. Norman, Maj Critchfield, Maj H.Q.A. Reeves
Sucker device	Mr F.A.O. Waren, Maj C.E.M. Critchfield, Maj H.Q.A. Reeves
Altimeter fuse	Mr G.J. Sutton
Oil nitrate incendiary	Dr C.H. Bamford, Mr D.L. Levi
Directional incendiary	Dr C.H. Bamford
Phosphorous iodine gel	Dr C.H. Bamford, Mr D.L. Levi
Magnesium flash incendiary	Dr C.H. Bamford, Mr D.H. Malan
Small pocket delay incendiary	Messrs D.W. King, A.R.D. Wilde, Maj O.J. Walker
Flash grenade	Mr D.W. King, Maj O.J. Walker
Jet Thermite bomb	Dr F. Panzner
Paper tube delay	Maj C.R. Bailey
Pocket smoke generator	Maj O.J. Walker
Tyesule	Col L.J.C. Wood, Dr F.A. Freeth
Welmine	Lt Col J.R.V. Dolphin, Mr E. Norman, Mr L. Berg
Remote control firing mechanism for pistol	Lt Col J.R.V. Dolphin, Mr E. Norman
Buoyant limpet	Maj H.Q.A. Reeves, Maj C.E.M. Critchfield
Tree spigot gun	Maj C.V. Clarke, Mr G.J. Sutton, Maj E. Ramsay Green
Tree spigot bomb	Mr G.J. Sutton, Maj C.V. Clarke, Capt J.P.B. Flowerdew, Col G.O.C. Probert

Tree spigot fuse	Mr G.J. Sutton
Tree spigot sight	Mr G.J. Sutton, Capt J.P.B. Flowerdew, Mr E.G.R. Welch
Plate spigot sight	Mr G.J. Sutton, Capt J.P.B. Flowerdew
Plate spigot gun	Mr G.J. Sutton, Mr E. Norman, Capt J.P.B. Flowerdew, Maj C.V. Clarke
ISRB Allways fuse	Lt Col H.H. King

APPENDIX C

ABBREVIATIONS

ACOS	Admiral Commanding Orkneys and Shetlands.
AFDC	Airborne Forces Development Centre.
AFEE	Airborne Forces Experimental Establishment.
C	The symbol of the head of MI6.
CCO	Chief of Combined Operations.
CD	Symbol of the executive director of SOE.
CIGS	Chief of the Imperial General Staff.
COHQ	Combined Operations Headquarters (London).
COS	Chief of Staff.
DMI	Director of Military Intelligence.
DMWD	Department of Miscellaneous Weapons and Devices.
DNC	Director of Navy Contracts.
DNE	Director of Navy Engineering.
DNI	Director of Naval Intelligence.
DNOR	Department of Naval Operational Research.
DSR	Director of Scientific Research.
EH	Electra House.
EM	Electrician's Mate.
ERM	Engine Room Mechanic.
FANY	First Aid Nursing Yeomanry.
FO(S)	Flag Officer (Submarines).
GS(R)	General Staff (Research) – later MI(R).
HADDA	High Altitude Delayed Dropping Apparatus.
IPF	Inshore Patrol Flotilla.
ISRB	Inter-Services Research Bureau (Cover name for SOE).
ISSU	Inter-Services Signals Unit (Cover name for SOE).
MGB	Motor Gun Boat.
MGOF	Master General of Ordnance Finance.
MI(R)	Military Intelligence (Research).
MO1(SP)	Military Operations 1 (Special Projects) (Cover name for SOE).
MTB	Motor Torpedo Boat.
NID	Naval Intelligence Department.
NNIU	Norwegian Navy Independent Unit.
PID	Political Intelligence Department.
PPS	Parliamentary Private Secretary.
PWE	Political Warfare Executive.

Appendix C

RAE	Royal Aircraft Establishment.
RAOC	Royal Army Ordnance Corps.
RE	Royal Engineers.
REME	Royal Electrical and Mechanical Engineers.
R/T	Radio Telephony.
SFDC	Special Forces Development Centre.
SHAEF	Supreme Headquarters Allied Expeditionary Force.
SIS	Secret Intelligence Service.
SO	Special Operations.
SRD	Services Reconnaissance Department. (Cover name for SOE's Australian counterpart.)
STS	Special Training School.
W/T	Wireless Telegraphy.

APPENDIX D

SUMMARY OF THE WORK OF THE ENGINEERING SECTION

The inventiveness and skill of the Engineering Section may be appreciated from this summary of its achievements. Up to the end of 1942 the following equipment had been invented and developed to a degree, though some items never went into production:

A silent .22 pistol, possibly a silenced version of the U.S. Hi-Standard pistol.
A .22 machine gun.
The Welgun.
The Welhit silent short-range projector.
Various underwater containers.
A collapsible ski-sledge for dropping by parachute.
Special marlin spikes for containing explosives.
Camouflaged oil drums containing depth charges.
Numerous camouflaged containers.
Collapsible ladders and steps. Two types of scaling ladders were designed at Station XII for use by the Commandos.
A rope climbing device for use on ½-in rope was tested in April 1943 and after one or two adjustments was sent for user trials.
A collapsible bridge.
A grapnel device.
A short time delay for a parachute canopy.
A release switch for a parachute canopy.
A smoke boat, a smoke screen to operate from a robot motorboat.
In October 1942 a metal case was designed to accept an ampoule of liquid which was to be broken and used to put searching dogs off the scent. Research into a suitable liquid had not at that time come up with an answer.

By the end of the war many more devices had been invented, which are listed below.

Appendix D

Underwater and Marine

The Welman one-man submarine.
The Welfreighter stores-carrying submarine.
The motorised submersible canoe 'Sleeping Beauty'.
Silencer for outboard motor.
Silent power unit canoe with flexible drive.
Containers, deep water, quick opening, Mks I and II.
Suction-adhesion device for limpets.
Nail firing device for charge adhesion to steel ships.
Nail firing device for charge adhesion to wooden ships.
Small arms and other weapons.
Silenced Sten gun Mk II
Silenced Welrod Mk IIa .32 in.
Silenced sleeve gun.
Silenced Welrod 9 mm.
Silenced M1 carbine (in conjunction with CSAR).

Miscellaneous

Welbike folding motorcycle.
Overhead wire cutter Type 6.
Skeleton keys.
Grease gun for use with abrasive grease for axle boxes.
Drive attachment for Welbike for battery charging generator.
Collapsible ladder.
Tyre cutter.

DEVICES WHICH WERE ISSUED FOR AD HOC OPERATIONS

Welsilencer, a silent .22 pistol.
Blowpipe.
Collapsible bridge.
Silent prison bar cutter.
Collapsible ski sledge for dropping by parachute.
Marlin spikes containing explosive.

DEVICES WHICH ENGINEERING SECTION DEVELOPED BUT WHICH NEVER WENT
INTO PRODUCTION FOR VARIOUS REASONS

Welmine (magnetic).
Welmine (percussion).
Welmine (jettison-head).
Towing container (water).
Welbum (motor attachment for swimmers).

Limpet (stream lined, scraper).
Small-calibre machine carbine.
Special .22 magazine (2/1).
Machine pistol Type I Mark II.
Silent 9 mm machine gun.
Silent 9 mm Luger pistol.
Gas gun.
Welpen (.22 fountain pen pistol).
Verey light fired from Spigot Pistol.
Silent killer (spring gun).
Device for crossing Dannert wire fence.
2-in mortar grapnel device for minefields.
Welbike trailer.
Smokescreen to operate from Welbike.
Underwater glider.

NOTE

This information was drawn from the appendices to the History of the R&D Section provided by kind permission of the SOE Adviser to the FCO.

APPENDIX E

EXAMPLES OF CAMOUFLAGED DEVICES

Camouflage Section could disguise almost any piece of military equipment as an innocuous everyday item. Furthermore, many of their products were actually booby-trap devices. The following are examples of the skills of this talented team.

Clever containers were made in the form of:

A metal drum inside a fish barrel.
Metal flagons.
Plaster logs.
Wooden logs hollowed out.
Packing cases for everyday items.
Plaster vegetables and fruit.
Driftwood and spars.
Cement bags.
Fish boxes.

Wireless sets were camouflaged as:

Bundles of faggots.
A Mumo adding machine.
Domestic wireless sets.
Portable gramophones.
A vacuum cleaner.
Rocks, for depositing wireless sets on a beach or in open countryside.
A rubber armchair which was inflated with a pump and the wireless set placed under the seat.

Concealment of various miniature communications receivers (MCRs) was achieved by disguising them as:

Antique German clocks.
A paper punch.
A German water bottle.
A Belgian tea can.

A German manual.
A German bible.
A brandy flask.

On the offensive front, explosives were incorporated into all kinds of articles to transform them into incendiaries or lethal bombs:

Hollow wooden nuts or bolts containing explosive would replace rusty old genuine ones.
Wooden logs could conceal an explosive charge which would detonate when thrown on a fire or into a furnace.
Chianti bottles.
Bicycle tyre pumps which would inflate a tyre when used with short strokes but explode when used normally.
Food tins could conceal a bomb. Research into explosive food tins revealed that the pneumatic type were considered too dangerous as an unintentional air leak would cause it to detonate.
Incendiary soap contained a cavity with metallic sodium in it. This ignited on contact with water.
A shaving brush could contain an incendiary device.
Cigarettes could be made to start a real fire.
An innocent-looking book could conceal a bomb.
Wooden road blocks could hide explosive devices.
Ships' fenders could be made to explode.
An anti-personnel grenade could be made to look like a normal torch.
Chinese stone lanterns could conceal either explosive or incendiary devices.
Copies of Balinese carvings were cast in solid high explosive.
Japanese sauce tins could be made to explode.
An incendiary briefcase (single lock) had wiring concealed in the lining of the case and a quilt of potassium nitrate to assist the combustion.
The incendiary attaché case and the incendiary suitcase were variations on the above theme.
The Thatched Barn produced 43,700 cigarettes made of incendiary or explosive material for use by SOE agents.

OPTIMISATION OF AIR SUPPLY EQUIPMENT

To apply the criteria discussed on page 173/4 quantitatively it is necessary to know how the speed of descent (v) depends on the load (M) and on the parachute size expressed either in terms of its diameter (D) or area (A). Because of the complex airflow round a parachute and the porosity of the fabric from which the canopy is made, any detailed theory would be very complicated. Nevertheless, valuable information can be obtained using simple theoretical arguments. First, using the mathematical technique of 'dimensional analysis', it turns out that, independent of the details of any theory, the rate of descent is proportional to the square root of the load divided by the diameter of the chute: v is proportional to $\sqrt{M}/D$. It follows that doubling the load increases the rate of descent by $\sqrt{2} = 1.41$; while doubling the diameter of the chute halves the rate of fall.

The important operational result is that, if for a mixed load of packages the load and chute sizes are chosen so the $\sqrt{M}/D$ (or $\sqrt{(M/A)}$ is the same for all loads, then they will fall at the same speed.

The ASR files contain the following table of recommended parachute sizes to be used for panniers of various weights. The origin of these figures is uncertain, but they were probably arrived at empirically. Maximum and minimum weights are given for each parachute size: attention here is directed to the upper weight limit for each parachute size.

Recommended Values of M and D for use with Panniers

M/lb	Up to 40	41–80	81–120	121–160	161–200	
D/ft	12	16	20	24	28	
A/ft²	113	201	314	452	615	*Mean value*
$(\sqrt{M}/D)/lb^{1/2}ft^{-1}$	0.529	0.561	0.546	0.529	0.505	0.534 ± 0.015
$\sqrt{(M/A)}/lb^{1/2}ft^{-1}$	0.595	0.633	0.621	0.595	0.571	0.602 ± 0.019

If the above quantities are converted to metric (SI) units then the mean values of $\sqrt{M}/D$ and $\sqrt{(M/A)}$ are 1.15 kg$^{1/2}$m^{-1} and 1.30 kg$^{1/2}$m^{-1} respectively.

The values of $\sqrt{M}/D$ and $\sqrt{(M/A)}$ for the various load/chute combinations are seen to be constant to within a few percent. So by accident or design loads conforming to the specifications in the table should fall at roughly the same rate. To obtain a value of the actual rate of descent a more detailed but still very crude theory is needed. This links the rate of descent to the density of air, and leads to the two equivalent equations.

$$v = 4.60 \sqrt{M/D} = 4.05 \sqrt{(M/A)}$$

Thus, using the mean values of $\sqrt{M/D}$ and $\sqrt{(M/A)}$ gives

$$v = 5.29 \text{ m per sec or } 17.2 \text{ ft per sec}$$

This is equal to the impact speed of a load dropped from a height of 1.42 m or 4.64 ft.

Similar calculations for filled C or H containers weighing 330 lb (150 kg) with a 28 ft chute give an impact speed of 6.3 m per sec, or 21.2 ft per sec: this is equivalent to the terminal speed of a drop from 7 ft. The same containers on a 22 ft chute would fall at 8.3 m per sec or 27 ft per sec. equivalent to a free drop from 11 ft.

It is not known whether in the parachute dropping trials at Henlow or Cardington any attempt was made to measure accurately the speed of descent of parachuted loads but by the end of 1943 work, mostly at Henlow, had established the optimum size of parachute in relation to load. As a reasonable compromise a parachute with a 22 ft canopy, carrying a net load of 220 lb (100 kg) (the C-type container weighed 96 lb (43.5 kg), the H-type 86 lb (39 kg)) and giving an impact velocity of 27 ft per sec was accepted. That this is in close agreement with the calculated value suggests that the simple theory is adequate for the purposes of calculating impact speeds.

NOTES

Chapter 1

1. Details of the spy Richter's short stay in England are in PRO files KV2/30–33, HO144/21576, and CRIM1/1350. Albert Pierrepoint's autobiography *Executioner: Pierrepoint* deals with his execution in Chapter 5 pp.135–138. Further details are contained in PRO file PCOM9/909.

Chapter 2

1. The term Fifth Column applies to enemy sympathisers who might provide active assistance to an invader and originates from the Spanish Civil War rebel collaborators in Madrid in 1936 when four rebel columns were advancing on the city. The fifth column were the sympathisers already in the city.
2. PRO file HS7/27.
3. *Secret Flotillas* by Brooks Richards.
4. *Winston Churchill's Toyshop* by Stuart Macrae.
5. *The Partisan Leader's Handbook* is reproduced in Appendix 2 of *SOE in the Low Countries* by M.R.D. Foot.
6. *SOE: The Special Operations Executive 1940–46* by M.R.D. Foot.

Chapter 3

1. Information from a leaflet by SmithKlineBeecham, the owners of The Frythe in the late 1990s, and recollections of Berkeley Mason.
2. J. Harmston, an estate worker living locally, in *Hertfordshire Countryside*, Vol. 32, No. 214, Feb 1977.
3. 'A Description of the Building and Equipment of the Thermostat Hut, Station IX', Ref. JTVR/4956, 11 July 1945.
4. PRO file HS7/27 History of AD/Z Directorate (Research, Development and Supply).
5. Hertfordshire County Archives AP/A7 Vol. 1–Vol. 3 and D/Esd T1.
6. PRO file HS7/286
7. Mrs Mary Fields, whose parents were in service at Bride Hall before and during part of the war, provided the domestic background for this section.
8. PRO file HS7/286.
9. Information from *The Book of Elstree & Boreham Wood* and *Elstree & Boreham Wood in Camera* by Stephen A. Castle.

Chapter 4

1. Stuart Macrae, *Winston Churchill's Toyshop* (1971).
2. Everett's involvement in wartime work at Oxford is of some interest since it illustrates the complacency which developed in some quarters of the Establishment between 1918 and 1939. A major scare had arisen early in the War when secret intelligence had indicated that the Germans were preparing to use arsenic trihydride (arsine, code-named ARTHUR) as a war gas. The cause of the panic was the discovery that while the German respirator gave protection against this gas, the British version, which had remained unchanged since 1918, allowed it to penetrate. The importance of this discovery did not seem to have been appreciated by the top brass at the Chemical Defence Establishment at Porton Down. When the research group from Oxford visited Porton in May 1940 to discuss their work they met the Military Commandant who gave them little encouragement. He dismissed their research, saying that 'attempts to improve the British service respirator were like gilding the lily'! This was not what these young scientists wanted to hear, but this did not deter them from working long hours into the night to develop a charcoal with catalytic properties to deal with arsine. Their call-up had been deferred and they were desperately keen to make a contribution to the war effort. (It must be said, however, that someone in the Home Office had taken the threat of gas warfare seriously and had, by October 1938, arranged for the design and production of the civilian respirator which was issued, in its cardboard box, to the whole population.) The further objective of the Oxford work was to seek an alternative source of raw material for active charcoal. Traditionally in the UK this had been coconut shell but this had to be imported by sea and an indigenous material was needed. Finely ground coal briquetted under high pressure was the solution, but the choice of coal was critical. After an extensive survey of British coals and various blends an appropriate solution had been found and, by incorporation of metal catalysts, copper and silver, resistance to a range of gases was achieved. It was then possible for those engaged in this task to be reassigned to other work.
3. For details see *SOE Syllabus – Lessons in Ungentlemanly Warfare, World War II* with introduction by Denis Rigden. Public Record Office 2001.

Chapter 5

1. *SOE in France* by M.R.D. Foot.
2. PRO file HS7/27.
3. *This Grim and Savage Game* by Tom Moon.
4. *Plotting Hitler's Death* by Joachim Fest. Also recounted by Rigden in *Kill the Fuhrer*, p. 169.
5. PRO file HS7/286.
6. PRO file HS8/774.
7. *Secret Agent's Handbook of Special Devices*, Public Record Office, 2000.

Notes

8. *Baker Street Irregular* by Bickham Sweet-Escott, p. 250, footnote.
9. *Danger UXB* by M.J. Jappy, Channel 4 Books, 2001. Also *The Truth About Dirty Tricks* by Chapman Pincher, 1991.

Chapter 6

1. From the personal recollections of Prof D.H. Everett, FRS.
2. Correspondence with Anthony Brooks, DSO, MC.
3. PRO file HS8/817.
4. Ibid.
5. PRO file PREM3/409/5.
6. Ibid.
7. *Coastal Command 1939–1942*, HMSO, 1943, p. 101.
8. PRO file PREM3/409/5.
9. PRO file HS7/145.
10. PRO file FO898/356.
11. PRO file HS7/286.
12. PRO file HS7/110.
13. PRO file CAB81/53.
14. Ibid.
15. PRO file CAB104/234.
16. R. Harris and J. Paxman, *A Higher Form of Killing*, Hill and Wang, 1982. G.B. Carter, 'The Legend of Fildes and the Heydrich Assassination', ASA Newsletter 96–4, 16 August 1996.
17. *British Security Coordination – The Secret History of British Intelligence in the Americas 1940–45*, with introduction by Nigel West.
18. A tiny metal sphere containing ricin was used by an Eastern Bloc agent to kill a Bulgarian dissident, Georgi Markov, in London in 1978. The sphere was fired into his leg from a weapon disguised as an umbrella.
19. PRO file CAB81/55.
20. PRO file CAB81/58.
21. PRO file HS7/210.
22. PRO file CAB81/19.

Chapter 7

1. *Sabotage! The story of Lt Col J. Elder Wills* by Leslie Bell, T. Werner Laurie 1957.
2. PRO file HS8/199.
3. See *Secret Agent* by David Stafford, pp. 55–57.
4. PRO file HS7/110.
5. PRO file HS7/46.
6. PRO file PREM3 409/5.
7. PRO file HS8/199.
8. PRO file HS7/46. Remainder of section from PRO files HS7/27, HS7/30, HS7/47, HS7/49.

Chapter 8

1. Information for this section has been drawn also from the appendices to *The History of the R&D Section* provided by kind permission of the SOE Adviser to the FCO.
2. PRO file HS7/286.
3. PRO file HS8/199.
4. *Soldier of Fortune* magazine.
5. Ladd and Melton, *Clandestine Warfare*.
6. PRO file HS7/110.
7. PRO file HS7/286.
8. John D Walter, *Secret Firearms. An Illustrated History of Miniature and Concealed Handguns*.
9. Ladd and Melton, *Clandestine Warfare*.
10. Details of the Welbike are from *British Forces Motorcycles 1925–45* by C.J. Orchard and S.J. Madden.
11. *SOE: The Special Operations Executive 1940–1945* by M.R.D. Foot, pp. 110–11.
12. PRO file ADM226/48.
13. PRO file HS7/47.

Chapter 9

1. *Cockleshell Heroes* by C.E. Lucas Phillips.
2. This appears to have been an adaptation of the Budig Wing, details of which are in PRO file AVIA13/549 and in the 11 December 1935 issue of *The Aeroplane*.
3. PRO file HS8/199.
4. *Underwater Warriors* by Paul Kemp, p. 67.
5. Ibid.
6. PRO file HS8/252.
7. PRO file HS7/286.
8. Ibid.
9. Ibid.
10. IWM photo archive negative HU56761.
11. *Secret Agent's Handbook of Special Devices*, Public Record Office.
12. PRO file DEFE2/958.
13. *Secret Flotillas* by Brooks Richards.
14. PRO file HS8/897.
15. PRO file ADM1/17161.
16. PRO file HS7/287.
17. PRO file HS8/798.
18. PRO file ADM1/13413.
19. PRO file DEFE2/1009.
20. PRO file ADM204/525.
21. PRO file HS1/232.
22. PRO file HS7/88.

23. PRO file ADM1/16297.
24. PRO file HS7/286.
25. PRO file HS7/287.
26. PRO file ADM1/17161.
27. Ibid.
28. *Cockleshell Heroes.*
29. PRO file HS7/286.
30. PRO file HS7/287.
31. PRO file HS8/199.
32. PRO file ADM226/48.
33. PRO file HS7/287.
34. Ibid.
35. Ibid.
36. PRO file HS7/175.

Chapter 10

1. Much of the detailed information in this chapter is from the scientific notebooks and personal recollections of the late Prof D.H. Everett, FRS.
2. PRO file HS7/27. 'History of the Trials Section' – Appendix A.

Chapter 11

1. *SOE: The Special Operations Executive 1940–1946* by M.R.D. Foot.
2. PRO file HS7/50.
3. Ibid.
4. *Secret Agent's Handbook of Special Devices*, Public Record Office.
5. PRO file HS7/50.
6. Ibid.
7. PRO files HS7/47, HS7/109, HS7/110 and HS8/418.
8. PRO file HS7/286.
9. As retold by J.T. van Riemsdijk in 2001.
10. PRO file HS7/286.
11. From the personal reminiscences of the late Prof D.H. Everett FRS.
12. Report DHE/A/4684 dated 27 October 1944.
13. Much of this section is based on the notebooks and personal recollections of Prof D.H. Everett FRS who was in charge of both the trials work and the Air Supply Research Section.

Chapter 12

1. Much of this section is drawn from the Sound Archives of the Imperial War Museum, Audio Tapes 11035/6.
2. PRO file AVIA22/2757.
3. PRO file HS7/46.
4. *'Jacqueline' Pioneer of the Resistance* by Stella King, 1989.
5. *The Vital Link* by Philip Warner.

6. PRO file HS7/37.
7. *The Giant-Killers* by John Oram Thomas, 1975.
8. PRO file HS7/36.
9. PRO file AVIA22/2757.
10. The Royal Signals Museum kindly allowed the author to photograph some exhibits.
11. The reminiscences of Mr Eric Slater, formerly in RCD, are also drawn upon.

Chapter 13

1. Much of this chapter is drawn from PRO file HS7/27.

Chapter 14

1. PRO file HS7/46.
2. *Baker Street Irregular* by Bickham Sweet-Escott, p. 44.
3. PRO file HS8/252.
4. PRO file HS7/46.

Chapter 15

1. PRO file PREM3/408/5.
2. PRO file HS8/775.
3. PRO file HS8/199.
4. PRO file PREM3/408/5.
5. PRO file HS7/287.
6. PRO file PREM3/408/5.
7. Ibid.
8. PRO file HS7/282.
9. PRO file HS7/280.
10. PRO file HS7/175 Appendix 'F'.
11. *Operation Epsilon: The Farm Hall Transcripts* introduced by Sir Charles Frank, Institute of Physics Publishing, 1993. For an alternative view of Germany's atomic bomb programme see Henshall, Philip, *Nuclear Axis*, Sutton, 2000.
12. From J.T. van Riemsdijk who was also involved at Station IX. An engineer, he recalls how, with his knowledge of French and Dutch, he was called upon to translate and re-draw sketches of targets obtained from agents in the field.
13. PRO file HS7/181.
14. Prof D.H. Everett FRS provided information for this section from personal recollections.
15. Joachim Fest, *Plotting Hitler's Death*.
16. J.C. Masterman, *The Double-Cross System*.
17. John Cloake, *Templer, Tiger of Malaya*.
18. *Between Silk and Cyanide* by Leo Marks was also drawn upon.

Notes

19. PRO file HS7/147.
20. PRO file KV4/69.
21. PRO file FO898/356.
22. *Templer, Tiger of Malaya*.

Chapter 16

1. PRO file HS7/88.

Chapter 17

1. PRO file WO33/2256.
2. Ibid.
3. Recounted by J.T. van Riemsdijk.
4. Recounted by Prof D.H. Everett, FRS.
5. PRO file HS7/27.
6. This anecdote appears in PRO file HS7/287.

Chapter 18

1. *The Infernal Grove* by Malcolm Muggeridge.
2. PRO file HS7/27.
3. *Operation Epsilon: The Farm Hall Transcripts* introduced by Sir Charles Frank, Institute of Physics Publishing, 1993.
4. The author, FB, was the ICI Engineer-in-Charge.
5. *Resistance: European resistance to Nazism 1940–1945* by M.R.D. Foot, 1976.

Appendix B

1. PRO file AVIA22/1588

BIBLIOGRAPHY

Bell, Leslie. *Sabotage! The Story of J. Elder Wills*, London, T.W. Laurie, 1957
Brown, George I. *The Big Bang. A History of Explosives*, Stroud, Sutton, 1998
Cloake, John. *Templer – Tiger of Malaya*, London, Harrop, 1985
Cruickshank, Charles. *SOE in the Far East*, Oxford, OUP, 1983
—— *SOE in Scandinavia*, Oxford, OUP, 1986
Dear, Alan. *Sabotage and Subversion*, London, Cassell, 1996
Fest, Joachim. *Plotting Hitler's Death*, London, Weidenfeld & Nicolson, 1996
Foot, M.R.D. *SOE 1940–46*, London, Pimlico, 1999
—— *SOE in France*, London, HMSO, 1966
—— *SOE in the Low Countries*, London, St Ermin's Press, 2001
—— *Resistance*, London, Eyre Methuen, 1976
Garnett, David. *The Secret History of PWE*, London, St Ermin's Press, 2002
Kemp, Paul. *Underwater Warriors*, London, Arms & Armour, 1996
King, Stella. *'Jacqueline' Pioneer Heroine of the Resistance*, London, Arms & Armour, 1989
Ladd, James and Melton, Keith. *Clandestine Warfare*, London, Blandford, 1988
Lorain, Pierre. *Secret Warfare*, London, Orbis, 1984
Lucas Phillips, C.E. *Cockleshell Heroes*, London, Pan Books, 2000
Mackenzie, Prof W.J.M. *The Secret History of SOE*, London, St Ermin's Press, 2000
Macrae, R. Stuart. *Winston Churchill's Toyshop*, Kineton, Roundwood Press, 1971
Marks, Leo. *Between Silk and Cyanide*, London, HarperCollins, 1999
Masterman, J.C. *The Double-Cross System*, London, Pimlico, 1995
Moon, Tom. *This Grim and Savage Game*, Cambridge, MA, Da Capo Press, 2000
Orchard, C.J. and Madden, S.J. *British Forces Motorcycles 1925–45*, Stroud, Sutton, 1995
Richards, Brooks. *Secret Flotillas*, London, HMSO, 1996
Rigden, Denis. *Kill the Fuhrer*, Stroud, Sutton, 1999
—— (introduction). *SOE Syllabus*, Richmond, Public Record Office, 2001
Seaman, Mark (introduction). *Secret Agent's Handbook of Special Devices*, Richmond, Public Record Office, 2000
Stafford, David. *Secret Agent*, London, BBC Worldwide Ltd, 2000
Sweet-Escott, Bickham. *Baker Street Irregular*, London, Methuen, 1965
West, Nigel. *Secret War – The Story of SOE*, London, Hodder & Stoughton, 1992
Wilkinson, Peter and Ashley, Joan Bright. *Gubbins and SOE*, London, Leo Cooper, 1993

INDEX

Index

Index

Index

Index

Political Warfare Executive (PWE) 10, 98, 246, 254, 262, 263
Pollard, Maj Hugh B 19
Pollock, Lt Sir George RN ret'd 141, 143
Pond, Maj D W 232
Poona 272, 276
Port Bannatyne 150
Port Moresby 151
Portal, Lord, Chief of Air Staff 169
Porteus, Eric 44, 45, 127
Portland Place, 36 8
Porton Down 80, 82–5
Post Office Research Establishment 223
Postscript 288
Potter, Sqn Ldr 262, 263
Pounden (Station 53b) 207, 223
Pressed Steel Company, Oxford 131, 133, 136, 140, 142, 239
Prestwick 186
Primacord 52
Principles for explosives initiating devices 52
Printing and Art Department 96
Prisoner 13961 1
Prisoners of war and forced workers 244–6
Production Section, Station XII 18, 27, 161, 228
Propaganda 4, 5, 255, 256
Psittacosis 83
Public Record Office (PRO) 2, 255, 259, 285
Puddefjord 248
Pulver, Claudia 95
Pye of Cambridge 213, 216
Pyle, Sqn Ldr 236

Q-Branch of AL Section 171
Quality Control (QC) 60, 161
Quality Control (QC) Section, Station XII 162
Quality Control Department 156, 232, 234
Queen Mary reservoir 22, 142, 235
Queen's Gate, 56 21, 22, 90, 92
Quilter delay opening mechanism 196
Quislings 105, 106, 269

Ree, Harry 49, 50, 170
Rabies 83
Radio Communications Division 176, 200, 207, 211, 216–7, 221, 223
Radio Gramophone Developments 223
Radioactive paint 78, 190
Rae, Tom 102
RAF Special Duties Flight 169
Rail transport 69
Railway demolition tests 163

Railway Executive 7
Railway switches 54–6
Ramsden, Lt 21
Ramsey Green, Capt E 228, 230, 234
Ration cards, counterfeit 98, 255, 264
Ration packs 87
Rats, infected 85
Ratweek 105
Reception Committee procedures (RC) 171, 174
Reception Committees 181, 187
Recommended values of M and D for use with panniers 301
Red Circle Escape Club 263
Reeves, Maj H Q A 44, 103, 106, 107, 145, 155
Regulated area 142
Remote controlled wireless transmission 220
Renfrew airfield 207
Renouf, Admiral 125
Research, Development and Supplies Directorate 2
Resistance Movements 169
Respirators, development work at Oxford 304
Revogne 266
Rheam, Lt Col G T T 35, 48
Rheinhold, Miss 236
Riach, Maj H F 223
Richter, Karel Richard 1
Ricin ('W') 84
Rickard, Capt 212
Riemsdijk, John T van 36, 37, 58, 193, 282
Rjukan 49, 203, 250, 251, 253
Roberts, Maj F J G 234
Roller conveyors for package despatch 171, 183, 188
Rothesay Bay 146
Rothschild, Lord 68
Rotol Ltd 222
Rottnest Island 146, 158
Rough handling tests 162, 172, 183
Rowat, Capt E I 19, 21
Rowlandson, Lt Col 133
Rowley, J 248
Royal Aircraft Establishment (RAE) 172, 177, 185, 186, 189, 196, 197, 199, 201, 216, 271, 279
Royal Arsenal, Woolwich 17
Royal Cruising Club 7
Royal Marines' Harbour Patrol Detachment 117
Royal Ordnance Factory, Elstow 233
Royal Signals Museum 2
Royal Small Arms Factory, Enfield 107, 109
Royal Society 6, 26, 33, 35, 37, 39, 40, 45, 288

Index

Index